CAROLINA FOLK-PLAYS

FIRST, SECOND, AND THIRD SERIES

✳

Edited and with an Introduction by

FREDERICK H. KOCH
Founder and Director of
The Carolina Playmakers

Foreword by
PAUL GREEN

NEW YORK
HENRY HOLT AND COMPANY

All of these plays have been successfully produced.

A royalty fee is required for each performance of any of these plays, either by amateurs or by professionals. Special arrangements must be made for radio-broadcasting.

No performance of these plays may be given without full acknowledgment to The Carolina Playmakers, Inc., and to the publishers. Acknowledgment should be made to read as follows: "From the *Carolina Folk-Plays* edited by FREDERICK H. KOCH, Director. Produced by arrangements with The Carolina Playmakers, Inc., and with the publishers."

The amateur acting rights to these plays are controlled by Samuel French, 25 West 45th St., New York, N. Y., to whom application should be made for production.

———

The plays in this volume can be read or played anywhere, upon payment of the royalty required. While it would be well for the actors to study the hints on pronunciation in Appendix V, The Language of the Plays, still, outside of the Carolinas, the parts can be effectively played by actors speaking more or less in the manner of the country folk in whatever state the play is being presented.

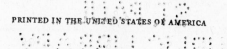

TO JEANIE

THE PLAYMAKERS' AIM

FIRST: *To promote dramatic art, especially by the production and publishing of native plays.*

SECOND: *To serve as an experimental theatre for plays representing the traditions and present-day life of the people.*

THIRD: *To extend its influence in creating a native theatre throughout America.*

CONTENTS

THE
CAROLINA PLAYMAKERS

By Frederick H. Koch

Founder of The Dakota Playmakers and The
Carolina Playmakers

North Carolina has witnessed a surprising renaissance of the drama during the past twenty-three years. With the formation of The Carolina Playmakers in the fall of 1918 a new era began. Before that time, Barrett Clark avers, the entire state was stricken from the mailing list of Samuel French, publisher of plays, as a dead state in its dramatic interest—so dead, in fact, as not to warrant the postage necessary for the mailing of their play catalogues. And H. L. Mencken had dubbed the South "The Sahara of the Bozart!"

There was no stage suitable for theatrical entertainment on the campus of the University of North Carolina in 1918. The performances of the dramatic club were given in Gerrard Hall on a temporary platform built out over the first row of seats. It must have been hard going for the actors in those days. They had to don their costumes and make-up in the Y. M. C. A. building near by and clamber into Gerrard by way of a side window, then huddle together in the "wings" to await breathlessly their time to go on.

Under the circumstances it seemed advisable to begin our adventure in playmaking in the auditorium of the Chapel Hill graded school building some distance from the campus. There, with volunteer assistants, I designed and constructed a stage and proscenium, installed a curtain and homemade footlights, and produced the first Carolina Folk Plays on March 14 and 15, 1919. The little homespun plays found an eager and lusty response.

Two of the plays included in that initial production of The Carolina Playmakers are reprinted in the present volume: *When Witches Ride*, about folk superstition in Northampton County, by Elizabeth Lay of Beaufort, North Carolina (now Mrs. Paul Green), and *The Return of Buck Gavin*, the tragedy of a mountain outlaw, by Thomas Wolfe. This little play was the first published work of the now immortal American novelist; and the first edition of the Second Series of CAROLINA FOLK PLAYS [1] in which it appeared originally is now cherished as a collector's item.

DAKOTA FOLK PLAYS

The new native plays of The Carolina Playmakers represent the culmination of twelve years of pioneer experiment at the frontier University of North Dakota, before the days of the Little Theatre movement. Maxwell Anderson, now distinguished American playwright, was one of the founders of our first dramatic society there, and out of the group of which he was a charter member, came The Dakota Playmakers and the first PRAIRIE FOLK PLAYS. On receiving a playbill of the first Dakota plays young Anderson wrote from California, where he was then engaged in teaching: "If there is anything that would bring me back to the old sod, it is a dramatic revival; and honestly, it seems to me that if the interest and enthusiasm keep up we may yet have one comparable to the recent flowering in Ireland. I would be willing to walk all the way back to the Dakota prairie to get in on that." [2] And when later he went to New York, the first play he wrote, you remember, was *White Desert*, a play of the vast winter plain of Dakota—its loneliness—a native play of the prairie. He had made a beginning.

The plays of Dakota were often crude, but they were honest. Simple folk plays, near to the good, strong, windswept soil—plays telling of long, bitter winters in the little sod shanty. But plays singing, too, of the prairie springtime,

[1] Henry Holt and Company, N. Y., 1924.
[2] January 25, 1917.

of unflecked sunshine, of the wilderness gay with wild roses, of the fenceless fields welling over with lark song. Plays of the travail and achievement of a pioneer people!

The Beginnings in Carolina

Thomas Wolfe, a lanky six-and-a-half-foot tall mountain lad with burning eyes, was the only male member of the original playwriting course at Chapel Hill in 1918. The other twelve members of the class were co-eds. After the meeting of the class that first day he said, by way of apology, "'Proff,' I don't want you to think that this Ladies Aid Society represents Carolina. We have a lot of he-men seriously interested in writing here, but they are all disguised in army uniforms now. I tried to get into one myself but they didn't have one long enough for me."

We couldn't find anyone to play the title rôle of the mountain outlaw, Buck Gavin, in Tom's first play. I tried to persuade him, "I guess you'll have to do it yourself, Tom. You may not know it, but you really wrote that part for yourself!"

"But I can't act, 'Proff,' I've never acted."

"You're a born actor," I assured him, "and you *are* Buck Gavin."

I shall never forget his first performance. With free mountain stride, his dark eyes blazing, he became the hunted outlaw of the Great Smokies. There was something uncanny in his acting of the part—something of the pent-up fury of his highland forebears.

In his foreword to *The Return of Buck Gavin* Tom wrote for all beginners: "It is the fallacy of the young writer to picture the dramatic as unusual and remote. . . . The dramatic is not unusual. It is happening daily in our lives."

Of his playwriting that first year he wrote: "I have written about people I have known and concerning whom I feel qualified to write. They have suggested a train of thought that intensely interests me, and is, I believe, of vital importance to me. My writing, I feel sure, has been made easier and better by their production.

"If they have affected my writing to this extent—if they have indirectly caused an analysis of my work, and a determination of my future course—are they not worthwhile, even though they be but the amateurish productions of a youngster?"

It is interesting to recall now the first efforts of the young writer. Like Anderson, he wrote what he knew. Though crude, those who have followed him through the years cannot fail to see in his first hastily written little plays the indications of his later achievement in *Look Homeward, Angel* and *Of Time and the River*.

The Carolina Folk Plays

As far as we have been able to determine, the first use of the term "folk play" in the American theatre was The Carolina Playmakers' announcement: CAROLINA FOLK PLAYS on the playbill of their initial production in Chapel Hill twenty-three years ago. Now the term is not unfamiliar in the expanding scene of our American theatre. Witness Paul Green's *In Abraham's Bosom*, Lulu Vollmer's *Sun-Up*, Dorothy and DuBose Heyward's *Porgy* and *Mamba's Daughters*, Jack Kirkland's dramatization of Erskine Caldwell's *Tobacco Road*, Lynn Riggs' *Green Grow the Lilacs*, Maxwell Anderson's *Winterset*, Thornton Wilder's *Our Town* and Robert Sherwood's *Abe Lincoln in Illinois*.

From the first our particular interest in North Carolina has been the use of native materials and the making of fresh dramatic forms. We have found that if the writer observes the locality with which he is most familiar and interprets it faithfully, it may show him the way to the universal. If he can see the interestingness of the lives of those about him with understanding and imagination, with wonder, why may he not interpret that life in significant images for others—perhaps for all? It has been so in all lasting art.

Four volumes of CAROLINA FOLK PLAYS by different authors and a volume of Paul Green's early plays, written in the playwriting courses at the University of North Carolina

over a period of years, have been published and widely produced in the United States and abroad. The materials were
drawn by each writer from scenes familiar and near, often
from remembered adventures of his youth, from folk tales
and the common tradition, and from present-day life in
North Carolina. They are plays of native expressiveness, of
considerable range and variety, presenting scenes from the
remote coves of the Great Smoky Mountains to the dangerous shoals of Cape Hatteras.

Our recent volume, AMERICAN FOLK PLAYS,[1] marks the
extension of our North Carolina idea of folk playmaking to
other American states, to Canada and to Mexico. It represents the work of twenty new playwrights, eighteen from the
United States—all the way from California and the Rocky
Mountain region to Florida and New England—one from
western Canada, and one from beyond the Rio Grande in
Mexico. The plays included were selected from hundreds of
scripts written and produced by students in playwriting at
Chapel Hill and in summer courses it has been my privilege
to conduct in some of our leading universities: Columbia,
New York, Northwestern, Colorado, California (both Berkeley and Los Angeles), Southern California, and four summers
now at the Banff School of Fine Arts in Alberta, Canada.

In writing of this anthology (in *The Saturday Review of
Literature* of July 1, 1939) under the caption, "The Native
Theatre," Stephen Vincent Benét notes: "Each Playmaker
has honestly tried to get to grips with some one aspect of
American life. It may be Davy Crockett or a farm woman of
the North Dakota prairies—it may be a cowboy comedy or
an Oklahoma tragedy—the same desire to work with native
materials and make something of them is obvious in them
all. It is an interesting and, in many respects, a remarkable
achievement." And the English reviewer of the *Literary Supplement* of *The London Times* wrote on September 9, 1939:
"Those who are tired of thrillers, drawing-room comedies
and film fantasies will find these tragedies, farces, and

[1] D. Appleton-Century Company, N. Y., 1939.

sketches from real life refreshing. . . . It would be worthwhile seeing whether similar 'folk' plays could not still be evoked from our English scene and so bring to the drama a fertilizing influence."

FOLK DRAMA DEFINED

The term "folk," as we use it, has nothing to do with the folk play of medieval times. But rather is it concerned with folk subject matter: with the legends, superstitions, customs, environmental differences, and the vernacular of the common people. For the most part they are realistic and human; sometimes they are imaginative and poetic.

The chief concern of the folk dramatist is man's conflict with the forces of nature and his simple pleasure in being alive. The conflict may not be apparent on the surface in the immediate action on the stage. But the ultimate cause of all dramatic action we classify as "folk," whether it be physical or spiritual, may be found in man's desperate struggle for existence and in his enjoyment of the world of nature. The term "folk" with us applies to that form of drama which is earth-rooted in the life of our common humanity.

For many years our playwrights of the South—indeed of all America—were imitative, content with reproducing the outlived formulas of the old world. There was nothing really *native* about them. Whenever they did write of American life, the treatment was superficial and innocuous.

When Augustus Thomas wrote *Alabama* and *In Mizzoura* optimistic heralds announced the arrival of the "great American drama"; but the playwright barely skimmed the surfaces of these colorful states. His next play, *The Witching Hour*, had something of the jessamine perfume of Kentucky romance, but the ghost of the old well-made melodrama was lugged in to resolve the plot. Then there was *Uncle Tom's Cabin*, a grand old theatre piece, but its treatment of the southern Negro, though sincere, was sentimental. Four native North Carolinians have contributed authentic drama of the Southern scene to the contemporary theatre: Paul Green, a challenging tragedy of the Negro race, *In Abraham's Bosom*; Lulu Vollmer and Hatcher Hughes, dramas of the mountain people, *Sun-Up* and *Hell Bent for Heaven;* and Ann Preston Bridgers, domestic tragedy in a small town, *Coquette.*

THE NEGRO DRAMA

Following Paul Green came Dorothy and DuBose Heyward with *Porgy* and *Mamba's Daughters*, of a Negro neighborhood in Charleston; and Roark Bradford's stories of *The Green Pastures* from Louisiana, to go singing along for five years all over America. The Negro theatre has come a long way in twenty-three years. I recall Paul Green's first Negro play written in the playwriting class at Chapel Hill, *White Dresses*, of a lovely Mulatto girl, Mary McLean—"a tragedy in black and white," he calls it.

Paul said, "I have written that part for you, Elizabeth," referring to Elizabeth Taylor who later played important rôles in Brock Pemberton's productions on Broadway for five years.

"I would love to do it!"

But the time was not ripe, although North Carolina was a leader among the Southern states in Negro education and in friendly race relationships. We had to wait. It was with great satisfaction in later years that this same play was brought to our Playmakers' stage by a visiting group of Negro players from St. Augustine's College in Raleigh.[1] And now we have flourishing Negro inter-collegiate and inter-high school dramatic tournaments each spring in North Carolina. The Jim Crow sentiment of the old South is gone and an audience crowded our big Memorial Hall to the rafters when Richard B. Harrison, formerly a teacher in Greensboro, North Carolina, came to Chapel Hill with *The Green Pastures.*

TENANT FARM DRAMA

Twenty-three years ago Harold Williamson, a student in the playwriting class from nearby Carthage, brought to our

[1] April 4, 1934.

makeshift stage in the high school the first play of the Southern sharecropper—hitherto undiscovered by the American
theatre as far as is known. It was a little tragedy about a
tenant farm girl, *Peggy.* The drab cabin that was her home
we had passed a thousand times as a dull sight, on the stage
became suddenly something new, something interesting,
something wonderful. Here the jaded farm woman, Mag, with
snuffstick protruding from the corner of her mouth, getting
supper of corn bread and fat back, singing the while snatches
of an old ballad, was no longer a commonplace figure. She had
been transformed by the magic of the theatre. The tragic fact
of her hard-won existence had become a reality to us—life
itself that moves and feels—a gripping drama! A neglected
chapter of the Southern scene had come to life on our stage.

A little later came Paul and Erma Green's little drama of
the grinding poverty of the sharecropper's life in *Fixin's* in
which the pent fury of the work-driven wife, Lilly Robinson,
is portrayed with grim and terrible reality. She craves a little
beauty, "purty fixin's." But her husband's eyes cannot see
beyond the sod he plows. The scene is a bare cabin home in
Harnett County, North Carolina, but the theme is universal
—the pitiful conflict of two natures which are irreconcilable.

The next morning after our Playmakers' tour performance
of *Fixin's* in Atlanta, before a sophisticated audience in evening dress, a man came to me and said, "I think I owe it to
you to tell you of the effect that little play, *Fixin's,* had on
me last night.—I come from New York, and I've been seeing
the best shows in the theatre there for thirty years. But that
little play last night *got* me so much that, before I went to
bed, I went to the Western Union office and telegraphed
some flowers to my wife in New York!"

And after a performance in western North Carolina, the
reviewer in the *Greensboro Daily News* wrote: "*Fixin's* presented a scene of such stark and terrible reality as to make at
least one person in the audience want to rise up and say,
'This thing has got to be stopped.'" The little play had gone
beyond the theatre into life itself.

Today the plight of this forgotten class of country people has been vividly portrayed in Jack Kirkland's sensational treatment of Erskine Caldwell's story of the degenerate poor white sharecropper of the backlands of Georgia in *Tobacco Road*. And the tragi-comic figure of an irrepressible Jeeter Lester has held the stage for more than five seasons now.

TROUPING

From the first The Carolina Playmakers have been interested in the making of a native theatre throughout the state and beyond their own borders. Traveling in their Show-Bus, with three sets of homemade scenery atop, portable lighting equipment, costumes, and stage properties, they have played all over North Carolina, in cross-roads villages in the mountains and in "neighborhoods" by the sea—in school auditoriums, old-time opera houses, and outlived town halls.

The Playmakers present trouping facilities offer a striking contrast to the first tour of The Dakota Playmakers over 800 miles of treeless plains when it was necessary to spend several hours at a junction point sometimes waiting for an "accommodation" train to take them to a little prairie town at the end of a branch line. Then the players drew lots to see who would peddle the handbills to advertise their arrival in town. Now The Playmakers ride in royal fashion over the hills and through the valleys of the Blue Ridge, blossoming with dogwood and flaming with the judas trees of a Carolina spring; now announced in three-sheet posters in gay colors, and by high praise in the newspapers, their coming is like a triumphal entry.

The thirty-seven tours of The Playmakers have not been confined to North Carolina. We have played in one hundred and thirty-one different towns and cities—all the way from south Georgia to Boston, Massachusetts, and as far west as the National Folk Festivals at St. Louis and at Dallas, Texas, playing three hundred and thirty-four performances to a total audience of nearly five hundred thousand. In their thirty-seven tours The Carolina Playmakers have played forty-six of the folk plays written and produced originally at Chapel Hill. They have played in the beautiful University Theatre at Yale, on three successive tours at Columbia University in New York City, and twice at the Fine Arts Theatre in Boston, where the troupe was greeted by Governor Frank Allen at the Massachusetts State House. On our first visit to Washington, D. C., we were cordially received at the White House by President Calvin Coolidge, who actually went so far as to say he thought our work was "very interesting."

Of The Playmakers first appearance in New York the reviewer of the *Theatre Magazine* wrote: "The rare characters and the homely qualities of these plays linger in one's memory long after some of the more sophisticated plays of Broadway have been forgotten. In fact, each time we witness a program of the CAROLINA FOLK PLAYS, we feel for the moment that we, too, are just 'folks'—along with those other folks on the other side of the footlights, who transport us for a brief but happy period back to their hill country, with its rich traditions, legends, and folklore." [1]

DRAMA IN EXTENSION

Simultaneously with the formation of The Carolina Playmakers at the University twenty-three years ago we organized the Bureau of Community Drama, as a unit of the Extension Division. At first the work was conducted by correspondence and by a play-lending and bulletin service. Later the demand was such that a traveling Field Director was provided to assist schools and rural communities in the writing and production of plays, pageants, and festivals. In 1925 the statewide Carolina Dramatic Association was formed which held its Eighteenth Annual Dramatic Festival and State Tournament in Chapel Hill the first week in April this year. The membership of the Association now includes one hundred and one college, high school, and country thea-

[1] M. E. Kehoe, "The Carolina Playmakers Come to Town," *Theatre Magazine*, Feb., 1929.

tres from all parts of North Carolina from the Great Smoky Mountains to the "banks" of Hatteras.

A remarkable development of the North Carolina state organization is the annual National Folk Festival held in this, the eighth year, in Washington, D. C. The founder of the National Folk Festival, Sarah Gertrude Knott, resigned as State Representative of the Bureau of Community Drama in North Carolina to become the founder and director of the nation-wide celebration of American folk arts. "If one state, North Carolina, can do it," Miss Knott asked, "why not the United States?" She has succeeded beyond all expectations.

PLAYS OF A COUNTRY NEIGHBORHOOD

In this connection it is interesting to note the achievement of Bernice Kelly Harris, author of *Purslane* and of a recent volume of FOLK PLAYS OF EASTERN CAROLINA,[1] of her own country neighborhood in Northampton County, North Carolina, not far from the Roanoke River. These plays of the simple lives and homely ways of her neighbors and friends were produced originally in her home town of Seaboard and brought in successive years to the annual festivals of the Carolina Dramatic Association at Chapel Hill. Bernice Harris, as a teacher of English in a rural high school, was a member of the first summer playwriting group in Chapel Hill twenty-three years ago. She was so captivated by her first adventure in playwriting that she was impelled to pass on to her boys and girls the new wonder she had found in folk playmaking. "I saw the beauty of a new sort of humanism," she has written of that first summer.

MEXICAN FOLK PLAYS

Since publishing five volumes of Carolina plays and a book of twenty American folk plays, The Playmakers issued in 1938 a volume of MEXICAN FOLK PLAYS [2] written at Chapel Hill by Josephina Niggli of Monterrey, Nuevo Leon, Mexico,

[1] University of North Carolina Press, Chapel Hill, N. C., 1940.
[2] University of North Carolina Press, Chapel Hill, N. C., 1938.

and produced originally in The Playmakers Theatre here. Plays of the humble lives of her own people, their restless history, their legends and the childlike wonder of their folkways. These Mexican plays have been widely produced throughout the United States and Canada, and many times abroad.

CAROLINA AND CANADA

Sometimes our home-grown plays of Chapel Hill are transplanted to far places. A play of the Canadian frontier, *Still Stands the House*,[1] which Gwendolyn Pharis of Magrath, Alberta, Canada, wrote here in 1938 was last year awarded the first prize of $100 as the best native play entered in the annual Dominion Drama Festival of Canada.

Another case: *Funeral Flowers for the Bride*,[2] written for The Playmakers in 1937 by Beverley DuBose Hamer of Eastover, South Carolina (who vowed at the first that she "couldn't write a play") won first place in England in the International One Act Play Competition of 1938 over one hundred and sixty-six plays entered. It was produced professionally in London at the Duchess Theatre on November 27 of that year.

A CHINESE PLAYMAKER

A Chinese boy came to Chapel Hill for playwriting: Cheng-Chin Hsiung of Nanchang, China.

"Hsiung," I inquired, "what kind of play do you want to write?"

"I want to write a play about the Chinese-American problem—a mixed marriage of a Chinese boy and an American girl."

"A good idea, but you can't do it.—We should like to have you write of your own people. You have a marvelous store of legend in old China. We are interested here in what we call

[1] *American Folk Plays.* D. Appleton-Century Co., N. Y., 1939.
[2] *Ibid.*

the 'folk play.' I wish you would write for us a Chinese folk play."

"If you let me write this Chinese-American marriage play first, then I will write for you a Chinese folk play."

"Hsiung," I said, "you know that you can't understand the mind of an American girl."

"Well, I have been in this country five years."

"Five years! Some of us have lived here fifty years, and we cannot do it! But go ahead, write your problem play first; then write a real Chinese play." So he wrote a play called *Poor Polly*—and it was well named!

Then he went to the storehouse of old China and wrote a charming play, *The Thrice Promised Bride*, in the manner of the Chinese stage—a play of romance, of comedy, of poetry. We were so much impressed with it that I sent it to the editor of *Theatre Arts*, who wrote back, "I like it so much that I want to publish it in our next issue." [1] There Frank Shay saw it and wrote for permission to include it in his anthology *Twenty-Five Short Plays, International*, as the only play in the volume representing China. There Henry Lanier, editor of the *Golden Book*, saw it and paid $105.00 for permission to reprint it in the issue of August, 1925.

So *Poor Polly* passed and *The Thrice Promised Bride* arrived. He wrote another Chinese play, *The Marvelous Romance of Wen Chun-Chin*, which was published in *Poet Lore*. [2]

Our Chinese Playmaker's plays have been favorites not only in the United States but especially in England, and we sent him a royalty check for a performance not long ago in far away Kuala Lumpur, Straits Settlements.

THE CAROLINA PLAY-BOOK

Besides publishing plays The Playmakers have issued thirteen volumes of a unique little quarterly, THE CAROLINA PLAY-BOOK, [3] devoted to the making of a native theatre. THE

[1] *Theatre Arts Monthly*, N. Y., October, 1923.
[2] *Poet Lore*, Autumn Number, 1924.
[3] *The Carolina Play-Book* is an illustrated quarterly of native plays and

PLAY-BOOK had the distinction of being included for two seasons in the International Exhibit of Periodicals at the Century of Progress Exposition in Chicago as one of only three American theatre journals—the other two being *Theatre Arts* and *Stage*. A valuable supplement to THE PLAY-BOOK is THE CAROLINA STAGE, an attractive publication in mimeographed form, designed to meet the practical needs of the members of the Carolina Dramatic Association.

THE PROFESSIONAL AND THE PEOPLE'S THEATRE

From the first The Carolina Playmakers have been interested primarily in the making of a people's theatre, and a host of our graduates have gone back to their home towns and cities near and far resolved to do their bit in the making of such a theatre in America. Of course a number of Playmakers have escaped to the professional theatre and found such there: more recently, Shepperd Strudwick and Eugenia Rawls on Broadway and Lionel Stander and Kay Kyser in Hollywood. Although successful on the New York stage in his early days, George Denny found a wider field for his talents. Now he is President of New York's Town Hall and director of the NBC "Town Hall of the Air," which he founded.

Shepperd Strudwick (from the village of Hillsboro, just twelve miles from Chapel Hill), after several years of struggle on Broadway, found a place in the New York Theatre Guild. More recently he has been the leading spirit in a group of young actors, The Surry Players. He has had considerable success with M–G–M in the pictures too. Not long ago I received an enthusiastic letter from him from Hollywood. "The more experience I have in the theatre," he writes, "the more strongly do I yearn for the theatre of Paul Green's *Johnny Johnson* and *The Lost Colony*, plays that excite me more than anything the theatre has had to offer for years. *Abe Lincoln in Illinois* and *The Grapes of Wrath* do it in the

articles, edited by Frederick H. Koch, and published since March, 1928, at Chapel Hill.

movies and I hope to get a shot at it here before I get through. . . . The times are ripe now to receive what The Playmakers have to give with a more open understanding than ever before. The times need The Playmakers badly now. That's why *The Lost Colony* project is so exciting to me."

COMMUNAL DRAMA OF AMERICAN HISTORY

Paul Green's *The Lost Colony*, you recall, was written and produced originally in the summer of 1937 to commemorate the 350th anniversary of the first English settlement in America. It has played for four seasons now on Roanoke Island to tens of thousands of people in an outdoor theatre on the actual site of the landing of our first English colonists. Brooks Atkinson in an article in *The New York Times* not long ago, "Ought We to Found a National Theatre?", is eternally right in saying that *The Lost Colony* has become a permanent part of the culture of the people on Roanoke Island. He goes on, "As long as they live, these people will have a grander notion of our heritage than they had before this reverent drama was written."

In November 1939 Mr. Green wrote a second drama for the American people's theatre, *The Highland Call*, commemorating the bicentennial of Scotch settlement in the Cape Fear River valley of southeastern North Carolina, the stirring events of Revolutionary times and the heroic leadership of bonnie Flora Macdonald. Extending the idea of communal playmaking in *The Lost Colony*, *The Highland Call* was produced in Fayetteville by The Carolina Playmakers in collaboration with the citizens of that historic town. It evoked such enthusiasm there that plans have been completed for its annual production.

Now Mr. Green is at work on the third drama of his trilogy of early American history for old Williamsburg in Virginia. Mr. Green holds that America was regarded by the underprivileged classes in the old world as a "land of opportunity," and that this was the compelling motive and promise which

brought all classes to our shores and which America must fulfill to validate her beginnings.

Brooks Atkinson observes further in the above-mentioned article that we are just coming to realize that our country is rich in folklore and "should yield an abundant harvest of drama, and a national theatre that will serve the entire country, should develop regional plays and contribute to a deeper national understanding." I know of no better way toward an imaginative, a spiritual expression of our tradition of democracy.

COMING OF AGE

From the first we have thought of our Playmakers as a fellowship of young people working happily together toward a single ideal—the making of a communal, a people's theatre in America. Walt Whitman happily expresses it, "An institution of the dear love of comrades." Important as the individual is in the theatre, it is well for us to remind ourselves constantly that the dramatic is essentially a social art. Whatever The Playmakers have achieved is due primarily to their holding fast together to such an objective. Whatever we have done, we have done together.

We have come a long way in twenty-three years. Beginning traditionally in the Department of English as a one-man theatre we now have a separate Department of Dramatic Art with a full-time theatre staff and, in lieu of the traditional research thesis in English for the Master of Arts degree, a student may submit an original play.

The Department has entered the field of cinema and radio, too. Films from the Museum of Modern Art library are shown regularly in The Playmakers Theatre, and old favorites from The Playmakers' repertory (and new scripts, too) are broadcast from the University radio studio over a national network.

We are wondering now how long it will be before we take on television!

The Carolina Playmakers celebrated the twenty-first anniversary of their founding in a Southern Regional Theatre Festival in Chapel Hill throughout the week of April 1, 1940.

The coming of age of The Playmakers showed a lusty cultural growth. Two thousand and nine hundred people came to Chapel Hill for the Festival. Groups of players came from seven Southern states to present their own native plays. They came from Kentucky, Virginia, South Carolina, Georgia, Alabama, Louisiana—and one all the way from Oklahoma—to celebrate the growth of a new "Drama in the South." Of particular significance was the presentation of an historical Negro folk drama, *Breeders*, by Randolph Edmonds of Dillard University in New Orleans, Louisiana. Among the distinguished visitors who came to Chapel Hill for the Birthday Party were playwrights Clifford Odets, DuBose Heyward and Ann Preston Bridgers; drama historian Arthur Hobson Quinn; Negro novelist Zora Neal Hurston; Barrett H. Clark; George Freedley; Robert Porterfield; and John Selby, Arts Editor of the Associated Press.

THOSE WHO COME AFTER

Time alone can tell what will be the effect of our folk playmaking. According to the editor of *Holland's, The Magazine of the South*, the influence of The Carolina Playmakers "has spread indubitably into the associated fields of the novel, the short story, and even nonfiction works. From the basic idea underlying their work and philosophy stem such writings as those of Caldwell, Heyward, Miller, Bradford, Faulkner, Stribling, and other and younger novelists. Not that many more influences have not impinged sharply and deeply on Southern writers and on Southern thought generally; but The Carolina Playmakers and their example have been a centralizing, crystallizing, and vitalizing force unequaled in Southern literature to date." [1]

[1] *Holland's, The Magazine of the South*, July, 1936.

From the first we have believed in North Carolina, in the South, and in America. We have held that America has something rich and strange to contribute, something of native honesty and of beauty. Dr. Albert Shaw in writing of the beginnings in Dakota and in Carolina interpreted our hope in an editorial article in *The American Review of Reviews* of September, 1919: "When every community has its own native group of plays and producers, we shall have a national American Theatre that will give a richly varied, authentic expression of American life. We shall be aware—which we are only dimly at present—of the actual pulse of the people by the expression in folk plays of their coördinated minds. It is this common vision, this collective striving that determines nationalism, and remains throughout the ages, the one and only touchstone of the future."

What of the future? I go back to a conversation of my high school days with one of Walt Whitman's friends. On his last visit to the Singer of America he remembered Old Walt standing in the door of his little home in Camden and calling out in farewell, "Expecting the main things from those who come after."

Chapel Hill, North Carolina
March 24, 1941

(*Top*) The Playmakers Theatre at Chapel Hill
(*Bottom*) The Forest Theatre at Chapel Hill.

(*Top*) The audience at an experimental production. The Director leading the discussion (in light suit, center)

(*Bottom*) Playmakers in the shop, constructing flats

(*Top*) Behind the scenes in The Forest Theatre
(*Bottom*) Off on a tour: Loading the Show-Bus

Thomas Wolfe as
"Buck Gavin"

Scene from *The Third Night*. "Captain Richard Harkins"
[Thomas Wolfe] at right

THE PLAYMAKERS AND OUR ART

By Paul Green

It is recorded in the Bible that Jesus once came upon some fellows lamenting the lack of anything doing. "Cast down your nets where you are," He said. And they did. We know what happened. This is the sort of parable that fits many things, not the least of all the lack and dullness of our section in any form of art, a condition lamented now for many a year. But the lamentations have been in the voice of the Pharisee. They have not been in earnest. Nobody has cried aloud and wept that he was undone.

From its beginning, three hundred years ago, until the present, North Carolina has made no lasting contribution to the art of the world, and what is said of this state can be said of most of our Southern states. Several millions of people have lived and died here, and no one has set himself aside in high-minded and intelligent devotion to record a single one of these lives, nor to propound in the devious ways of art any of the hopes, struggles, disappointments and attainments that made up the sum of their existence. And from knowledge of the past it would seem that such a record is worth while.

This state has never produced a single great work of art. I am not talking about the factories, railroads, agricultural and commercial industries and the many and one creations of what is more or less called the practical mind. In a way they are forms of art too. At least they have their æsthetic side— their pattern, their fulfilled design and completed function and, in addition, the pleasure resulting to the maker and planner. But one must remember that they have also produced their slaves—even more slaves than creators and free men, and so therewith stand somewhat in condemnation. What I am especially concerned with here is the so-called finer arts. And as far as they count we can call the hogs till our tongues drop out and there will be no stir in the pasture.

Have we had a great painter? A great musician? A great sculptor? A great architect? A great poet, novelist, dramatist, essayist, biographer—a great anything so far as the subject of art is concerned? We have not. We've not had even an adequate one in any of these. Other states in the Union, to limit the matter nearer to hand and to souls of not so heavenly stature, have had their Emerson, Longfellow, Thoreau, Poe, Whitman, Mark Twain, Henry Adams, Whistler, Saint Gaudens, Winslow Homer, Henry James, Stanford White, Theodore Dreiser, Mrs. Wharton, Miss Cather, Edna Millay, Sinclair Lewis, Robinson Jeffers, Upton Sinclair, Eugene O'Neill and many, many others. I mention these simply at random. But we North Carolinians have had no one. True, we've had O. Henry in the short story, and have named cigars, drug stores, mattresses, candies and hotels after him, but still, if I may say so, he remains for me a man without a vision, not a great writer, his life seeming in itself to be much more significant than his books. In nearly everything he wrote he played his characters about at will. And when a writer creates characters he might do it with reverence and honor—even awe. To him they should be living souls, people in their own right, and should never be switched and pop-whipped in the clutch of the author's plot or design. O. Henry never so treated his creations. He was an ingenious man, not a great one.

And how explain this lack, this dullness of the records of our lives and days? For it is true that we have had plenty of records, plenty of thus and so, and about it and about, but nothing great and real, nothing surpassingly enlightened or enlightening. We've had numerous poets, would-be novelists, columnists, dabblers in water-colors and bangers on instruments. None of them have had much meaning for you and me nor for the world at large. We haven't bred the real thing. And why? Nobody knows. There are a thousand and one possible suggestions and theories but they are no more than partial descriptions and come along after the train's done gone. There was no explanation as to why those fellows in the parable were in the midst of dull business except the simple one that they were not really fishing. And the only answer to our lack and dullness is the simple one that we haven't been at the real business of production. Then how can we produce art? Nobody knows. Why we haven't done it and how we may do it—both are mysteries. It all is part of that strange matter known as living. As the Scriptures put it, and as Hamlet put it, and as the old farmer, eyeing the sky for rain, puts it, "It will come when it will come." But be it ever so mysterious, we don't profit by laying the burden on God or on the weather. There are aids—some in the form of prayers and some in the form of everyday matters. They are only aids though, and can never be more. The cause and source will forever be mysterious and so discussion is pretty much worthless *except* as it concerns these aids and the individual who strives to use them.

One of the first and most apparent helps towards an escape from this artistic lethargy and emptiness is to become acutely conscious that such is our condition. That is relatively a simple matter. We only have to look squarely at the facts. They are written down in the records and a blind man running can read them. As soon as we know what we are and have been so long, it is unthinkable that we shan't try to improve. The second and realest help is the most difficult and yet the most necessary, if we are to do our duty before God and man—the duty of building monuments in the name of what is finest and most beautiful in the lives of human beings. And that also is a becoming conscious. It is the becoming conscious of the marvel of being alive. It is not a moral matter, nor a practical matter. It rather is more nearly that something symbolized and denoted in the word spiritual—the word that had significance for souls in Victorian days. Now how can we so become conscious? If it were as difficult as it seems at first sight, certain and many of us would be condemned to hell from the beginning. But it so happens that here there is in this no dogmatic division of sheep and goats, of lost and saved. For all people (even idiots maybe) have this consciousness, this sense of beauty, to be specific. But they have it more or less. And the whole burden and responsibility rests upon our making the less more.

And how can that be done? How can there be progress towards such a coming to pass? There is no definite answer, for it is individual with every individual. In the main he must work it out for himself. The institutions of education, the technologies of industries that minister to man's comfort cannot give it, cannot of themselves increase it. They can but be used as partial means in this process. Again, it is a personal matter of a man's own living. He has the privileges of choice from books. He can draw from wind and weather, from inspiring lives about him, from the broken and the oppressed, from the triumphant and successful—from all that walk on God's green earth and under God's high heaven. He can draw sustenance from all that is around him. He can increase within him more and more the light that lighteth. And for all men there is this strange way of salvation, and no one can save him but himself. So cast down your nets where you are if you dwell by the sea. Or if a laborer in the field, go forth with strength and song. Push on, let heads be raised and faces set to the rising sun. In the cool of the evening God will walk there and a blessing will remain on the lifted or the bowed.

At least it seems so.

And so I for one hold that this work of The Carolina Playmakers in the publishing of their folk-plays and touring with them, in the putting out of a new magazine—*The Carolina Play-Book*, in the founding of dramatic clubs and in the state-wide organization of The Carolina Dramatic Association with tournaments and an annual Festival, study groups, clubs and more clubs, discussion and re-discussion—all is good. They are working along with and in a sound way are supplementing the schools and colleges; they are gradually making literature and other forms of art things of concern with us generally and are serving to help us get our eyes open. And don't we need it? We need to stir our will-power, revivify our senses, shake our minds out of their deadness. Rise and shine, as the Negroes sing. And the more we shine the more power we have to shine—that's our blessed miracle. And that alone so far as I can see is our proper excuse for being. If that is true—and it is true—the Bible and the Victorians still have much worth our study and appreciation. Go to it—all is part of our world, and the world is for our appreciation or it remains wasted upon us. In the words of a revised version, grow in grace. So will it to be and struggle to bring it to pass, and our heavy responsibility is somewhat discharged. Then upon a day iron palings that divide will be less cruel. I believe that. And the fear of the low for the powerful will be lessened. The slave will see some easement in his chains, and the pitiful and lost will have the records of their lives set down. And they the more will not have lived in vain. For it is by such living records, records and more records that we can pack up, store up and hand down accumulated living unto those that shall come after, and they thereby shall be made more aware of the power and glory of man and the universe in which he struggled for a season. They will have more food to feed upon, more possibilities of quickening their lives to wonder and joy.

And what material we have had and put to no use!—Material for music, poems, pictures, novels, songs—matter for dreams. But we've had no dreamers. Where is the man, where are the men? Come out of your hiding-place. Strike up the harps, let the bands play. Where shall we find him who shall light up the struggles of our people? Who will tell of the builders, the road-makers, the pioneers, the builders of cities, or railroads? Their records stand unsupported in themselves. Let them have their place in story and song—in the illumination of art.—These are high-sounding phrases, but they have some meaning, I hope.—Who among us has told the story of the lonesome seashore, of the early settlers along that ocean, of the wrecks and disasters there? Nobody. Along the empty sand-banks lie rotting ribs of many a ship, the disappearing records of struggle and death. In that wide and barren land of sand and battered trees there are symbols of man and his bravery, enough to move an army. And yet through all these years they have failed to touch the heart of a single North Carolinian. I mean touch him so that he had to cry out. And the light and darkness among those sounds and shallows there, and the wonders in the sky above. Where is our painter there, and the wonders in the sky above. Where is our painter? He is not yet born, or he is away from home. Maybe he is in Greenwich Village talking of formations, or copying his own fever-dreams. Ride among the sand-hills in the evening. Who has painted a sunset in Moore County? Nobody. Who will make it his business to speak to the brethren in the valley? Little men, big men, where are you hiding? . . . Who has sung of our mountains? Spring or autumn, they cry for a voice. One Wordsworth among them would carry inspiration to millions before the curtain came down. Who tells the romance of the farmer's life among his tobacco, his cotton and corn? Nobody. And the Negro and his life that was and is to be? I hear no answer. Or the great winter migration of John Smith and his family in search of a better home over there in Sampson or up in Harnett or down in Pender? Call the roll of the chosen ones. Who recounts the drama of the country doctor and his fight against ignorance and poverty, flies and dysentery and typhoid fever—his devotion to the needy in freeze and flood? Who has told his story? Nobody. And the matters of statecraft and politics, an epic tale of wisdom and gentleness, of cunning and graft, of bribery and dealings at the pie-counter? Where is our Balzac or Tolstoi or Hauptmann? Asleep or gone on a journey? The dinner bell rings, the house burns down, but no one comes. . . . It is too evident then that everywhere around us, both here and yonder, is work for willing hands to do, hands that will shape and build to the finer uses of a living art.

And The Carolina Playmakers are to be commemorated in that they have dedicated themselves to the uses of this living art. Let us go the way with them.

Chapel Hill, North Carolina.
June 19, 1928.

POSTSCRIPT: 1941

Since Paul Green lamented the dearth of fine arts in North Carolina in 1928 we have witnessed a dramatic renaissance and the beginnings of a new people's theatre. A glance at the list of our Carolina Playmakers' productions, published plays, and thirteen volumes of *The Carolina Play-Book* in the Appendices of the present volume will suggest to the reader something of the beginnings and remarkable growth of a new native drama in North Carolina.

In the Introduction to this collection of *Carolina Folk-Plays* I have noted the contributions of some of our Playmakers as playwrights and novelists, as actors and directors on Broadway, in Hollywood and in Little Theatres all over the United States, and as teachers in schools, colleges and universities in many states.—*F.H.K.*

March 24, 1941

WHEN WITCHES RIDE

A Play of Folk Superstition

BY

ELIZABETH A. LAY

1

WHEN WITCHES RIDE

When Witches Ride by Elizabeth Lay (now Mrs. Paul Green), was the first play written in the University playwriting course to be presented on the improvised Playmakers' stage in the auditorium of the Chapel Hill High School building on March 14 and 15, 1919.

The characters and the superstition in this play were drawn largely from the author's observation as a country school teacher in Northampton County, North Carolina. The idea of the plot is based on the following account of the actual character, Phoebe Ward, given in an article by Professor Tom Peete Cross of the University of Chicago on "Folk-Lore from the Southern States," published in *The Journal of American Folk-Lore*, Volume XXII (1909).

"The early years of Phoebe Ward, witch, are shrouded in mystery. . . . She lived here and there, first at one place and then at another in Northampton County, North Carolina. She stayed in a hut or any shelter whatsoever that was granted her.

"She made her living begging from place to place. Most people were afraid to refuse her, lest she should apply her witchcraft to them. . . . Hence the people resorted to a number of methods to keep her away. For instance, when they saw her coming, they would stick pins point-up in the chair bottoms, and then offer her one of these chairs. It is said that she could always tell when the chair was thus fixed, and would never sit in it. Also they would throw red pepper into the fire, and Phoebe would leave as soon as she smelled it burning. . . .

"Among her arts it is said that she could ride persons at night (the same as nightmares), that she could ride horses at night, and that when the mane was tangled in the morning it was because the witch had made stirrups of the plaits. She was said to be able to go through key-holes. . . . She was credited with possessing a sort of grease which she could apply and then slip out of her skin and go out on her night rambles, and on her return get back again."

3

CAST OF CHARACTERS

As originally produced on The Playmakers' Stage, Chapel Hill, North Carolina, March 14 and 15, 1919.

UNCLE BENNY, *owner of the crossroads store,*
George McF. McKie

ED, *his son,*
Walter H. Williamson

JAKE, *formerly a railroad engineer,*
George Denny

PHOEBE WARD, *witch*
Alga E. Leavitt

SCENE: The storehouse of a crossroads store. The action takes place in the back country of North Carolina, near the Roanoke River, at a time when the people of Northampton County still believed in witches. A stormy night.

SCENE

The storehouse of a crossroads store.

The room is a typical log cabin, roughly built. Red peppers, herbs, and dried vegetables hang from the low rafters. Boxes and bales are piled in disorder among farm implements, kitchen utensils, and miscellaneous articles from the stock of a crossroads general store. Dust and cobwebs are everywhere. In the back wall at the right a small opening cut in the logs serves as a window, with a rough shutter hinged loosely at the right side. The door in the back wall at the left is hidden by a dirty sheet, hung over it to keep out the cold air. In the right side-wall is a huge stone fireplace in which a hot fire blazes, the opening being nearly filled with logs. A large supply of wood is piled beside the fireplace at the right. A big jug of liquor stands on a box in that corner. There is a rough bench in front of the fire. In the front at the left is a table. Three lighted candles, a small straw-covered jug, mugs of liquor, and coins are on the table.

ED, JAKE, and UNCLE BENNY are seated around the table, playing cards and drinking. Outside the storm is gathering.

UNCLE BENNY is very old. His face is wrinkled and weather-beaten. He has no teeth and is nearly bald. He wears an old shirt and rusty trousers.

ED is middle-aged, red of face, very tall and lank. His shoulders droop and his whole appearance is that of slouchiness. He wears a dirty shirt with sleeves rolled up, and ragged overalls.

JAKE is older than ED. He is burly and strong, commanding respect from the others who fear his bad temper. He is something of a bully. He wears a dark coat over his overalls. An old engineer's cap is on his head.

UNCLE BENNY (*speaking in a high, nervous voice*). This here's mighty good liquor, ain't it so, Jake?

JAKE (*pours himself another glass*). Uh-huh. (*Gruffly.*) It's your play, Ed.

5

UNCLE BENNY. I reckon you might's well pour me some more, too, while you're 'bout it. (JAKE *pours while* UNCLE BENNY *holds his cup. Suddenly a loud crash of thunder is heard.* UNCLE BENNY *starts up and jerks his hand away, nearly spilling the contents of the jug.*)

JAKE (*grabs the jug and sets it down with a bang*). Drat your hide, ol' man! Do you want to waste all this good whiskey? What's the matter with you? Hey?

UNCLE BENNY. Thar now, Jake, I didn't mean no harm.

JAKE. I reckon you nigh about wasted all this here liquor!

ED (*drawling, testily*). Well, 'tain't none of your liquor, is it?

JAKE (*turning on him*). An' what're you jumpin' in about? You're both 'bout to jump out'n your skins! What you feared of? 'Tain't nothin' but thunderin' a mite.

UNCLE BENNY. But it's an awful night, Jake. It's witch weather—thunder an' lightnin' on a cold night like this here—jest the night for witches to be ridin' an' sperits to be walkin' an' I can't leave off from feelin' that bad luck's a-comin' to us here. (*A very loud thunder clap is heard as the storm grows more fierce.*) Oh, lordy! lordy!

ED. Hit's one powerful queer storm, sure, but brace up, Pop, 'n have another drink. (*The mugs are filled again.*)

UNCLE BENNY. Mighty strange things has happened on a night like this here, an' right nigh the Roanoke River here, too. I mind as how 'twas jest sech a storm as this when a ol' witch rid my ol' woman to death. Yes, suh, when she woke up in the mornin' they was dirt in between her fingers, an' her hair was all tangled up whar the witch had done made stirrups of it for to ride her through the briars. She was nigh about wore out, an' all she could do was to stare an' gape an' mumble 'bout goin' through the key-hole. . . .

JAKE (*scornfully*). Aw, shucks! Your ol' woman drunk herself to death an' I reckon it didn't take much ridin' to finish her, neither. If you'd been drivin' a railroad engine nigh about all over Carolina an' into Virginia like I have, you'd 'a seen so many sights that it'd take more'n any ol' hag to give you the shakes. Any ol' back-country witch like Phoebe Ward can't scare me off from a good dram like this here, let me tell you all that!

ED. They do say ol' Phoebe herself is prowlin' round in this neighborhood, her'n that durned ol' toad she carries round. She slept 'cross the river last night an' Jeff Bailey seen her cuttin' through the low-grounds 'bout dawn.

JAKE. Wal, I'd jest like to see ol' witch Phoebe one more time an' I'd finish for her. 'Clare to goodness the last time she come roun' to my house I fixed her good an' purty. (*Laughing loudly*.) I chucked the fire right full of red pepper pods an' she nigh about sneezed her head off. It didn't take ol' Phoebe long to pick up that toad of hers an' clear out of there, damned if it did! I reckon she won't come soon again to stay with me!

UNCLE BENNY (*fearfully. Rolling thunder is heard*). They do say as how she was married to the Devil hisself once. I've heared 'em say he's comin' hisself an' carry her off one of these days when her time's come.

JAKE. I reckon he'll get us all when our times comes, for all that. (*Laughing coarsely*.) Aw, brace up, Benny! I'd like to get my hands on that ol' toad. (UNCLE BENNY *looks around fearfully as though dreading her appearance. He gets up and shuffles slowly to the fireplace, speaking as he goes*.)

UNCLE BENNY. I've heared tell it was her toad that's her sperit. The varmint leads her to a place an' then sets on the hearth stones 'twell it's time for her to move. She won't stir from that place 'twell her ol' Gibbie commences to hop off first.

JAKE. She didn't wait for her toad to hop last time she visited me, let me tell you-all that!

UNCLE BENNY. You'd best to mind how you rile ol' Phoebe, Jake. They do say as him what angers her will be witched. They say her spell'll pass on him, an' Gibbie'll be his sperit. He'll have to move when that toad commences to hop jest the same as ol' Phoebe.

JAKE. Aw, I'd like to see any ol' toad-frog make me move on. A good jug of liquor's the only thing'd put a spell on me!

ED (*rises and speaks to* UNCLE BENNY *who is warming his hands at the fire*). Let's have another dram, Pop. (*As they stoop over the big jug in the corner to the right, a terrific thunder crash is heard. They drop the jug with a bang and* JAKE *strides over to them in a rage.*

The witch has entered unseen, having slipped through the curtain over the door. PHOEBE WARD *is very old, and bent, and wrinkled. Her dress is wrapped around her in rags and on her head she wears an old bonnet which does not hide her wizened face. There are two pockets in her skirt. She stands rubbing her hands, pinched and blue with the cold.*)

JAKE (*with his back to the door. He has not seen* PHOEBE). Damn you, give me that jug, you two ol' fools! Are you goin' to waste all the liquor yet? (*The others are bending over the jug, paralyzed by the sight of* PHOEBE, *who advances slowly into the room.*) What're you starin' at? (*He wheels around, sees* PHOEBE, *and starts back in amazement.*) The witch! (*There is a dead silence while* PHOEBE *shivers toward the fire.*)

ED (*hoarsely*). Good Lord! How'd she get in?

UNCLE BENNY (*cowering in fear*). Sure's you're born she's done come through the latch-hole!

JAKE (*hesitating*). What you doin' here?

PHOEBE. (*She ignores* JAKE *and comes down centre.* ED *and* UNCLE BENNY *cross to the left as she advances, and retreat behind the table in fear. She speaks to an object concealed in her pocket.*) Sh, now, Gibbie, quit your hoppin'. (*She takes the toad out of her pocket, shuffles slowly to the right and puts the toad on the end of the bench.*) Sh, now, this here's whar you'll leave me rest a bit now, ain't it? Thar now, toad-frog. (*She crosses to the right of the table.*) Uncle Benny, I'se powerful tired. I'se done come nigh onto ten mile from the river. Leave me rest a spell, me'n Gibbie?

UNCLE BENNY. Sure, now . . .

JAKE (*takes a step forward, menacingly*). Get out of here, you damned witch! (ED *and* UNCLE BENNY *regard his boldness with alarm.*)

PHOEBE (*slowly turns to* JAKE, *watching the effect of her words, which make even* JAKE *draw back*). 'Tain't no good luck it'll bring to you, Jake, if you drives me out again into the storm. My spell'll pass on him 'at harms me, an' the sperits'll be drivin' him like they drive ol' Phoebe. For it's my ol' man, the Devil, you'll be reckonin' with this time. It's the demons what're ridin' in the storm. Them an' Gibbie, they'll be drivin',—ain't it so, Gibbie? Drivin', drivin', an' never restin' 'twell Gibbie rests! Won't you leave me warm myself a bit, poor ol' Phoebe what the sperits has been drivin'?

ED. Don't rile her, Jake, don't rile her.

JAKE (*grudgingly, as he goes to the back of the room*). Wal, set down, Phoebe, an' warm yourself—(*Turns on her*)—but you got to ride yourself off presently, you hear me? (*He comes down toward the table.* PHOEBE *sits down on the bench, looking very helpless and old.*)

PHOEBE. 'Tain't as if I'll ever warm myself again, Jake. 'Tain't as if I'll ever set again an' watch the flames a-snappin' an' the sap a-sizzlin' in the hickory logs! When my Gibbie starts to hoppin' off from me this time, poor ol' Phoebe's 'bliged to go. She'll be gone for good, Jake, an' this here's the last time you'll lay your eyes on this poor ol' woman, Jake, this here's the last time . . . this here's the last time . . . (*Mumbling.*)

JAKE. What're you talkin' about, Phoebe? Are you studyin' for to ride off home to hell with your Ol' Man, the Devil?

UNCLE BENNY (*hoarsely*). She's goin' to ride us all to death, Jake. Don't make her witch us. Leave her be!

PHOEBE. (*a loud crash and roll of thunder is heard as the storm increases. The shutter and door rattle loudly in the wind.* PHOEBE *looks around wildly*.) I done hyeard the Black Uns callin' in the thunder. (*She rises and goes to the window*.) The Devil's ridin' on the fiery blaze o' lightnin' an' the Black Uns are a-screechin' in the wind. (*Frenzied*.) Oh, they're straddlin' on the storm clouds an' they're leanin' down an' stretchin' out an' callin' for ol' Phoebe. Don't you hear 'em, Jake, don't you hear them voices shriekin'? (*The wind blows loudly*.) Don't you hear them demon claws a-scratchin' at the door? They're callin' me, ain't they, Gibbie? An' when my time's done up, I'll go ridin' through the storm clouds an' this here's the last time you'll be seein' me on this earth. This here's the last time, ain't it, Gibbie? (*She mumbles to herself*.)

ED. Aw, what's she mumblin' 'bout? (*The candles flare in the draft*.)

UNCLE BENNY. Look! Look, Jake, we've got three candles a-burnin' an' it's a sure sign of death in this place. (*Quavering*.) Don't let her curse us all by dyin' in this place! (*He goes to* JAKE *and seizes him appealingly*.)

JAKE. Aw, I ain't no witch doctor!

PHOEBE. Be you feared I'll leave this here ol' corpse behind me when I go? Oh, the Black Uns'll be callin' when my time's done over here an' the Devil hisself'll take me to be ridin' by his side. I'll be ridin' on the storm clouds as they thunders through the sky! I'll be ridin' off in lightnin' an' you won't see no trace o' Phoebe left behin'. . . . Jest a little while . . . jest a little while. . . .

ED (*less frightened*). Aw, stay an' warm yourself, Phoebe, an' don't mind Jake. He's sort of queer hisself, I reckon. (*They watch as* PHOEBE *pulls the bench nearer to the fire and settles herself, crouched over the warmth. They sit down as far away from her as possible but* ED *and* UNCLE BENNY *are still uneasy. Thunder is heard*.)

PHOEBE. Gibbie, you been a-wrigglin' 'round an' hoppin'.

Don't be signin' me to go right yet. Jest leave me set a spell an' get a rest an' warmin'. Set still, Gibbie, set still, set still. . . .

UNCLE BENNY (*staring fascinated at the toad*). I don't like these here goin's-on, I don't. I don't like that varmint of hers!

ED. I sure wish that ol' toad would hop off from here an' sign the hag she's got to move on. I hope to God this here *is* the last time for ol' Phoebe!

PHOEBE (*lies down on the bench*). Set still, Gibbie, set still.

UNCLE BENNY (*quavering*). I—I don't like to stay in this place, Jake. 'Tain't no good luck comin' from three lights in a room an' I'm feared of that varmint. It's a demon, sure. One of us'll be witched if we stays! Let's us go!

JAKE (*shaking off any fears and speaking with studied gruffness. Rolling thunder is heard*). An' let the screechin' devils get you from the clouds!

ED. That ol' toad makes my flesh crawl. Somethin's goin' to happen!

JAKE. Aw, come on, boys. I ain't goin' to let this here hag an' her dirty ol' toad spoil my good liquor. I'm goin' to have a drink. (*He fills the jug and pours more whiskey in the mugs. As he goes to the corner to the big jug he looks defiantly at* PHOEBE.) She's done gone to sleep as peaceful as you please. (*He sits down to drink and the others recover a little.*) I ain't goin' to let ol' Phoebe witch me. I ain't feared of her.

ED (*looking intently at* JAKE). They do say as how witches cain't harm them as is like themselves. (*Insinuating.*) They do say they's men witches, too.

JAKE. (*Begins to show drunken bravado. He speaks sarcastically.*) Well, now, mebbe I am a witch. I ain't never thought about it before. I never did know jest how to call myself, but mebbe that's jest what I am, a witch. (*Laughing, with a swagger at* UNCLE BENNY.) You'd better look out for me, Benny!

UNCLE BENNY. Aw, now, Jake, I ain't never done nothin' agin' you, Jake. Now you know I ain't, Jake.

ED (*half maliciously*). They do say there's somethin' queer when a man ain't a-feared of a witch an' her demon.

JAKE. Naw, I ain't feared of her. (*He takes another drink. All show the effects of the liquor.*) An' I'll tell you-all what I'll do. I'll go right up to the old hag an' snatch that cap right off'n her head, I will! (*He rises.*)

ED. They do say she keeps a heap of money in that ol' bonnet o' hers.

UNCLE BENNY (*he rises*). Don't tech her, Jake. Don't rile her. Leave her be. (*As* JAKE *advances to the bench where* PHOEBE *lies.*) Aw, Jake!

JAKE. I'll see if this here ol' bundle is full o' demon witch-spells or jest good money. (*He puts out his hand toward the cap.*)

UNCLE BENNY (*jumps up, trembling with horror, as a crash of thunder is heard outside*). Don't, Jake! Look at that witch! Look thar! That ain't nothin' but her skin layin' thar. See how shrivelled 'tis. Oh, lordy, Jake. She's done already slipped out'n her hide an' she's ridin' through the sky. She left her skin behind! (*With despair.*) Oh, lordy, lordy.

JAKE. Aw, drat you, Benny. Quit your shriekin'. You'll jump out'n your own skin next. This here's Phoebe Ward an' all of her, too,—(*With a swagger*)—an' I'll show you! (*Before* UNCLE BENNY *can stop him he reaches out and lays a finger on* PHOEBE's *hand. He draws back, awestruck.*) Wal, I'll be damned! (*Touches her again.*) My God, Benny, if she ain't dead! Get a lookin' glass, Ed. (ED *brings a cracked glass from the mantel shelf.* JAKE *holds it before* PHOEBE's *mouth.*) Yes, sir, sure's you're born, Phoebe Ward's done blew out. She's had her last ride for sure.

UNCLE BENNY (*wildly entreating*). Cover her up, Jake. Cover her up! I don't want to see her no more. Them three lights was a sign. Oh, lordy, lordy!

JAKE (*goes to the door and pulls down the old sheet, throws it over* PHOEBE). Thar, now, that'll do. (*He goes to the table and drains his glass.*) Here, brace up, all, an' have a drink. (*They drink in silence.*)

ED. Wal, she's gone.

JAKE. Say, you-all, ol' Phoebe's dead an' I reckon we might's well drink her wake right now. Fill up, all. (ED *pours the whiskey while* JAKE *takes the candles from the table and places two at the head and one at the feet of the "corpse."*)

ED (*gulping*). Here's you, Jake! (*He drinks.*)

JAKE. Here's to ol' Phoebe. (*He drinks, laughing coarsely.*)

UNCLE BENNY. Oh, Lord, help us. (*He drinks.*)

ED. This place's gettin' cold—needs some more wood on the fire. (*The fire has burned low and the light is dim.*)

JAKE. Wal, *you* put it on.

ED (*solemnly*). I wouldn't go nigh that there witch's corpse, not if her ol' cap was plumb full of gold!

JAKE. Aw, I'd shake hands with her ol' man, the Devil his-self, to-night. (JAKE *gets up and goes around the bench to the woodpile, with his back to the "corpse."* PHOEBE *sits up, very slowly, and feebly pushes aside the shroud. The thunder is heard above the storm outside. The shutter bangs and the candles are puffed out.* JAKE *drops his load of wood into the fire and turns toward the bench as he hears the sound behind him. He leans against the side of the fireplace. All stand spellbound, gazing at the witch.*)

PHOEBE. Uncle Benny, gimme a drap o' liquor. It's mighty cold over here. (*Shivering, she gets up and shuffles toward the table.* ED *and* UNCLE BENNY *retreat in horror.*) I'm done frizzed clean through . . . jest one little drap . . . before I go! This here's my last time! (*She picks up a cup and gulps hurriedly as if fearful that she will be forced to go before it is finished.*) This here's my last time!

JAKE (*infuriated*). This here's your last time, is it? Warn't you dead? Ain't we done drunk your wake? Ain't it time to bury you now? You git yourself out'n that thar door, Phoebe Ward! You're dead for sure an' I'm going to bury you now. (*The storm outside grows fiercer, with the heavy sound of thunder. Flashes of lightning are seen through the window as the shutter swings in the wind.*)

PHOEBE (*menacingly to* JAKE). You'd best to leave me be, Jake! 'Tain't in your hands to dig a grave whar Phoebe'll lie. 'Twon't be no good that'll follow him as sees me ride the clouds to-night!

JAKE (*frenzied, he dashes her aside and strides to the door*). You won't ride the clouds no more'n I will, you damned witch! You're dead an' it's time you're buried! (*He stumbles through the door.*) Come on out, or I'll come back an' drag you out when I get your grave dug. (*Vivid lightning is seen through the door as* JAKE *strides out. Loud crashes of thunder sound near by.*)

PHOEBE (*exalted, listening as she moves to the door*). Oh, I hear the Black Uns thunderin' down the pathways of the sky! I hear 'em whirlin' through the clouds an' dartin' flames of fire! It's all of hell is risin' up to carry me away! (*Strong wind and rolling thunder are heard.*) Oh, they're screamin' out for Phoebe an' they're wild to sweep her through the storm with the Devil at her side! 'Tis the Devil hisself is waitin' an' he's scorchin' up the blackness with the lightnin's of his eyes! (*As though in answer to a call from without.*) I'm comin', I'm comin'! I'll be ridin'! I'll be ridin'! (*She stands in the open door, facing the room, and a terrific flash of lightning throws her figure into dark silhouette. Then she retreats backward and the door bangs behind her.* UNCLE BENNY *and* ED *are left crouching by the table.*)

UNCLE BENNY. She's gone. She'll get Jake.

ED. Oh, Lord, where's her toad? Where's her sperit? (*There is a wild crack and crash of thunder, the door bangs open and there is another blinding flash of lightning.* JAKE *stumbles through the door in terrible fright. His hands are over his eyes, as if he is blinded. He gropes, stumbling, to the table and falls into a seat.*)

JAKE (*stunned*). I seen 'im! I seen 'im!

UNCLE BENNY. My Lord!

ED. What— What was it, Jake?

JAKE (*wildly*). I'm witched! Oh, I seen all the Black Uns in Hell, I seen the Devil hisself! I seen 'im, I seen the Ol' Man! The heavens done opened like a blazin', roarin' furnace an' the storm clouds wrapped ol' Phoebe 'round an' snatched her up in fire! An' all the clawin' demons out'n Hell rid roarin' past my ears. Oh, they've blinded me with balls of fire an' knocked me to the ground. An' the Devil hisself done carried off ol' Phoebe for to ride among the witches. I seen 'im, I done seen 'im!

ED. My God, he seen the Devil! He's witched sure.

UNCLE BENNY. (*Moves back trembling and steps against the toad, which has moved near to the table. He jumps in fright and stares at it in horror.*) Oh, good Lord, the spell's here!

ED. What do you see?

UNCLE BENNY. The toad!

JAKE. My God! She left her toad!

ED. It's done moved! It's moved from where she put it.

UNCLE BENNY. Her spell's passed on Jake. Her demon's witched him! Oh, lordy!

JAKE. It's moved, it's moved! (*Struggling as with a spell.*) Oh, I got to go too. The witch's toad's done got me an' I got to go. (*Retreating from the toad with his hands to his eyes as before.*) I'm comin', Gibbie, I'm comin', I'm comin'. . . . (*He turns at the door and stumbles out into the night. The door remains open on blackness and a roaring wind blows through the room, leaving it nearly in darkness as* ED *and* UNCLE BENNY *stare at the toad and retreat in horror.*)

ED. It done got him!

UNCLE BENNY. The Devil took him! Oh, Lord, help us. Oh, lordy, lordy! (ED *and* UNCLE BENNY *fall on their knees and crouch in abject terror. The sound of thunder is heard rolling in the distance.*)

CURTAIN

PEGGY

A Tragedy of the Tenant Farmer

BY

HAROLD WILLIAMSON

17

PEGGY

Peggy is a little tragedy of tenant farm life written by Harold Williamson of Carthage in eastern North Carolina. Here the drab cabin that we had passed a thousand times as a dull sight, was suddenly transformed—something new, something strange, something wonderful! Here the jaded farm woman, Mag, with snuffstick protruding from the corner of her mouth, getting supper of cornbread and fatback, singing the while snatches of an old ballad, was no longer a commonplace figure. She had been changed by the magic of the theatre. The tragic fact of her hard-won existence had become a reality to us—life itself that moves and feels—an exciting drama!

The characters in this play were drawn from life. "Although far from typical of North Carolina, such conditions as are here portrayed are not uncommon in some localities," the author writes. "The action of the play is a true transcript of the family life of the characters in the play, as I have known them in real life."

As far as I know, *Peggy* was the first play to be written about the poor sharecropper of the South. Later came *Fixin's* by Erma and Paul Green. Today the plight of this forgotten class of country people has been vividly portrayed in Jack Kirkland's sensational treatment of Erskine Caldwell's story of the degenerate white tenants of the backlands of Georgia in *Tobacco Road*.

Fred Howard of Black Creek in eastern North Carolina, in his one-act tragedy of the Negro tenant, *New Nigger*,[1] and his later full-length *Sharecropper*,[2] presents the revolt of the Negro against the white plantation owner in the Carolina tobacco country.

[1] Produced by The Carolina Playmakers, Chapel Hill, N. C., April 26 and 27, 1935. Included in their thirty-third tour, November 13–26, 1935.
[2] Produced by The Carolina Playmakers, Chapel Hill, N. C., February 24, 25 and 26, 1938.

19

CAST OF CHARACTERS

As originally produced on The Playmakers' Stage, Chapel Hill, North Carolina, May 30 and 31, 1919.

WILL WARREN, *a tenant farmer*,	George McF. McKie
MAG WARREN, *his wife*,	Elizabeth Taylor
PEGGY, *their daughter, aged 18*,	Virginia McFayden
HERMAN, *their son, aged 6*,	Nat Henry
JED, *a farm hand, in love with Peggy*,	Harold Williamson
JOHN MCDONALD, *the landowner*,	George Denny
WESLEY MCDONALD, *his son, a University student*,	
	George Crawford

SCENE: A tenant farm in North Carolina. The bare living-room of a two-room cabin.

TIME: The present. An April evening, about seven o'clock.

SCENE

The scene is laid in one of the two rooms of a tenant shack. In the centre of the room is a square eating-table with an oil-cloth cover. On each side of the table is a straw-bottom chair. A small, worn cook-stove is in the left corner and beside it a wood-box. At the right of the stove is a rectangular table on which are a dishpan and other cooking utensils. Against the back wall is a cupboard which holds the meagre supply of tableware. On top of it are several paper sacks and pasteboard boxes containing cooking materials. A door in the right side leads from the eating-room into the only other room of the shack, used as a sleeping-room. A door at the back on the left leads outdoors. Through this doorway can be seen a crude string lattice-work partly covered by a growing vine, and a shelf supporting a bucket and gourd. A small window is at the right in the back wall. The floor and walls are bare. Everything has a fairly neat appearance but suggests the struggle against a degrading poverty.

As the curtain rises MAG WARREN *is busily preparing supper, singing as she works.* HERMAN *is sitting on the floor tying a piece of rope to the end of a broom handle.*

MAG WARREN *is a thin, bent, overworked woman of forty-two. Her face reveals the strain of years of drudgery. Her thin hair is drawn tightly into a knot on the back of her head. She wears a cheap calico dress and a faded checkered apron. In the pocket of her apron is a large snuff can. A protruding snuff-brush claims the right corner of her mouth.[1] She beats up a batter of cornbread, pours it into a pan on the stove, and after pouring some water into a large coffee-pot, she begins to slice some "fatback."* [2]

[1] The habit of "dipping snuff" is common among the poor whites in all sections of North Carolina. A twig is chewed into shreds at one end and is known as a snuff-stick or "tooth-brush." This is dipped into the powdered snuff and then rubbed over the gums and teeth. The women seem to get much satisfaction from this practice.

[2] "Fatback" is fat salt pork which, together with cornbread, forms

21

Mag's Song

A rich man lay on his
Three years rolled by and the

vel - vet couch, He ate from plates of
rich man died, He de - scend - ed to fiery

gold; ___ A poor girl stood on the
hell, ___ The poor girl lay in the

mar - ble steps, And said, "So cold, so cold." ___
an - gel's arms, And sighed, "All's well, all's well." ___

Herman is an under-sized boy of six years with a vacant expression on his pinched face. He wears a faded shirt, and a lone suspender over his right shoulder gives scanty support for his patched pants, which strike him midway between the knee and the ankle. He is barefooted. When he finishes fixing his " horse," he gets up, straddles the stick, and trots over all the unoccupied part of the room.

HERMAN. Git up, Kit . . . whoa . . . ha. (*Whipping the stick.*) What's the matter? Cain't you plow straight? (*In his trotting he runs into* MAG *at the stove. She turns on him angrily.*)

MAG. Git out'n my way an' git over thar in the corner. (*Utterly subdued,* HERMAN *goes and sits in the corner while* MAG *goes on with her work. Presently she turns to him.*) Go git me a turn o' wood, an' don't you take all day about it neither. (HERMAN *goes out.* MAG *continues to sing, moving* the main part of the diet of "hog and hominy" eaten by poor whites the year 'round.

about between the table, stove, and cupboard as she prepares the meal. JED SMITH *enters. He is a tall, lanky, uncanny-looking fellow of twenty-four. He is dressed in the shabby shirt and faded blue overalls of an ordinary poor farm-laborer. He walks in slowly and lazily and says nothing. As he goes to the table* MAG *looks up at him from her work.*)

MAG. I thought you was Will, Jed. (*She continues her work.*) Seen anything o' Pegg? Hit's a-gittin' mighty high time she's back here.

JED (*pulls out a chair from the table, flops down in it, and begins whittling on a stick*). That's what I come to see you about, Mag.

MAG (*stopping her work and looking around at* JED). Ain't nothing' happened, air there, Jed?

JED. Nothin' to git skeered about, but ol' man McDonald's boy come in from one o' them 'air colleges th' other day an' I jest seen Pegg down yonder a-talkin' to him an' a-lookin' at him mighty sweet-like. 'Tain't the fust time neither.

MAG (*goes up nearer to* JED). So that's what's been a-keepin' her?

JED. Yeah, an' if you don't watch out, Mag, there's a tale goin' to git out an' ol' man McDonald'll drive you off'n the place.

MAG. You're right, Jed. Jest wait till me an' her pa gits through with her. We'll put a stop to it.

JED (*nervously*). Now don't go an' tell her I told you, Mag.

MAG. You needn't be skeered. I been a-thinkin' as much myself. She's been powerful uppity lately, but I didn't know what about. Her pa's allus said that perty face o' hern would be the ruinin' of her. Don't you know Wes McDonald wouldn't be a-havin' nothin' to do with Pegg 'lessen she was perty?

JED. Naw.

MAG. She's clear out'n his class an' ain't got sense enough to know it. (*She turns the corn cake in the pan.*) An' it's a perty way she's a-doin' you, Jed.

JED (*drearily*). Yeah, I reckon she ain't likin' me no more. (HERMAN *returns with the wood and throws it in the box.*)

MAG. Ain't she said she'd marry you?

JED. Aw, she did onc't.

MAG. An' you're a good match for her, too. Will's a-been a-sayin' how good you are at the plow.

JED. I'd shore like to have her, Mag.

MAG. Well, if you want her you can git her, Jed. She's done a right smart o' washin' an' a-cookin' an' a-hoein' in her day an' I reckon she'll make you a good woman.

JED. I ain't a-worryin' about that.

MAG (*looking out of the window*). Yonder she comes now. Ain't no tellin' what fool notions that boy has been a-puttin' in her head, but you jest wait till me an' her pa gits through with her.

JED (*rising nervously*). Reckon I'll be a-goin' now, Mag.

MAG. Ain't you goin' to wait an' see Pegg? 'Pears like you'd be a-pushin' yourself.

JED. Naw, I . . . I'll come back after I eat.

MAG. Well, you come back. Me an' her pa'll have her in a notion then.

HERMAN (*stops* JED *as he is going out*). Gimme some terbaccer, Jed.

JED (*feels in his pockets*). I ain't got none, Herman. (*He goes out.*)

MAG. What'd I tell you about axin' folks for terbaccer? When you want terbaccer ax your pa for it.

HERMAN. He won't gimme none.

MAG. Well, it don't make no odds. You don't do nothin' but waste it nohow. (HERMAN *sits down on the floor to the front and begins to play aimlessly.*)

PEGGY *comes in, flushed and happy. She is a pretty girl of*

eighteen years. She has attractive features, is of medium height,
slim and lively. Her hair is light and becomingly disheveled.
Her dress is extremely simple but shows signs of care.

PEGGY. Supper ready, ma?

MAG. Cain't you see it ain't? Why ain't you been here long
ago a-helpin' me to git supper?

PEGGY (*putting the milk bucket she has brought in with her on
the table, she goes over to the left to hang up her bonnet*). I
couldn't finish milkin' no sooner.

MAG. You needn't tell me you been a-milkin' all this time.
Where you been anyhow?

PEGGY. I stopped to help Lizzie Taylor hang out her wash.

MAG. Been anywheres else?

PEGGY. No'm.

MAG. Well, git busy a-fixin' that table, an' tell me what fool
notions Wes McDonald's been a-puttin' into your head.

PEGGY (*she tries to look surprised*). I don't know nothin' 'bout
Wes McDonald, ma.

MAG. Don't you lie to your ma like that, Pegg. You think
I don't know nothin' 'bout it, but you cain't fool your ma.
He's been a-settin' up to you, ain't he?

PEGGY. No, ma, he ain't said nothin' to me, he . . .

MAG. Now be keerful.

PEGGY. He jest spoke to me, an' I jest axed him how he liked
to go off to school an' he said he liked it an' he axed me why
I wasn't goin' to school an' I told him I had to work.

MAG. Didn't he say nothin' 'bout your bein' perty?

PEGGY (*proudly*). Yes, he said I was perty. Said if I had book-
learnin' an' lived uptown I'd be the pick o' the whole
bunch.

MAG. That's what I was a-thinkin' he'd be a-puttin' into
your head. You keep out'n Wes McDonald's way. He ain't
a-keerin' nothin' for you and besides he'll git you into

trouble. Wait till your pa hears o' this. (*There is a silence while* MAG *goes on with her work.*)

PEGGY (*looking out of the window, wistfully*). I reckon it'd be nice to go to school.

MAG. Mebbe it is. If you'd a-been rich, schoolin' might a-done you some good, but you ain't rich an' schoolin's only for them as is rich. Me an' your pa never had no schoolin', and I reckon you can git along 'thout any yourself. (*She goes to the door and looks off anxiously across the fields.*) Hit's high time your pa was a-gittin' home.

HERMAN. I'd like to see pa myself. Want some terbaccer.

MAG. (*comes to the front. Solemnly*). I been mighty skeered 'bout your pa ever since the doctor told him he had that 'air misery round his heart.

PEGGY. Did he say 'twas dangerous?

MAG (*going back to the stove*). Well, he said your pa was liable to keel over most any time if he ain't mighty keerful. Ol' man McDonald's got him down yonder in that 'air new ground a-bustin' roots an' it ain't a-doin' your pa no good neither.

PEGGY. I jest seen pa an' Mr. McDonald a-talkin' together an' both of 'em was mighty mad about somethin'.

MAG. I reckon your pa struck him for a raise, an' he ought to have it. A dollar an' a quarter a day ain't enough, workin' like your pa does, but ol' man McDonald'd see your pa clear to hell afore he'd pay him a cent more. (*She goes to the door, takes the snuff-brush from her mouth and spits out the snuff. She puts the snuff-brush in her pocket, takes a drink of water from the gourd and washes her mouth out with it, spitting out the water. She speaks to* PEGGY *as she turns back to the stove.*) There's them cabbages your pa told you to hoe an' you ain't done it, have you?

PEGGY. No, ma, I ain't had time.

MAG. You had a-plenty o' time to let Wes McDonald put a lot o' fool notions in your head. You'll have a perty time a-tellin' your pa you ain't had time. (*There is a pause.*) Jed said as how he might come around after he's eat. Hit's a perty way you been a-treatin' Jed an' he ain't a-likin' it neither.

PEGGY. I don't care if he likes it or not. 'Tain't none o' his business.

MAG. Hit ain't? Ain't you done told him you was a-goin' to marry him?

PEGGY. I might have onc't, but I've changed my mind.

MAG (*angrily*). What's come over you anyhow?

PEGGY. Nothin', ma.

MAG. Well, I'd like to know what you think you're a-goin' to do? 'Tain't every man a woman can git, an' you ought to thank the Lord Jed's given you the chanct.

PEGGY. I ain't a-wantin' it. I ain't a-goin' to marry Jed an' have to work like a dog all my life—besides, I got to love the man I marry.

MAG (*scornfully*). Love? What's love got to do with your bread an' meat? You been a-readin' some o' them magazines as they git down at the house. I'd like to know what you think you're goin' to do?

PEGGY (*resolved*). I'm goin' to git me a job uptown an' *be* somebody!

MAG. There ain't nothin' you could do there. You was raised on a farm, an' I reckon that's jest about the place for you. You don't think you're better'n your ma, do you?

PEGGY. No, ma, but I could git me a job in the Five an' Ten Cent Store. Mary Cameron's got her a job there, an' she's a-wearin' fine clothes an' got a lot o' fellows.

MAG. Yes, an' there's a lot a-bein' said as to how she got them clothes. I tell you, me an' your pa ain't a-goin' to have nothin' like that.

PEGGY. But, ma, I——

MAG. Shet up. You behave yourself like you ought to before Jed. If you don't, you better.

PEGGY. I'll treat him all right but I ain't a-goin' to marry him.

MAG. Me an' your pa'll say if you will or not, an'——

PEGGY. The bread's a-burnin', ma!

MAG (*running quickly across the room she jerks the bread off the stove and dumps it into a pan on the table*). Good Lord, now don't that beat you? An' there ain't no more meal. (*She looks out of the door.*) Yonder comes your pa, too. Hurry up an' git that table laid while I git a bucket o' water. (*She takes the pail and hurries off.*)

WILL WARREN *comes in heavily. He is a slouchy, hump-shouldered man of fifty years. His hair is long and his face unshaven. He wears an old, dirty, sweat-stained black hat with a shaggy brim; a faded blue denim shirt; brown corduroy pants, worn slick, attached to a large pair of suspenders by nails; and brogan shoes with heavy gray socks falling over the top. He drags himself in and stands propped against the side of the door. His face is white and he appears entirely exhausted.*

HERMAN (*going up to* WILL). Gimme some terbaccer, pa. (WILL *pays no attention to him.*) Pa, gimme some terbaccer.

WILL (*giving* HERMAN *a slap on the face that sends him to the floor*). Git to hell away from me. (*He comes into the room slowly and unsteadily, pulls off his hat and throws it into the corner, and falls into a chair by the table, breathing heavily and staring blankly. He says nothing.*)

PEGGY. (*She notices* WILL'S *heavy breathing and is alarmed.*) What's the matter, pa, ain't you feelin' well?

WILL (*struggling for breath*). Gimme . . . some coffee . . . quick!

PEGGY. (*Quickly pouring a cup of coffee and giving it to him. He gulps it down and appears considerably relieved.*) You ain't sick, air you, pa?

WILL. Naw. . . . It's another one o' them durned miseries round my heart. (*He gulps the coffee.*) I ain't a-goin' to

work another day in that durned new ground. I told Mc-
Donald I wouldn't an' damned if I do.

MAG (*who has now come back, and has overheard his words*). I
don't blame you for sayin' so, but there ain't no use in
flyin' off'n the handle like that.

WILL. Well, I said it an' I'll do it. These here money men
like McDonald think as how they can work a poor man
like me to death an' pay me nothin' for it neither, but
durned if I don't show him.

MAG. What'd he say when you axed him for a raise?

WILL. Aw, he said he was a-losin' money every year. He
allus says that. Says he ain't a-raisin' enough to pay for
the growin' of it, but don't you reckon I know how much
he's a-raisin'? He's a-gittin' thirty cents a pound for his
cotton an' two dollars a bushel for his corn, an' then he
says he ain't a-makin' nothin'. He cain't lie to me, he's
a-gittin' rich.

MAG. Course he is. Ain't he jest bought another one o' them
automobiles th' other day?

WILL. Yeah, an' while him an' that no'count boy o' his'n
are a-ridin' around in it I'm down yonder in that 'air new
ground a-gittin' a dollar an' a quarter a day for killin'
myself over them durned roots. Jest afore quittin' time I
come mighty nigh givin' out.

MAG. (*brings the cornbread and "fatback" and puts it on
the table.* PEGGY *busies herself at the table and cupboard.*)
You better take keer o' yourself. You know what the doctor told you.

WILL. Yeah, but how in the devil can I help it like things
are now? I told him what's what a while ago, an' damned if
I don't stick to it too. (*He looks over the table.*) What you
got for supper? (*Seeing the burnt bread, he picks it up and
hurls it to the floor.*) What kind o' durned cookin' do you
call this you're doin', anyway?

MAG. It wouldn't a-happened if Pegg hadn't been
a-pesterin' me.

WILL (*angrily to* PEGGY). Well, what you been a-doin'?

PEGGY. Nothin', pa.

MAG. In the fust place, you told her to hoe them cabbages.

WILL. Ain't you done it?

MAG. No, she ain't done it, but she's been down yonder a-lettin' Wes McDonald put a lot o' fool notions into her head about her bein' perty, an' now she says she ain't a-goin' to marry Jed.

WILL (*savagely to* PEGGY). You ain't, air you?

PEGGY (*half crying but defiant*). No, pa, I ain't. I've seen you an' ma a-workin' from sun-up to sun-down like niggers an' jest a-makin' enough to keep us out'n the poorhouse, an' I ain't a-goin' to live no sich life with Jed. He couldn't do no better.

WILL. Well, durn your hide . . .

MAG. An' she says she'll git her a job uptown like Mary Cameron's got. You know what's a-bein' said about Mary! (*To* PEGGY.) Don't you know we ain't a-goin' to have nothin' like that? (*She shakes her finger at* PEGGY.)

PEGGY. But, ma, I . . .

WILL. Shet up. We've raised you up here an' it's us as'll say what you'll do. Jed axed you to marry him an' durn it, you'll do it, too.

PEGGY. I won't.

WILL (*rising from the chair*). You won't? Don't you let me hear you say that agin.

PEGGY (*wildly*). I won't, I won't, I won't!

WILL (*in uncontrolled rage*). Then, damn you, you can git right out'n this house right now an' . . .

MAG. Hush, Will, hush.

WILL (*breathing heavily and struggling in his speech*). An' don't you . . . let . . . me ever . . . see you . . . agin . . . (*Clutching his hands to his heart, he gasps, staggers backward, then falls heavily to the floor. The women stand stunned for a moment, then* MAG *rushes over, kneels by him, and shakes him.*)

MAG. Will, Will, . . . answer me, Will, . . . say somethin'. (*Turning to* PEGGY, *who has not moved, and speaking dully.*) Lord, Pegg, he's dead, . . . your pa's dead . . . he's gone. Send for somebody . . . quick!

PEGGY (*excitedly to* HERMAN). Run tell Mister McDonald to come here quick. He's down at the house. Go git him quick! (HERMAN *runs out.* MAG, *shaking with sobs, crouches over the body. Her head is buried in her apron.* PEGGY *tries to comfort her mother.*) Don't carry on like that, ma. It ain't a-doin' no good. (*Hopefully.*) Mebbe he ain't dead.

MAG. Yes, he is. He's gone. . . . Oh, Lord . . . I knowed it'd git him. (JED *appears at the door and stands stupefied for a moment.*)

JED (*coming into the room*). What's the matter? (*Going nearer to the body.*) What's the matter with Will?

MAG. He's gone, Jed, he's gone. O Lord!

JED. He ain't dead, is he? Who done it? (JED *kneels over the body and examines it for signs of life.* MAG *rises slowly, shuffles to a chair on the other side of the table and sits sobbing.*)

PEGGY (*appealing*). Is he dead, Jed, is he dead?

JED. I don't know. Git some camphor, quick. (PEGGY *runs into the other room for the camphor bottle.*

JOHN MCDONALD *enters, followed by his son,* WESLEY. *The farm-owner is a tall, prosperous-looking man of forty-eight. He has a hard face and stern, overbearing manner.*

WESLEY *is a rather handsome young fellow of twenty-one, a typical well-dressed college boy.*)

MCDONALD (*to* JED, *taking in the scene at a glance*). What's the matter? Is he dead?

JED (*rising*). I believe he is, Mister McDonald.

MCDONALD. How did it happen?

JED. I don't know.

MAG (*sobbing*). He's gone, Mister McDonald, he's gone. . . . He had another one of them fits with his heart jest like the doctor said he would, an' he went all of a sudden afore I knowed it.

McDONALD (*examining the body*). Well, he's dead all right, sure. (PEGGY *runs in with the camphor bottle.*) That's no use, he's dead. Jed, let's put him on the bed in the other room. (*They carry the body off the stage,* MAG *following.*)

WESLEY. I'm awfully sorry, Peggy. Tell me how it happened.

PEGGY (*crying*). He got mad with me because I said I wouldn't marry Jed, an' he jest got madder an' madder an' told me to leave an' never come back. An' then he put his hands up to his heart like this, an' fell over.

WESLEY. Did he have heart trouble?

PEGGY. Yeah, I reckon so. He's been a-havin' pains in his side, an' a-chokin' for wind, an' the doctor said he'd have to be keerful.

WESLEY. And he wanted you to marry Jed?

PEGGY. Yeah, he said I'd have to.

WESLEY (*understandingly*). And you didn't want to?

PEGGY. No, if I married him I'd have to work like a dog all my life, an' I ain't a-goin' to do it.

WESLEY. I don't blame you, Peggy, but what are you going to do?

PEGGY. I'm goin' to git me a job uptown.

WESLEY. You mustn't go there, Peggy. You couldn't get along there.

PEGGY (*looking to him wistfully*). Well, what can I do?

WESLEY (*thoughtfully*). I don't know. . . . I guess you'd better marry Jed. (*There is a pause.* PEGGY *goes over to the window and looks out hopelessly.*) If everything was different I'd . . . Oh, I didn't mean that. You see such a thing would be impossible.

PEGGY (*turning to him, hopefully*). But I could . . .

WESLEY. Stop, Peggy. . . . I think a lot of you but don't you see I couldn't do more? It's impossible. Don't cry that way, Peggy. I'm sorry I said what I did this afternoon. I didn't mean to upset you like this. Go on and marry Jed. He's all right and I'll see that he gets a good showing.

PEGGY (*desperately*). But I don't want to. I know how it'll turn out. (MCDONALD *and* JED *return, followed by* MAG.)

MAG (*without hope*). What's a-goin' to come of us now?

MCDONALD (*brusquely*). I don't know, Mag.

MAG. You ain't a-goin' to make us leave, air you?

MCDONALD. Let's not talk about that now.

MAG. But tell me, Mister McDonald, will we have to leave?

MCDONALD (*impatient*). Well, if you just must know right now, Mag, I'm sorry to say it, but I don't see how I can keep you here.

MAG (*imploring him*). For God's sake don't make us leave the place!

MCDONALD. Now don't get foolish, Mag. You see it's a business proposition with me. With Will gone there's nothing you and your family could do on the farm that would pay me to keep you here. It's the man I need, especially now when there is so much plowing to be done, and as soon as I can I will have to get another man to take Will's place. Of course he will have to live in this house.

MAG (*resentful*). After Will has worked for you steady for sixteen year you ain't a-goin' to turn me out now, air you?

MCDONALD. I'm sorry if you look at it in that way, Mag, but business is business, and I can't afford to keep you here.

MAG. But, Mister McDonald, we ain't got nowhere else to go . . . an' we'd starve to death. (*She turns away sobbing.*)

MCDONALD. You ought to be thankful for what I've done for Will. He was about the sorriest hand I ever had. There's absolutely nothing you can do. I can't keep you.

WESLEY. But, father, you can't turn them away like this.

McDONALD. It's time you were learning that business is not a charitable institution, Wesley. I'm trying to run a farm, not a hard-luck asylum.

JED. Mister McDonald, let me see you a minute. (*He goes over and whispers to* McDONALD.)

McDONALD (*to* JED). Well, if you do that everything will be all right! (PEGGY *looks up hopefully. He turns to* MAG.) Jed has just said that if Peggy would marry him he will let you and the boy stay here in the house with them. If you want to do that it will be all right with me. (PEGGY, *disheartened, sits down by the table and buries her head in her arms, crying.*)

MAG. You'll marry Jed, won't you, Pegg? You'll do it for your ma, won't you?

McDONALD. Well, I'll leave that for you to decide. You can let me know later. (*Going to the door.*) Come, Wesley. I'll send to town for something to put him in, and Jed can get help to dig the grave. If you want anything, let me know. (McDONALD *and* WESLEY *go out.* WESLEY *hesitates in the door a moment, looking with sympathy at* PEGGY).

JED (*he goes slowly and uneasily over to* PEGGY). You ain't a-goin' to turn me down, air you, Peggy?

MAG (*imploring*). You'll marry Jed, won't you, Pegg? You ain't a-goin' to see your ol' ma go to the poorhouse, air you, Pegg?

PEGGY (*after a moment of silence she raises her head and speaks in broken sobs*). I reckon . . . it's the only way . . . for me.

CURTAIN

DOD GAST YE BOTH!

A Comedy of Mountain Moonshiners

BY

HUBERT C. HEFFNER

DOD GAST YE BOTH!

This is a play dealing with moonshiners of western North Carolina. It is a comedy of folk characters lifted out of contemporary life and portrayed through the medium of drama.

A group of mountaineers, lounging around a blockade still which nestled in a thicket of rhododendron and laurel on the side of Grandfather Mountain, one summer day not long ago decided to play a trick on old Noah Setzer, a moonshiner and boss of the Ridge, by telling him that his daughter Mary had "fell" for a certain suspicious stranger who had come into those parts and who was believed to be a "revenooer." Out of this prank and the results that came from it, the plot was developed.

After writing the play, the author took it back to the Hills and read it to Noah one winter evening by his still. To find himself in a play and to hear his very words spoken again quite amazed and delighted the old man. He laughed as he heard again how he had been fooled into getting a "revenooer" for a son-in-law. As he got up to stir his mash, he said, "But hit was a kind o' unnad'ral joke to pull on me atter all!"

One summer on the occasion of a subsequent visit to the scene of his play, Mr. Heffner, the author, found old Sank, the bootlegger for old Noah (whose part he himself played in the original cast) in jail for moonshining.

CAST OF CHARACTERS

As originally produced on The Playmakers' Stage, Chapel Hill, North Carolina, April 30 and May 1, 1920.

NOAH SETZER, *a mountain moonshiner,*	George Denny
WALT, *his son, an ex-member of the A.E.F.,*	Wilbur Stout
MARY, *his daughter,*	Ione Markham
BILL SPIVINS, *a rough mountaineer,*	Bergin Lohr
MOSE, } *frequenters of the still and boot-*	{ Chester Burton
SANK, } *leggers for Noah*	{ Hubert Heffner
LAURENCE ABNER, *a "revenooer,"*	George Crawford

SCENE: A dense thicket in the mountains of North Carolina. TIME: Four o'clock in the morning. The spring of 1919.

SCENE

A typical mountain moonshiner's retreat in a remote cove in the mountains of western North Carolina.

The whole scene is hedged in on all sides by a thicket of tall rhododendron. At the back runs a small, trickling brook which supplies the water for distilling purposes. On the left is the still proper, to the right at the rear, the mash tub. Boards are nailed between some of the trees to form rough benches. Near the front of the stage three modern, high-powered rifles are stacked against a tree. The ground immediately around the still shows signs of much tramping.

When the curtain rises WALT *is discovered, standing by the mash tub, leaning idly on his paddle and smoking a cigarette.* SANK *is stretched out on a bench at the right, fast asleep and snoring loudly.* MOSE *sprawls on the ground near the still, smoking an old cob pipe.*

MOSE *is a heavy-set, rough mountaineer. He is dressed in a blue shirt, patched coat, and dirty khaki pants, stuffed into heavy laced boots. There is almost a week's growth of stubby beard on his face.*

SANK *is a thin, shriveled old man of about sixty years, so bent as to appear little. He is dressed in dirty khaki trousers, blue shirt, worn coat and heavy shoes, with blue knit socks hanging down over his shoe-tops. His beard is very scant—thin as is his shrill, effeminate voice.*

WALT *is a lank, lazy-looking fellow of about twenty-two. An ex-member of the A.E.F., he still wears his overseas cap and military breeches.*

WALT (*looking at his heavy turnip watch*). 'Bout four o'clock. Soon be through. So the cops give ye a hard run of it, did they, Mose? (*He stirs the mash.*)

39

Mose. Yeah, since that thar pro-ser-ser-bition . . . they're gittin' tighter'n a rum jug. I used to could take a run o' brandy to Lenore an' measure hit out right on the streets, but ye can't do it no more.

Walt. Guess ye took the preachers their half o' gallon per, all right, did ye?

Mose (*speaking with a drawl, between the puffs of his pipe*). Yeah, ever' sanctified one of 'em. They can't preach their hell fire and brimstone sermonts if they ain't got their fiery spirits. Hit's about time th' ol' man was comin' back. He's had time to send in the watchers, an' he seemed to be so anxious to finish up an' go home. Ye'd better git to stirrin' that mash.

Walt (*smoking idly*). Oh, well. Mary'll meet th' ol' man if she went by the back way. What ye reckon she came fer, anyway, Mose? 'Tain't nothin' here she wanted this time o' night, an' she didn't git nothin'.

Mose. Dunno. (*He puffs his pipe a moment.*) Walt, since that revenoor is come in these parts, I don't like fer yer ol' man to send in the watchers like he allus does afore we git the run off.

Walt. Oh, well, but I don't reckon thar's any danger. He's been at it fer 'bout forty year an' hain't got took yit. I'll say sumpin' to him about it afore long.

Mose. Ye'd better not to-night. Th' ol' man's mad as a hornet to-night. Ever'thin's gone wrong an' he's a-bilin' over.

Walt. Ye needn't worry. I know th' ol' man better'n that. (*There is a sound of heavy footsteps outside as* Noah *stumbles in the thicket and mutters an oath.*) That's him comin' now. Don't ye say a word 'bout Mary's bein' here, hear?

Mose. Yeah, but some o' these nights he's goin' t' send in his watchers too early fer th' last time.

Walt. Don't reckon so, but if'n he does—then au re-war! (*The sound of tramping draws nearer and* Noah *stamps heavily in. He is a stocky mountaineer, sixty-five years of age—heavy-set, active and muscular. He wears dirty breeches, stained with mash, rough laced boots, a worn hunter's coat and blue shirt. His bushy gray hair sticks through the torn crown of the old hat which he wears jammed down on his head. His face is covered with a stubby gray beard. He looks crabbed and sullen.*

SANK *snores on.* MOSE *smokes in silence. As* NOAH *enters,* WALT *stirs the mash industriously, but he stops and leans lazily on his paddle as the old man goes to the still and begins fussing with the fire, muttering to himself.* NOAH *glares at him several times, then bursts out.*)

NOAH. Walt, durn yer lazy hide! Stir that mash an' git a move on ye.

WALT. Oui, oui, mess-sure. But, pa, what ye want t' rush so fer? I'll git this mash ready toot-sweet, 'fore ye're ready fer it.

NOAH. Stop yer durn toot-sweetin' an' git t' work. How the devil d'ye 'spect to git this run done 'fore mornin' if ye ain't a-goin' to work! (NOAH *continues to work at the still.* WALT *stirs the mash for a few moments and then leans idly on his paddle once more.*

MOSE (*still sprawling on the ground*). T'other night, like I was a-tellin' ye, Walt, when I was comin' back from takin' that run o' brandy down to Lenore, I heared that man Abner had been kind o' hangin' roun' yer sis Mary.

WALT. Who tol' ye that? (*He pokes his mash paddle at* SANK'S *nose.*) Wake up thar, Sank! Fall out! (WALT *laughs.* SANK *sleepily strikes at the paddle and begins to yawn and stretch.*)

MOSE. I heared it down to Patterson when I was a-comin' back, but I disrecollec' who tol' it.

WALT. Pertite madamerzelle! D'ye hear that, pa? (NOAH *works on, sullenly refusing to answer.* SANK *is now sufficiently awake to catch the last remark.*)

SANK. Hear what, Walt? Hear what, ye say?

MOSE. Hear that Mary's been a-carryin' on with that Abner. Ye hyeard it.

SANK. Yes, Walt, that's right, so 'tis, so 'tis. I heared Jinkins, the Post Office man, down to Patterson say, says he, that this here Abner was a revenooer fer he got letters from the givermint, so he did—an' that he's a-carryin' on with Mary, so he was.

NOAH (*unable to remain silent any longer, turns and glares at* SANK). That's a ding-busted lie!

WALT. No, 'tain't, pa. I seed Mary talkin' to 'im.

NOAH. Then why in hell didn't ye . . .

WALT. 'Twon't do, pa. I thought about it, but I larned when they took me to camp that it was beaucoo hell to pay fer gittin' one o' his kind. Then over thar in France one time . . .

NOAH. Dad-durn France! Hit don't make a dang what ye larned in France. Hit's a-goin' down the Ridge thar that this here Abner is a revenooer.

WALT. Parlay voo! How'd ye git like that, pa? (NOAH *again turns to his work in surly silence.*) Say, pa, air ye sure o' that? (NOAH *refuses to answer and* WALT *points to him, laughing.*) That mess-sure no parlay Fransay. (*He picks up a can of liquor near him and drinks from it, then offers it to* MOSE *and* SANK. *Both refuse.*)

MOSE. Too early in the mornin' to drink. Want my liquor in the daytime or in the fore part o' the night. 'Bout time Bill was comin' fer his liquor.

SANK. Yes, it be, an' it be. He ought to soon be here.

MOSE. Bill's ol' 'oman said that Mary was purty well took with that Abner feller.

SANK. She must be, yes she be. My ol' 'oman said that Bill's ol' 'oman said that Mary sees a right smart o' that feller.

WALT. How d'ye know Mary sees 'im?

MOSE. I heared said that Mary meets him in the day time while ye're sleepin', Noah.

SANK. Yes, she do, an' she do.

WALT. Pa, d'ye hear that?

NOAH (*unable to hold in any longer, now bursts out in a rage*). Dod gast her divilish soul, a gal o' mine carryin' on with a revenooer! She ain't been the same since she came back from that thar ding-busted school over thar to Boone. Dod-burn her durned hide! I's allus agin' her goin' over thar, but her ma sent her, an' then layed down an' died on me, an' left her fer me to ten' to.

WALT. You ain't tended to her, much, pa. Ye been tendin' to this here most o' yer time.

NOAH (*furiously*). Who in hell axed ye to speak? Stir that mash, damn ye, stir that mash. (WALT *goes to work as* NOAH *fumes on.*) So ye think I'd let a gal o' mine marry one o' them danged revenooers, do ye?

WALT. No, pa, but . . .

NOAH. Shet up, durn ye, shet up! (*Stamping about in a rage.*) I'd see her in hell first! I'd . . .

SANK. That's right, Noah. So 'tis, so 'tis. I don't blame ye, so I don't, so I . . .

NOAH (*turning on him*). Shet up! Who axed ye t' speak?

SANK (*fawningly*). Well, Noah, I . . .

NOAH. Shet up, I said. What're ye doin' here anyhow?

SANK. Ye tol' us to come an' git this run o' liquor to take to Patterson, so ye did.

NOAH. How ye goin' to 'spect me to git this run off an' ye an' Mose settin' aroun' runnin' yer mouths. Git that thar bucket an' go fotch some water. If'n I's as ding-busted lazy as the rest o' ye, I never would git 'nough juice made fer them thar judges an' lawyers, not to say nothin' 'bout them thar preachers. (MOSE *and* SANK *hurry off with a bucket.* NOAH *continues to fume around the still.*)

WALT. Pa, t'other day when we's a-talkin' 'bout that thar man, Abner, bein' a revenooer, Mary comes in an' says that he wa'n't no revenooer, an' that he's some kind o' magerzine scribbler, or somethin', an' we axed 'er how she knowed it, an' she said she jes' knowed he wa'n't. (NOAH *pays no attention to him.* MOSE *and* SANK *enter with the water.*)

SANK. Yeah, that's so, so 'tis, fer Mary tol' my ol' 'oman that you all was tellin' lies 'bout that thar man Abner, she did, so she did. An' she said that Abner's a better man than any of us 'uns, she did, so she did . . .

NOAH (*breaking out*). Consarn ye! Bring that thar water here. (*He grabs the bucket.*) What ye standin' thar fer? (*He goes to pour the water into the still, but in his anger he spills it on the fire, almost putting it out. He turns on* SANK *furiously.*) Dod-limb ye, Sank! Dod gast ye, ye goozle-necked ol' fool ye! What ye a-goin' an' puttin' that thar fire out fer? Ding-bust ye, yer . . .

SANK (*cringing*). I didn't put it out, Noah, so I . . .

NOAH (*sputtering*). Ye . . . ye . . . ye hum-duzzled . . .

SANK (*shrinking from him*). Leastwise I didn't go fer to do it, Noah, so I didn't.

WALT. Pa, ye put the fire out yerself, an'—

NOAH. Shet up, ye whing-duzzled yaller boomer ye! Ye ain't no better'n yer sis! Both o' ye be a bunch o' cowards, an' ye . . .

WALT. Oo la-la! Sweet pa-pa!

NOAH. Dod gast ye! Stop that thar la-la-in' an' pa-pa-in' or I'll wring yer neck!

WALT. Aw, pa, I didn't go fer to—

NOAH. Shet up them jaws o' yer'n! D'ye hear me?

MOSE. Noah, my ol' 'oman said that that thar gal o' yer'n went plum' down to the rock to meet that thar Abner, an'—

NOAH. Ding-dang her! I'm a-goin' home right now an' see if'n she'll . . . (*He starts off right just as three owl hoots ring out in the distance, followed by a shrill "Bobwhite."* NOAH *hesitates a moment.*)

Mose. Thar comes Bill fer his brandy. That's his call. I'll give
him the come-on. (*He returns the call.*)

Bill (*singing drunkenly as he approaches from the left*).

Way up on Clinch Moun-tain I

wan-der a - lone. I'm as drunk as the

Dev-il Oh, let me a - lone.

Banjo Accompaniment

I'll eat when I'm hungry,
En drink when I'm dry;
En if whiskey don't kill me,
I'll live till I die.

O Lulu, O Lulu!
O Lulu, my dear!
I'd give this whole world
Ef my Lulu was hyer.

Jack o' diamonds, jack o' diamonds,
I know you of ol'—
You rob my pore pockets
O' silver an' gol'.

Sank. Ah-hah. Drunk agin'!

Bill. (*entering from the left.* Bill Spivins *is a rough, careless
mountaineer. He wears clothes of the same drab tone as those
of the other men. His big, bloated face marks him as a heavy
drinker and he shows in his singing and in his speech the*

effects of his liquor. He calls after NOAH.) Hey, thar, Noah . . . whar be ye a-goin'? . . . I wanna git my brandy afore ye leave . . . Ye done an' sint yer watchers in, ain't ye? Whar be ye a-goin'? . . .

NOAH (*coming back*). That dod-gasted gal o' mine's been carryin' on with that thar damned revenooer, Abner, an' I jes' started to give her hell, an' make her stop it. A gal o' mine carryin' on with a revenooer!

BILL. Hit must be so then . . . I been down the Ridge . . . an' when I come back my ol' 'oman said that yer gal, Mary . . . was a-carryin' on with him . . .

WALT. What else did she say, Bill? Mary allus tells yer ol' 'oman ever'thin'.

BILL. Wal, she said that Mary said that . . . this here Abner wa'n't no revenooer . . . an' that she had met him over thar to Boone . . .

NOAH. She's a-lyin'! That Abner gits letters from the giver-mint.

SANK. An' he ain't never been to Boone. He's a furriner in these parts, an' he's a ding-busted revenooer.

BILL. My ol' 'oman says Mary wants to run off with him . . . but she's skeered to, fer she knows what ye'd do, Noah. . . . An' she says he ain't no revenooer an' she's goin' t' show us he ain't . . . an' that she's a-goin' t' marry him.

NOAH. Dod gast her! I'll be the one to say about that. My gal run off with a revenooer! No, by the holy damn, I'll see her in hell first!

BILL. My ol' 'oman said that Mary was jes' like her ma . . . an' that she's up to somethin' now . . . an' if'n ye didn't watch out she'd marry that revenooer yit.

SANK. Yes, she will, Noah, so she will. Ye'd better watch her, so ye had.

NOAH. Shet up, Sank, ye ding-busted ol' jay-hawk ye, shet up!

BILL. My ol' 'oman said . . . that yer ol' 'oman allus had her way 'fore she died . . . an' that she didn't listen to ye when she didn't want . . .

NOAH. Dod gast yer ol' 'oman! She's allus sayin' too much. Gimme yer jug. (*He takes the jug, fills it, and hands it back to* BILL.) Don't ye fergit to bring me them 'taters to pay fer this. Ye owe me two bushels now.

BILL. My ol' 'oman said that that man Abner's up in these parts to-day . . . an' thet yer gal met him over to the rock, an' that she believed they's up to somethin'! Mary ain't been home to-day. . . . Ye'd better watch her, Noah. . . . She'll git ye yit.

NOAH. Dad burn ye, git out o' here! A gal o' mine an' a revenooer git me! Ye ding-busted yaller-livered fool, git out! Ain't I the best man on this side o' the Ridge? Ain't I boss here?

SANK. Yes, ye be, Noah, so ye be. (BILL *reels out with his jug.*)

MOSE. Noah, t'other night down to Curtis's store I heared that Abner was sent here by the givermint to git ye fer killin' that other revenooer a few years ago.

NOAH (*startled*). What's that? What're ye sayin', Mose? Ye're a liar! That's what ye are. Ye're a liar, I say! Ye're . . .

MOSE. Stop that, Noah. I's givin' ye straight talk, an' ye ain't to be callin' me a liar. I don't have to work fer ye, an' I ain't a-goin' to. . . .

NOAH (*more calmly*). I didn't mean it 'zactly like that, Mose, but . . . but . . .

MOSE. That's the truth, Noah. Ol' man Jinkins tol' hit hisself.

SANK. Yes it be, so it be. I heared him myself, so I did.

WALT. Pa, that's why he's been hangin' roun' Mary. He's tryin' to pick it out o' her, so he c'n git us, an' he's caught her. That's hit. (*At this moment* MARY SETZER *carefully peers through the rhododendron branches at the right. She is a*

*pretty mountain girl, simply dressed in a plain but becoming
pink gingham. Without having been seen, she withdraws
noiselessly into the bushes again.*)

NOAH. Gol ding her, she ain't got no more sense 'n to let him
ketch her an' then let him be hangin' 'roun' to spy an' larn
all he can.

WALT. Pa, hadn't we better skip an' git out'n this?

NOAH. An' leave all this an' be skeered to come back to git
it? No, I ain't goin' t' let no revenooer run me. They ain't
never done it yit an' they ain't never goin' t' do hit. I'll go
down thar to Patterson to-morrow, an' I'll take ol' Beck
over thar (*pointing to his rifle*), an' I'll fix this here dod-
gasted, ding-fuzzled revenooer like I did t'other'n. An'
then I'll take that gal o' mine . . . (NOAH *is interrupted by*
LAURENCE ABNER, *who breaks through the thicket at the
right, followed by* MARY SETZER, *who keeps a safe distance
in the rear, yet is on the alert, ready to assist him if necessary.*
ABNER *is a good-looking young man, trimly dressed in clothes
suitable for mountain wear.*)

ABNER (*firing a shot and then covering the moonshiners with a
pistol*). Hands up, gents! (*They turn, startled.* WALT *and*
MOSE *spring toward the rifles but* ABNER *stops them.*) None
of that, gents. It'll mean death if you try it again.

NOAH. Dod gast ye!

ABNER. First time a revenuer ever had the ups on you, isn't
it? Now, gents, kindly move over to this side and remove
your coats so that I may see that you are not armed. (*The
men obey his orders as he motions them over to the left with his
pistols.*) No tricks, remember! I learned to shoot pretty
straight in the army.

WALT. Larned to shoot in the army, huh? Wal, that hain't
nothin'. While I's over thar in France I captured 'bout
forty Bochers, three big rumble-bumble guns, an' a dozen
or more rifles an' . . .

MARY (*advancing*). Aw, now, Walt, ye wa'n't never up at the
shootin' line. Ye said ye peeled 'taters all the time.

WALT. Parlay whippay dally doodle doo! Air *ye* here, Sis?
Wal, ye jes' watch the ol' man.

NOAH (*seeing* MARY). Dod gast ye, gal! Ding-damn ye!
Here's that damned ol' jay-pipin' horn frog what ye been
a-hangin' aroun' with—ye see now if he ain't a revenooer,
don't ye? Dad-burn yer hum-duzzled soul! Consarn the
dod-limbed hide o' ye! Ye see whar yer pa is, do ye?
Damn ye, I'll fix ye. . . . (*He starts toward* MARY, *but*
ABNER *motions him back with his pistol.*)

ABNER. Hold on there! You want to be careful and not forget
that I've got you at present, and the law doesn't deal any
too lightly with your kind, especially since prohibition.
(WALT *slinks around behind the mash tub and picks up a
club. The "revenooer" is occupied watching* NOAH, *and*
WALT *steals closer to him, while the old man rages.*)

NOAH. Damn ye, ye yaller-back 'tater bug ye! Ye got me
now, but ye jes' wait. What ye goin' t' do with us?

ABNER. What would you give me to let you off?

NOAH (*surprised*). What! What's that ye say? (WALT *has now
crept up close behind* ABNER. *He raises his club and springs
forward, but* MARY *seizes his arm.*)

MARY. Don't try nothin' like that, Walt. Hit won't work.

NOAH (*regaining his voice, he sputters in his uncontrolled rage*).
Ding-damn ye! Dod gast ye . . . ye . . . ye . . . consarn ye . . . ye . . . damn ye . . . ye be helping this
here revenooer to take yer own pa. So that's what ye come
here fer, ye durn yaller boomer ye! Ye divilish dog! Ye
allus was jes' like yer ma. Ye said he wa'n't no revenooer,
so ye did. Well, ye lied, gal, ye lied, an' I'll git ye. . . .

ANBER. Hold on a minute. You seem to forget that I've got
you all just at present, and I'm likely to keep you. But just
for the fun of knowing—what would you give me to let you
go?

NOAH. Ding-bust ye! By that rotten mash over thar . . .

ABNER. Don't swear by the mash, I've captured it, too.

SANK. So he has, Noah, so he has.

NOAH. Dad durn ye, Sank! Damn ye—Walt—if ye'd do somethin'—if ye'd drag him off—he wouldn't be standin' there with his gun drawed on us. But ye stand thar a-runnin' yer clop-trop mouths an' doin' nothin'. Why don't ye . . .

WALT. Holy scents of sweet smellin' asserfiditty! Why don't ye do hit yerself, pa?

ABNER. Here now, let's come to business. If you're not going to make me an offer, I'll make you one. If you'll let me marry your daughter, we'll call this off. What do you say?

NOAH (*amazed*). What's that? (*Beginning to understand, he stamps the ground in a rage and advances toward* ABNER, *who motions him back with his pistol.*) Marry my gal, a revenooer marry my gal! Ye dod gasted pole-cat ye! Ye ding-busted stinkin' possum skunk! Ye bow-legged 'tater bug ye! I'll see ye in Heck's ol' pine field twenty miles t'other side o' hell first. I'll . . . I'll . . .

ABNER. Just a minute before you go on. Listen to this—if I take you down the Ridge, as I certainly will if you don't do as I say, think of the days in prison. You're an old man and you would probably die there between the walls, behind the bars. People would come to see you, and point their fingers through the bars at you as they do the animals at the circus, and they'd say, "There's Noah Setzer. He used to be the leader on this side of the Ridge, but a revenuer gets them all, and one got him." Then there'll be your son and all these other fellows in cages beside you . . .

SANK. That's right, Noah, so 'tis, so 'tis. He'll take us all, so he will, an' . . .

NOAH. Shet up, ye . . .

ABNER. And then there's another thing I want to tell you before I take you. I have the proof that you and your son were the men who killed the revenue officers four years

ago. At your trial I shall turn the evidence against you
both. That means death for you.

NOAH. Wh-wh-what's that . . .

ABNER. Just think! They'll lead you, the boss of the Ridge,
in like a cow, and sit you down in a chair. And then they'll
turn on just enough juice to burn you, and let you know
how it feels. Then gradually they'll turn it on full force and
your bones will snap and it'll cook the flesh off your live
body!

SANK. Give him yer gal, Noah, give him yer gal!

MARY (*glancing at* ABNER *with a smile*). Pa, he's got ye, so
ye'd better give in. If ye don't, jes' think what the Ridge'll
say when he takes ye to jail. Ye'll be the only Setzer they've
ever got yet! I'm willin' to marry him, an' if you'll let me,
it'll save us all. I'm goin' t' marry him, anyhow.

NOAH. Well, marry him an' . . . damn ye both!

ABNER (*lowering his pistol, and laughing*). Thank you, Mr.
Setzer.

NOAH. Damn ye . . . don't "Mister" me! An' I don't want
none o' yer thanks. . . . (*To* MARY *and* ABNER, *who are
now both convulsed with laughter*.) What're ye laughin' at?

ABNER. Well, you see I'm not a revenue officer after all. I'm
just a magazine writer up in these mountains collecting
materials and—incidentally (*Smiling at* MARY)—a wife.
This has been the first real fun I've had since the Boston
Police Riot.

NOAH. Ye're not a . . . a . . . dod gasted . . .

MARY (*who has been standing by* ABNER's *side, now steps forward*). No, he ain't, pa. We wanted to git married, but I
couldn't think of runnin' away like Laurence wanted me
to, an' the whole Ridge a-thinkin' that me, a Setzer, had
run away with a revenooer. An' then, I couldn't a never
come back, fer ye'd 'a got us.

SANK. Yes, he would-'a, so he would-'a.

MARY. An' we wanted to be married right away, but we

couldn't think o' no way to prove that Laurence wa'n't no revenooer, so we—

ABNER (*breaking in*). Mary happened to remember a hold-up like this which she told me about when we were over at Boone, and then—

WALT (*interrupting, with a loud guffaw*). And then ye planned all this jes' to git us? (MARY *and* ABNER *nod a smiling assent.*)

ABNER. Yes, and I'm going to get a corking good story out of it, too.

WALT. Pa, ye said a revenooer wa'n't never goin' t' git ye! Why he ain't even a revenooer's picter an' he's got ye!

NOAH (*unable to restrain his rage*). Dad burn ye! Ding dang ye, . . . an' ye hain't no revenooer . . .! If I'd a knowed that . . . dad burn ye . . . by jumpin' Jupiter's horn snake, I'll not stand fer hit. . . . I'll . . .

MARY. Hold on, thar, pa, ye've done give yer promise, an' Walt an' Mose an' Sank all heared ye.

SANK. Yes, ye did, Noah, an' ye did!

MARY. We got ye, pa, an' ye can't go back on yer promise. So we're goin' to git married an' stay on right here.

NOAH (*violently*). Damn ye! Dod-limb ye . . . ye hum-duzzled . . . (*He recovers his composure, takes a quart bottle, goes to the still and fills it from the worm.*) I'll git even wid ye. Jes' wait, I'll git ye, durn ye! (*He hands the bottle to* ABNER.) Here, take this here quart, an' clear out o' here, an' stay out, an—(*He stands, shaking his fists at them as they go off laughing. There is just the trace of a grin on his face*)—an' dod-gast ye both!

CURTAIN

OFF NAGS HEAD

A Tragedy of the North Carolina Coast

BY

DOUGALD MACMILLAN

53

OFF NAGS HEAD

In the winter of 1812, according to the legend, a pilot boat drifted ashore at Kitty Hawk, near Nags Head, on the coast of North Carolina. In the cabin, among other evidences of the presence on the boat of a woman of wealth and refinement, was found a portrait of a lady. The "bankers," the rough, half barbarous inhabitants of the islands along the North Carolina coast, cut off from the moderating influences of mainland civilization, were in the habit of regarding all drift-wood, regardless of its size or condition, as their own property. They fell upon deserted vessels and demolished them. This small pilot boat was treated in the customary manner. The portrait fell into the hands of a fisherman, on whose walls it hung for many years.

In 1869, Dr. William G. Pool was called in to see, near Nags Head, an old fisherwoman, who was sick. He found the portrait, secured possession of it and its story, and later identified the subject as Theodosia Burr, daughter of Aaron Burr.

In a small pilot boat, *The Patriot*, on December 30, 1812, Mrs. Theodosia Burr Alston sailed from Georgetown, South Carolina, for New York, where she expected to join her father who had just returned from exile. *The Patriot* did not reach New York; neither it nor any of its crew or passengers was ever heard of again.

"It is not improbable that *The Patriot* during a night of storm was lured ashore by a decoy light at Nags Head, and that passengers and crew fell into the hands of the land pirates in waiting, who possessed themselves of the boat and everything of value it contained."[1]

[1] *The Eyrie and Other Southern Stories* by Bettie Freshwater Pool. New York. 1905.

CAST OF CHARACTERS

As originally produced on The Playmakers' Stage, Chapel Hill, North Carolina, April 30 and May 1, 1920.

AN OLD FISHERMAN,	Jonathan Daniels
THE "GAL," *his daughter*,	Mildred Sherrill
THE SICK WOMAN, *the fisherman's wife*,	Aline Hughes
THE DOCTOR,	David Reid Hodgin
THE OLD WOMAN,	Elizabeth Taylor

SCENE: A fisherman's hut on the sand dunes of Nags Head on the North Carolina Coast.

TIME: September, 1869. A stormy night.

SCENE

A fisherman's hut on the North Carolina sand banks, at Nags Head.

The roar of the surf and the distant clanging of the bell buoy can be heard before the curtain rises on a room furnished meagrely and not very neat in appearance. There is a door at the back to the left, opening out on the beach; to the right a small window, closed by a rough shutter. Between the door and the window, on the back wall, hangs an old portrait in a tarnished gilded frame. It is a handsome painting of a young woman. At the beginning of the play it is covered by a coarse woolen cloth.

There is a fireplace in the left side wall and in that corner a table with a water bucket. On the right a door opens into the adjoining room. A lantern, hung on a nail by the fireplace, gives a flickering light.

It is nearly dark on an evening in September and a storm is piling up mountains of spray in the surf, some distance across the beach. Throughout the entire action the roar of the surf and the ringing of the bell buoy can be heard. It is far away, but you can hear it at any time; only, when some one is talking, you do not notice the distant clanging. From time to time the wind howls around the house, and every now and then the smoke blows out of the fireplace, in which a fire of driftwood is struggling to overcome the draft down the chimney.

A woman is lying on a low bed in the corner of the room to the right. She is moaning as if she were suffering acutely. The old FISHERMAN *is standing by the bed with a conch-shell of water in his hand. He touches the woman on the shoulder.*

FISHERMAN. Here, want a drink o' water? (*The woman moans and raises her head slightly. The* FISHERMAN *holds the shell to her lips. She drinks a swallow and sinks back on the bed. The* FISHERMAN *puts the shell on top of the water bucket and,*

57

crossing to the fireplace, begins to mend a shrimp seine lying across a chair. He sits down with the seine in his lap. The SICK WOMAN *moans again and moves restlessly. He turns toward her.*) Doctor Wright'll be here purty soon. The gal's been gone long enough to be back. (*After a moment of silence the door at the back opens and the* GIRL *comes in with an apron full of driftwood that she has picked up on the beach. She has a shawl drawn tightly around her shoulders and her colorless hair has been blown into wisps about her freckled face. She whines in a nasal drawl when she talks. Dragging her heels, she shuffles over to the fireplace and drops the wood in a pile on the hearth. The* FISHERMAN *turns to the door as she comes in, speaking anxiously.*) Is he comin'?

GIRL. Doctor Wright's gone over to Jug Neck an' won't be back till to-morrow. I foun' a docto' at ol' man Stokes's though. He come thar to-day from Raleigh. He's comin'. (*She hangs her shawl on a hook behind the door and goes to the* SICK WOMAN.) Is it bad? (*The* SICK WOMAN *groans.*)

FISHERMAN. Did you see the ol' 'oman?

GIRL. Naw. Is she gone?

FISHERMAN. Been gone 'bout an hour.

GIRL. Which way'd she go?

FISHERMAN. Toward the inlet.

GIRL (*she rises from bending over the* SICK WOMAN *and goes to the door for her shawl*). M . . . hm. Time she was back. I'll go hunt 'er.

FISHERMAN. Wait. Maybe she'll come in in a minute. I'll go hunt. How high is the tide now?

GIRL (*hangs up her shawl again but speaks anxiously*). Them stakes fo' Jones's shack is covered an' it's washin' up under the seine racks.

FISHERMAN. M . . . hm. Purty bad.

GIRL. An' it's so misty you can't see the Topsail Light. (*She goes to the fireplace and crouches there, warming her hands.*)

FISHERMAN. Huh. This is a worse storm'n we've had in a long time. (*He goes to the door and looks out. The bell buoy clangs.*)

GIRL. Listen to that bell buoy. It makes me feel so quar. (*She shivers.*)

FISHERMAN. Don' you take on like that. The ol' 'oman's bad enough.

GIRL (*she takes an old, round, iron kettle and fills it with water from the bucket by the door*). She's been bad all day—like she was las' storm we had when she tried to jump off'n the landin'! She might try again. We better look for 'er. (*She hangs the kettle over the fire and crosses to the* SICK WOMAN.)

FISHERMAN. I reckon so. You look out for yo' ma.

GIRL. The ol' 'oman's been a-doin' like she done that day when she tried to run in the surf with the picter.

FISHERMAN. Has she? (*As though he doesn't quite understand why.*) She sets a lot o' store by that picter.

GIRL. I'm kind o' skeered she'll do somethin' bad some day.

FISHERMAN. She ain't gonna jump in the surf no more. Not on a col' night like this un. You take care o' yo' ma thar. I'll hunt th' other un. (*He starts toward the door and opens it. The* OLD WOMAN *is seen outside just coming in. She has been tall and might have been imperious. She speaks with a more refined accent than the others. She is demented and they humor her. The* FISHERMAN *speaks to her from the doorway.*) Well, we was jest a-comin' to look fo' you! Thought you might 'a fallen overboard or sumpthin'. (*He sits down again by the fire. The* GIRL *takes the* OLD WOMAN'S *shawl from her shoulders and hangs it by the fireplace to dry. The* OLD WOMAN *does not seem to notice the others but speaks as though to herself.*)

OLD WOMAN. I've had so much to do.

FISHERMAN. Well, now that's bad. You mustn't work too hard. It's bad for you.

OLD WOMAN. It's better to work than to think. (*She smiles in a vague sort of way. Her eyes are expressionless.*) There are times when I think and I hear things. They keep calling me on the boat and the bell buoy rings——

GIRL (*to the* FISHERMAN). Ain't it time the doctor was comin'?

OLD WOMAN. I see many things. There is the cheery crowd on the boat and they keep calling, for all is dark and everything reels—the light comes close and all is dark again. Listen! my baby boy calls—the water roars and we all get wet. . . . But I still have my work. I must not give up—I still have my child and my picture to work for. (*She goes toward the curtained portrait.*) My dead boy and you—(*She pulls the curtain aside, displaying the beautiful old painting. Her voice is more cheerful and less troubled as she speaks to the* FISHERMAN.) It is a picture of me! Don't you think it is good? It was done by the best artist. I am taking it to my father in New York.

FISHERMAN (*humoring her*). Yes, yes. You done tol' us that a lot o' times.

GIRL (*to the* FISHERMAN). I wonder why the doctor ain't come.

OLD WOMAN (*interrupting and still speaking to the* FISHERMAN). So I have—so I have. Well, I must keep on working. I've had a message from my father. (*More brightly.*) I'm going to leave soon. (*She starts toward the room at the right, then turns to the* FISHERMAN, *speaking anxiously.*) Take care of her. Don't let anyone get her. (*Speaking to the portrait.*) I am going to take you with me when I go to New York to see my father. (*She goes out, glancing back from the door at the portrait.*) I'm coming back soon.

FISHERMAN. She's so scared someun's gonna steal her picter. . . . Is the lamp lit in thar?

GIRL. Yeah. I lit it. (*There is a knock on the door.*) It must be the new doctor. (*She opens the door and the* DOCTOR *comes in. He is an elderly man, wearing a long cloak and carrying a satchel. His manner is brisk and cheerful and he is rather talkative, the old family doctor type.*)

FISHERMAN. Come in.

DOCTOR. Thank you. I had some trouble finding the house. There is so much mist you can't see very well. I believe this is the worst storm I ever saw.

FISHERMAN. Yeah. It's bad. You can't even see the Topsail Light.

DOCTOR (*taking off his hat and cloak and laying them on a chair by the fire*). Do you often have storms like this one? This is my first trip down here. Mr. Stokes asked me down to go fishing with him.

FISHERMAN. This un is right bad.

DOCTOR. Now, where is the sick woman?

FISHERMAN (*pointing to the bed*). Here.

DOCTOR. Oh, yes! Your wife?

FISHERMAN. Yes, suh.

DOCTOR (*sitting by the bed*). How do you feel? (*The* SICK WOMAN *moans.*)

FISHERMAN. She don' say nothin'. She's got a misery in her chist.

DOCTOR. I see. How long has she been this way?

FISHERMAN. Since this mornin'.

DOCTOR (*to the* GIRL, *who stands by the door to the next room*). Will you bring me some water, please. (*She goes out. He opens his satchel and takes out a bottle, pouring some medicine into the cup which the* GIRL *brings him, and gives it to the sick woman to drink. The* FISHERMAN *and the* GIRL *look on in silence. He speaks reassuringly.*) She'll be comfortable in a few minutes. It is not serious this time, but she must not work too hard. (*He rises and crosses to the fireplace for his cloak.*)

FISHERMAN. Will you set down an' rest yourself an' git dry? It's a long walk back to Stokes's.

DOCTOR. Why, thank you, I believe I will. (*They sit before the fire and light their pipes. The* GIRL *goes out.*)

FISHERMAN. You ain't been here befo', Doctor?

DOCTOR. No. This is my first trip. I've always wanted to come but never had a chance before. There are lots of interestin' tales told about your beaches and islands around here.

FISHERMAN. Yeah. I reckon thar's a lot o' tales.

DOCTOR. Captain Kidd is said to have buried money on every island on the coast.

FISHERMAN. Yes, suh. Right over thar on Haw's Hammock my pa dug up a chist.

DOCTOR. Was there anything in it?

FISHERMAN. No. (*He smiles.*)

DOCTOR. That's often the way. (*He laughs, then stops to listen to the wind, which is increasing in volume and intensity.*) Listen to that! This would be a good night for the land pirates that used to be around here. Did you know any of them?

FISHERMAN. I don' know what you mean.

DOCTOR. Oh, is that so? Why, they say there used to be a band of men around here that hung lights on a horse's head and drove the horse down the beach. From a distance it looked like a ship. Ships at sea were often fooled by it and ran aground. When they did, the men on shore plundered them and killed the crew. That's how Nags Head got its name.

FISHERMAN (*showing some confusion*). Is that right?

DOCTOR. Why, you are old enough to know about that. I'm surprised that you didn't know some of those old rascals.

FISHERMAN (*turning away*). We don't talk much in these parts.

DOCTOR (*becoming interested in his tale*). A very famous case, I remember—one that has been talked about for a long time. I heard it from my mother, was that of a boat named the . . . *The Patriot*. She was bound for New York from Georgetown, I believe. An illustrious lady, Theodosia Burr, was on board—the daughter of Aaron Burr. The boat disappeared somewhere along this coast. That was about fifty years ago, and none of the crew has been heard of since. (*The* FISHERMAN *is silent, looking into the fire. The* DOCTOR *rises.*) Well, let's have another look at the patient. I'll have to get back pretty soon. Stokes gets me out early these days to get the blue fish on the right time o' the tide. (*He knocks out his pipe against the chimney and turns toward the bed. The* FISHERMAN *rises. The* OLD WOMAN *enters unnoticed, crosses to the fireplace and stands there watching the others. The* DOCTOR *starts to the bed but stops suddenly, astonished. He has seen the portrait!*) Why, hello, what's that?

FISHERMAN. What?

DOCTOR. The portrait. Where did it come from?

FISHERMAN. Oh, we found it on a derelict that drifted in one day.

DOCTOR (*becoming excited*). Why that looks like the picture that was on *The Patriot.* I remember distinctly, I once saw a copy of the lost portrait. It must be the portrait of Theodosia Burr! (*The* OLD WOMAN *watches them intently.*)

FISHERMAN. Who's she?

DOCTOR. The woman that was lost. Where were the crew and passengers on the boat?

FISHERMAN. I don' recollect no people on 'er. I reckon thar wan't no people on 'er.

DOCTOR. Where were they?

FISHERMAN. I don' know.

DOCTOR. Was the boat named *The Patriot?*

FISHERMAN. I can't say, 'cause I don' exactly know. She might 'a been *The Patriot* or she might 'a been the *Mary Ann*—I can't say. (*He has become sullen.*)

DOCTOR. Come, now. Tell me about it.

FISHERMAN. I don' know no more. We jest found it. (*He turns away.*)

DOCTOR. Then I must have the portrait. I'm sure it's the key to the Theodosia Burr mystery. Will you sell it? (*The* OLD WOMAN *watches him, frightened.*)

FISHERMAN (*looking at her*). I dunno as how we would. We sets a lot o' store by that picter.

DOCTOR. I'll pay you for it. How much do you want? (*He starts to take the picture from the wall. The* OLD WOMAN, *who has been moving toward it, seizes his arm, excitedly.*)

OLD WOMAN. Sell her! Sell my picture! She is one of the things I work for—my dead boy and my picture. You shall not take them from me. (*She lifts the portrait from its place and holds it tightly in her arms, talking to it.*) I am taking you to my father in New York. He wants it. (*More wildly, speaking to the* DOCTOR.) You shan't have it. . . . They shan't take you from me. . . . It is all that I have. I've been cruelly treated. My baby boy died. He is out there. . . . (*She points to the sea.*) He often calls me to come to him but I must stay here, for I still have my picture to work for. (*She turns away.*)

DOCTOR. Who are you?

OLD WOMAN. (*Smiling. She seems to look at something far away.*) Ah. . . .

DOCTOR. Who are you? What do you know about the picture? It must be a portrait of Theodosia Burr!

OLD WOMAN. Burr? Theodosia Burr? (*Almost frenzied as she suddenly remembers her identity.*) Why, she's the person that I stand for! I've been thinking—she keeps talking to me. That's who I stand for!

DOCTOR. What?

FISHERMAN (*with a significant nod*). Don' mind her. She ain't right.

OLD WOMAN. I must be going now. They are tired of waiting. I've stayed here long enough. . . . I'm coming, father. (*She starts to go into the next room.*)

DOCTOR (*stepping in front of the door, he speaks gently*). Where are you going?

OLD WOMAN (*turning back into the room*). Maybe the boat's fixed now. I wonder where the others are.

DOCTOR (*persuasively*). Yes, tell us where the others are.

OLD WOMAN. Oh, I remember. They're gone. They were killed. Hush, don't you hear them . . . listen! . . . *They* took all the things on the boat, but I have saved you. (*She clasps the picture closer and stares before her.*) It was an awful storm like this one. A false light, we ran on the beach. It was horrible! Yes . . . yes, *they* were there— *they*, they killed them all!

DOCTOR. Yes, yes! Don't get excited. We'll fix everything all right. Don't let it worry you. Sit down and tell us all about it.

OLD WOMAN (*moving to the right of the room*). I am going away very soon now. . . . I saw a sign to-day. I have been sent for. They have sent for me to come to see my father in New York. He has been waiting so long. I must go—— (*She goes out into the adjoining room, muttering. The* DOC- TOR *turns to the* FISHERMAN.)

DOCTOR. What do you know about this?

FISHERMAN. Nothin', I tol' you.

DOCTOR. How did she get here?

FISHERMAN. We took 'er in one time. (*He speaks sullenly.*)

DOCTOR. Yes, but where did she come from? You know more about this, and you're going to tell me. If you don't, I'll have you arrested on suspicion. You'll be tried and maybe you'll be hanged. Now, tell me what you know.

FISHERMAN. Wait—(*He is beginning to be afraid*)—I don't know nothin', I tol' you.

DOCTOR (*threateningly*). Yes, you do. Do you want to get into court?

FISHERMAN. No! No!

DOCTOR (*raising his voice*). Then tell me what you know about it. I'll——

FISHERMAN (*interrupting*). Be quiet, I'll tell you. Don' make no noise . . . I was a boy . . . they used to hang a lantern on a horse . . . then when the ship run aground they got all the stuff off'n 'er . . .

DOCTOR. Land pirates! I thought you knew! Go on.

FISHERMAN. That's all.

DOCTOR. What became of the people on these boats?

FISHERMAN. They got drownded.

DOCTOR. How? Don't take so long.

FISHERMAN. Jes' drownded.

DOCTOR. Did you kill them?

FISHERMAN. No. They was jes' drownded.

DOCTOR. And where did the old woman and the portrait come from?

FISHERMAN. They was on one o' the boats an' we took 'em in. She ain't been right in 'er head sence. Her baby boy died that night.

DOCTOR. Where did she go? I want to talk to her again. (*He goes toward the door.*)

FISHERMAN. You ain't a-goin' t'——

DOCTOR (*interrupting*). No, I won't send you to jail. Go get the old woman. (*He moves to the fireplace.*)

FISHERMAN. She went in thar. (*He goes to the door and looks into the next room.*) She ain't in thar now.

DOCTOR. Then where could she be?

FISHERMAN. I dunno. (*The* GIRL *comes in, very much excited and frightened. She enters by the door at the back and as she opens it the roar of the surf and the ringing of the bell buoy may be heard more distinctly.*)

GIRL. I tried to stop 'er, but she jest went on! I can't do nothin' with 'er.

DOCTOR. What do you mean?

GIRL. She run out a-huggin' that picter. I couldn't stop 'er. She said she was goin' away!

FISHERMAN. Where did she go?

GIRL. I dunno. She's been so bad all day, a-talkin' 'bout the bell buoy a-ringin' for 'er—(*She goes to the* FISHERMAN.) I'm skeered o' what she'll do! (*Above the roar of the surf can be heard faintly but clearly, a high-pitched, distant cry.*)

DOCTOR. What's that?

FISHERMAN. I dunno . . .

GIRL. I wonder if it's . . . (*The* DOCTOR *and* FISHERMAN *go to the door at the back.*)

DOCTOR. We'd better go look for her.

FISHERMAN (*as they run out into the darkness across the beach*). I hope she ain't . . . (*The* GIRL *stands in the open door watching them. The* SICK WOMAN *moans. The roar of the surf and the ringing of the bell buoy are heard more distinctly. After a moment the* FISHERMAN *comes in, breathless and wild-eyed.*)

FISHERMAN. Gi' me the lantern! She's run in the surf an' it a-bilin'.

GIRL (*taking the lighted lantern from a nail by the fireplace*). She said the bell was a-ringin' for 'er. . . . Is she . . .

FISHERMAN (*takes the lantern, pausing a moment in the doorway*). She's drownded! She done washed ashore! (*The* FISHERMAN *goes out and the light from his lantern disappears in the night. As the* GIRL *stands in the doorway looking toward the sea, the bell buoy can still be heard above the storm.*)

CURTAIN

THE LAST OF THE LOWRIES

A Play of the Croatan Outlaws of Robeson County, North Carolina

BY

PAUL GREEN

THE LAST OF THE LOWRIES

In *The Last of the Lowries*, the first play written by Paul Green in the University playwriting course to be produced by The Carolina Playmakers, the author tells the story of the famous Carolina outlaw, Henry Berry Lowrie, who carried seventy pounds of firearms on his person and on whose head there was a reward of $50,000.

The play is based on the account given by Mrs. Mary C. Norment in *The Lowrie History* (Daily Journal Print, Wilmington, N. C., 1875). Part of the action is not historical. In reality Steve Lowrie and not Henry Berry was the last of the gang.

The Lowries were a famous band of outlaws of mixed blood, part Croatan Indian. In the latter part of the Civil War many of the Croatans in Robeson County were opposed to the conscription of men by the Confederate Government for work on the fortifications along Cape Fear. Among these were the Lowrie boys, who killed an officer sent to arrest them for evading the law. After this, the Lowries concealed themselves in Scuffletown Swamp where they were supplied with food by their sympathizers. As the gang grew in size it began to act on the offensive instead of the defensive, and soon it spread terror throughout the county, robbing, plundering, and killing when necessary. For more than ten years the gang held out against the officers of the law and only in 1874 was the last Lowrie killed.

No particular effort is made to follow the intricacies of the Croatan dialect. But the following characteristics of pronunciation will be of aid in giving the play local color.

The typical Croatan of 1874 spoke with a peculiar drawl in his voice, most often pronouncing his *t* like *d*, as "better," *bedder; c* or *ck* was pronounced like *g*, as "back," *bag;* short *a* like short *o*, as "man," *mon.* Sometimes *g* was sounded as *d*, as "loving," *lovind.* Even now there is little change in the dialect of the uneducated Croatans.

CAST OF CHARACTERS

As originally produced on The Playmakers' Stage, Chapel Hill, North Carolina, April 30 and May 1, 1920.

CUMBA LOWRIE, *the aged mother of the Lowries,*
Elizabeth Taylor

JANE, *her daughter,* Ruth Penny
MAYNO, *Cumba's daughter-in-law,* Rachel Freeman
HENRY BERRY LOWRIE, *last of the outlaw gang,*
Ernest Nieman

SCENE: The rough home of the Lowrie gang in Scuffletown, a swampy region of Robeson County, North Carolina.
TIME: A night in the winter of the year 1874.

SCENE

The kitchen of the Lowrie home.

The interior is that of a rude dwelling built of rough-hewn timbers. At the right front is a fireplace in which a fire is burning. Pots and pans are hung around the fireplace. A rocking chair is drawn up in front of the fire. At the right rear is a cupboard. At the centre rear a door leads outside. Above it are several fishing poles and a net resting on pegs fitted into the joists. To the rear at the left is a loom with a piece of half-finished cloth in it. A door in the centre of the left wall leads into an adjoining room. To the right of it is a window. At the front on that side is a chest. In the centre of the room is a rough, oblong eating-table and several home-made chairs with cowhide bottoms. A spinning-wheel stands at the front left. On the table is an unlighted candle in a tin holder.

The play opens with MAYNO LOWRIE *spinning at the wheel. She stops, folds her hands aimlessly across her lap, and stares idly into the fire. She is a full-blooded Croatan, about twenty-five years old, of medium height with skin a tan color, almost copper, prominent cheek bones, short flat nose, and black shifty eyes. Her coarse raven hair is wound into a knot at the back of her head. She is dressed in a polka-dot calico. Her shoes are somewhat heavy but comfortable looking. Around her neck she wears a string of shiny glass beads. Several cheap rings adorn her hands.*

For a moment she sits idle, and then begins to spin lazily, at almost every revolution of the wheel stopping to glance at the rear door, then at the door to the left, as if expecting someone to enter. She listens. From afar off comes the lone hoot of an owl. She shakes her head and starts the wheel going again. Then she goes to the fireplace, turns the bread in the spider and with a long-handled spoon stirs the peas in the pot. After this she goes back to her chair at the wheel.

Three knocks are heard at the rear door. MAYNO *hurries to remove the bar.* JANE LOWRIE *enters with a bundle under her arm. She throws the bundle on the table, takes off her bonnet and cape and hangs them on a peg near the door at the left.* MAYNO *goes to the bundle, stares at it half curiously and fearfully.* JANE *comes to the fire without speaking. She is a tall Croatan girl, dressed more plainly than* MAYNO *in a dress of homespun, with no ornaments. Her shoes are covered with mud. She is about twenty years old, with heavy black hair, light tan-colored skin, and regular features. Her face is more open and intelligent than* MAYNO'S. *Her whole figure expresses weariness. She looks anxiously at the door of the adjoining room, then turns to* MAYNO.

JANE. Has she asked for me?

MAYNO. Not but once. I tol' her you'd stepped over to Pate's for a little flour, and she seemed to pearten up at that. Said mebbe they'd be a letter from the boys 'way yander. (*She smiles scornfully. Still standing at the table, she looks at the package.* CUMBA'S *voice is heard calling from the room at the left.*)

CUMBA. Jane, Jane, is that ye?

JANE (*going to the door at the left*). Yes, muh, I'm jes' back from Pate's with the flour.

CUMBA. All right, honey. (JANE *goes into the room. Their voices can be heard indistinctly.* MAYNO *looks at the package, reaches and touches it. Then she tears a hole in the paper, peers at it intently and draws away.* JANE *comes back.*)

JANE. Mayno, they're . . . his'n!

MAYNO. Whose? . . . Yes, they must be his'n.

JANE (*lighting a candle and placing it on the table*). Yes, Mayno, they's Steve's all right.

MAYNO. How'd you git 'em, chile?

JANE. I got 'em from the sheriff.

MAYNO. And I thought you were goin' to see Henry Berry

'bout Steve's money and find where they put 'im. (*She opens the package and takes out a coat, a pair of trousers, and a black felt hat. The garments are slashed and stiff with blood.*)

JANE. I did—two hours proguin' down through the black swamps an' the bramble br'ars, and when I foun' Henry Berry he said them sher'ffs what killed Steve got his money, and as for where they put 'im, nobody knows. (CUMBA *is heard groaning as she turns in her bed.* JANE *lowers her voice.*) And then I went to the sheriff for his clothes. I knowed that some day when she—(*Nodding to the room at the left*)—finds it out she'll be wantin' his clothes, them she made with her own hands like th' others. And the sheriff wouldn't tell me where they buried 'im.

MAYNO. Took his money, did they? That's the way with them white folks. They do all they kin agin' us poor Croatons, 'cause we's jes' injuns, they says—though we knows better.

JANE. They don't hold nothin' agin' us; hit's agin' the boys.

MAYNO. They killed yo' daddy and William and Tom and Steve for being robbers and cut-throats and they robbers and cut-throats theyselves. (*Fiercely.*) And me needing new dresses and the like. But they's one left they won't git, the last an' best of 'em all. The day they lays Henry Berry cold they'll be more of 'em got than has been.

JANE (*wearily*). Hush, Mayno; with your jawing you'd wake the dead. She'll hear you.

MAYNO (*throwing down the clothes and coming to the fire*). Well, why you want to keep pushing trouble from her? What's the good o' it? She'll find it out somehow. She's suffered now 'til you cain't hurt her no more. And ain't I suffered too, with my man dead on me? What call has she got to . . .

JANE. No, we ain't a-goin' to tell her now. She ain't got much longer, and let her keep on b'lieving Steve and

Henry Berry's safe in Georgy. No, they ain't no use o' letting her on to it now. (JANE *sits at the spinning-wheel.*)

MAYNO (*vehemently*). Ain't Henry Berry going to *try* to git them sher'ffs back for killing Steve? If I's a outlaw like him I'd a done paid 'em. And he'll pay 'em, too! He's the best o' the Lowries and he'll 'venge them that's been murdered in cold blood like Steve and the rest.

JANE. No, Mayno, he won't nuther. His time's drawin' nigh. He knows it. They're settin' for him everywhere. They's men watchin' this house to-night. I seen it in his face to-day that he's layin' down. He was wrong from the first. He knows it now.

MAYNO. What's that!

JANE. Yes, he's a-quittin', but if them sheriffs hadn't agged him on ten years ago when he wanted to quit and be quiet he'd a been livin' in peace here to-night. But it's too late now. Too many men's been killed. And he's putting up his guns at the last. They'll git him 'fore many days. . . . He tol' me so.

MAYNO. You're a-lyin', gal. You know he's goin' to bring 'em down for Steve, him as was the strappingest man o' the gang. It ain't his way to be a-backing down and not pay 'em.

JANE. No, he ain't. He's a-puttin' it by, I tell you. They'll ketch him 'fore long.

MAYNO. Then what you goin' to do 'bout her in there? You cain't keep on a-foolin' her forever with your letters and money and mess from Georgy.

JANE. Well, we c'n fool 'er till she gits better, cain't we? And if she don't git better, then she'll go out happier, won't she . . . believin' Steve and Henry Berry's safe and livin' as they ought—(*She rises and goes to the cupboard*) —she so old and fearful at the door hinge skreaking even and the red rooster crowing 'fore the glim o' dawn, you know, Mayno. (*She brings some butter and the molasses pot from the cupboard, takes the spider from the fire and puts supper on the table.*)

MAYNO. Well, go on if you will, but you cain't keep it up much longer. It'll be jes' like I said. Henry Berry'll come broozin' around some night. Sposen so?

JANE (*frightened*). You reckon he'd do that. . . . No he couldn't. I tol' him about how it was with her, and besides he knows the house is watched.

MAYNO (*shaking her head*). I dunno. He mought. You know the time he slipped through a whole passel o' them sher'ffs jes' to come here and git a shirt she'd made 'im? And by this time he must be a-wantin' to see her powerful bad.

JANE (*terrified*). You reckon he will? No, he won't! He couldn't do that. (*Old* CUMBA *is heard calling* JANE). Put them things in the sack with th' others, Mayno, and put 'em in the bottom, too. You c'n be fixin' her supper while I ten' to 'er. (*She goes into the rear room.* MAYNO *takes up the clothes, opens the chest at the left, pulls out a bulky burlap sack and crams the trousers, shirt and hat into it. Shutting the chest, she goes to the cupboard, takes out three plates and some knives and forks and lays them on the table. Then she begins preparing* CUMBA'S *supper on a plate.* JANE *comes to the door and speaks.*) You needn't bring her supper in here, Mayno, she's going to git up, she says. (JANE *goes back into the room.* MAYNO *shrugs her shoulders, sits down and begins to eat.* JANE *comes in supporting old* CUMBA. *She speaks to* MAYNO.) Fix her chair by the fire, Mayno.

MAYNO (*rising reluctantly from the table*). Gimme time, cain't you? (*She pulls* CUMBA'S *chair nearer to the fire.* CUMBA *is a bent, emaciated old woman, about seventy years of age. Her face is scarred with suffering. She is a mixture of Negro and Portugese, somewhat darker than* JANE. *She is feeble and shakes with palsy.*)

CUMBA (*pausing, as* JANE *leads her to the fire*). Did you say they warn't nary letter from the boys 'way out thar?

JANE (*looking at* MAYNO *as she settles* CUMBA *in her chair*). No'm, there warn't no letter this time, but they'll be one soon. You see they cain't write often, not yit. They mought be ketched on account of it. 'Tain't quite time for another'n yit.

CUMBA. Mebbe so, mebbe so. But I thought they mought 'a been one. How long is it they been out thar, chile?

JANE (*placing the plate of food on her lap*). Two months now, muh. And they's livin' straight and 'spectable, too. And 'twon't be long 'fore the big Governor'll pardon 'em, and they'll come back to you, and you'll be happy agin, you will that.

CUMBA (*brightening*). And I'll be at the loom then, a-weavin' 'em the good shirts, won't I? And they'll be working in the fields and comin' home to a good dinner, won't they? And at night Henry Berry'll be a-playin' of his banjo like old times, won't he? (*She stops suddenly. All the brightness goes out of her face. She lets her knife fall to her plate.*) But they won't be but two of 'em, will there, Janie? Jes' two. When thar was Allen, my old man—they shot 'im over thar in the corner. (*She turns and points.*) They's a blood spot thar now. Then thar was Willie and Tom. And they ain't no tellin' how they put 'em away, chile . . . chile . . .

JANE. Now, muh, you mustn't do that!—Eat your supper. You got to git well, time Steve and Henry Berry gits back. They's allus grief with the children going, but you still got two of the boys and me. (JANE *butters a piece of bread and hands it to her.*)

CUMBA. Mebbe so, mebbe so, chile. But . . . (*She stops*) Whar's that letter that come from the boys last month? I wants it read agin.

JANE. But, muh, you got to eat. I'll read it after while. Let me fry you a egg. (MAYNO *leaves the table and begins spinning at the wheel.*)

CUMBA. I ain't hongry, chile. Take them thar rations and

put 'em back and read me the letter. It's enough to hear it . . . hearin' that the last of my boys is safe and ca'm and livin' once more as I'd lak 'em to.

JANE. Well, I'll git it then. (*She goes, searches in the cupboard, and at last draws out a greasy envelope. From this she takes a sheet of paper and comes back to old* CUMBA.)

CUMBA. Read it, honey. It's the blessin' of the Lord that I's spared to learn that two o' my boys is shet of sin. But they's been a heap o' blood spilt, chile, a heap o' blood spilt . . . but they's been more tears spilt by they ol' mammy, too, and mebbe at last they'll ketch a chance to come back to her. Read it, chile.

JANE (*glancing at* MAYNO *and then looking at the letter*). They says they's a-gitting along well and makin' money an' . . .

CUMBA. Don't read it like that. Read what they says!

JANE. Well, I'll read it then. (*She reads.*)

"Dear Mammy:
"We writes to let you know we're in Georgy at last, safe an' sound. We're both workin' in a store an' makin' good money. They ain't nobody knows what we done back there, an' the people is good to us. 'Twon't be long 'fore the Governor'll pardon us, and we can come back and take care o' you.
"Your lovind sons,
"Steve and Henry Berry."

CUMBA. You left out somethin', child. Don't you know they sent some money with the letter and they spoke about it.

JANE (*confused*). Yes'm, that's right. I forgot it. It's on the other side, mammy. Yes'm, here it is. It says, "We're sendin' you twenty dollars to buy meat and flour with."

CUMBA. Good boys they is, they ain't never meant no harm. Willie and Tom was jes' that-a-way. Every cent they used to make a-hoein' cotton 'roun' they'd give it to they ol' mammy, an' the good Lord knows whar they's sleepin' to-night . . . but they's two spared me an' I hadn't ought to complain, I reckon. Is the money all gone, Janie?

JANE. No'm, there's some left yit, and they'll be sending more in the next letter. (*She puts the letter back into the cupboard and begins cleaning up the dishes. Old* CUMBA *leans back in her chair, gazing into the fire. The hooting of an owl is heard. She stirs uneasily in her chair.* MAYNO *and* JANE *stop their work and listen. They both look at each other and then glance at old* CUMBA, *who is trembling and gripping the arms of her chair.* JANE *begins to rattle the dishes.* MAYNO *spins rapidly.*)

CUMBA (*turning to* JANE). Ain't that a owl squeechin', Jane?

JANE (*looking at* MAYNO). What? . . . I . . . I don't hear nothin'. (*The hooting is heard again.*)

CUMBA. Ain't that it agin?

MAYNO. Aw, it's nothin' but that ol' swamp owl. He hollers 'most every night. Don't take on 'bout it. (*She shivers and stirs the fire.*)

CUMBA (*shrilly*). It sounds like some o' my boys a-makin' o' they signals down thar in the night; but 'tain't them though. The only two that's left is a long ways off, and mebbe won't never come back.

JANE. Now, they will too.

CUMBA. 'Way back yonder I loved to see 'em 'round me here, the warm fire a-burnin' and Allen thar a-working at his gear, and them that was little uns then a-playing on the floor. I didn't mind it them times. (*Her voice grows shriller.*) And now where are they? My ol' man and all the house gone from me.

MAYNO. Aw, Ma Lowrie, what's the use of all them carry-ing-ons? You reckon you're the only one that's had trouble in this world?

CUMBA. And when the rain and the wind come raring down and the cypress trees is moanin' in the dark and the owls a-honing through the night, I think on them three lyin' dead thar in the woods and the water washin' over them, and me with nothin' but their clothes to remember on and show for them I was prided for. (*Again the hooting of the owl is heard.* JANE *leaves the dishes suddenly and comes to the fire, lays more wood on, furtively wiping the tears from her eyes.* CUMBA *still looks in the fire.*)

JANE. It's time for you to lay down now.

CUMBA (*without noticing her*). At times in the dark night I dream on 'em and they ain't nothin' happened and it's all like it used to be, and then I wake a-callin', and they don't answer, for they're sleepin' out naked in the cold.

MAYNO (*shrugging her shoulders*). Jes' listen at her!—Ma Lowrie, cain't you be quiet a bit? (*Lowering her voice.*) Lord, you're as techous as a old hen!

JANE (*half sobbing*). What makes you carry on like that? It cain't do no good. Ain't Henry Berry tol' you a hundred times that he's buried all three of 'em down thar in the swamp? And he's skeered to tell the place for fear them sher'ffs'll dig 'em up and git the money for 'em. Don't take on so. They's put away with praying, and you'd better lie down now. (*She looks at* MAYNO.)

CUMBA. Yes, they mought be buried in the swamp down thar, and when it rains the river rises and washes over 'em, them that used to pull at my dress when I was at the wash— But Old Master sends the sun and the rain, and the Book says we ought to be satisfied. (*The owl's hoot is heard again.* CUMBA *looks at the door and shivers.*) Help me in now, chile. I didn't mean to say all that, but I'm done. An ol' woman's heart is a foolish thing . . . a foolish thing. . . . (JANE *helps her into the room at the left. A moment later she reappears. She looks at* MAYNO *inquisitively.*)

MAYNO. Sounded like Henry Berry's hootin', didn't it?

JANE. Yes, I'm afraid it's him, after all I tol' him. Oh, what makes him do it? But it's like I said. He's givin' in now, he's quittin' at the last. And he's set on seein' her once more or it's some of his quair notions, somethin' he's wropped up in gittin'. (*Three knocks are heard at the door.* JANE *runs and lifts the heavy bar, and* HENRY BERRY LOWRIE *walks in.*)

MAYNO. Henry Berry! (*He starts to speak but* JANE *lays her finger on her lips and leads him towards the fire. He takes off his hat and bows wearily to* MAYNO.

He is a man of handsome personal appearance. The color of his skin is a mixed white and yellowish brown, almost copper-colored. Just below his left eye is a crescent-shaped scar. Despite the look of weariness, his countenance is expressive in a high degree of firmness and courage. His forehead is broad and high, his eyes large and keen, his hair thick and inclined to curl. He wears a black beard. From appearances he is about twenty-six years of age, a little above medium height, well-knit, broad-shouldered, and well-proportioned throughout. He wears a broad, black felt hat, brown corduroy coat, dark woolen trousers, and calf-skin boots. In a belt around his waist he carries two pistols. From this belt a strap passes upward and supports a repeating rifle behind. He also carries a long-bladed knife stuck in his belt. He takes a seat at the fire, putting his rifle in the corner, but retaining his other arms. JANE *runs to the door at the rear and makes sure that it is closed tight. Then she hurries to* HENRY BERRY.*

JANE. Brother, what made you do it! The house is watched an' . . .

HENRY BERRY. I know it, Sis, but I had to come. I'm quittin' . . . to-night. Is she asleep? (*He jerks his head towards the room at the left.*)

JANE. No, I've jes' helped her in. That's the reason we couldn't make no sign with the light.

HENRY BERRY. I couldn't figure what the trouble was. I hooted till my heart hurt. But I was goin' to risk it anyhow.

JANE. What'll she think if she sees you! Oh, hurry and go away!

HENRY BERRY. Naw, I got to see her. After to-night 'twon't matter. Bring me a bite to eat, Sis. How is she?

MAYNO. I reckon she's on the mend. . . .

JANE (*frightened*). Will they git you to-night? What do you mean by sich talk?

HENRY BERRY. Never mind. They'll git me . . . when I'm dead, all right, no doubt o' that. I'm taking the gear off at last. The ol' man's gone, Willie and Tom's gone, and they got Steve last week, and I'm the last o' the gang. I'm tired, damned tired of it all, Sis.

JANE. But I tell you, you cain't give up like that. You got to keep on fightin' till you git a chance to git away!

HENRY BERRY. Naw, it's too late now. If they'd 'a let me, I'd 'a lived straight, but after the first trouble I had to keep killin' to live. Well, I'm done killin', now . . . 'cept one man, and they ain't no use of you knowin' who it is. You'll know soon enough. One man can't stand it allus, and they'll scrush him at the last. (JANE *sits in her chair weeping softly.* HENRY BERRY *lays his hand gently on her head. Trying to appear cheerful, he turns to* MAYNO.) Mayno, bring me a bite to eat. (*He sits at the table, facing the front.* MAYNO *gets a plate of food and puts it before him. He eats hungrily.*)

MAYNO. Whar'd they put 'im, Henry Berry?

HENRY BERRY. I ain't been able to find out, Mayno. Piled him in some of their rotten graveyards, I reckon, when he loved to run the woods with th' other wild things like him.

MAYNO. What'd they do with his money?

HENRY BERRY. I dunno. Got that, too, I reckon. But you needn't to worry. Jane! (JANE *looks up.*) Here, I've fixed for you-all. Here's money enough to last you three after

I'm gone. (*He stops eating and pulls a bag of money out of his pocket.*)

JANE. But, brother . . .

HENRY BERRY. Never mind, take it and take care o' her. It's the last thing I c'n do for her and you.

JANE. But she won't use it, knowin' how you come by it.

HENRY BERRY. She won't?

JANE. No, she won't. She'll starve first, and you know it. You know all them fixin's you sent her. She give 'em all away, the stove and the stool with three legs and everything. And when she thought you and Steve was livin' straight in Georgy, she give away that gold chain you brung her. She's feared you hadn't got it honest.

HENRY BERRY (*softly*). Yes, yes, she's allus been too good fer us. (*He leaves the table and takes a seat near the fire.*) Still that chain was bought honest. . . . But you three's got to live, ain't ye? Take that money, and don't tell 'er. (JANE *puts the money in the chest.*) Mayno, is my ol' banjo still here?

MAYNO. Yeah, in thar.

HENRY BERRY. I been wantin' to knock her a little for a long time. And I want to knock her a little the las' night.

JANE. The las' night! It ain't the las' night! If you'd go now you'd git away. Why do you talk like that? (*She is interrupted by a loud cry. Old* CUMBA *stands in the door at the rear.*)

CUMBA. It's you, it's you, Henry Berry! Come back from Georgy. I knowed you'd come. I knowed. . . . (*She totters to* HENRY BERRY *and throws her arms around him. He kisses her on the forehead. Her look is one of unmingled joy. Suddenly the hurt look comes back into her face.*) Why you come back a-wearin' of your guns?

HENRY BERRY (*helping her to the fire*). I'm just wearin' 'em. I didn't want to be ketched empty. I'm leavin' in a few minutes and le's us enjoy ourselves, and forgit about Georgy.

CUMBA. No, they's somthin' wrong. Whar's Steve?

HENRY BERRY (*looking at* MAYNO *and* JANE). He's waitin' for me . . . out thar. (*He points toward the swamp.*)

CUMBA. Why didn't he come in wid you? Is he well and strong? How I'd love to see 'im!

HENRY BERRY. One of us had to wait for th' other'n, and he's all right. How you feelin', mammy? Is your haid better now?

CUMBA. Yes, I'm gittin' better now. I wants to git well time you and Steve comes home for good. (*Stroking his hand.*) Has the Gov'nor pardoned ye already?

HENRY BERRY. No, mammy, not jest yit. But it'll be all right soon. . . . Steve and me's jest passin' through. . . . Now le's us enjoy ourselves. I got to be movin' in a minute. Steve's waiting for me. . . . Mebbe we'll talk about Georgy some other time. . . . Mayno, bring me my ol' music box.

CUMBA. Yes, yes, git it and let 'im play for me. (MAYNO *brings the banjo from the next room.* HENRY BERRY *tunes it.* CUMBA *sits gazing in the fire, a troubled look on her face.*)

HENRY BERRY. You want me to play 'bout Job's Coffin hanging in the sky? (*Strangely.*) That was Steve's piece.

JANE (*nervously*). Don't, don't play that. It's too lonesome. (*She shivers.*)

HENRY BERRY. What piece you want me to play? (*To* CUMBA. *She makes no reply.* HENRY BERRY *looks at her. He strums several bars, his face gradually losing its tense expression.*) What you want me to play, muh?

CUMBA. Play anything. Some o' the ol' pieces.

HENRY BERRY. I'll play that piece 'bout poor John Hardy. (*He plays and sings three stanzas of the ballad "John Hardy."*)

John Hard-y was a mean and — dis-per-a-ted man, He tot-ed two guns ev-'ry day. He shot him-self a man in — New Or-leans — Town John Hard-y nev-er lied to his guns, poor boy.

He's been to the east and he's been to the west
And he's been this wide world round,
He's been to the river an' been baptized,
An' he's been on his hanging ground, poor boy.

John Hardy's father was standing by,
Saying, "Johnnie, what have you done?"
He murdered a man in the same ol' town,
You ought a-seed him a-using of his guns, poor boy.

(*He stops and gazes pensively before him.*)

CUMBA (*looking anxiously at* HENRY BERRY). What's the matter, son? You don't play it like you used to.

HENRY BERRY. It ain't nothing. I'll play yo' other piece now, that Florelly song.

CUMBA. Yes, play it. Allen allus said 'twas a good piece.
HENRY BERRY.

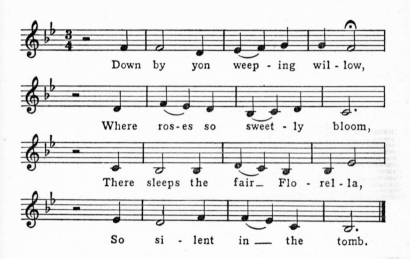

Down by yon weep-ing wil-low,

Where ros-es so sweet-ly bloom,

There sleeps the fair_ Flo-rel-la,

So si-lent in __ the tomb.

> She died not broken hearted,
> No sickness her befell,
> But in one moment parted
> From all she loved so well.

> Down on her knees before him,
> She begged 'im for her life,
> But deep into her bosom
> He plunged the fatal knife.

*(Before the last verse ends, owl hoots are heard outside.
HENRY BERRY stops, listening. The banjo slips through his
hands to the floor. All three look at him questioningly.)*
CUMBA. What is it, boy? Don' look that-a-way. *(Again the
hooting of an owl is heard.* HENRY BERRY *rises to his feet,
takes his rifle from the chimney corner and stands an instant
tensely silent. Slowly his defensive attitude changes to one of*

*despair. They watch him anxiously as he comes back to his
former place in the room, looks down at his banjo, makes a
move as if to pick it up, then turns to* CUMBA.)

HENRY BERRY. Well, I'm goin'. I've sorto' tried to be a
fitten boy to you, but I reckon I made poor outs at it.
(*He bends and kisses her. She rises and clings to him.*)

CUMBA. You ain't a-goin' air ye? It'll be for the las' time
and I know it.

HENRY BERRY. Yes'm, I got to go. Didn't you hear Steve's
signal? He's a-waitin'. (*Making an indefinite motion with
his hand toward the swamp, he loosens her hold, kisses* JANE
and makes a sign for MAYNO *to follow him. They both go
out.* CUMBA *wrings her hands and follows him toward the
door. Then she becomes calm.*)

CUMBA. Let him go off now, an' I'll never see 'im agin. His
sperit's broke and he won't be a-goin' back to Georgy. I
see it in his face that he's quittin' it all.

JANE. No'm he ain't, he's a-goin' straight back. . . . He
and Steve is.

CUMBA. No, he ain't a-goin' back. Cain't I see what's in his
face? They'll git 'im and 'twon't be long, and then Steve'll
be shot down next, and there'll be only a handful o' their
clothes for me to look at. (JANE *weeps silently.*) Whar's
Mayno?

JANE. She's jes' stepped out a minute. She'll be back.

CUMBA. Yes, and I know, they're goin' to git 'im. They's
a-setting for him thar in the black night.

JANE. No'm, they ain't, I tell you. They'll never git Henry
Berry. (OLD CUMBA *shakes her head mumbling. She goes to
the chest at the left and takes out the burlap bag. The lid of
the chest falls.* JANE *starts up.*) Put it back, put it back.
You mustn't look at 'em to-night. Come back to the fire.
(*She tries to take the bag from her.*)

CUMBA. No, chil', I ain't. I'm goin' to look at all that's left
of 'em.

JANE. Let 'em be!

CUMBA (*waving her off*). No, git away. Soon Henry Berry's 'll be in there, too. (*She stops and looks at the bag.*) Janie, who's been foolin' wi' this? What's . . . (*She hurries to the table and holding the sack close to the candle, opens it. She catches hold of a coat sleeve and draws out Steve's coat. A gasping dry sound comes from her throat. She drops the bag and holds the coat in her trembling hands.*) It's Steve's! How come it here? It's Steve's!—one I made 'im myself.

JANE. Oh, muh, let . . . What ails you?

CUMBA. I s'picioned it! And they been foolin' me.

JANE (*hopelessly*). Yes'm, it's Steve's. (CUMBA *sways to and fro.*)

CUMBA. You been foolin' me! You been foolin' me! (*She stands rigid for a moment, then speaks in a hard, lifeless voice.*) It warn't right to fool me like that. . . . When'd it happen?

JANE. Las' week. . . . They got 'im down on the big road by the swamp, an' . . .

CUMBA. Hush! Don't tell me 'bout it. I'm afflicted and defeated enough now. They's only one left and they'll git 'im soon. . . . Did they put Steve away like a man?

JANE. I dunno. The sheriff give 'is clothes to me. (*A shot is heard in the distance, followed by a woman's scream.*)

CUMBA (*starting up and speaking in a shrill voice*). They got 'im now! They got 'im now! The last un's gone! (*She tries to go out at the door.* JANE *stops her.*)

JANE (*catching her by the arm*). Don't do that! (CUMBA *goes back to the sack, picks up* STEVE's *coat and stares at it dully.*)

CUMBA. They tuck 'em all now. They tuck 'em all.

JANE. Muh, it had to come. An' it's better that-a-way.

CUMBA (*dully*). Better that-a-way?

JANE. Yes, it's better like that. They was wrong from the jump.

CUMBA. Wrong! My boys was good boys. They ain't never . . . (*Raising her hands above her head, she speaks fiercely.*) May Ol' Master send his fires on them that done it! An' . . .

JANE (*sobbing*). Oh, why'd they do it!

CUMBA. No. It says as how we'd ought to love 'em 'at does us wrong. (*She closes her eyes, swaying slightly from side to side.*)

JANE. Let me help you to lie down now!

CUMBA. Yes, it's better that-a-way, I reckon. (*Her face shows resignation to sorrow. She speaks with a sort of joy in her voice.*) An' I won't be livin' in hope and fear no mo', will I? (*Slowly.*) And when the owls hoot through the swamp at night, and the whippoorwills sing in the thicket at dark, I won't have cause to think that's one o' my own a-givin' of 'is signals, an' tryin' to slip back to 'is ol' home, the only place he loves,—will I? (*She drops down into the chair behind the table.*) An' I won't lie awake at night, thinkin' they're in danger . . . for He's done give 'em His peace at last. (MAYNO *enters running.* OLD CUMBA *stands up.*)

MAYNO. He shot 'isself. He shot 'isself! He give me this coat to give to you, an' then the sheriffs crope from the thicket at 'im, but he shot 'isself 'fore they got to 'im, and they tuck 'im and toted 'im off! (*She drops into her chair exhausted, rocking to and fro.* OLD CUMBA *takes the coat from her, looks at it, and then puts it in the sack. She puts* STEVE'S *coat in also and stands looking down at the bag.*)

CUMBA. Thar's all that's left o' them I loved . . . a bundle o' clothes to show for my man an' four grown sons. (*She stops an instant.*) And you'll all sleep quiet at the last. (*She stands a moment silent, then shrilly.*) But they're all gone, and what call hev I got to be living more. . . . (*She raises her hand as if in a curse. But her face softens, and as the curtain falls, she stands with both hands outstretched on the clothes, blessing them.)*

It is interesting to note that the actual story of the old Lowrie mother somewhat parallels that of Maurya in Synge's *Riders to the Sea*. In the one case the mother sees her sons sacrificed before the power of the law. In the other she sees them claimed by the terribleness of the sea. So far as the suffering is concerned, the forces in both cases might be the same.

CURTAIN

TRISTA

A Play of Folk Superstition

BY

ELIZABETH A. LAY

TRISTA

The author of *Trista* comes from Beaufort, a little town by
the sea, which still retains the spirit of colonial times. She
knows the sturdy lives of the fisher-folk and understands the
meaning of their wondering beliefs. These she holds to be as
much a part of our heritage as the religion brought from
England by the first settlers. What is now looked upon as
worn-out superstition, in *Trista* is restored to its original
meaning and beauty.

Witches were usually conceived as ugly old hags, but
Trista is a young woman, fair, akin to the sirens of the
Greeks and to the fairies of all times. Here a legend of an
outlived past is interpreted for its human significance.

THE CHARACTERS

As originally produced on The Playmakers' Stage, Chapel Hill, North Carolina, December 2 and 3, 1921.

Eph Hunter, *a young trader in the settlement,*
Le Grand Everett

Kezzie, *his good-natured mother,*   Katharine Woodrow

Gaffer, *the old grandfather,*   Hubert Heffner

Dr. Trask, *a minister of the Church of England, sent as a missionary to the Colonists,*   Robert Frasier

Trista, *Eph's young wife,*   Katherine Batts

Scene: Eph's log-cabin home in a settlement on the North Carolina coast.

Time: A spring night in the early Eighteenth Century, when the superstitious but lenient Southern colonists firmly believed in witchcraft.

SCENE

The room is comfortable in spite of the rudeness of the house. The furniture is simple but well made, and the family posses- sions brought across the sea only a few years before, help to give the colonist's home a look of prosperity and comfort.

The light from the fireplace in the left wall casts dark shadows about the room, lighting but dimly the open cupboard in the corner which contains bright pewter and old blue china dishes. The bed in the right corner is covered with a hand-woven bed- spread. A patchwork quilt is folded across the foot. The table, covered with a fringed cotton cloth, is in the center of the room. On it are two unlighted candles in old pewter candlesticks. There are several chairs about the table and one near the fire- place. In the right corner at the front is a spinning wheel. A cradle stands by the fireplace. A door at the right leads into another room.

A rough board door in the rear wall, to the left, opens out-of- doors. The latch-hole is stopped with a cotton rag and, in place of the latch, a fastening has been contrived from a wooden peg and staple. Through the small open window over the bed there may be seen a glimpse of budding trees against a starry sky. When the door at the rear is open the new moon may be seen and the far-off line of the river.

When the curtain rises, KEZZIE, a placid-looking middle- aged woman, is sitting by the fire rocking the cradle with her foot and humming an old psalm tune. She wears a plain dress of homespun and a white apron. Her knitting lies in her lap but she is too nervous to work on it. She glances anxiously at the door and at the child, to be sure he is asleep. Then she rises and goes softly to the cupboard to get some dishes from it. There is a sound of shuffling footsteps outside. KEZZIE goes quickly to the door and opens it. GAFFER enters.

He is bent and shriveled—a pitiably feeble old man. He has long hair and a long white beard which nearly covers his face. His clothes of homespun are disorderly, his short trousers baggy, and he holds an old shawl tightly about his shoulders and advances feebly, leaning on a cane and appearing not to see KEZZIE. *His eyes are very bright and glisten with the unearthly expression of one who imagines he sees strange things.*

GAFFER (*mumbling*). Trouble, trouble, trouble. . . .

KEZZIE (*coming closer to him and speaking anxiously*). She ain't a witch, Gaffer? What is it? The trial's over, Gaffer, is it?

GAFFER. She's a-goin' to leave us. She's a-goin' to leave us. The time's come.

KEZZIE (*impatiently*). Dear life! If he was jes' right in his head! (*She turns to* GAFFER *and speaks coaxingly.*) Gaffer, the judge at the trial . . . listen, Gaffer. You rec'lect the man with the wig and the black gown. Didn't he say she's not a witch, Gaffer? Didn't he say she's not a witch? (*She turns from him despairingly as he sits down by the fire and continues mumbling, stirring the fire with his stick.*)

GAFFER (*suddenly bursting out, almost sobbing*). They say she ain't a witch, she ain't a witch.

KEZZIE. Oh, there ain't no sense in any of your words, good or bad.

GAFFER. They say she ain't. Oh, trouble, trouble, trouble!

KEZZIE (*lighting the candles from the fire*). Hush, Gaffer. For shame to take on so if sech is true. We all should praise the Lord that Trista's free.

GAFFER (*suddenly rising*). Oh, I've turned the dead coals in the fire an' I've turned trouble close to my heart. (*He gets up and hobbles toward the door.*) An' I've seen the new moon through the trees to-night an' it's a sure sign of evil.

KEZZIE (*following him to the open door*). You cain't go out in the dampness agin this night. (*She closes the door and leads him back to the fire.*) Set down thar, Gaffer, an' be still till

I change my dress a bit. They'll be comin' back from the trial an' if she's cleared they're goin' to baptize her. (*Speaking gently.*) They're goin' to baptize her, Gaffer, in the faith, jes' same's her little baby thar—hers . . . an' Eph's. (*Her voice has become almost broodingly gentle. She looks out of the window as she crosses to the right. Then she turns to the old man.*) Thar's lanterns comin' down the river now. The trial's over sure, an' I'll be learnin' the truth 'bout Trista. Set still, Gaffer, an' mind you don't wake the child. (*She goes hurriedly into the next room.*)

GAFFER. They say she ain't a witch, an' she'll be leavin' us now. She'll ride off an' leave us, for she *is* a witch; she is a witch. An' they won't guard her now. They can't hold her here. Fools an' blind, fools an' blind. . . . Yer mother be a witch, my child, a witch. Aye, we see it, an' we see the far-off signs—signs an' wonders! Signs an' wonders! (*He rises.*) She'll ride away, she'll ride away. An' you'll be left to grow an' work an' I'll be left to die. . . . Oh, trouble, trouble, trouble. (*He sinks back into his chair.*) There'll be no one left to see things then, an' we'll forgit, we'll forgit. . . . (*There is a pause, then he becomes wilder.*)
   Will we leave yer mother ride away, will we leave her go, child? (*He laughs.*) She have eyes like an ol' man an' eyes like a child, eyes to see, eyes to see. . . . We'll hold her here, we'll hold her here. . . . (*He hobbles to the door and his face becomes crafty. He points to the latch-hole.*) While the latch-hole is stopped, child, the spell's on her an' she cain't ride away. We'll hold her here. She's a witch, a witch! . . . The spell, the spell will hold her here! (*He stands over the child with his arms upraised in exaltation.*)

KEZZIE. (*Opens the door at the right and enters hurriedly. She has freshened her gown with an old lace collar and taken off her apron. She runs to* GAFFER.) Gaffer, Gaffer, leave the child be! (*At her entrance* GAFFER *lowers his arms and shrinks into a chair at the back of the fireplace.* KEZZIE *pats him hastily on the shoulder.*) Now, you set down thar,

Gaffer, an' be still. (*She looks anxiously at the cradle.*)
The child's still asleep, praise be!

GAFFER (*mumbling*). They's signs of sorrow an' trouble. They
say she ain't a witch. . . .

KEZZIE. (*goes to the cupboard and brings out bread, ham, a
jug of wine and some cakes. She places them, with some
dishes, on the table. Sounds are heard of people approaching,
talking cheerfully but with earnestness.* KEZZIE *runs quickly
to the door and opens it, calling to some one outside.*) Is that
you, John? Tell me quick. Is . . . is the hearin' over? Is
Trista . . . is she free . . . ?

(JOHN's *voice answers.*) Yes, all over, Mistress Hunter.
She's free an' Eph's a-bringin' her home from court.

(*Other voices call.*) We be thankful she's cleared. She
ain't a witch.

No, an' I never was one to say it, neither. The dissenters
that accused her. . . . (*The people pass by.* KEZZIE *closes
the door and comes to the table.*)

GAFFER (*continuing monotonously*). They say she ain't a
witch. They say she ain't a witch. . . . (*The refrain
catches the attention of* KEZZIE. *She speaks as one would to
a precocious child.*)

KEZZIE. Why, so 'tis, Gaffer. (*She laughs contentedly.*) An'
you knowed it. No, Trista ain't diff'rent from any of us
an' the jedge has said she kin go free.

GAFFER (*suddenly vehement*). Fools, fools! She is a witch!
You are blind, blind!

KEZZIE (*reprovingly*). No, no she ain't, Gaffer. An' now you
hush. (*She leans close to him as though trying to make him
understand.*) Let's leave her forget all them strange notions
of her'n an' be jes' like other folks now. . . . You been
talkin' craziness to her 'nough to make her turn quair, too.
Nobody believes she's any hag! (*As* GAFFER *continues
she takes the easiest way of silencing him.*) Here, Gaffer,
take this piece of bread an' eat it an' be still. (GAFFER
refuses.) Well, be still then, anyways. (*She moves about the*

room setting the table. Sounds of footsteps and voices are heard outside and she goes quickly to the door. EPH *enters with* TRISTA, *supporting her.*

He is a good-natured young man of about thirty, rather earnest and matter-of-fact. His face is good and honest, though commonplace in expression. He has the appearance of a man who has succeeded and will settle into a comfortable middle age. He wears clothes, evidently his best, neat but not handsome.

TRISTA *is a tall, lithe girl. There is something elfin in her graceful figure. Her face is too thin to be beautiful but her eyes have an unearthly look about them which makes them seem almost too large. Her expression is wistful and hauntingly sweet, sometimes desperate like that of a hunted wild thing, sometimes wearied and hopeless. Her straight fine hair is drawn loosely back into a heavy coil at the back of the head. She wears a gown of homespun and a long gold chain of strange design. When she enters she is completely hidden by a cloak with a pointed hood.*

DR. TRASK *enters behind them. He is a mild-looking man, rather small. He wears clothes of dark color, with a white stock, and a bright-colored waistcoat. His hat is a flat-brimmed, clerical hat, but the rest of his costume is that of any gentleman of the time.*)

KEZZIE (*going joyfully to* TRISTA, *she kisses her and leads her into the room. She turns to* DR. TRASK). Come in, Dr. Trask. You've brung us a blessin', sir.

DR. TRASK (*bowing*). Mistress Hunter! You stood godmother to the child last Sabbath. Yes, indeed, I remember.

KEZZIE. 'Tis good to see you again, sir, at such a time.

EPH. Ma, Trista should rest a spell now, afore the baptizin'. She's that tired out.

KEZZIE. Yes, Eph. She'll want to freshen up a bit. You'll excuse us, sir. 'Twon't be long.

DR. TRASK. We would wait until another day for the baptism, Mistress Hunter, but I must leave for Virginia in the morning. They are expecting me there for services.

KEZZIE. Jest come in here, Trista, with me. (*She turns to* TRISTA *who was standing listlessly beside her a moment ago, but has slipped away now and crossed to the cradle where she stands staring down at the child, a worried expression on her face. She does not hear* KEZZIE *nor rouse from her reverie until* KEZZIE *crosses to her and takes her hand. Then she looks up in terror. She shrinks down over the cradle shielding her child with one arm. As* KEZZIE *takes her hand she looks at her with a blank expression for a moment, then seems to come to herself and follows listlessly into the next room.*

EPH *has been helping* DR. TRASK *remove his cloak. He now goes over to the cradle and looks at the child.*)

DR. TRASK (*following* EPH *to the fireplace*). And this is your only child? The one I baptized last Sabbath?

EPH. Yes, sir. We been waitin' an' hopin' a minister of the Established Church 'd come to the settlement an' now you've come. But it's been five year since the last one was here. Trista an' me was married by the jedge three years a-gone.

DR. TRASK. She has never been baptized, you say?

EPH. No, sir, not unless it were before she come to us an' she don't never speak o' that time. It's like she's forgot it all.

KEZZIE (*entering*). Trista'll be ready soon. She wants to be alone a while. Eph, ain't you even asked Dr. Trask to have some supper? He must be hungry.

DR. TRASK. No, I thank you. I have already supped.

KEZZIE. I've had my bite to eat, too. Eph, you'll want to wait for Trista. Set down, Dr. Trask. You must have had a tedious day. (KEZZIE *sits down at the right of the table,* DR. TRASK *at the back.* GAFFER *in his corner mumbles unnoticed.* EPH *stands awkwardly, oppressed by the difficulty of expressing his thanks to the preacher.*)

Eph (*very sincerely*). There's . . . Dr. Trask . . . there's no ways I can say how to thank you for what you done for us this day. The folks hereabouts has never been terrible bitter in accusin' Trista of servin' the Devil— like the dissenters in some places. But we thought it was best to have her brought to trial to lay the talkin' for good an' all . . . an' you examinin' her an' . . .

Kezzie. They's nothin' they can say agin' her now—now that a minister of the gospel has examined her before the court an' the jedge has said she ain't a witch.

Dr. Trask. It's been a blessed privilege to be able to examine her, and to clear her from this charge, my good friends. And, when she's joined God's church, she'll have no cause to be thought of but as all godly women of this colony. . . . You people have been true to her from the first, I hear.

Eph (*speaking resolutely, after a pause*). It's right, sir, for me to tell you as how when she fust come we *all* thought she's here through some spell . . . that . . .

Dr. Trask. You didn't believe yourself that she was a servant of the Devil?

Kezzie. God forgive us. We thought she's a witch.

Dr. Trask. What is that? The working of the dissenters! 'Tis no wonder that such superstitions should flourish in Salem and in all *New* England, but in Carolina and among the members of the Established Church! (*Almost sternly.*) I fear this settlement is indeed in sad want of spiritual guidance, of a minister from England. . . . When I set forth for America they told me of the many ungodly dangers I should encounter in my ministering journeys among the colonists. Ah, it is true. . . . Tell me, you believed this maid . . . your wife now. . . .

Eph. (*Sitting down. He speaks wonderingly.*) It does 'pear strange-like now. 'Twas on account of the quair way she come to us.

Dr. Trask. How was it I did not hear of that?

KEZZIE. We ain't talked of it to others. But it all come through Gaffer, my old father thar, sir. He went out'n his head in the great sickness on the ship, when we come across the water from England, an' he ain't been right since.

DR. TRASK. He found the girl?

KEZZIE. Yes, sir. The way she come did seem right quair then. . . . Three years a-gone it was. . . . One night he was in that thar bed, sir. We was all asleep, when he screamed out mos' fearful like. We both come runnin' in here, Eph an' me, an' Gaffer was a-babblin' that a witch had been a-hantin' him and that he'd stopped up the latch-hole an' done kotched her. The witch couldn't get out 'cept by the key-hole, he said, an' he'd done kotched her with the stoppin' of it. We heared a moanin' sound an' somethin' beatin' on the door soft-like. Gaffer cried out that it was a witch, an' we was a-feared, I can tell you. But Eph brung a light—an' thar was Trista . . . a-faintin' by the door!

EPH. She was that faint an' poor we all pitied her, an' we took to carin' the world an' all about her. Gaffer allus talked about her bein' a witch. But he follows her 'roun' an' won't hardly let her get out'n his sight.

KEZZIE. He talks about her bein' a witch, an' ridin' off some day if we don't watch out. He takes on so, we allus have kep' the latch-hole stopped to keep the spell on her. It's been jes' like you see it now, sir, stopped up. An' somehow . . . I sorter . . . It's quair, but I sorter feel it's safer.

DR. TRASK. But she is no witch.

EPH. We did believe she was, sir. But ma an' me—we couldn't turn her out, even so.

KEZZIE. She was lost an' sick an' dazed-like, an' we didn't know what to think of the strange things she'd talk on and the spells she'd have.

EPH. Even after she got right in her head she couldn't say jes' how she come. But thar was a ship come into harbor

down the river that same night, an' we 'lowed she'd come
across the seas on that. She must 'a' lost herself, an'
wandered in the door. It's like the long sea voyage turned
her mind in the sickness, like it done Gaffer. Some folks
allus said thar was somethin' quair 'bout Gaffer's allus
babblin' o' spells an' sech. She'd talk about seein' things
same as he do, an' we all thought she's a witch. . . . But
then . . . I married her, spite of all.

DR. TRASK. You truly believed she was a witch? Believed
she was a servant of the Devil?

EPH. Well, she was so harmless-like, an' jes' that sweet an'
purty an' good. . . . I dunno how I ever thought she's a
witch.

KEZZIE. Eph 'lowed he had to have her, witch or no. An'
they ain't a sweeter nor a purtier gal in all the river
settlements, after she got by havin' spells. Then we
knowed she's all right. I've prayed forgiveness that I ever
thought she's a witch.

DR. TRASK (*musing*). 'Tis a sad tale of unholy beliefs. But
she is cleared now before God and the law. That is all past.
And there is no need for such charms as the stopped
latch-hole. 'Tis wicked.

KEZZIE (*protesting*). Ah, 'tis only a notion.

EPH (*rather shamefaced*). 'Twas stopped up to keep her here,
sir, the night I fust saw her. I have a feeling' . . . an'
surely 'tain't no harm—

DR. TRASK (*rising and speaking sternly*). No, my friends,
these practices must be stopped. 'Tis acknowledging the
rule of witchcraft in this house. 'Tis tempting God to
punish. The young Mistress Hunter is no servant of the
Devil. She is like all the other wives of the Colony, and
needeth only her duty as wife and mother to hold her here.
This unholy sign must be removed at once, before I may
baptize her into the fold, according to God's Holy Word!

EPH (*convinced and penitent*). 'Twas a sin, sir; I see it now.
(*He rises.*) But Gaffer thar— (*He starts toward the door.*

Gaffer, *who has been watching them intently, intercepts him.*)

Gaffer (*hysterically*). She'll be gone; she'll be gone. She'll ride away from us all. She's a witch, she's a witch!

Dr. Trask (*commanding, his hand on the latch-hole*). Stand aside, old man!

Kezzie (*pleading to the minister*). Don't cross him, sir, in his notions. He's that fond of Trista; an' he takes a deal of store in his charms an' sech. But he's old an' crazed an' he'll soon forget. Jes' wait a bit.

Gaffer (*wildly, as he throws himself against the door, with appealing eyes to the minister*). The old an' young can see, can see. But they forgits, they forgits.

Kezzie. You see how he talks, sir. (*At this moment the door at the right opens and* Trista *enters. She wears now a gown of rich but faded silk. The same gold chain is around her neck. There is a look of wistful hopefulness in her face.* Eph *goes quickly to her, and leads her to a chair at the table.* Kezzie *speaks to* Dr. Trask *as he turns from the door.*) You won't eat a bite, Dr. Trask? (*He shakes his head, bowing.*) Then would you please to come in here, sir? There's fresh water an' you'll want to see what vessel to use.

Eph. You'll pardon us if we eat a bit first, sir. Trista's that weak an' faint.

Kezzie. Be quick, son. It's a long journey Dr. Trask has before him in the morning. (*She and the preacher go out at the right.* Eph *closes the door behind them, then turns to* Trista *who has risen and is looking at him as if searching for something lost.*)

Eph (*reprovingly*). Trista, why do you wear that gown?

Trista. Why, 'tis my prettiest gown, Eph . . . an' besides . . . I wore it when we were married, Eph. (*She speaks softly.*)

Eph. But it minds me of the time when you fust come here;

when you used to see strange sights an' we all thought you's . . .

TRISTA (*quickly*). But, Eph, you married me even so an' . . . (*She goes toward him.*)

EPH. We must put them things by, Trista, with the thoughts of those old days. (TRISTA *goes to the window and stands gazing out at the moonlight.*)

TRISTA. Those old days!

GAFFER (*moaning, as he bends over the fire*). There's no rest, there's no rest! Fools and blind! Fools and blind. . . .

EPH (*sitting at the table*). Hush, Gaffer, you'll wake the child. (TRISTA *walks listlessly to the door, opens it and looks out. EPH sees her and turns around from the plate of food at the table. He speaks impatiently.*) Trista, come eat your supper, an' don't keep Dr. Trask waitin'. (TRISTA *does not move from the door. EPH speaks more gently.*) Ain't you hungry, Trista? . . . Trista!

TRISTA (*in an expressionless voice*). No. (*There is silence for a moment, then* TRISTA, *with a swift movement, runs to* EPH *and puts her hands on his shoulders. There is a thrill in her voice.*) Eph, Eph! (*She seems transformed.*) Eph, come with me! Come out into the night, Eph, where the moon is making pathways on the river. Eph, the wind is calling —Hear! . . . and the clouds are flying, flying past the moon! (*Worn out by the stress of her emotion, she drops to her knees beside him. He bends over her, trying to quiet her.*) Eph, Eph, where are you? You used to love to go with me . . . an' now . . . an' now . . . (*She sinks down on the floor.*)

EPH. There, there, child. Forget all them quair notions. Why, I'm here, Trista,—an' there's your little baby, child. (*He leads her over to the cradle. She kneels and gazes at the baby with a troubled look. EPH goes back to the table and brings her some bread which she refuses.*)

TRISTA. What is it? What have you done to my child?

EPH. There, there, Trista. Be still an' rest.

GAFFER (*as* EPH *resumes his seat*). Only the young and the old kin see strange sights, an' they forgits, they forgits. (TRISTA *rises and goes softly and swiftly to the door. As* EPH *turns and sees her, she speaks.*)

TRISTA. I'm goin' down to the river, Eph.

EPH. No, you ain't, child. It's too cool. You ain't goin' to look at the river to-night. (*Trying to lead her back to the table.*) Come an' set here with me.

TRISTA. I've got to go out, Eph. . . . Just a piece of the way.

EPH (*emphatically*). No, you ain't, Trista. You got to forgit them there quair notions now. They ain't nothin' to see, nohow. (*He shuts the door.* TRISTA *crosses to the window and stands looking out.*)

GAFFER (*mumbling*). Fools and blind . . . fools and blind . . .

TRISTA. It's just . . . just the new moon shinin' on the river, Eph. You seem to think it's nothin' to look at now.

EPH. I kin look at the moon an' tell the weather that's comin', but that's all thar is in it. You don't see all them strange things you used to talk on, an' it's time you forgot 'bout 'em. It's wrong to think on sech things.

TRISTA. Oh, Eph, you didn't use to think it wrong to look at the starlight on the river. You used to love to . . .

EPH (*laughing shamefacedly*). That's 'cause I liked to look at you, child. But now we don't have to go out in the night. I kin set here an' see you, an' we don't need to be goin' down by the river. (TRISTA *runs to the door and throws her arms out longingly towards the stars.* EPH *turns.*) Don't, Trista, don't! (*He closes the door.*) Hit's bad luck to look at the new moon through the trees. (*He leads her to the fire.*)

GAFFER (*mumbling*). Bad luck for some is good luck for others.

EPH (*gently*). You're tired out, child. You jes' set still an' rest. I'll go fetch the minister, Trista, so you kin go to bed soon. (*As he goes out*, TRISTA *follows him with out-stretched arms, but he does not see her. As the door swings shut behind him*, TRISTA *throws herself against it with a wild little sobbing cry.*)

TRISTA. Eph, Eph, come back, Eph, an' tell me we can see wonders together! (*Dully.*) He's gone, he's gone. He said I must be just like the rest now. (*She goes over to the child and looks down, troubled. Then she drops on her knees, speaking to* GAFFER.) Gaffer, Gaffer, what has happened? My baby, my child! The beauty and the strangeness is gone. He'll be just like the others, they say. And then he'll sit in by the fire and sing psalm tunes, and never gaze at the stars and the river and . . . Gaffer. (*She rises and speaks close to his ear.*) Gaffer, let me out, let me out!

GAFFER (*unheeding*). The new moon has brought trouble, trouble.

TRISTA. Quick, Gaffer, let me out. (*She leans closer and speaks compellingly.*) Unstop the latch-hole, Gaffer. Take off the spell and let me go. . . . See, I will give you my gold chain, Gaffer. Just let me go.

GAFFER. The witches are ridin' and dancin' and shriekin', but one is not there, one is not there. . . .

TRISTA. I cannot stay here. I . . . I . . . (*She sinks on her knees before the cradle.*) See, I'll leave you my child, Gaffer. I will leave you the baby, just let me go.

GAFFER. The river is shinin' . . . an' shinin' . . . an' shinin' . . . but she cannot go, she cannot go!

TRISTA. I must go. I'll die here. I'll die! They say I am just like the rest. They are blind. They cannot see what I am. . . . (*Wildly.*) I am a witch. I must go! (*She darts to the door*, GAFFER *following. There she stops as though hurled back by some strange force. She cowers.*) The spell, the spell! (*She clings to* GAFFER.) Oh, unstop the latch-hole, Gaffer. I am a witch. I cannot stay here longer. (*Slowly she sinks down by the door.*) Eph sees me like one of the rest and I'll die if I stay. He loved me for a witch, and now they say I am just like . . . Oh, I'll die here.

GAFFER. Love dies when the wonder is gone, aye, love dies. But we hold her still. The latch-hole is stopped. The witch-mother shall not leave us alone in the night . . . alone . . . alone. . . . (EPH *enters quickly from the next room and goes to* TRISTA.)

EPH. Trista! What ails you, Trista? Trista, speak!

KEZZIE (*entering, followed by* DR. TRASK). Gaffer has frightened her. (*She leads him to his seat.*) It do try me how foolish he be! Come here, Gaffer, an' set down. (EPH *has knelt by* TRISTA. *She rises, very pale.*)

EPH. Thar, now. 'Tis all over now. (*He leads her to a chair at the fireplace.*)

KEZZIE. She's that weak from the trial, sir.

DR. TRASK. We shall have the services at once, then. (*They start toward the door of the bedroom.* GAFFER *has crept over to the stopped latch again.* DR. TRASK *sees him.*) But first, unstop the latch-hole, Mistress Hunter. 'Tis not right that such signs of the dominion of darkness should be seen at this time. We have no witch here nor need for strange spells.

EPH. Oh, sir, 'twill do no harm, but . . . (*He goes to the door*) as you say, there is no need for spells to hold Trista. She's no different from us all. (TRISTA, *near the fireplace, watches intently. As* EPH *puts out his hand to the latch-hole,* GAFFER *throws himself against the door.*)

GAFFER. She is a witch, a witch. Don't loose her. She'll ride away, she'll ride away. She'll be gone!

KEZZIE. He's out'n his mind, sir. (*She goes to* GAFFER, *trying to soothe him.*) (TRISTA *watches them intently, while she moves, unnoticed, to the table.*)

GAFFER. She'll ride off on the winds and clouds and she'll never come again. The new moon's a-shinin' an' the

witches are a-ridin' an' she'll never come again . . .
she'll never come again. . . .

EPH. Oh, hush, Gaffer. Be still. (*He reaches out and unstops
the keyhole. At that instant,* TRISTA *utters a wild cry and
falls forward, dragging the tablecloth with her to the floor.
The candles are extinguished. In the darkness the people are
heard groping about.*)

KEZZIE. Where is she? Has she fainted? Trista!

EPH. I felt something touch me! Trista! The door—where
is she?

GAFFER. She's gone, she's gone. . . . And she'll never come
again. . . .

EPH. I can't find her. (*Desperately.*) Trista! (*He lights the
candle from the coals of the fire and stands with it held over
his head. He speaks in dumb wonderment.*) She is gone!

KEZZIE. But the door is shut. What . . . What . . .

DR. TRASK. Oh, heaven protect us all. "From all evil and
mischief, from wrath, from the crafts and assaults of the
devil, good Lord, deliver us."

EPH (*repeating dully*). She's gone. I let her go.

GAFFER. Only the old folks and the very young kin see
strange things an' they forgits, they forgits. . . . (*He
sinks down by the cradle.*)

CURTAIN

THE RETURN OF BUCK GAVIN

GAVIN

The Tragedy of a Mountain Outlaw

BY

THOMAS WOLFE

113

THE RETURN OF BUCK GAVIN

This little play is the first published work of the now distinguished American novelist. Thomas Wolfe—or better, just plain "Tom" Wolfe, as he was familiarly known here on "The Hill," was born in Asheville in the mountains of western North Carolina. *The Return of Buck Gavin* was his first play. It was written in the fall of 1918, the year of the beginnings of The Carolina Playmakers, for our initial performance. "Tom" himself played the part of Buck Gavin— no one else could be found to do it—no one who knew the life as he knew it. He had never acted before, but a glance at the picture of him at the front of the book will indicate how completely he embodied the character of his rugged hero. He was scarcely eighteen years of age then, but he had found himself as a "playmaker" in his own play.

I have before me as I write, the original manuscript of the little play, and his illuminating foreword—good counsel for the young author. "When the dramatic possibilities of this incident flashed upon me," he says, "I immediately started to work with a set of mountain characters, the principal being Buck Gavin, an outlaw. It is a fallacy of the young writer, I believe, to picture the dramatic as unusual and remote. It is therefore but natural that he should choose for the setting of his first effort a New York apartment house, the Barbary Coast of San Francisco, or some remote land made dramatic by all the perfumes of Arabia. . . . But the dramatic is not the unusual. It is happening daily in our lives. Some of us, perhaps, toil on a mountain farm, and when we relax from the stolidity of mind and allow ourselves thought, it is to think bitterly on the unvaried, monotonous grind of our existence. Here is material for drama in the true sense."

THE CHARACTERS

As originally produced on The Playmakers' Stage, Chapel Hill, North Carolina, March 14 and 15, 1919.

Buck Gavin, *a mountain outlaw,*	The Author
Mary Gavin, *his sister,*	Lelia Nance Moffatt
The Sheriff,	Frederick Cohn

Scene: The cabin home of Buck Gavin in a remote cove of the Carolina mountains.

Time: The present. An afternoon in May.

SCENE

The living and dining room of the log cabin home of BUCK
GAVIN.

*The furnishings of the room are more pretentious than are
usually associated with mountain cabins. This is explained by
the fact that* GAVIN *is a mountain chief, the leader of a clan—a
kind of tribal leader, if you like. The interior is rude, but comfortable, with not a little taste displayed in the arrangement.
A woman's presence is denoted by blue chintz curtains at the
windows and a covering of the same material on the table in the
center of the room. A shaded lamp, several weekly newspapers,
and a knitting basket are on the table. At the left a crackling
wood-fire burns in a large stone fireplace. In the right corner is
a home-made cupboard. Skins are tacked to the wall here and
there. The garish lithographic display usually found in mountain cabins is lacking here. Several hand-made, splint-bottom
chairs are grouped around the hearth. The outside door is in
the rear wall at the center, with small windows on either side
of it. In the right wall is another door, leading into the bedroom
and thence into the kitchen shed. There is a rocker by the table.*

MARY GAVIN *is seated in this rocker, knitting. She has a
face not old, but worn—not by toil, we should say, but care-
worn. It is a good face—attractive, possessing a sensitiveness
of feature remarkable for a mountain woman. Although she is
not more than thirty-five years of age, her hair is even now
streaked with gray. As she knits, her back to the door, it opens
softly, slowly. A man steps quickly into the room and shuts the
door as quietly as it was opened. The man is* BUCK GAVIN,
*master of the house, a fugitive from justice, wanted on charges
of illicit distilling and murder. He has returned by stealth after
being hunted for six weeks.*

BUCK GAVIN *is a great, powerfully built fellow, aged forty
years, or thereabouts. He has a strong, heavily-lined face,*

covered by a beard of the Van Dyke type—although he would not call it that. He has piercing black eyes and heavy black hair. In his swift silent movements there is a suggestion of a veiled panther-like power. This seems characteristic of him; he moves always with the same decisiveness. He is dressed in a dark flannel shirt and loose corduroy trousers stuffed into rough laced boots.

GAVIN (*stands quietly a moment surveying the scene; then he speaks casually, quietly*). Howdy, sis.

MARY (*springing from her chair and turning quickly*). Buck! Buck! My God! What air you doin' here? Why did you come back?

GAVIN (*simply*). I had to, sis.

MARY. But, my Lor', man, they've been lookin' fer you high an' low. There's nary a nook ner corner 'bout these hills they haven't scoured fer you.

GAVIN. Don't you reckon I know it? But I come, an' thar's an end to it. (*Speaking impatiently as she starts to interrupt him.*) Don't argue with me. I come . . . an' you know why, I'm thinkin'.

MARY (*sullenly*). Yeah. I calc'late I knowed why. (*Going to him.*) But 'twarn't no use, Buck, 'twarn't no use for you to risk yer neck after all's over.

GAVIN (*with quiet emphasis*). Thar's the rub. 'Tain't all over. There's one mo' leetle job to be done, an' I reckon I'll git to see that through . . . least-ways, I'd better. For they'd never o' caught me whar I was, an' I don't calc'late to come more'n two hundred miles jes' to be caught. I reckon they'll git me soon, anyway; they're so powerful smart.

MARY (*contemptuously and proudly*). Bah! They never could o' caught you in the ol' days, Buck, no matter how powerful smart they were. You'd allus fool 'em, Buck.

GAVIN. The ol' days is gone—the good ol' days—an' all that made 'em good. But now . . . now . . . well, I'm jes'

not in the foolin' mood. (*Moving away from her.*) . . .
He's gone . . . they got him, an' I'd ruther that it'd
been me. I reckon you know it. . . . But they got him,
damn 'em, an' now . . . now . . . (*Passionately.*) Aw,
what's the use? (*Striding restlessly across the room.*) A lot
I'd keer if they'd come now . . . only . . . only . . . I
want a leetle mo' time . . . jes' a leetle.

MARY. Buck! Buck! Perk up, man, you mustn't act this
way. What's come over you?

GAVIN. Oh, don't worry 'bout me. . . . (*He speaks softly.*)
Where'd you put him, Mary?

MARY. On the top o' big Smoky. You know he allus liked
the view up there . . . said kind o' jokin' that that was
where he wanted 'em to plant him.

GAVIN (*almost in a whisper*). I . . . rec'lect.

MARY. So the rest o' the boys built a kind o' box an' carried
him up there. 'Twarn't easy neither, for it's a good ten
mile from the Gap to the top o' the Smoky. But we all
felt sort o' like it was doin' the right thing by Jim. Allus
was different, was Jim, from the rest of us. He'd have
them dreamy times when he wanted to be left alone.

GAVIN (*sits down at the table and gazes before him*). He was
plumb foolish over the view from the Smoky. Called it a
leetle bit o' God's country. Used to go up there an' stare
off 'cross the valleys till the sun got low an' everythin' was
blurred an' hazylike. Didn't want to talk to no one when
he got that-a-way. But one time, when we was up there,
he set a-lookin' out awhile an' he turned to me an' says,
says he, "Buck, this is shore purty. We're powerful close
to heaven, Buck. . . ." I reckon you done the right
thing to plant him there. . . . Good ol' Jim. It's 'bout
all we could do. But the best warn't good 'nough fer him.

MARY. On the box we carved out his name . . . jes' carved
"Jim." Somehow it seemed more nat'ral-like to have it
"Jim" than "James Preas." An' over the grave—at the
head, I mean—we stuck a wooden cross that the boys

made . . . an' on it we carved "Jim Preas—He asked no favors from revenooers an' he died with his boots off."

GAVIN (*sharply*). What's that 'bout his boots?

MARY. Oh, that's the funny part of it. He had his leetle joke right to the end. You know he allus calc'lated he'd have his boots off when he died. Well, when the Sheriff an' his dep'ties found him, he was lyin' up agin' a rock with his boots off, with his gun in one hand, an' grinnin' a funny leetle grin as if he was sayin', "I had the last laugh, hey?"

GAVIN (*quietly after a pause*). How . . . how many did we git?

MARY. Three dep'ties.

GAVIN (*with savage satisfaction*). Good . . . good, damn 'em, they had to pay. A lot o' good it does me, though. (*He goes on reminiscently.*) I won't forgit the fight out there on the hill-side, an' how they got him. He gives a funny leetle cough an' crumples up an' quits pumpin' his gun. "Buck," he says, grinnin' that crooked grin of his'n, "Buck, my boy, I reckon they've settled my hash. . . . 'Tain't no use, big feller," says he when I starts to carry him, "They've got me, an' I'm done fer. You can't help me, so for God's sake, help yourself. Now git." So I left him jokin' an' grinnin' an' pumpin' lead at 'em. He was a great joker, was Jim. . . . (*They are both silent.*) Mary, I reckon I ought to git some flowers. Could you git 'em fer me?

MARY (*puzzled by the question*). Why, yeah, I reckon I could. I got some here picked fresh this mornin', but what on airth d'you want . . . Buck, you can't be meanin' to go up there with 'em. Why, man alive, you cain't—they're searchin' high an' low fer you.

GAVIN (*doggedly*). No matter if they air—I'm goin'. That's what I come fer.

MARY. D'you mean to tell me, Buck Gavin, that you come all this way to risk your neck fer . . . fer . . . sech? . . .

GAVIN (*with quiet determination*). Yeah, I mean to tell you jes' that. That's what kep' pullin' me home; that's all I hanker to do an' after that's done let 'em come an' git me . . . an' to hell with 'em.

MARY. All right, Buck, I reckon you know. I'll git 'em.

GAVIN (*to himself*). With his boots off, hey? (*He sits down at the table.*) By cripes, that was like him, jes' like ol' Jim. Allus was a joker. (*He chuckles.*) I reckon that tickled him. Oh, Lord, that was a man fer you! (*He rises and strides across the room.*)

MARY (*returning with a large bunch of arbutus*). Reckon these'll do, Buck?

GAVIN. Guess so—too many, though. Here, le' me have 'em, I'll fix 'em. Say, how 'bout some vi'lets, got any? Jim was plumb daffy over 'em—the big blue uns. You know the kind, Mary?

MARY. I know where they's a sight of 'em. I'll go git 'em. 'Twon't take long. (*She goes out.*)

GAVIN (*sitting by the table, he speaks disjointedly as he arranges the flowers*). No, an' 'twon't take long fer you either, Gavin, my boy. . . . Your goose is 'bout cooked, I'm thinkin'. Fine way of cookin', too. Jim's was the right way after all. . . . Wish I'd stayed with him now. A purty sight I'll be with a noose 'round my gullet—first Gavin to be hung—a disgrace to the family. . . . They'll git me—they allus git us. We've fit 'em time an' time, an' they git us in the end. Lord, I reckon we'uns is all fools. . . . (*Holding the bunch of arbutus at arm's length.*) . . . There, that's purty now. (*Now the door opens slowly and a short, thick-set fellow steps into the room. The badge of an officer of the law can be seen under his coat. In his hand he holds a revolver. He is the* SHERIFF.)

THE SHERIFF (*smiling ironically*). Welcome home, Buck. (GAVIN *wheels swiftly, his hand moving to his hip pocket. He stops short on seeing the* SHERIFF'S *gun.*)

GAVIN. Aw. . . . Hell. . . .

THE SHERIFF (*genially, highly pleased with himself*). Quite a surprise, eh? Knew you'd be back, my boy, so I jes' laid low fer you. You never had a chance.

GAVIN (*slowly*). Yeah, you got me I reckon, Sheriff, but I ain't worryin' 'bout it. Fact is, I'm glad you come—only . . . only I wish to God you'd been a leetle later.

THE SHERIFF (*surprised*). Why?

GAVIN (*sullenly*). Aw . . . nothin'. Come on, let's be travelin'. My sister'll be back any minute now, an' I don't want her to see the kind o' company I've took up with.

THE SHERIFF (*in a high good humor*). Jes' as you say, Buck, jes' as you say. (*They start toward the door as* MARY *enters with a large bunch of violets. She sums up the situation at a glance.*)

MARY. Oh, Buck, Buck, why did you come? I told you. An' now they've got you. I knowed it! (*She sinks into a chair and buries her face in her hands.*)

GAVIN (*he speaks gently and clumsily tries to soothe her*). There, there, little sis, you mustn't carry on so. This is sartin' the best way out an' I'm not worr'in'—look at me. I'm glad, sis. What's in the game fer me now? My pal's gone an' there ain't no mo' fun in playin' it without him. . . . Tell the boys hello an' good-by fer me, an' tell 'em I says—But you needn't t' mind. . . . As fer you . . . (*Going to her*) . . . you needn't to worry 'bout nothin' no mo'. I've fixed things up fer you.

MARY. Oh Buck, you needn't o' been caught. You could've got away.

GAVIN (*with quiet emphasis*). It is the law. You cain't buck it. (*There is a pause. The* SHERIFF *stands with bowed head, his jesting spirit gone. Then* GAVIN *speaks awkwardly as he prepares to leave.*) Well, I reckon that's about all, so I'll be a-goin'. Be good to yourself, sis. (*He notices the arbutus and the violets on the table and picks them up, muttering under his breath.*) I would've liked to 've took 'em up there, an' . . . an' . . . sort o' looked 'round. (*He looks at* MARY, *deeply moved.*) But . . . well, I reckon I cain't go now . . . but ol' Jim'll know . . . jes' the same. Sis,—you take 'em. (*He places the flowers in her lap.* MARY *does not raise her head. He pats her hair gently, clumsily, once or twice, then turns to go with the* SHERIFF. *At the door he turns and gives a last look around the room. His gaze rests finally on his sister. Then he goes out quietly.* MARY'S *head is pillowed in her arms. The flowers are in her lap.*)

CURTAIN

THE THIRD NIGHT

A Play of the Carolina Mountains

BY

THOMAS WOLFE

A HITHERTO UNPUBLISHED work of Thomas Wolfe written when he was a student in the playwriting course at the University of North Carolina nearly twenty-three years ago. *The Third Night* was produced by The Carolina Playmakers on their original improvised stage in the auditorium of the Chapel Hill high school building on December 12 and 13, 1919.

THE THIRD NIGHT

The untimely death of Thomas Wolfe recalls the striking figure of a lanky, wild-eyed, six-and-a-half-foot-tall mountain lad striding across the Chapel Hill campus twenty-three years ago. It was the first year of The Carolina Playmakers. In those dramatic beginnings Tom played a leading rôle both as playwright and actor.

It was the autumn of 1918 when the campus of the University of North Carolina had been converted into a student army training camp and the dormitories labeled, "Barracks A, B, C, etc.," Tom was too young to get into the war and was the only male student in the original playwriting group of thirteen. He was a great joker. There was never a student gathering where he was not the chief speaker. Characteristic of his humour in his speech-making is a phrase I recall, "than which there is no whicher." It was always accompanied with a twisted little smile and a chuckle. An outstanding figure, he was easily the most popular man on the campus. A keen and scintilant wit, a Shavian satirist, his talk was shot through with a pyrotechnic exuberance which hypnotized his youthful audiences.

His first play—and his first published work—*The Return of Buck Gavin*,[1] a tragedy of a Carolina mountain outlaw, was included in the initial production of our native plays on March 14 and 15, 1919. He was the protagonist, and again in his next play, *The Third Night*, he took the leading rôle—the romantic adventurer, Captain Richard Harkins, a degenerate Southern gentleman haunted by the ghost of "The Old Man" he had robbed. Again Tom scored as an actor in his brittle and sardonic characterization. The play is here published for the first time in book form. It was printed in *The Carolina Play-Book* of September, 1938.

[1] See p. 113.

In an autobiographical sketch at the end of the play-writing course in 1919 Tom wrote about his youthful enthusiasm for George Bernard Shaw, and the change that had come over him in his attitude toward his writing:

"When I see the influence Mr. Shaw has unconsciously exerted on me it is but natural that I should analyze his plays to find the reason why. And I have reached this conclusion: Shaw's satirical writing has influenced me only so far as his brilliant, scintillating wit has compelled my admiration.

"By no stretch of the imagination could I picture myself as a satirist. Indeed, I started my modest career as a 'Play-maker' by attempting a satiric comedy. It was a false start. It was a dismal failure. . . ."

From Chapel Hill he went to Harvard to study with Professor Baker and worked hard at his playwriting for three years. There the 47 Workshop produced a one-act play of his, *The Mountains*, and his first full-length play, *Welcome to Our City*. Then he went to New York hoping to break into the professional theatre. But he was unable to find a producer for his stirring drama of the race conflict in his home town, Asheville (Altamont in the play), North Carolina. Theresa Helburn of the New York Theatre Guild assured me at the time that the Guild was much interested in the play and in the young playwright's talent. But for some reason nothing came of it.

In New York, several years later, I found him still enthusiastic over his playwriting. We were walking up Fifth Avenue when he turned to me and said, "What we need 'Proff,' is a robust drama! There are too many dilettanti in the theatre." He was striding along in the keen October air, towering high above me, and I could not help but think of the schoolboy, Tom, of the Chapel Hill campus and of Buck Gavin, the mountain outlaw.

He came up to my hotel room and read to me several scenes of the first draft of a new play, *Mannerhouse*, mentioned later in *Of Time and the River*. I remember his restless rocking

back and forth as he read from the pencil-scrawled yellow
sheets. Especially the fine dramatic prologue in which the
ceaseless files of African slaves build the Big House out of the
Carolina jungle. Also, the whimsical satire of "An Interlude
in Heaven," in which the old slave, Uncle Tom, is shown
climbing the golden ladder to secure a choicer seat in Heaven
than his former plantation master. Of the prologue he writes
in the novel: "This was a fine scene, and should have been
beautiful and moving on the stage."

The New York Theatre Guild thought very favorably of
this play too, and seriously considered producing it. I
mentioned it to Sheldon Cheney, who was at that time
directing the policies of the Actor's Theatre. He was much
interested but the Actor's Theatre failed and Tom Wolfe,
the playwright, missed again.

On January 10, 1925, he wrote to me, "It would give me
infinite pleasure to witness the success of my new play because it was written in the silences."

It was a discouraging time. "For two years now," he
wrote, "I have worked and traveled alone, ordering the
events of my life as courageously and honestly as I could. . . .
In that time the honey flies who found me lacking in the
promise of instant victory have turned away and forgotten
me. But a few people have never forgotten; they have given
unbounded loyalty to a mad fellow who made loneliness his
mistress. . . ."

In the Foreword to *Of Time and the River* he expressed the
same unrest. ". . . of wandering forever and the earth
again. . . . Where shall the weary rest? When shall the
lonely heart come home? What doors are open for the
wanderer?"

As far as I know this was his last venture in the theatre.
To Eugene in *Of Time and the River*, the mother speaks,
"Pshaw, boy, your life's not ended just because you find
out that you weren't cut out to be a playwriter."

I remember the grateful letter he wrote me from Paris
upon receiving the first $4.00 royalty check I sent him for a

performance of his first student play, *The Return of Buck
Gavin*. "Thank God, 'Proff,' it's the first real money I ever
had for my writing!"

On October 9, 1933, he wrote: "If you come to New
York, I hope you will let me know, so that we can arrange
to get together and have a talk. I want to say something to
you about this play for which you have sent me a royalty
check. . . . I am very proud to call myself one of the Playmakers and to remember that I belonged to the first group
you ever taught at Chapel Hill, and had a part in writing
and producing some of the first plays. I want to tell you
also that no one is prouder than I of the great success the
Playmakers have achieved and of the distinguished work
which has been done by them. The fact that I was associated
with that work at its very beginning, even in an obscure
and unimportant fashion, is another fact I am proud of.
I am also proud to remember that two little one-act plays
that I wrote were among the first plays put on by the Playmakers and that I acted in them and helped produce them.
I was a boy of eighteen when I wrote those plays and I wrote
each of them in a few hours, because I did not understand
what heart-breaking and agonizing work writing is. I think
those plays show this and are fair samples of the work of a
boy who did not know what hard work was and who wrote
them in a few hours. . . . I should like to be remembered
as a Playmaker and as one who had the honor to be a member
of that pioneer first group. . . . Please let me know when
you are coming to New York."

When I saw him in New York a little later the first question he asked was, "How is everything going with you all down
there?" His eyes flashed, "You know there's no place on
earth like North Carolina—there's adventure in the air
there!" He talked about the early days and recounted some
amusing incidents in connection with our earliest productions
on the simple, improvised stage in the auditorium of the
Chapel Hill high school building.

"You must come back to see our Playmakers Theatre

now—our fine lighting system, and complete stage equipment. You must come back to the 'Hill,' Tom, and recall some of your student adventures for us. We'll pack the theatre to the doors for you. They won't all be able to get in."

"No," with a quiet drawl, "I don't want to appear on the stage there. I just want to slip in and see the old place for myself without anybody noticing me."

That is just what he did the next spring. "Do you mind if we run by the Old Well first and take a look at that," as he darted from the car in front of the South Building. "My God, this is a swell place to live in—it hasn't changed a bit!"

Now he has come home to stay—"Where the weary of heart can abide forever, where the weary of wandering can find peace, where the tumult, the fever, and the fret shall be forever stilled."

On the day Tom died in Baltimore, October 3, 1938, came a royalty check for $4.00 for a production of his first little play and his first professionally published work, *The Return of Buck Gavin*. It was a strange coincidence. At the funeral in Asheville his classmates,[1] Paul Green, Jonathan Daniels, Elizabeth Lay Green, and I tried to get some violets for Tom like "the big blue ones" the home-coming Buck Gavin wanted to put on his pal's grave high up in the Smokies. But there were no violets to be had in October. Instead we found for him a bunch of flaming bitter-sweet and a mass of palm-like leucothoë from his native mountains.—*F. H. K.*

[1] The Carolina Playmakers produced Paul Green's first play, *The Last of the Lowries*, in the same year with Thomas Wolfe's *The Third Night*. Jonathan Daniels, author of *A Southerner Discovers the South*, played Dorset in the original production of *The Third Night*. Elizabeth Lay, now Mrs. Paul Green, was the author of *When Witches Ride* produced on the initial bill of The Carolina Playmakers with Thomas Wolfe's *The Return of Buck Gavin*, March 14 and 15, 1919.

THE CHARACTERS

As originally produced on The Playmakers' Stage, Chapel Hill, North Carolina, December 12 and 13, 1919.

CAPTAIN RICHARD HARKINS, *a degenerate Southern gentleman*,	THE AUTHOR
DORSET, *his henchman*,	Jonathan Daniels
COGSWELL, *a mulatto*,	Fred Cohn
THE OLD MAN	Chester Burton

SCENE: The living room of a dilapidated dwelling of the "Old Man" in a deserted mountain section of North Carolina, some miles west of Asheville.

TIME: A stormy night in the autumn of 1858.

SCENE

The gloomy living room of a decaying country house in a dark mountain valley of the Blue Ridge. The plaster is cracked; great patches of it have fallen from the high ceiling. The rear wall is broken by a single uncurtained window at the right and an open doorway at the left, through which another room is partly visible. At the right, downstage, is an ample fireplace with a rude table and two chairs before it. A door at the left leads outside.

A smouldering fagot gives a half light to the bare, gaunt room; the corners are almost in darkness. Before the fireplace in the room at the rear THE CAPTAIN *is sitting, his profile silhouetted by the glow of the hearth.*

COGSWELL *and* DORSET *are seated at the table.* COGSWELL *is playing a game of solitaire with a pack of greasy cards.* DORSET *is thumbing the pages of a well-worn family photograph album with an air of detached curiosity. The light is just sufficient to accentuate the lines of each man's face.* COGSWELL'S, *the face of the degenerate, is weak but sensitive and mobile. He is a young man, half negro. In him have cumulated many of the superstitions of the black race.* DORSET *is thickset, unemotional, unexpressive—ox-like, as he sits in squat stolidity, thumbing the pages of the album with pudgy fingers. He looks over at* COGSWELL *out of his little, pig-like eyes. The two men are strongly contrasted.* DORSET *speaks ponderously with a slow drawl,* COGSWELL *with nervous rapidity. Both are roughly dressed. They are without coats and wear heavy boots.* COGSWELL *is smooth-faced;* DORSET *has a short, unkempt beard.*

There is a dark silence except for the moaning of the storm outside. COGSWELL *plays a card or two.*

DORSET (*thumbing the album*). This is the third night, ain' it, an' we're still here.

133

COGSWELL (*looking up with a nervous start, as he puts down a card on the table*). The third—the *third*, you say? The third . . . since we done it?

DORSET. Sure. Had you lost track?

COGSWELL. The third— that's bad; we should 'a' left befo'.

DORSET. That's the Cap'n—that quair way of his'n. (*He motions toward the door at the rear—then turns to* COGSWELL, *eyeing him intently.*) What's wrong, Cogswell? We're right enough here, ain't we?

COGSWELL (*half embarrassed*). I reckon . . . only—God, Dorset, listen to that rain . . . listen to that wind howl!

DORSET (*indifferently*). Yeah. Purty bad storm, I reckon. (*There is silence for a moment.* DORSET *turns a page in the album.*

THE CAPTAIN *enters. He is very tall and slenderly built, fashionably dressed in the style of his period. He is a dark, handsome man of aristocratic bearing and fine, but somewhat dissipated, features. He wears a well-groomed moustache.*

He goes to the window and looks out at the storm, then turns, looks intently with sinister foreboding at COGSWELL *and* DORSET, *and goes back into the rear room.*)

COGSWELL. I don't like the way he acts.

DORSET. He don't mean nothin'. 'S his way, you know.

COGSWELL (*after a pause*). What's that book you're readin'?

DORSET. 'Tain't no book. It's a album.

COGSWELL. What's that?

DORSET. You put picters of yer folks in it—a photygraph album, they calls it.

COGSWELL (*in a subdued voice*). Was it . . . was it the . . . Old Man's?

DORSET. Yeah, I reckon. Found it upstairs while I was rummagin' 'round today. Found his picter in it—a lot of 'em. See here—(*He pushes the album over to* COGSWELL *and traces with his finger.*) Here's one with "sixteen" under it—this boy, you see here—that's the old duck at sixteen.

Another'n here at twenty-three. Here's one at forty—you can tell him here all right.

COGSWELL (*with a shiver*). Yeah, that's him . . . that's him . . . he was a lot older but y' can tell that's him, all right. (*He shudders.*) I can't forgit how the ol' bird looked when the Cap'n killed him, how he laughed all up in his throat when the Cap'n shot him . . . a bloody gurgle it were.

DORSET (*bluntly*). Forgit it. I ought to 'a' been here to do it for you an' not a-traipsin' down the mountain for grub that night.

COGSWELL (*not heeding*). An' the funny part is that he knew the Cap'n—

DORSET (*staring at him in astonishment*). What's that?— You're crazy!—Knew the Cap'n? Why he couldn't. He ain't never been in these parts before. Said he hadn't.

COGSWELL (*glancing nervously toward the rear room where* THE CAPTAIN *is pacing up and down*). He did all the same, he spoke his name. (THE CAPTAIN *comes to the open door. He pauses a moment and looks into the front room—a cynical, half-brooding look. The men sense his presence. They are silent but glance nervously at each other and fidget under his gaze, not daring to look up until he retires.*)

COGSWELL (*looking craftily toward the door before he speaks*). Damn him! I wish he wouldn't look at us like that. 'Tain't like he's human. No, it ain't.

DORSET (*defending his chief*). He's all right . . . (*There is a pause.*) You say the Ol' Man spoke the Cap'n's name? Tell me about it. I wa'n't in here when it happened.

COGSWELL. The first thing that struck me funny was the noise the Cap'n made when he come in. An' him knowin' all the time that the Ol' Man was asleep upstairs. Right over his head!

DORSET (*unbelieving*). You say he made a noise, an' him as soft-steppin' as a cat?

COGSWELL. I know, I know, but he did. Went clumpin' over the floor like no one was 'round, like he didn't care. I says "Cap'n, be keerful, you'll wake the Ol' Man."

DORSET. What did he say?

COGSWELL. Nothin'. He looked at me an' grinned that mean little grin of his'n. 'Bout that time th' ol' bird heard us. He hit the floor an' come thumpin' down the stairs . . . thought we were after his money, an' he wa'n't far wrong. I tell you he was a funny sight in his night shirt, an' his red night cap, an' his ol' shanks like two sticks as he come down a-glarin' at us.

DORSET (*almost eagerly*). Go on, man. The Cap'n, the Cap'n— what did he do?

COGSWELL. When he heard the Ol' Un' comin', he turned his back.

DORSET. What?

COGSWELL. Yeah, that he did! An' then the Ol' Un' come down the stairs into the room an' started screamin', "What do you want? Who are you? Burglars, by God!" An' he ran over to the stone where his money is . . .

DORSET (*impatiently*). Go on, go on!

COGSWELL. The Cap'n turned an' faced him, never sayin' a word. An' the Ol' Un's eyes nearly popped out'n his head— he was that put to it . . .

DORSET. What did the Cap'n do then?

COGSWELL. In a minute th' Ol' Man croaked out, "Richard Harkins—Richard Harkins—Richard Harkins!"

DORSET. An' the Cap'n, what did he say?

COGSWELL. Nothin'. Jes' grinned his mean grin, the one that makes you fidgety, you know.

DORSET (*dully*). Yeah, I know. . . . Go on, Cogswell.

COGSWELL. Finally the Ol' Man starts laughin', jes' stands there laughin' . . . a gaspin', gurglin' kind o' laugh . . . make yo' blood freeze.

DORSET. Didn't he talk none?

COGSWELL. Yeah. Finally he says, still laughin', "I fooled you, didn't I, Captain Richard Harkins; I fooled you, hey? You thought you'd take her but I fooled you. An' now she's gone, she's dead. I took her away from you an' she died, she died!" An' with that he started laughin' his bloody laugh again. The Cap'n shot him then. Standin' still an' cold as ice, the Cap'n shot him through the neck. He fell still laughin'—right by that stone where his money is. (*He shudders at the recollection.*)

DORSET. Yeah, I know. I was comin' back when I heard the shot an' I hurried in. The blood spots are still there—but why didn't you tell me this before, Cogswell? Why didn't you? (THE CAPTAIN *is heard pacing in the adjoining room.*)

COGSWELL (*whining now, as he gazes in that direction*). It was him, damn him! I'm afeard o' him an' the way he looked at me that night, an' I swore to myself I wouldn't tell no one if I got out of here. But—(*Listening to the rain as it drives against the house.*) God, Dorset, this is the third night! (*He is almost whimpering as his overstrained nerves give way.*) The Cap'n done it, Dorset; I didn't know 'bout it or I wouldn't 'a' come along. The Cap'n killed him, Dorset. It wa'n't no work o' mine, Dorset, and this is the third night. . . . We oughtn't to be here!

DORSET (*eyeing him curiously*). What's in the third business, Cogswell?

COGSWELL. Third is bad all the time. On the third night the hoot owl screeches; the third time the dog barks; the third night—

DORSET. Bah! That's the nigger in you showin' up. (COGSWELL *springs up furiously with clenched fist, but in a moment sinks sullenly back into his chair, cowed by* DORSET'S *threatening contempt.* DORSET *turns away, meditating with his sluggish mind on* COGSWELL'S *account of the killing. While* COGSWELL *fools nervously with the cards, he turns the pages of the album, muttering.*) The Ol' Man talked of a girl, huh . . . that's funny . . . damn funny—(*Half indifferently.*) Now, I wonder . . . (*Suddenly he stiffens in his seat as his glance rests on a certain photograph in the album. He speaks hoarsely.*) Good God! The picture, the locket picture; it's the girl!

COGSWELL (*frightened, stares at him*). What . . . what do you mean?

DORSET (*excited*). Here it is! . . . Why didn't I see it when you tol' me 'bout the Ol' Man's talk of the girl . . . an' him knowin' the Cap'n?

COGSWELL. What . . . what are you talkin' 'bout?

DORSET. The Cap'n carries a locket 'round his neck. Got a girl's picter in it. When he's drinkin' he takes it out an' curses under his breath, slow an' soft an' steady—awful, I tell you.

COGSWELL. He's drinkin' now.

DORSET. An' it's the same as this picter here, the Ol' Man's daughter. . . . Don't you see, Cogswell? It's plain as the nose on your face. (COGSWELL *shakes his head.*)

DORSET. Why the Cap'n come back to kill 'im. That's what he come for. Why, I don't even believe he wanted his money. The Ol' Man must've took his daughter away from the Cap'n long ago. Don't you see?

COGSWELL (*in an awed tone*). God, Dorset, is that it?—How long you been with that man, Dorset?

DORSET. Five year. He picked me up in Memphis. Five year last week it was, when we picked you up in Asheville.

COGSWELL (*interrupting*). I had nothin' to do with it, I tell you. I never knew there was to be a killin'. I just come to show you the way.

DORSET (*grinning at him*). Yes, you did. You'd heard of the Ol' Man's money, that's what you wanted.

COGSWELL (*sullenly*). Well, mebbe you're right. . . . But it wa'n't no work o' mine.

DORSET (*taunting him*). Anxious to git out of it, ain't you?

COGSWELL (*whining again*). You would be too, if you knew all 'bout the Ol' Man.

DORSET. What's that?

COGSWELL (*lowering his voice and glancing around nervously*). They say 'round here he was a witch-man—half-way crazy, he was. Whenever anything went wrong with farmers or when there was a big drouth, they put it on the Ol' Man.—Mind, I'm not sayin' they're right. I'm jes' tellin' you. . . .

DORSET. Forgit it. He'll have a hard time witchin' anybody now, from his bed six feet under his wood pile. I reckon we fixed his witchin' business when we throwed dirt in his face. (*He laughs coarsely.*)

COGSWELL (*quaking*). Fo' God's sake, don't talk that way. (DORSET *laughs at him. Then both are silent and listen to the storm outside.* DORSET *continues ruminative, hardly noticing his companion.*) What do you know 'bout it? (*He rises and goes to the fireplace.*) The Cap'n, the Ol' Man, and the locket girl—all hooked up together! This is a funny worl'. An' after all this time, the Cap'n comes back an' gits him. It must've been a long time, too. I been with him five year now. . . . Five year with that man. . . .

DORSET (*reflectively, standing with his back to the fire*). Five year up an' down an' 'round about. Gamblin', that's the Cap'n's line. Smooth an' slick, that's the Cap'n! On river boats he used to fleece 'em right an' left. At the race track in New Orleans—in Memphis . . . five year with him . . . an' . . . an' yet . . . I might 'a' knowd somethin' was up.

COGSWELL. Why'd you know?

DORSET. I been with 'im five year an' this is the first time he's ever . . . (*He pauses.*)

COGSWELL (*finishing it*). Killed? That what you mean? (DORSET *nods.*)

DORSET. That's what.

COGSWELL. Who *is* he, anyhow?

DORSET (*with grim humor*). You ought t' as'd the Ol' Man. He could've tol' you. (*Leaning toward him confidentially.*) Why, at times, Cogswell I think the Cap'n's crazy. (*He jerks his finger toward* THE CAPTAIN *who is now sitting before the fireplace in the rear room, his back to the two.*) Sometimes he gits out by hisself an' talks—talks, mind you, when there's nobody 'round. I found him that way one time. "Cap'n," I says, "what are you doin'?" "Talkin'," he says short-like, and walks away. He's crazy, or he's a funny way of jokin', I tell you.

COGSWELL (*shivering*). What's keepin' us here now? Why does he stay in this ol' house, Dorset?

DORSET. He's all right. Waitin' till the Asheville stage comes by tomorrow.—Just comes twice a week, don't it?

COGSWELL (*eagerly*). Do we leave tomorrow then?

DORSET. I reckon. (*Ruminating.*) I wonder how the Cap'n 'll split! I wonder what our share will be? (*As if in answer to the question* THE CAPTAIN *now enters the room. They stare at him, almost in awe.*)

THE CAPTAIN (*in a cold, severe tone, looking at neither of them*). We leave here tomorrow morning.—We will divide the money now.

COGSWELL (*cringing, yet eager*). Cap'n, (THE CAPTAIN *does not look at him*) . . . now, can't we go *now* . . . tonight!

THE CAPTAIN (*sharply*). That would be foolish, in this storm. Besides—(*For the first time* THE CAPTAIN *observes* COGSWELL's *twitching face.*) Eh! Do you wish to go now, Cogswell?

COGSWELL (*almost tearfully*). Yes . . . damn it, I do!

THE CAPTAIN. Very well. Lift the stone, Cogswell. (THE CAPTAIN *goes to the window and gazes out at the storm, indifferent to the division of the money.* COGSWELL *drops eagerly to his knees and lifts the hearthstone, looking nerv-*

ously at the blood stains on it. An iron money box fits neatly into the cavity below. COGSWELL *lifts the lid easily. The box is filled with coins and paper money, the* OLD MAN'S *hoard.* COGSWELL *gives a long exultant sigh as he leans forward, half raising his arm.* DORSET, *looking at the gleaming mass, bends swiftly forward. His eyes glitter. Outside the storm is still raging.*)

COGSWELL (*after a moment*). Cap'n . . . for us two, about how much?

THE CAPTAIN (*speaking carelessly, over his shoulder*). As much as you like. (*The two men, dazed at their good fortune, gaze stupified at each other. Then with a gloating laugh,* COGSWELL *delves both hands into the box, letting the coins ripple through his fingers.*

Suddenly there is a blinding flash of lightning, followed by a roll of thunder which increases in volume until it fills the room. Out of the thunder comes a low, throaty chuckle. THE CAPTAIN *recoils. In a moment the sound passes.* COGSWELL *is paralyzed.* DORSET *passes a hand before his eyes. He forces a grim smile.*)

COGSWELL. God help us all . . . the laugh . . . the Ol' Man's laugh!

DORSET (*evasively*). It was the thunder.

COGSWELL. You fool!

THE CAPTAIN (*ironically, cold*). Why don't you take your share, Cogswell?

COGSWELL (*whimpering*). I'll have none of it, I swear I won't! (*The room has darkened but* COGSWELL *and* DORSET *are vividly silhouetted in the hearth glow.* THE CAPTAIN *stands in semi-darkness near the window. He is very erect.*)

DORSET (*staring at* THE CAPTAIN—*dully and slowly*). Let's leave it, Cap'n, let's leave it be.

COGSWELL (*whining, rubbing his hands pitifully*). Yes, yes, Cap'n . . . Let's leave it be, let's leave it be. . . . The Ol' Man'll git us! I tell you he will, Cap'n. (THE CAP-

TAIN *laughs sharply. There is a brilliant flash of lightning, followed by a loud peal of thunder which converges in the room.* THE CAPTAIN *walks slowly over to the hearth and faces the door. He appears not agitated, but resolved. The men kneeling on the hearth are stupified.* COGSWELL *is beginning to whimper with fear.* THE CAPTAIN *does not notice them. He opens his shirt bosom and rips from its chain a locket which he wears around his neck. Then laughs harshly.*)

THE CAPTAIN (*very softly*). Journey's end. (*He hurls the locket into the ashes and rebuttons his shirt. He stands waiting with an intense, listening attitude. The two men stare up at him with open mouths. The wind and rain are heard beating violently against the old house. The door at the left blows open and the rain drives into the room.* THE CAPTAIN *bends forward, losing his composure a little. He speaks with repressed emotion.*)

THE CAPTAIN. All right! What is it . . . what is it, I say? What do you want? (*He crosses the room slowly, moving toward the door. A vivid flash of lightning which sustains itself for some time makes him turn instinctively toward the window. Dimly outlined through the misted window pane, appears the face of the ghastly* OLD MAN—*even as they killed him. From beneath his red flannel nightcap long stringy white locks may be seen, and in his throat a small bluish hole from* THE CAPTAIN'S *gun. He is looking at* THE CAPTAIN *and chuckling, a horrible soundless chuckle now. But, as the light disappears and the thunder rolls again, it swells to the awful throaty chuckle converging gradually until it fills the entire room, then dies away slowly in the storm.* THE CAPTAIN *is leaning intently toward the window, fascinated. He regains his composure and his dignity quickly, however, and stands facing the spectre in the window. The figure passes slowly by—around the house.*)

THE CAPTAIN (*very proud and straight, strides resolutely out of the room*). I am coming . . . now. . . . (*The thunder*

*rolls. There is another flash and it converges in the room—
the triumphant laugh of the* OLD MAN! COGSWELL *whimpers
softly on the hearth.* DORSET *is silent. The ghostly chuckle
recedes and is heard faintly in the distance.*)

CURTAIN

GAIUS AND GAIUS, JR.

A Comedy of Plantation Days

BY

LUCY M. COBB

GAIUS AND GAIUS, JR.

The chief character in *Gaius and Gaius, Jr.*, by Lucy M. Cobb of Chapel Hill, was drawn from life—from descriptions of him given by his kinsmen and neighbors, and from the family portrait. Mr. Gaius Mayfield was an irascible old gentleman of the old school, a great-great-uncle of the author. He was absolute master of his household—hot-headed and dictatorial—though kindly, for all his blustering.

The incident recorded in the play—that of the town protesting against his working his Negroes on Sunday—and his constant fear of dying are true to the facts. The author has given us a realistic portrayal of the spacious Southern plantations in the days before the devastating War Between the States.

In production the comedy of *Gaius* is irresistible. On many State Tours—from the tiny mountain towns in the west, to Elizabeth City on the coast—it has been greeted with "tumultuous applause," as one of the newspaper reviewers phrased it.

THE CHARACTERS

As originally produced on The Playmakers' Stage, Chapel Hill, North Carolina, November 16 and 17, 1923.

GAIUS MAYFIELD, *a plantation owner*,	George Denny
MRS. MAYFIELD, *his wife*,	Margaret Jones
GAIUS MAYFIELD, JR.	Theodore Livingstone
DR. FOSTER	Robert Pickens
BEN, *a young slave*,	Tom Quickel
TOM, *an old slave*,	James Hawkins

SCENE: Demopolis, North Carolina. The plantation home of Mr. Gaius Mayfield.

TIME: The fall of 1859.

Scene 1. Saturday evening—about 8 o'clock.
Scene 2. Sunday morning—shortly before 5 o'clock.

The scene is a spacious sitting room of plantation days. The windows are draped with lace curtains under cornices of gilt. In the rear wall is a door leading into the hall-way. A door in the left wall leads into GAIUS MAYFIELD, JR's. bedroom. A mahogany sewing table, mahogany chairs upholstered in horse-hair, a round table with marble top, and a what-not furnish the room. On the right is a fireplace with bookshelves on either side of it. On the mantelpiece is a row of medicine bottles, two medicine glasses, two spoons and a small glass pitcher half-full of water. Over the mantel is a steel engraving of the "Sign-ing of the Declaration of Independence." In the center of the room on the marble-topped table stands a lamp hung with glass pendants. MR. MAYFIELD'S comfortable arm chair is at the right of this table before the fireplace.

MR. and MRS. MAYFIELD have settled down to a com-fortable Saturday evening. He is sitting in his arm chair read-ing "The Atlanta Constitution." MRS. MAYFIELD is sitting in a small rocking chair at the left sewing.

MR. MAYFIELD is a portly gentleman of fifty-odd years, self-willed, hot-tempered and dictatorial. He is older than his wife, his hair and pointed beard already white. He is impeccably dressed in a well-tailored, black broadcloth suit of the period. MRS. MAYFIELD is a charming, delicate lady—rather pretty in a faded way. She is dressed in a full-skirted lavender silk dress, worn over a hoop skirt. She wears a round, white, lace collar, pinned with a miniature of her husband. One can see by her manner that circumstances and her husband's overpowering will have made her subservient to him.

GAIUS, JR. (*calling from his room*). Mother!

MRS. MAYFIELD. Yes, son.

GAIUS, JR. Did Mammy do up the shirt I told her to—that new-fashioned one I got from New York?

Mrs. Mayfield. Yes, son, look in the lower bureau drawer and——

Gaius (*he speaks abruptly and peremptorily*). Let the boy find his own things. Why is he dressing this time of night, anyway?

Mrs. Mayfield. Emily Winn is giving a dance for her cousin Jessamine, and Gaius is invited.

Gaius. Well, does the young fool have to go because he's invited? When I was young——

Mrs. Mayfield (*interrupting him*). Now father, you know when you were young you were the best dancer in the country.

Gaius (*somewhat appeased*). Well, I didn't dance when there was something better to do.

Mrs. Mayfield. Well, Gaius has finished the book work you gave him.

Gaius. Great Scott, Madam! What is a little bookkeeping to a Carolina college man? In my day when men left the University they assumed grave responsibilities. I took charge of this plantation before I was twenty-one.

Mrs. Mayfield. Gaius is only twenty.

Gaius. Yes, and the young jackanapes must have his boots from London, his broadcloth clothes made by a New York tailor—made from the same piece as his father's!

Mrs. Mayfield (*soothing him*). But, Father, you must see him in them when he is dressed! You'll be proud of your son. None of the young beaux at the party will match him.

Gaius. Humph! He'd better not come back and tell me he's been attentive to that Foster girl. I'll——

Mrs. Mayfield. Mr. Mayfield, don't threaten. You know what happens when you get excited.

Gaius. Madam, I'm *not* excited. I tell you my heart is all right. An ignoramus like that Foster doesn't know what he is talking about. But to be on the safe side, I will take a few of my drops. (*Going to the mantelpiece, he pours out the medicine into a spoon, then into a glass, mixing it with water, and takes his dose.*) This section has reached a most deplorable condition, a most deplorable one, when a know-nothing doctor like Foster can practice here, and his daughter be received in polite society. Tells me nothing is the matter, when I know I've nearly died several times! Only urges no excitement. Bah! Gentlemen's sons ought to study the art of medicine. Who wants a rank plebeian admitted into his family circle?

MRS. MAYFIELD. I'm sure——

GAIUS (*impatiently*). Sure—excuse me, Madam, you women are always sure about things of which you know absolutely nothing. (LIZ, *a young negro maid dressed in black, with white kerchief and red and yellow head-rag, appears at the hall door and drops a curtsy.*)

LIZ. Massa . . .

MRS. MAYFIELD. What is it, Liz?

GAIUS. What do you want, girl?

LIZ (*she trembles as she speaks*). Please ma'am, please sir, Ben wants to know kin he speak to you?

GAIUS. Tell him to come in. (LIZ *drops another curtsy and goes out.* BEN *comes in. He is a half-grown negro boy, dressed in plaid blue and red shirt, and nondescript trousers. He holds a ragged cap in his hand and stands first on one foot, then on the other, rolling his eyes, afraid to speak.*)

BEN. Please . . . sir . . . de conjure woman says ez how if we all don' stop wuckin' on Sunday, the "Old Boy" gwine ter get us sure! Me an' Sam . . . we's 'pinted to axe you 'bout quittin' it, sir.

GAIUS. Oh, confound you and Sam and your conjure woman! You young niggers are just too infernally lazy to lift one leg above the other. This is an emergency, I tell you, an emergency! You know you never do work on Sunday. But you'll work *this* time. . . . You do nothing the other six days of the week.

BEN. But, Massa, de black cats am a-scratchin' at de yearth, and de squinch owls am a-squinchin', and ever' time us niggers crosses de road from de south field, a rabbit runs across our paf.

GAIUS (*charging on* BEN). Oh, damn you black Africans and your superstitions; it'll take more than black cats and owls and rabbits to make me let you stop work, you lazy nigger. Get out o' here, and don't you come back here with your conjure tales! . . . Get out, I say! (BEN *slinks out more frightened than ever.*)

GAIUS (*sitting again with some difficulty in the big chair, and gasping for breath*). Maria, give me my medicine—quick. These black rascals will be the death of me yet. (*Sputtering.*) If I die . . .

MRS. MAYFIELD (*soothing him*). Oh, Father, don't talk of dying. (*Going to the mantel, she takes up a small bottle, drops a few drops of medicine into a glass, pours in water and takes the glass to her husband. He gulps down the contents of the glass.*)

GAIUS (*still gasping, but somewhat relieved*). Zounds, Maria, maybe these darkies are right. . . . I'll reconsider this Sunday business. I'd hate to die (*gasping*) and . . .

MRS. MAYFIELD (*patting him on the shoulder*). There, there, Father! I'm glad for you to do the right thing. You remember you were sorry and sick after that road affair.

GAIUS (*getting up*). I'm better now. (*Stretching himself.*) I'm all right. I'll be . . . I'll be . . . Oh, confound it!—Excuse me, Maria,—but I'll be *consarned* if I do remember. ——No! these lazy niggers shall work when I say so. Did they have any Sunday in Africa, Madam? Tell me that? (MRS. MAYFIELD *is about to retort, but closes her lips firmly and goes on with her sewing.*)

GAIUS, JR. (*Entering. He is dressed in a new black broadcloth suit made in the same style as his father's. He is a youth of twenty, tall as his father, but slender. He is faultlessly dressed, and is evidently proud of himself.*) Mother, does your son's appearance suit you? (GAIUS MAYFIELD *puts down his paper and glares at his son over his spectacles.*)

MRS. MAYFIELD (*surveying him approvingly*). Yes, son, you look——

GAIUS (*sputtering out*). 'Tis not his appearance I'm interested in, but his deportment. I hope sir, you'll have the grace to remember the honor of your forebears, and pay no attention to that upstart, Betty Foster.

MRS. MAYFIELD AND GAIUS, JR. Father!

GAIUS, JR. Don't call her an upstart, Father. She is a charming girl!

GAIUS. Charming, fiddlesticks! From such ancestry! Humph! Your judgment is worth just that of any other foolish young puppy.

GAIUS, JR. Her father is a reputable physician, who attends you when you're sick.

GAIUS. Only because I can get no *gentleman* in this God-forsaken country. He doesn't even know enough to tell when I'm desperately ill! (*He resumes his reading.*)

GAIUS, JR. Mother am I dressed correctly?

MRS. MAYFIELD. Just as you should be, son. (*She surveys him proudly, smiles approvingly, flicking a bit of imaginary dust from his coat.*) Son, you look so well, I wonder if this wouldn't be a good time to tell your father about the trouble with Simeon Hatcher.

GAIUS, JR. (*in despair*). Is there *ever* a good time to tell him troubles—unless he thinks he's dying, and so is repentant?

MRS. MAYFIELD. Be careful what you say, son. He's had to have his medicine twice in the last half-hour.

GAIUS, JR. Dr. Foster says we needn't fear for his heart. He's hot-headed. That's his only real trouble!

MRS. MAYFIELD. Hush! He may hear you.—Now, son, please do as mother asks.

GAIUS, JR. Father. (GAIUS MAYFIELD *puts down his paper, surveying him.*) Can't we let up on this Sunday work? Sim

Hatcher says Uncle Enoch and all the older darkies are giving him trouble about working that south field on Sunday.

GAIUS. It is only in an emergency like this after a spell of dry weather when the ground gets right do I make them work. If they get too uppety I told Sim to use the lash.

MRS. MAYFIELD. Poor old Enoch!

GAIUS. Don't get sentimental, Madam. You know our darkies are seldom whipped. We are too good to them, that is the trouble.

GAIUS, JR. But, Father, whipping does them no good. They say the devil will get them if they work on Sunday.

GAIUS. African superstition! Gad, they are mine and I'll do as I damn please with them.—Excuse me, Maria!—As I *please*. A young buck of a nigger came to me just now, and here you're pleading for the old ones.

MRS. MAYFIELD. Father, I said no good would come from this work on the Lord's Day.

GAIUS, JR. Both old Annie, and the conjure woman say "the portents are a-p'inting at trouble" and have been since that first Sunday the niggers worked. And all the darkies stand by old Annie.

GAIUS (*blustering out*). Am I afraid of such confounded superstitions? One day is as good as another if the weather is right for hoeing.

MRS. MAYFIELD. Father, I don't like to remind you——

GAIUS. Then don't do it, Madam.

MRS. MAYFIELD. Father, I must. You remember, when you thought you were going to die last fall, how sorry you were for the Jefferson affair!

GAIUS. Gad, Madam, the new road is shorter than the old one.

MRS. MAYFIELD. To think a Mayfield would disturb public worship with the creaking of his wagons, and the cursing of his darkies! I hate to feel the unspoken reproach of our neighbors and friends.

GAIUS. Humph! I haven't found much of it unspoken. If they didn't like the sounds of honest toil, they needn't have put their church-house by the road.

GAIUS, JR. Father, I am humiliated that they had to write in their records of incorporation, that they incorporated their town to keep your wagons out on Sunday; but this Sunday field work is even worse than that.

GAIUS (*starting up*). And since when has a son had the right to insult his father by talking of humiliation? Gad, young man, you'd better clear out to your infernal party or I'll make you clear out! (*Rising*). Where is my cane? (*He stalks angrily around the room.*) You rely on the mildness of my temper to excuse you for your insolence!

MRS. MAYFIELD. Son, say something to him.

GAIUS, JR. Father, I didn't intend to make you angry.

GAIUS. You didn't, eh? Well, get out of here!—Now, mind you, you're to be back at 12 o'clock. Honest working folks like me get up at 5 o'clock. I don't want any young whipper-snapper disturbing my rest.

GAIUS, JR. I'll go up the back stairs.

GAIUS. Gad, sir, do as I tell you!

MRS. MAYFIELD. Yes, son; I'll leave a fire for you.

GAIUS, Jr. Thank you, Mother. Good-by. (*He goes over to his mother and kisses her.*) Good-by, Father.

GAIUS (*growling*). Good-by. (*He resumes his reading.*)

MRS. MAYFIELD. Good-by son, have a good time. (GAIUS, JR. *goes out.*) And, son, be sure to hang your new suit in the hall wardrobe when you come in.

GAIUS, JR. All right, Mother, I will.

MRS. MAYFIELD (*beseeching*). Father, you'll do as Gaius asked, won't you?

GAIUS. Mrs. Mayfield, I've given my orders; I'll be obeyed.

MRS. MAYFIELD. You gave your orders about the hauling, but when the Lord sent that sickness upon you, you grew sorry. You promised then to stop breaking the Sabbath.

GAIUS. Who says I'm sick now? Because I played the fool and weakened once, do you think I'll continue to do so? No, Madam, your husband is no old fool. An occasional emergency must be met with common sense.

MRS. MAYFIELD. Poor old darkies, they're too feeble to work seven days in the week.

GAIUS. Feeble! Humph! It's just that foolish conjure woman's talk. Those old darkies can put in a better day's work now than many of their grandchildren. I tell you, Mrs. Mayfield, no time can be wasted on this plantation when you encourage your son to dress in the style of his father. Time was when such extravagance was not permitted. Black broadcloth—made in New York—just like his father's! Bah! . . . I must say the young scamp looked well when he left just now. You, Madam, are bad enough, but I shall not tell him how handsome he has become.

MRS. MAYFIELD. Yes, hasn't he? Why, my dear, just the other day, Mrs. Tallichet said to me, "How strikingly like his father young Gaius is growing." (GAIUS *strokes his chin and smiles his agreement.*) He is, too.

GAIUS. Um-m . . . Mrs. Tallichet is a very observant woman.

MRS. MAYFIELD. She saw Gaius and Betty Foster together and said, "What a handsome couple!"

GAIUS. Madam, please do not couple the name of my son with that of old Foster.

MRS. MAYFIELD. Father, after that last spell when you thought you were dying, you said you'd not interfere if Gaius really loved Betty.

GAIUS. There you go again reminding me of illnesses. Don't I suffer enough without that? Madam, it may be, "No

fool like an old fool," but I say, "No fool like a sick man."
I'll keep no promises extorted from me on my dying bed.

MRS. MAYFIELD. Extorted, my dear? You freely offered to
accept the girl.

GAIUS. Well, I will not. No Mayfield has yet married a de-
scendant of old Abe Foster, and, while there's breath in
my body, none shall.

MRS. MAYFIELD. You've grown to depend on Dr. Foster to
keep it there.

GAIUS (*rising and starting to the door*). Madam! I shall go to
bed.—With a son going against his father's wishes and
his mother abetting him in his disobedience, it's no wonder
that I often come near death's door. It's no wonder that
I . . . Good night, Mrs. Mayfield. (*He goes out.*)

SCENE 2

*It is 5 o'clock on the following morning. The room is almost
dark.* GAIUS MAYFIELD *is heard groaning off stage.* MRS.
MAYFIELD *enters from the hall with a lighted candle and lights
the table lamp. She is in negligee.* GAIUS *staggers into the room
and drops into his chair. He is dressed in black broadcloth as
before, but his white shirt front bulges out and his waistcoat
and trousers will not meet. He is collarless.*

GAIUS. (*With great perturbation. His manner is now humble
and sanctimonious in strange contrast with his former defiance.*) Oh, oh! My dear—(*Groaning.*) Call Gaius! Tell
him to ride at once to Dr. Foster. I am desperately ill!

MRS. MAYFIELD (*leaving him, she goes to the door and calls*).
Gaius, Gaius!

GAIUS, JR. Yes, Mother.

MRS. MAYFIELD. Your father is sick. Dress quickly and ride
for Dr. Foster.

GAIUS, JR. All right, Mother, I will.

GAIUS. Come to me, my dear one. Take my hand. I may not

be here when the doctor comes. (*With pathetic appeal.*) Look at my body. See how I am swelling! (*Touching his body.*)

MRS. MAYFIELD. My dear, be calm. It does not seem swollen.

GAIUS. But it *is*, Maria. (*Excited.*) Don't you see . . . my clothes will not meet? Maria, hold my hand. This may be the last time you will look on your poor, patient, suffering husband.

MRS. MAYFIELD. No, my dear. No.—Where does it hurt? Can I give you some drops? (*She lets go her husband's hand, and starts toward the mantelpiece.*) There are none for the swelling.

GAIUS (*in despair*). Oh! Don't let me die! Suppose you mix *all* the bottles. (*She pours out medicine from each of the three bottles into a glass of water and gives it to her husband.*)

MRS. MAYFIELD. Here it is. (*He drinks.*) Now don't you feel better?

GAIUS. Better, my love? I cannot be better till the good doctor comes. (*In despair.*) Oh! I shall die before he gets here . . . (*Humbly.*) The *good* doctor!

MRS. MAYFIELD. Is there any pain?

GAIUS. Of course there is pain, for I am getting bigger! (*He feels about on his body with both hands.*) God a'mighty, where *is* the pain? . . . I must be in pain for I'm dying . . . of . . . dropsy!

MRS. MAYFIELD. No, no, there! (*Soothing him.*) Your temperature is all right. You have no fever. You can't be very sick.

GAIUS (*his voice rising*). But I *am* very sick! I must be dying! Madam, will you let your husband *die?*

MRS. MAYFIELD. Calm yourself, Mr. Mayfield. The doctor will soon be here.

GAIUS (*vehemently*). Calm! Calm! How can I be *calm* when I am swelling up . . . like a balloon! Careful, Maria, careful—Oh, Lord! . . . I shall die! I cannot stand this!

Oh, my God! *Don't* let me die. I'll let my niggers rest on Sunday, hard times or no hard times. Don't let me die, Lord! Call old Tom, Maria.

Mrs. Mayfield. The doctor will soon be here. Don't be excited. (*She goes to hall door and calls.*) Tom! Tom!— There now. . . . Calm yourself, my dear!

Gaius. Calm myself . . . in the face of death! This is no time for calmness; I must talk to the Lord.—Oh, Lord, I'll let the niggers never work on Sunday, and do any other thing you want if you'll just stand by me now! Don't let me . . . burst before the doctor comes! (*He writhes in his chair, feeling parts of his body as before. Uncle Tom, Ben and Liz have come in. They stand in respectful attitudes. Liz drops a curtsy and speaks.*)

Liz. What kin I do, Missus?

Mrs. Mayfield. Put on a kettle of water. Have Tom fix the fire. Get some cloths from the press in the other room.

Liz (*curtsies, and goes*). Yes, Missus.

Gaius (*sitting up straight in his chair*). Tom, Tom, come here!

Tom. Yes, sir, Massa, here I is.

Gaius. Tom, you old niggers needn't work any more on Sunday.

Tom. Thank y', Massa, thank y', suh.

Gaius. Ben!

Ben. Yes, suh, Massa.

Gaius. Ben, what's that in your hand?

Ben. Jes' er rabbit foot, Massa. Nothin' but a rabbit foot.

Gaius. Ben, you needn't be afraid of that black ape of a conjure woman . . . you nor the rest of you young niggers. There'll be no more Sunday work!

Ben. Thank y', suh, thank y'.

Gaius. Oh, Lord, I'm damned, I'm damned. What else do you want? Maria, am I going down any?

MRS. MAYFIELD. You certainly are not swelling any more.

GAIUS. Oh, Lord, let me go down . . . just a little.—That would be a vile end for a gentleman like me! To burst!!

MRS. MAYFIELD (LIZ *brings cloths and a kettle of hot water*). Let me put some hot cloths on you.

GAIUS (*pushing her away*). No, no, if I get hot, I might burst like a . . . *baked apple!* Take those damnable cloths away! Take them away! Do you want your husband to *explode?*—Oh, Lord, send the doctor.

LIZ. Heah he come now, Missus. (DR. FOSTER *enters with young* GAIUS. *He is about forty-five, fair and fat, with a shrewd twinkle in his eye. He looks as if he can't believe the situation is serious.*)

DR. FOSTER. How do you do, Mrs. Mayfield. (*Putting down his bag, he goes over to* GAIUS *and feels his pulse.*) Good morning, Mr. Mayfield. . . . Your tongue. (GAIUS *puts out his tongue.*) Umm. . . . (*He thumps the patient's body on both sides, listens above his heart, thumps him on his stomach.*)

GAIUS. Oh! oh! . . . Careful, doctor, careful!

DR. FOSTER (*to* MRS. MAYFIELD). What time was he taken?

MRS. MAYFIELD. He got up at five. When he couldn't make his clothes meet, he called me—about 5:10, I suppose.

GAIUS. Five! Zounds! It was two!

DR. FOSTER. Um—um—about three quarters of an hour ago. What have you done for him?

GAIUS (*interrupting*). Done, doctor, done? Not a damned thing!—Oh, Lord, forgive me!—Do something, doctor, quick!

MRS. MAYFIELD. I've given him his drops.

DR. FOSTER. How many times?

MRS. MAYFIELD. At least three times. I mixed them all together once.

GAIUS. I know I am dying! I am going to explode!

Dr. Foster. Mr. Mayfield, are your affairs in order?

Gaius. My affairs? Good God, man! (*He realizes he must be very sick, now that it is confirmed by the doctor.*)

Dr. Foster (*winking at* Mrs. Mayfield). Have you no messages to leave? No sins to repent of?

Gaius. (*In desperation. Now quite penitent.*) Oh, Lord, let me live to do it. Don't let me die till the niggers rest next Sunday.—Wife, wife, send the Jefferson church that organ money. (*Groaning.*) Oh, Lord, Lord!—Where is Gaius?

Gaius, Jr. Here I am, Father.

Gaius. Gaius, do you really love that girl?

Gaius, Jr. I swear I do!

Gaius. Then, boy, marry her . . . with my blessing.

Dr. Foster. Mr. Mayfield, try to be calm. Such moments of reparation seldom come. Do you wish to put in writing what you have just said?

Gaius. In writing! Yes, in any d—— in any thing. Can this poor dropsied hand write?—For God's sake, doctor, you write it. I'll sign whatever you write.

Dr. Foster. Mrs. Mayfield, take care of him while I write. (*He winks at* Gaius, Jr. *and* Mrs. Mayfield, *goes to table, and writes.* Mrs. Mayfield *stands behind her husband and smooths back his hair.*)

Gaius. Careful, careful, Maria.—Is the skin on my forehead stretched?

Mrs. Mayfield. It seems to be about as usual, dear.

Gaius. Oh, what a good wife you have been—with never a cross word between us. Oh, Lord, let me show her I love her before I—Dear Maria, you know I love you.

Mrs. Mayfield. Yes, Father, I——

Dr. Foster (*interrupting*). This paper promises the Lord and man that if he is allowed to live, he'll treat his niggers kindly, and give them no Sunday work. The Jefferson church shall have the promised money, and Gaius, Jr.

shall marry whom he pleases. Is that all right? . . . Now sign here, Mr. Mayfield.

GAIUS. Oh, Lord yes, I promise you all this and everything else you want. (DR. FOSTER *hands him the paper which he signs. Then with a supreme effort he continues.*) Gaius, put on your broadcloth coat, and send for the girl and the preacher. I'll see you married before I pass away.

GAIUS, JR. (*cheerfully*). Father, you are good for many a day, yet.

GAIUS. No, my hour has come. Put on your broadcloth and fetch Betty. . . .

DR. FOSTER. Your father is in no immediate danger. Do as he tells you if it pleases him.

GAIUS. Go, son, go quick!

GAIUS, JR. (*as he goes into the hall*). Very well, Father.

GAIUS. He's a fine son, doctor . . . a *fine* son . . .

GAIUS, JR. (*calling from the hall*). Mother, Mother! Where are my new broadcloth clothes—the one like father's?

MRS. MAYFIELD. In the wardrobe where you put them when you came from the party last night, I suppose.

GAIUS, JR. (*enters, carrying his father's broadcloth suit*). No, they aren't. Here are *Father's*, with his watch in his pocket. But where are mine? (GAIUS, *at the word "watch," feels in his pocket.*)

DR. FOSTER (*chuckling*). Where did you get your new suit, Mr. Mayfield?

GAIUS. My new suit? I have no new suit.

DR. FOSTER (*laughing heartily*). What do you have on, then?

GAIUS (*he picks up one of his coat tails and feels in his pocket*). Well, I'll be—is this Gaius's coat? Is this *his* waistcoat? God a'mighty! Then I'm *not* dying? I shall not burst?

DR. FOSTER. Not a bit of it. You're a perfectly well man.

GAIUS. But all that medicine I took? Won't it kill me?

DR. FOSTER. Colored water, mostly. If it'd kill you, you'd been dead long ago.

MRS. MAYFIELD. Oh, my dear! You're really not sick! (*She kisses his forehead. He pats her hand.*)

GAIUS. Well, well . . . I . . . I . . .

GAIUS, JR. Then, Father, your promise doesn't hold?

GAIUS. Hell, it doesn't!—O Lord, forgive me!—Who said it doesn't? I think I've learned my lesson. (*He holds out his hand to* DR. FOSTER.) Your hand, doctor. Tell your little girl I beg her to be my daughter.

CURTAIN

FIXIN'S

The Tragedy of a Tenant-Farm Woman

BY

ERMA AND PAUL GREEN

FIXIN'S

Fixin's, by Erma and Paul Green, is a study of the grinding poverty of tenant-farm life, which the authors have observed from childhood. Here the pent fury of the work-driven woman, Lilly Robinson, is portrayed with grim and terrible reality. She craves a little beauty—"purty fixin's." But her husband's eyes cannot see beyond the sod he plows. The scene is a bare cabin home in Harnett County, but the theme is universal—the pitiful conflict of two natures which are irreconcilable.

In all the towns of The Playmakers' itinerary this play has had a powerful appeal. The editor of *The Smithfield* (Johnston County, N. C.) *Herald* expressed it: "*Fixin's* went straight to the hearts of those present. Too many times had that scene been enacted before their eyes in real life. The simple story of the tenant farmer's wife was too true to mean actual enjoyment to the spectators. The scene might just as well have been in Johnston County as in Harnett. It was typical of this, the cotton section of North Carolina."

The next morning after our Playmakers' tour performance of *Fixin's* in Atlanta, before a sophisticated audience in evening dress, a man came to me and said, "I think I owe it to you to tell you of the effect that little play, *Fixin's*, had on me last night.—I come from New York, and I've been seeing the best shows in the theatre there for thirty years. But that little play last night *got* me so much that, before I went to bed, I went to the Western Union office and telegraphed some flowers to my wife in New York!"

THE CHARACTERS

As originally produced on The Playmakers' Stage, Chapel Hill, North Carolina, February 8 and 9, 1924.

ED ROBINSON, *a young tenant farmer*,	Charles Pritchett
LILLY ROBINSON, *his wife*,	Frances Gray
JIM COOPER, *his landlord*,	Aubrey Shackell

SCENE: The kitchen of the Robinson farmhouse in Eastern North Carolina.

TIME: The present. An Autumn evening, about half-past six o'clock.

SCENE

*The kitchen of the Robinson home, the bare cold room of a
tenant farmer. In the rear wall is a door leading to the outside,
a small window to the right of it. A door on the left leads into
the only other room of the house, both a bedroom and sitting
room. At the right is a cooking stove, and in the center of the
room is an eating-table made of rough timbers and covered with
a checkered oil-cloth. Between the table and the wall is an old-
fashioned bench. There is a chair near the table and another
near the stove.*

The scene opens with ED ROBINSON *preparing supper at
the stove. He is a stockily-built man of twenty-five or thirty,
with a plain, honest face, but a face that shows strength and
will and maybe a violent passion when aroused. His movements
with the supper are awkward and detached, showing that he is
unused to the job of cooking and, too, that he is thinking of
something besides his present task. He is dressed in overalls, a
rough jacket, and heavy shoes. As he is cutting the meat, steps
are heard on the porch. He stops and listens. The door is
pushed slowly open, and* JIM COOPER, *a broad-shouldered,
pushing, genial man, past middle-age, comes in. He is blunt
and outspoken.*

COOPER. Heigho, Ed, havin' it all by yerself, uh?

ED (*turning from the stove*). Why, how you, Mr. Cooper?
Come in and have a che'r. (*He pushes a chair towards*
COOPER *who sits at the left of the table.*)

COOPER (*looking around the room*). Thanks. Sort o' lonesome
here by yerself, you know, ain't it, Ed? (*Hurriedly.*)
Course some folks likes it that-a-way . . . but . . .

ED. Yeh, 'tain't no picnic mebbe. . . . (*He lapses into
gloomy silence, stares at his knife-handle a moment, then*

169

begins putting the meat quickly into the pan, stirring around as if anxious to forget something that is worrying the life out of him.)

COOPER. Well, I thought I'd come over and have a settlement about the cotton before you got off some'r's or went to sleep. (*Watching him closely.*) But you ain't no night-hawk fer traveling, are you?—Not lately anyhow.

ED. Nope, I stick clost about. (*He taps on the pan with the knife-blade.*)

COOPER. You shore do, and that's the God's truth. But just because she's gone off making a fool of herself, you needn't. (ED *straightens up and stands listening, threatening.*) Never mind—'scuse me, Ed—you know I will talk. My daddy was a great hand fer it. . . . (*Pulling out a pencil and paper and leaning over on the table.*) Cotton was bringing thirty cents to-day—got thirty fer Lilly's bale.

ED (*with a show of interest*). Quair it run up so—boll weevil, I reckon, 's e't it all up from Texas to I don't know where.

COOPER. That's it, I 'spect. Fine on us though, fer it ain't hurt us none as yet. (*He lays down his pencil and pulls a roll of money from his pocket.* ED *sits on the opposite side of the table.*) Your bale weighed 505 pounds, the seed $20, all told $171.50. Your half comes to $85.75. (*He counts out the money and lays it on the table.*) There it is, Ed, a right smart pile. If you turn this money over to her, I reckon she'll cut a splu'ge.

ED. Thank y', Mr. Jim. I'll put it away soon's I finish my cooking. How much I owe you fer the hauling?

COOPER. Nothing, nothing. Glad to do it fer you; we'll strike off even fer that day you holp me pull stumps. (*He gets up, as if to leave.*)

ED. All right, sir. Suits me, if it does you.

COOPER (*making as if to go, but plainly in no hurry*). You

got . . . got any certain thing you want to sink this money in, Ed?

ED. Not exactly. . . . I had been thinkin'—least-ways Lilly's been thinkin'—you see 'tain't my money, it's hers.

COOPER. I know what's she's been thinking. (*He sits back down decisively.*) Look-a-here, Ed, seems like a good time fer you an' me to talk business.

ED (*uncertainly*). Yes, sir. . . .

COOPER. I'm plumb good an' ready to sell you that land. The $400 you lent me is due about now. Course I can pay it back. (*Edging his chair nearer.*) But I got a note over in Lillington to pay off next Sat'd'y for $500. Tell you what I'll do. Pay me $80 down now and I'll credit you with a plain five-hundred on the land.

ED (*hurrying to turn his meat*). I dunno just exactly. . . . That's Lilly's money. . . .

COOPER. Lilly's nothing. You use' ter talk right sharp about that trade, and last spring fer a while—But you ain't 'peared to take much stock in it lately.

ED (*fingering the money*). Well, this here's the first time cotton's been bringing anything since Lilly an' me got married. And I'd sorter been thinkin' . . .

COOPER (*filling up a clay pipe and lighting it*). Thinking what?

ED. Oh, nothin', mebbe. I had sorter begun to git out'n the notion of the land business.

COOPER (*dropping the burning match with a smothered exclamation of pain*). Who put you out'n the notion, Ed?

ED (*sitting down again*). Nobody . . . that is . . . well, I just got out'n the notion, that's all.

COOPER. I know who done it. Ed, I remember, same as yesterday, the day you and Lilly drove off to git married. What had you been talking about before that,—buying you a place of yer own, that's what. You talked the same way the year after—even went so far early this fall as to lend me the four-hundred with the land matter in mind. And now you're all changed. What's the matter?

ED. Land costs a whole sight more'n it use' ter.

COOPER. Yes, but cotton's bringin' a terrible high price and going higher. You know, Ed, I want you to have that 25 acres. Drat it, I can git rid of it to-morrow fer cash money, but—well, you've been good to wait on us all—sickness, cold, hot or whatsoever—and Mary says herself that if that piece o' ground is ever sold, she wants it sold to you two.

ED. That's shore good of her—of you too. She's tuk a sight with my Lilly.

COOPER. Well—business is business and feelin's is feelin's —but if you want that place you can——

ED. Mr. Jim, Lilly . . . she ain't——

COOPER (*stamping the floor*). Of course it's Lilly behind it all—knowed it from the fu'st—everybody knows it! (ED *looks at the floor, then goes to his cooking. His complete silence makes* COOPER *uneasy and he speaks in a more placating tone.*) What does Lilly say, Ed?

ED. Mr. Jim, you remember that time at Tom Atkins's saw-mill when I forgot myself and nearly come to—to—scrushing in his head——

COOPER. Lord, Ed, I didn't mean to rile you.

ED (*quietly*). That's all right, I hadn't ought to git mad either. And they ain't no harm in my telling you that Lilly ain't tuck with farming no more. In place of land, she wants to buy fixin's and sich, and purty up the house.

COOPER. Wants to buy furniture, and graffyfoans, and lace curtains, and the like, uh?

ED. Somethin' like that, I reckon, if you say so.

COOPER. And all that there talk o' hern's caused you to change yer mind?

ED. The main reason, I 'spect, Mr. Cooper.

COOPER. Well, Ed, I'm goin' to talk ter you plain, man to man, and I don't want you to git stirred up nuther.

ED. What's . . . what you want to tell me?

COOPER. Well—Lilly ain't treating you right, and that's the p'int-blank truth.

ED (*going to him*). What you mean?

COOPER. Now don't git on a high horse. I'm goin' ter say out my say.

ED (*stubbornly*). All right, sir.

COOPER. Lilly wants to move to town, don't she?

ED. Well, she's plumb wore out with choppin' cotton and pickin' till her fingers drip blood. (*Bursting out.*) And who can blame her?

COOPER. I can, fer one. Women ain't made jest to be dolls and kept in a show-case, and Lilly Robinson ain't never hurt herself at work, now has she?

ED. I said I'd let you tell what you wanted to.

COOPER. And I will too. She's been over in Dunn now for nigh three weeks, ain't she?

ED (*controlling himself*). She was needin' a change. It's been hard . . . hard on her since . . . since little Charlie died.

COOPER (*kindly*). Yes, yes. (*Sternly.*) But not as big a change as she's gittin' from what I hear.

ED. Do, how?

COOPER. Oh, I know you've promised to give her that money to buy flim-flams fer herself.—Yes, you have.—And what's she doing? . . . Lloyd Mangum told me to-day that she's over there in Dunn riding around with a traveling man, some sort o' agent, one of these guys, I reckon, that squirts cologne on hisself and wears two or three rings at a time.

ED. Lloyd Mangum is a damn liar, and I'll wring his damn neck.

COOPER. What 'n the thunder you want to git het up so

sudden fer? I ain't talkin' up fer Lloyd, or fer you, or anybody. But he's never been known to have a loose tongue, now has he?

ED (*muttering to himself*). God a'mighty, she cain't be doing that! (*He bows his head, staring at the floor.*)

COOPER. It's fer your own good I'm telling you this. You know well enough Lilly ought to be here helping you git out your cotton—right in the busiest time o' the year too —and she gallivantin' 'round! And Lloyd Mangum ain't the only one that's been talkin' and seein' the truth, with you as blind as a bat. Mary got a letter to-day from Marthy Sikes over in Dunn, and she spoke about Lilly's ridin' around and goin' to movin' pictur' shows with that feller. It's true, Ed, true as gospel that she ain't a-doing you right.

ED (*starting up*). I'm going to Dunn to-night!

COOPER. Your meat's burning up, Ed. (*Going to the stove.*) And you ain't going to no Dunn to-night.

ED (*sitting down, rolling the dish-cloth in his hands*). It's a passel o' lies somebody's startin'. It shore God is!

COOPER. Lies or no lies, that's not the question. It's this. Ed—Are you goin' ter let her with her honey-sugar ways keep you from being a man? She studies herself.—Oh, yes she does, and you needn't deny it.—If I was you I'd put on the britches and wear 'em awhile. (*He walks angrily about the table.*) Good Lord! do you reckon I'd let a bright-haired looking glass hugger run over me like that? And, Ed Robinson, if you've got any guts in you, you'll not. (*He takes up the burning meat and sets it off the stove.*)

ED. Oh, I hear what you say about my wife, Mr. Jim Cooper. And I don't want to hear any more of it.

COOPER (*shouting*). Don't want to hear any more of it? Well, you will all right!

ED (*standing up, holding the knife in his hand*). That I won't. Stop talking about my wife like that. (*He dashes the knife on the table, and stands closing and unclosing his enormous hands.*)

COOPER (*laughing bitterly*). Stop talking? You order me to stop talking. Well, my boy, if I wanted to I could tell you a streak, before I finish. Why in this world you want to go around with your eyes shut and seein' nothin', never suspicionin' what everybody has talked over and over a thousand times, I can't see!

ED (*slumping down in his chair, and sitting with bowed head*). All right, say what you think then.

COOPER (*coming out of his flood of anger, and speaking more kindly*). I ain't doing you right, I reckon, Ed. But I couldn't wait no longer. I just had to say what I felt fer onct. (*They are both silent a moment. Then* COOPER *goes towards the door.*) I got to be goin' now. Mebbe I done wrong talkin' to you so, and beggin' you to buy that piece of ground. (*Turning back.*) But, Ed, think of the *bargain* I'm offerin' you. Why this evening at the gin, Joe Langdon offered me $3000 fer that piece. And . . . I tell you what I'll do—I'll let you have it fer $2500, and five years to pay fer it. Count what you lent me and the eighty, as five hundred. (ED *sits hunched over.*) Shore 'nough, Ed, don't take on so about that little piece o' news.

ED. It ain't no little piece o' news. (*Throwing his hands out before him helplessly.*) Why, Mr. Jim, she's so . . . so . . . well, it's all lies, that's what.

COOPER. Well, poke up yer chin, and don't git down—don't you now. Everything will come out fer the best. It always does. (COOPER *stands with his hands on the door-knob. They are both silent.*) Well? . . .

ED (*turning, and pushing the money across the table*). Here it is, Mr. Jim.

COOPER. (*Coming again back into the room. He sits down at the table and picks up the money. Then he takes out his pencil and writes on a piece of paper.*) Here's a receipt for the full five-hundred, Ed. Come over in the morning and we'll fix up all the papers. (ED *mechanically takes the receipt from him.*)

ED. Much obliged to you.

COOPER (*blustering*). Keep your thanks, boy. I'm more tickled over it than you seem to be. I feel like a man who has done a bit of missionary work, or something. Say, come on and walk home with me now and take supper at our house. Mary'll be plumb glad to have you in. Reckon she thinks old Bloody-bones's got me, or something. Come on.

ED. I cain't. I'll git my supper here . . . don't mind. (COOPER *turns around awkwardly, then moves to the door.*)

COOPER. Well, good-by. Take care o' yerself.

ED. Thank y'. . . . You do the same. (COOPER *goes out. ED sits staring before him. The receipt drops unnoticed to the floor. He gets up, looks ruefully at the burnt meat, and punches up the fire in the stove. He leans back against the table, his hands shoved deep into his pockets, and begins whistling "Oh, Sally dear. . . ." He sees the receipt on the floor, picks it up, crams it into his pocket, sits back heavily against the table, knocking over a vase of dried flowers. After looking intently at the vase for a moment, he takes it up and, without any show of emotion, hurls it into the corner, smashing it into bits. He punches the fire up once more, and stands warming his hands. He hesitates a moment, then suddenly hurries into the room at the left. Almost immediately he returns carrying a suit of clothes on a coat-rack and a pair of shoes. He drops them on the table, takes off his overall jacket and begins to take off his shoes. Light footsteps are heard coming up the porch. He stops, an incredulous look on his face which gives way to one of joy and anger. He watches the door in a sort of stupefaction. There is a fluttering of knuckle knocks on the door, and a voice calls, "Ed!". But ED makes no response. The door opens, and LILLY ROBINSON comes in, carrying a cheap suitcase in her hand. She is a tall young woman of twenty-three or twenty-four years, dressed in plain, becoming clothes—white waist, dark skirt and lacy collar. She has a fresh sweet face and youthful manner; yet behind her apparent gayety and child-likeness there hides a strong will and a hint of recklessness, now hidden in weariness.*

As she enters, ED *begins lacing up his shoes and putting his overall jacket on again. He does not look at her after the first glance of recognition.* LILLY *stands, undecided, in the doorway, waits an instant, then moves into the room, closing the door behind her.*

LILLY. Ed, I was sorter expecting you to meet me. (ED *makes no reply, but picks up his clothes and carries them back to the room at the left.* LILLY *watches him uncertainly.*) Was you going somewheres, Ed?

ED (*reappearing*). No, not now.

LILLY (*dropping her suitcase on the floor and standing, undecided*). Ed. . . . I didn't mean to stay an extry week . . . but I wrote you why I wanted to. You got my letter; didn't you?

ED (*glumly*). No, I hain't heard a word from you. (*Picking up the dishcloth and moving to the stove.*) But I've heerd *about* you.

LILLY. What, what have you heard?

ED (*dully*). Have off yer things, and make yerself at home.

LILLY (*mechanically pulling off her coat and hat and laying them on the table*). What'n the world ails you, Ed? You ain't mad about something, are you?

ED. I reckon I'm not.

LILLY. I wrote to you, Ed, and told you to meet me in Angier this evenin'. If it hadn't been for Mr. Jake Turlington coming this way, I don't know how I'd 'a' got home.

ED (*after a pause*). I ain't had no letter from you.

LILLY. I give it to Mr. . . . Mr. . . . Ryalls to mail for me. (*Thinking.*) No, I declare, I plumb forgot to mail it. It's lying on the bureau at Aunt Margaret's.

Ed (*a hard note slipping into his voice*). Who is Mr. Ryalls?

Lilly. He was just a man who boarded there at Aunt Margaret's. I got acquainted with him over there.

Ed (*turning to look her full in the face a moment*). How *well* did you git acquainted?

Lilly (*in surprise*). I . . . I don't know just what you mean.

Ed. He don't happen to be a fellow you knowed last spring when you was over there, does he?

Lilly. Why, no, I never saw him before this time. And . . . he . . . he was purty nice to May Belle——

Ed. And how about you?

Lilly. Well . . . why he treated me all right.

Ed (*suddenly flaring out*). By God, I reckon he did! (*And he goes on with his cooking.*)

Lilly (*startled*). Ed, what you so upset about? You said you'd heard about me. What . . . what have you heard?

Ed. I reckon you been enjoying yerself all right.

Lilly (*dubiously*). Yes, I sure have. (*Turning quickly to him.*) What's all this you're driving at?

Ed. Nothing. (*After a moment.*) Looks like you could help me git a little supper—if you ain't above it. (*She leans against the table a moment, looking at her hands. Her brow is wrinkled in thought. Suddenly she looks up at his broad back with a touch of fear in her face.*)

Lilly. Oh, what am I thinking about.—Here, you set down and let me fix for you. My goodness, you've burnt your meat slam to pieces! (*She bustles around the stove, putting in wood, cutting meat, and straightening the table, laying out dishes, etc. Ed sticks the dishcloth towards her, sits down in a chair and begins drumming on the table.*) How you been getting along?

Ed. Oh, purty good. How's Aunt Margaret and all of 'em over there?

LILLY. All right. (*Fumbling in the cupboard.*) Cain't we have some eggs? (ED *makes no reply.*) Oh, here they are. My, my, the hens must have been a-laying! Must 'a' tuk a notion and started in all of a sudden. Ain't been eating many of 'm, have you?

ED (*beginning to whistle a low meaningless tune and tapping with his fingertips on the table*). No, not many. (*He goes on whistling.* LILLY *turns from her work now and then to glance at him. Her quickening movements show her nervous perturbation. She goes on talking.*)

LILLY. Has the little white pullet we set come off yet? She was to come off sometime this week.

ED (*mechanically*). Uh huh. (*He continues whistling and tapping.*)

LILLY (*begins breaking the eggs into a dish*). How many eggs did she hatch? You know we put twelve under her. (ED *makes no reply, his eyes narrowing to slits and his jaw taking on a more and more firm look. His whistle is more pronounced and the tapping on the table sharper and more staccato. As* LILLY *moves around the table, she crunches a piece of the broken vase underfoot. Suddenly she stoops, finds the remains of the vase and flowers, and with an exclamation of pain and hurt, she gathers them up. She turns sharply towards* ED *with a defiant and bitter word on her lips, but his inner absorption deters her for the moment. Tears of anger glisten in her eyes. She stirs the eggs more and more rapidly. At last with a stifled sob she whirls upon him.*) Who . . . who broke my purty blue vase? (*He makes no answer. She bursts out more shrilly.*) Ed Robinson, I want to know who broke my vase?

ED (*suddenly bringing his fist down on the table in a shattering blow and roaring out his words in a rage*). Damn it to hell, I want to know what you been doin' with that Ryalls fellow over there at Dunn?

LILLY (*laying the remnants of the vase on the table and back-*

ing away from him). I . . . I ain't been doing nothing. What . . . you . . . mean?

ED. Yes, you have been doing something, or else. . . . (*She looks miserably into his face, his words dying away into a mutter. They both are silent a moment.* LILLY *twists the dried flowers in her hands.*)

LILLY. What in the world's got into you? Somebody's been telling lies, that's what. Well—(*Defiantly.*) If you want to think *that* about your wife, go ahead and think what you please. I ain't done nothing I'm ashamed of, and that's the truth if I ever spoke it.

ED. Well, what you doing ridin' 'round with that Ryalls fellow—or whatever his name was?

LILLY. They wa'n't no harm in that. And, besides, he took May Belle around a sight more'n he did me.

ED. You went around enough to set everybody talkin' about you.

LILLY. 'Tain't the first time they've talked about me, and— (*recklessly*) it may not be the last, if you cain't treat me any better than you have to-night.

ED. What . . . you . . . mean?

LILLY. I mean that I ain't goin' to be stormed at and driv 'round like a dumb brute by a slave-drivin' husband— that's what!

ED. You needn't to r'ar so. Why'd you stay away another week, and me here with the cotton all fallin' out and nobody to pick it? Ain't no other woman in the neighbor-hood'd treat her man so.

LILLY. No, they ain't. They're all plumb fools! (*She turns to the stove, her lips trembling in anger, and begins putting the supper on the table.*)

ED (*presently*). Lilly, I've tried to treat you right, but a man cain't stand everything.

LILLY (*now and then wiping the tears from her eyes*). Come on and eat yer supper. (*She waits for him.*)

Ed. I don't want nothin'.

Lilly. Ed, come on and eat. (*After a moment.*) Cain't we have a little peace? Seems lak . . . seems lak . . . (*Stifling a sob.*)

Ed. (*Moving to the table and slouching his heavy arms down on it. He begins eating in huge mouthfuls as if he would drown his wrath with food. He lays down his knife and looks at her, sitting in her chair near the stove.*) Ain't you goin' ter take a bite yourself?

Lilly. I ain't hongry nuther.

Ed. Oh . . . well . . . (*He goes on eating. Presently he shoves his plate from him and leans his head on his hands.*) You . . . don't seem glad much to be back home.

Lilly (*cleaning the dough from her fingers with a hairpin*). You shore don't seem glad to see me back either.

Ed. Well . . . I reckon I am, too . . . but—(*He lapses into silence. Suddenly he flares out.*) I want to know what in the devil is up 'tween you and that man?

Lilly (*laughing nervously*). Well you won't know, 'cause they ain't nothin' betwixt us. But I can tell you this, if it'll do you any good, he knows a heap sight better how to treat a woman than you do.

Ed. I reckon he does—if she's the kind of a woman he wants to treat.

Lilly. Watch out what you're sayin', Ed Robinson.

Ed. I am watchin'. They ain't no woman with a grain o' sense in her head 'd be flying around with a fellow lak that, and her husband at home workin' his head off. And you orter know that.

Lilly. He took me to a pictur' show onct or twice, and give me a good time, and that's more than you've ever thought of doing the five long years I've been married to you. (*A pause.*) There you set in that there chair, laying down the gospel to me. Well, I'm goin' ter tell you a thing or two right now. You'd *kill* any woman God ever made, with your hard, stingy ways. (*She rises from her chair and stands before him.*) Oh, yes you would. You don't care for nothin' but a mule to plow in the day time and a shuck mattress to sleep on at night—that you don't; and always a-laying up for land, always a-talking about it, and lettin' me and everything I want go with never a thought.

Ed (*weakening*). Well, Lilly, you hadn't ort to——

Lilly. Hadn't ort to what, I'd like to know. I've worked for you, washed your clothes, hoed your grassy corn, and you off fishing, stayed here at night, with you and Jeems Atkins 'possum huntin' in the swamp and me so lonesome I jest lay there listenin' to the wind whistlin' through the trees. And I've set out your rations over this here table three-hundred and sixty-five days in the year for five long winters and summers, and I ain't never heard a dozen sweet words out'n you the whole time. God *help* me! Who wouldn't go crazy for a sight of a town and purty things onct in a while?

Ed (*mumbling*). I cain't see why you always got to be thinkin' o' somethin' better'n you got—that I cain't.

Lilly (*swallowing her sobs*). That you cain't. You're blind as a bat. All you study is yourself.—Look at Jim Cooper— worked his head off—after you to do the same, though the Lord knows you don't need no coaxing about saving money. Look at him. And then, look at his wife. She's nothing but a ghost of a woman. She won't cast a shadow in the sun she's so thin. He's run her to death, the dirty devil!

Ed (*with a show of anger*). She's been a good wife to him, that's what. She ain't never had no crazy notions about gettin' fixin's, and movin' to town and dressing up in finery, and smearing herself in paint—like them hussies in Dunn. And you might ca'm yerself and not fly complete off'n the handle.

Lilly. How you know she ain't? What do you men know

about a woman's wants anyway?—Nothin', not nothin'. She ain't never had the heart to go ag'in his wishes, poor thing. But Ed Robinson, here's one ain't goin' ter be druv' lak that. I come back home to tell you that. Leonard Ryalls showed me that they's things in this world you ain't never dreamt of. And I've made up my mind from now on to have my way about a few things, I will that!

ED (*with a hurt in his voice*). God a'mighty, ain't you had your way! They ain't another man in the country would let his wife go off and stay three weeks and him pickin' out her own cotton.

LILLY. How much o' yourn have I picked, I'd lak to know? Don't you say nothin' to me about work, don't you! (*She drops down in her chair and begins sobbing.*)

ED. Now you needn't think crying'll git you anything. (*He moves around the room, kicks at the table, seats himself again.*) Shet up yer crying, Lilly. (*She rocks in her grief. He watches her a moment.*) Shet up, I tell you! They'll hear you slam over to Mr. Jim's. (*He picks up a biscuit and begins chewing on it. LILLY bursts out into another tirade.*)

LILLY (*in shrill anger*). Let them hear me! I don't care if the whole world was a-watching me. I got reason to cry, I have. (*Then she grows more calm, and speaks with more control but with more bitterness.*) I'm goin' ter say something to you now, Ed Robinson, I ain't never said to nobody before. (*She pauses a moment, swallowing hard.*)

ED. Say it if you want to—but it seems you've said enough fer one night.

LILLY. (*Getting up and going to the door, she opens it and stands looking out into the darkness. Quietly.*) I can see way yonder that clump o' pines black against the sky.

ED (*uneasily*). Come on back, Lilly, and eat a bite o' supper.

LILLY. I can see them trees there looking all thick and dark and . . . (*turning back vehemently into the room*) you know what I'm thinking of—you know well enough.

ED (*getting up quickly and closing the door, pushing her gently away*). You quit that lookin' out thar. (*Kindly.*) Come on, gal, drink some coffee . . . or somethin'. (*He stands at the stove stirring a pan idly.*)

LILLY. I'm goin' ter tell you. (*A pause, twisting her dress in her hand.*) Who was too stingy to have a doctor? Who said they wa'n't no use putting up screens in the house? Who said all them newfangled idees 'bout baby food and taking care was foolishness? You did, you did! And that's the reason he's out there dead and buried under them pines, with his little white dress all wet and rotten. You killed him, that's what you did, you *killed* him! (*She sits down in her chair with the tears rolling down her face.*)

ED (*in a stifled voice*). Lilly . . . Lilly, don't——

LILLY. I jest wanted you to know that you are just as much a murderer as if you shot a man down in the road—yes, and a sight worse!

ED. I didn't . . . I didn't know . . . Lilly . . . (*He looks at her in pain.*)

LILLY. Thank God, it hurts you a little bit. (ED *sits down at the table, staring before him with set face.* LILLY *speaks very quietly.*) Now that I've told you how I feel about it maybe you won't think it so quair that I want to git away from you onct in a while.

ED (*uncomprehendingly*). You don't mean . . . you don't believe all that, do you, Lilly? Do you feel that way about it? Shore enough? . . . (*He turns away, choking.*)

LILLY. So you did like him some yourself, didn't you? But you see it's too late now. You see, Ed, you can tap on the table and make a funny gooin' sound, and he won't answer you from over there in the corner on his pallet. (ED *looks up perplexed.*) Try it and see. He can't, you know, for he's dead . . . dead . . . dead . . . dead.

ED. What . . . what you mean? (*He stares at her blankly.*)

LILLY. You watch me now. (*She goes to the door, opens it, and calls.*) Charlie! Charlie, come here! (*Her voice goes out across the dark.* ED's *amazement increases. She closes the door softly and turns back to him.*) You didn't hear him answer, did you, Ed? No, I could call, and call, and call, and he wouldn't make a sound. Oh, yes, I used to call when you was out in the fields workin'—oh yes, I did. But you didn't hear me then. But you hear me now, don't you?

ED. What'n the name o' God ails you?

LILLY. You couldn't understand if I told you. (*She looks around the room.*) Ed, did you bring in my flowers off the porch at night the way I told you to? (ED *makes no reply. She goes out and brings in a pot.*) No you didn't. Here's my purtiest geranium all frost-bitten. (*She crumples up the leaves in her hand.*) All the others is dead . . . dead. You see how it is, Ed. You kill things you tech.

ED. Lilly, I forgot all about them flowers.

LILLY. No, you mean you didn't never think of 'em. (*She sits down wearily, thinking. They both are silent. Presently* ED *begins watching her.*)

ED. Say something. Don't set there—so still lak.

LILLY. I was jest thinkin' that . . . it'd take a long time to git any flowers growing agin lak them you killed.

ED. I told you I forgot 'em, and I didn't kill 'em. Don't lay that to me.

LILLY. It'd take too long, wouldn't it? . . . And I guess we've about come to the end of our rope, hain't we, Ed?

ED. I don't un . . . der . . . stand. What . . . you . . . mean?

LILLY. I didn't think you would. (*She sits tapping her fingers.*)

ED (*unable to endure the silence any longer*). Le's don't keep on lak this. Mebbe I ain't done you . . . well—mebbe not just right. Mebbe nuther of us 's done tother'n jest right.

LILLY. Maybe not. That's mighty hard to do as I've found out . . . after a long time.

ED. Le's sorter forgit about all this mix-up, and go on. Things'll turn out better; they always do.

LILLY. I didn't expect to hear you say that.

ED. But, Lilly, that fellow—shore you didn't mean nothin' by goin' around with him, did you?

LILLY (*thoughtfully*). I mought 'a' meant a lot,—who knows?

ED (*bitterly*). You talk lak that an' 'spect me to be humble as a dog.

LILLY. You needn't worry about him. He and May Belle was married to-day before I left. I helped 'em decorate all the week. That's what I wanted to stay over for.

ED (*a joy breaking in his voice*). Is that so? I knowed somehow they was talkin' out'n their heads when they said all that about you. (*Sincerely.*) I'm sorry as kin be about that vase. But I'll git you another one, that I will.

LILLY (*with gentle irony*). There's a bed-room suite over there in Holiday's store I was looking at for seventy dollars. It's priced at a hundred; but he said I could have it for seventy, if I'd send for it in the morning. Do you think you could go for it in the morning, Ed?

ED (*quickly*). I mought. (*Dubiously.*) But that's a heap o' money to put in on sich fixin's.

LILLY. But they ought to be enough of my cotton money to buy that. And I was wondering if you couldn't take off my cotton then and sell it.

ED. But . . . Lilly . . . I . . .

LILLY. Well, you needn't to, if you don't want to. But I was just thinking. . . .

ED (*blurting out*). I sold it to-day.

LILLY (*still going on in her even voice*). You did?

ED. Yes, and . . . and . . . I tell you . . . I let Mr. Jim have that money.

LILLY (*a flame in her voice for a moment*). Oh, yes, the same way you done time and time ag'in—give me a cotton patch, and then by hook or crook get me to believing you needed it worse'n I did. Women don't need money lak men, do they?

ED. But I kin git it back; I know I kin. He begged it out'n me to fix up the deal about . . . about the land. I'll go over thar right now and get him to break it off. (*He stirs in search of his hat and old overcoat.*)

LILLY (*pleasantly*). You needn't bother about it. (*Almost yawning.*) 'Tain't no use now.

ED (*again perplexed*). Lilly, what ails you anyhow? You act quair at times.——(*Hurriedly.*) But I'll go and get it right now. (*He pulls on his coat. There is a noise of stamping feet on the porch. Ed slips off his coat.*)

LILLY. There's somebody coming in. (*She picks up her coat and puts it on. There is a knock on the door.*)

ED. Come in. (JIM COOPER *enters.*)

COOPER. What'n the world's all this racket over here about? We heard it clean over home. (ED *stares at the floor.*) Oh, hello, Lilly. Come back, have you?

LILLY (*pulling on her hat*). Yes, but I'm passing by. . . .

ED. Mr. Jim, I just started over to your house to see you. Lilly ain't satisfied about that trade. She wants her money back. Mebbe I ain't done jest right about it anyhow.

COOPER. I'll swear. Goin' ter let her run over you ag'in? Lilly, ain't you got no sense? Cain't you quit thinking about yerself long enough to help Ed git a start in the world?

LILLY. I ain't asked him to get it back. It'd be fine if Mis' Mary could ask you a question or two, wouldn't it?

COOPER (*blinking*). None o' yer sassy talk.

ED. Mr. Jim, I'll have to back out about that trade. That

was Lilly's cotton money, and if you'll give it back, I'll fix it somehow. (LILLY *picks up her suitcase and moves towards the door.*) What you mean? (*In alarm.*) Where you goin'?

LILLY (*blankly*). I'm . . . jest . . . goin'. You all can fix up about the money to suit yourselves. I don't want none of it.

COOPER. What'n the thunder is all this foolishness about? (ED *stands with his hand on the knob of the door. The two men eye her in astonishment.*)

LILLY. I told Ed a minute ago that we had come to the end of our rope. (*Turning to* COOPER.) You know what that means, don't you? Maybe you don't, but Mis' Mary does. Ask her when you get back home. Good-by to you, Ed. . . .

ED (*amazed*). Where you goin' this time o' night? What? . . .

LILLY. It don't matter. I'm a-goin' all right. And I ain't never coming back never . . . never . . . never. (*She pronounces the words with the same intonation as "dead . . . dead . . . dead."*) Good-by ag'in to you all. (*She goes out, closing the door behind her—singing, as she goes.*)

Oh, Geor-gie Buck is dead, and the last word he said, was "Nev - er let a wo - man have her way."

Repeat Refrain
"Never let a woman have her way."

COOPER (*puzzled*). Ed, what ails her? You ain't goin' ter let her go off lak that, are you, traipsing out into the night?

ED (*blankly, dropping down into a chair*). I dunno . . . what she means.

Cooper (*taking the money from his pocket*). Here—here's yer money, Ed. I ain't anxious about that trade if you ain't.
. . .

Ed. I dunno . . . I dunno . . . exactly. . . .

CURTAIN

THE BEADED BUCKLE

A Comedy of Village Aristocracy

BY

FRANCES GRAY

THE BEADED BUCKLE

In *The Beaded Buckle*, Frances Gray of Chapel Hill gives us an intimate glimpse of present day small-town "aristocracy." The actual name of the town where the scene occurs, and the real name of the heroine, are withheld—for obvious reasons. The real Mrs. Agnes Miller, however, still flourishes as the leader of the "smart set" of her Glendale and still fascinates all who know her with her irresistible charm. "Her soft, beguiling voice is very sweet," the author confesses, "and I am still under her spell." The other characters of the play are still in Glendale—her genial neighbor, Louise; her darling boy, Joe; old Herb Shine, keeper of the "Metropolitan Store"; and "the little clerk," Leona King.

This was Miss Gray's first play on the Playmakers' Stage. She was a very young playwright, in fact only eighteen. Besides writing *The Beaded Buckle*, she distinguished herself as a player of much promise—especially in the exacting rôle of Lilly Robinson, in *Fixin's*.

THE CHARACTERS

As originally produced on The Playmakers' Stage, Chapel Hill, North Carolina, February 8 and 9, 1924.

MRS. AGNES MILLER, *a charming widow,*   Anne Majette
JOSEPH CONROY MILLER, *her son, a University student,*
                                                     Marion Dixon
MRS. LOUISE BAILEY, *a neighbor,*   Vinton Liddell
MRS. BERKELEY, *a gossip,*   Polly Wells
HERB SHINE, *proprietor of the "Metropolitan Store,"*
                                                     Claudius Mintz
LEONA KING, *his clerk,*   Miriam Sauls

SCENE: Mrs. Miller's living room, Glendale, North Carolina.
TIME: The present. An afternoon in May.

SCENE

The scene is the living room of Mrs. Agnes Miller. *A door and window in the rear wall look out upon the village street. The room is furnished to conform to* Mrs. Miller's *aristocratic taste: old portraits on the wall, a vase of fresh roses from her garden on the small table at left; a large sofa, a whatnot and several chairs of Colonial design—family heirlooms, evidently. The telephone is on the table at the left. Beside the table is a large chair in which* Joe Miller *is seated, reading a popular magazine and smoking a collegiate-looking little pipe. He is a well-built, handsome youth hardly out of his teens.*

Mrs. Louise Bailey *enters hurriedly. She is a woman of forty-five, inconspicuously but a bit carelessly dressed in a dark blue voile. Her manner and appearance suggest her generous outlook on life. She has evidently come on an important errand.*

Louise (*calling*). Agnes, oh Agnes! (*She sees* Joe *who has risen.*) Hello, Joe, what are you doing at home?

Joe (*goes to greet her*). How're you Miss Louise, mighty glad to see you. I just hopped off for the week-end. I don't know where mother is. But sit down and wait, she'll be in pretty soon, I reckon.

Louise (*sitting in* Joe's *chair*). Yes, I will stay, Joe. I've got something very important to tell your mother. I suppose she's still at Sadie's tea.

Joe (*drawing up a chair for himself*). Well, I wish she'd come on home. Seems like a year since I've seen her.

Louise (*laughing*). It hasn't been quite a year since the Easter holidays, but I know Agnes will be glad to see you. How'd you leave the Hill?

195

JOE. Oh, quite as I found it. Very pleasant, but slightly monotonous.

LOUISE. Chapel Hill isn't exciting, but it's a mighty sweet old place. . . . Studying hard?

JOE. Yes'm, I'm keeping my nose to the grindstone. You know I entered the law school this quarter.

LOUISE. Yes, so your mother told me. I'm glad that you did, Joe. If you're as much like your father on the inside as you are on the outside, you ought to make a good lawyer.

JOE. Thank you, ma'am. Daddy was a good lawyer. And I thought it was the natural thing to do; a legal mind kind of runs in the family.

LOUISE. I declare it's a pity that Joe, senior, couldn't live to see you grow up. He was so proud of you.

JOE. I wish I could remember Daddy better. Mother says he had the strongest mind and the clearest vision. . . .

LOUISE. He was a born lawyer, and he was just as fair as the day is long.

JOE (*fervently*). That's my idea of greatness. To be fair, to be above prejudice, to have an unerring sense of elemental justice!

LOUISE (*quietly*). It's a great thing to have.

JOE (*rising*). I want to be able to stand on a mountain and look at the whole show and see all sides dispassionately. To be ruled by no emotion!

LOUISE. We couldn't live without emotion, Joe.

JOE. But emotion doesn't have to obscure the truth. I want to be so just that I could judge the most charming person in the world without being biased—so just that I could judge my own mother!

LOUISE. My! What law book did you get that oration out of?—I wish your mother'd come on home.

JOE. So do I. I sure do want to see her. What's she doing these days?

Louise. Oh, she's flirting outrageously with Colonel Haywood, whom she has no idea of marrying.

Joe (*laughing*). The one with the bay window?

Louise. You ought to see the way Agnes "strings" him. She smiles up at him like he's the only man on earth. She'd put a sixteen year old school girl to shame!

Joe. You know I marvel at mother. The way she keeps so young, and she's such good company.

Louise. Yes, Agnes is a good companion.

Joe. She's the best I've ever seen. And she's pretty. No wonder the Colonel fell for her.

Louise. Well, Agnes always had plenty of beaux, but she's devoted her life to you, Joe.

Joe. She's been wonderful. She's been a mother and father both. . . . (*Meditating.*) And she's got a conscience like a man's. She's the soul of honor!

Louise. But she always gets what she wants.

Joe. Because she's lovely. Everybody falls for her charm. She could get away with murder.

Louise. Yes, . . . I believe she could.—I wish she'd come on; it's getting late, but I've *got* to see her.

Joe. If you're in a hurry I'll take a message.

Louise. Thank you, no. I'd better wait. But, (*Hesitating.*) Joe . . .

Joe. Ma'am?

Louise. I suppose I ought to tell you, too. . . . People are saying things about Agnes that I don't like.

Joe (*abruptly*). Do you mean that some one has said something uncomplimentary about my mother?

Louise. Hold your horses, Joe. You can't do me any good if you fly up.

Joe. Well, I shan't permit——

Louise. Please give me a chance to talk. Can't you think quietly about this?

Joe. I hope I am old enough to be cool.

Louise (*sitting on the sofa*). I hope so too. Come sit down, and let me tell you about it. You remember that lavender dress your mother had summer before last—the one with the fringe?

Joe. Yes'm.

Louise. Well, she had it dyed and she wanted a distinctive ornament for it.

Joe (*perplexed*). Well—what under——

Louise. But she couldn't find anything in town that wasn't ordinary.

Joe. Naturally.

Louise. Then day before yesterday, it seems, she went into the Metropolitan Clothing Store and she saw a very commonplace dress, oranmented with a beautiful beaded buckle.

Joe (*impatiently*). Did she buy the dress?

Louise. She didn't want the dress, Joe. She wanted the buckle; but when she asked the clerk to sell it to her, she refused to sell it without the dress.

Joe. Those clerks are the dumbest!

Louise. Agnes finally sent her to ask the manager, but the manager said that he wouldn't take the buckle off the dress.

Joe. And poor mother couldn't get anything?

Louise. Agnes was very much irritated. So she went to the back of the store with the clerk to ask the manager again to sell it.

Joe. And he refused *again?*

Louise. Yes, he refused again. So your mother just left them back there and walked out of the store. But, Joe,— the next time they looked at the dress *the buckle was gone!* (*There is a silence.*)

Joe. You reckon the sales-girl took it?

LOUISE. Probably. . . . Though she's a mighty nice girl.
Leona King—you know her.

JOE. Yes, she was in my class at High School. Too bad.

LOUISE. But of course she doesn't admit it. She and old
Herb Shine say that . . . Agnes *stole* the beaded buckle!

JOE (*dumfounded*). That *my mother stole a buckle?* (JOE *rises,
visibly angry.*)

LOUISE. Isn't it preposterous? But the worst part is that
to-day Agnes walked into the "Metropolitan" wearing
the spit image of the lost buckle.

JOE. Was old Herb Shine impertinent to her?

LOUISE. Oh, no. He hasn't nerve enough to be impertinent.
He just asked Agnes where she got her buckle.

JOE. And what did mother say?

LOUISE. Why, she said she ordered it from Raleigh.

JOE. I reckon old Shine took a back seat then.

LOUISE. But he didn't. He and Leona started telling the
town that Agnes stole——(JOE *starts toward the door.*)
Why, Joe, where are you going?

JOE. I'm going to kill Herbert Shine!

LOUISE (*restraining him*). Now listen to me, Joe. You be
calm, and wait——

JOE. Do you think I can be calm while the scum of the earth
is slandering my mother?

LOUISE. You'd better wait and consult your mother before
you do any killing. (MRS. AGNES MILLER *enters. She is a
gracious woman of forty, combining the freshness of a girl
with the poise of a matron. Her soft beguiling voice is very
sweet, and her arrogance is an inherent part of her charm.
She wears a delicate lavender gown with a vivid beaded
buckle on the hip. She pauses in the doorway when she sees
Joe; then, with a little cry, she rushes to him.*)

AGNES. Oh Joe! Where did you drop from, you precious
lamb, you . . . (*Embracing him.*) Oh, you're so strong;

you'll break every bone in my body. . . . Why didn't you let me know you were coming? I'd have had a party for you.

JOE. I didn't want a party, Mother. I wanted to see *you*.

AGNES. Aren't you the quintessence of gallantry? (*She holds him at arm's length.*) Stand off there and let me look at you . . . just let me look at . . . Isn't he beautiful, Louise? (LOUISE *smiles indulgently.*) Do you know I haven't seen him since Easter?—Isn't he perfectly lovely? Son, you're so beautiful I just can't stand it! . . . Look at me straight in the eyes and tell me the truth, Joseph.

JOE. Yes, Mother, my word is as good as my bond.

AGNES. Are you getting enough to eat?

JOE. Yes'm, absolutely! On my honor!

AGNES (*surveying him*). I don't know . . . you look a little wan. Don't you think so, Louise?

LOUISE. Well, no—not particularly, Agnes.

AGNES. But you're perfect anyway. You're just perfect! Why are you so perfect, son?

JOE (*joking*). Because Miss Louise is my godmother, I guess.

LOUISE. No, I don't take any of the credit, Joe.

AGNES. But what have I ever done to deserve such a son?

JOE. If you had your deserts——

AGNES. Did you ever see a boy so unconscious of his own beauty? (JOE *admits this.*) See how straight he holds himself! I love him to distraction! Come here, angel, and kiss your poor old down-trodden mammy.

JOE (*kissing her fondly*). Mother, you look like a full-blown rose.

AGNES. Isn't it a blessing to have a dear appreciative child in your old age? Especially when he's all you've got in the world. Lou, do you think you could ever love one of yours like I love Joe?

LOUISE. Oh, I think I love 'em enough. But I *know* that if

I raved about my six like you rave about Joe they'd think I was crazy.

AGNES. But he's so perfect!

LOUISE (*laughing*). They all are.

AGNES (*going over to the table discovers* JOE'S *pipe*). I thought I smelled this horrible old thing. That's all right, Joe. If you can't "smell up" your own mother's house, whose house can you smell up? (*Removing her hat.*) Don't you like my dress? (JOE *and* LOUISE *exchange glances.*)

JOE. Yes, mother, but——

LOUISE. Agnes, I came to tell you about that dress. Everybody is talking——

AGNES. What's the matter? Has some old gossip-monger discovered that it's about a hundred years old?

LOUISE (*hurriedly*). Agnes, I might as well tell you. . . . Mr. Shine and Leona King say that you stole that buckle!

AGNES. That I *stole* this buckle!

LOUISE. They say that you went in their store.

AGNES. Yes, I went in their store. I admit I went in their store. I went in their store because there are no decent stores in this town to go in!

LOUISE. And you wanted them to sell you a beaded buckle.

AGNES. Yes, it was the only pretty thing in the store, and they refused to sell it to me without a tacky little dress. Refused to sell *me* a buckle! When it's only my patronage and that of my friends that has kept the doors of that store open at all. It's the insolence of it that I despise. I can remember when old Herb Shine was——

LOUISE. They say that after you left they looked at the dress and the buckle was gone!

AGNES. And therefore I took it. I took their beaded buckle! It's pitiful how the insignificant love to slander their superiors. I suppose they will attempt to blackmail me.

JOE (*passionately*). I'm going to beat up that swine——

AGNES. No, Joe, no! You can't do that and get all this in

the papers. Your mother's name in the papers in such a story. We can't court publicity. We'll have to hush this thing up. Of course that little Leona has lied to all her friends, and that stratum of Glendale society considers me a thief——

JOE. The low-down blood-suckers—the gully dirt—the——

LOUISE. Joe, I thought it was you who were orating to me about level-headedness. Calm down and try to see their point of view.

JOE. They have no point of view—they——

LOUISE. Oh, yes, they have. The buckle is gone. Of course it's ridiculous for old Shine to say that Agnes took it, but he thinks he's right. There's nothing to be mad about.

JOE. Mad! Of course I'm mad! I'm fighting mad! I'm mad because they have displeased my mother!

AGNES. I'll have to see them myself. I'll have to see that this thing is stopped immediately. It isn't fair to Joe to allow his mother's name to be——

LOUISE. I wouldn't go down there if I were you, Agnes.

AGNES. No, indeed. They shall come up here, and I shall tell them to be quiet. I go down there indeed! They must come to me. I'll make them go down on their knees! I'll —— (*She sweeps to the telephone.*) One, seven, eight, please. May I speak to Mr. Shine? . . . How do you do, Mr. Shine? This is Mrs. Joseph Conroy Miller of Myrtle Hill. I wish you and Miss King to confer with me at my home immediately. . . . No. . . . To-morrow will not do. . . . No, I shall not be free to see you this evening. . . . Very well, Mr. Shine, but I think it would be to your advantage to come immediately. . . . I shall expect you in a few minutes, then. Thank you. (*She hangs up the receiver and turns to* LOUISE *and* JOE.) The idea of their refusing to sell me a buckle in the first place. I needed that buckle to complete my costume! What does he keep his messy little store for anyway, if it's not to serve me?

JOE. Oh, Mother, I can't stand it!

LOUISE (*by the window*). Agnes, there goes Mrs. Berkeley looking like she's full of a mean tale.

AGNES. Oh, I bet she's spreading the buckle story. We'll call her in. (*She rushes to door.*) Oh, Mrs. Berkeley, come in a minute. (*To* JOE.) Joe, she's a newcomer trying to break into society and she has the most abominable tongue in town. (MRS. BERKELEY *at the door.*) Why, how do you do, Mrs. Berkeley. Come in, I want to show you my jewels.

MRS. BERKELEY (*observing the buckle*). Your jewels? . . . How do you do, Mrs. Bailey.

AGNES. Yes; my child, and my first roses! This is my son Joseph. How do you like him?

MRS. BERKELEY (*coyly*). I'm afraid that, if I told him, I might embarrass him.

JOE. I am not easily embarrassed. . . . I go to the University.

AGNES. He's really quite nice when you know him. But oh, Mrs. Berkeley, I have a choice bit of gossip. (*She motions her to a chair.*)

MRS. BERKELEY. What is it? Do tell me, my dear.

AGNES (*sitting beside her*). It's about this beaded buckle. It seems I stole it.

MRS. BERKELEY. You stole it!

AGNES. So I hear. It seems that I went into the Metropolitan Store, knocked the clerk down, snatched the buckle, and ran out of the store with the whole works crying after me, "Stop thief!" Can you imagine that?

MRS. BERKELEY. How absurd.

AGNES. Yes, it would be amusing, if it were somebody else. The little sales-girl evidently took it. I'm not going to say anything about it, though. I really feel sorry for her.

Starved for beauty, I suppose. (*Sweetly.*) Of course all this is confidential.

MRS. BERKELEY (*eagerly*). Of course.

AGNES (*rising and taking the roses from vase*). And Mrs. Berkeley, as you go, I want you to take these; they're the first from my garden.

MRS. BERKELEY. Why, they're lovely. It's awfully sweet of you.

AGNES. Oh, can't you and Mr. Berkeley drop in for bridge to-night?

MRS. BERKELEY (*flattered*). We'd be very pleased to come!

AGNES (*she has ushered her to the door*). I shall expect you then—about eight. And remember, don't breathe that buckle story to a soul.

MRS. BERKELEY. Oh, no! That's confidential. Good-by. So glad to have seen you. (*She goes out, passing by the window.*)

LOUISE. That settles her. She'll spread your version.

JOE. She looks like a cat.

AGNES. She'll spread my side; but there'll always be people in town who'll believe that I stole that buckle!

LOUISE. It's horrid for you. But I believe old Shine and Leona will soon need more sympathy than you do.

JOE. If mother'll let me alone, Shine will.

LOUISE (*starting out*). Well, I'll run before the fight begins. My cook got married last week and——

AGNES. Louise, you're just lovely to come tell me. You're the living example of true friendship.

LOUISE. Oh, Agnes, don't take on so. I've got to run and fix supper.

AGNES. I don't see how anybody can be a cook and a lady at the same time. But you could step right off of an ash can and say the right thing at the right time——Oh, by the way, dear, the Colonel is coming to dinner this evening, and he has a plebeian passion for boiled onions. And oh,

Lou, should you mind if I sent them over to your house to be boiled? They make the house smell so bad.

LOUISE. Why——Agnes Miller! You certainly can flatter and insult in the same breath. But, no, I don't mind. Send them along. Bye bye. (*She goes.*)

AGNES. Louise is pure gold! But, Joe, isn't it strange how some people can be born and bred with no conception of honor? Like that little Leona King——people who don't even know it's wrong to lie, or, if they do, as your Great-uncle Sam said to your Great-uncle Fred, "the worst of it is, they don't give a damn!"

JOE. Mother, say "damn" again. You do it so charmingly!

AGNES. Why, dear, you know I never said "damn" in my life! . . . Joe, did you think your own mother would ever be called a thief?

JOE. Mother, please let me *kill* that man.

AGNES. No, no, not for the world. But—as if it would have been stealing if I had taken his old buckle! Why the thing wasn't worth two dollars and it's only my patronage— and then to be rewarded in this way!

JOE. That stripe of trash doesn't know the word gratitude.

AGNES. By the way, dear, what's the law about libel?

JOE (*hesitatingly*). We haven't taken that up yet. (*There is a knock at the door.*)

AGNES. Answer it, Joe. And wait, dear, be kind and firm. Hold up your shoulders and remember that you have the best blood of North Carolina in your veins. (*A second knock. JOE opens the door. HERB SHINE and LEONA KING enter. He is old and wizened. LEONA is pretty in an unrefined way.*)

AGNES (*sitting on the sofa*). Good afternoon, Mr. Shine. How do you do, Leona?

SHINE (*bowing and scraping*). Good evenin', Mrs. Miller.

LEONA (*coyly*). How 'do. Heyo, Joe.

JOE (*formally*). How do you do, Miss King.

AGNES. Won't you sit down? (*They sit.*) I called you here, Mr. Shine and Leona, because I hear that you have been maligning my character.

SHINE (*embarrassed*). You don't want to believe all you hear, Mrs. Miller.

AGNES. Am I to understand that you have not said, Mr. Shine, that I took from your store a beaded buckle?

SHINE. Wal now, Mrs. Miller——

AGNES. Mr. Shine, do you think that there is any sane person in Glendale who would believe that I stole a buckle from you? Don't you realize that to refuse to sell me a buckle in the first place was insolence? Don't you?

SHINE. Mrs. Miller, we've always been good friends—and I'd like to have given you the buckle but——

AGNES. Mr. Shine, I have never taken a gift from you and I never expect to. You know, I suppose, that it is from me and my friends that you get your bread and butter. Your little old store isn't any good. You never keep anything fit to wear. We always have to go to Raleigh in the end. But we keep on trading with you out of kindness— that's all that keeps you out of bankruptcy. And, in offending me, you have offended the best people in Glendale.

SHINE (*cringing*). They ain't any reason to get offended, Mrs. Miller. I've allus been your friend. 'Twas jus' two winters ago that I knocked five dollars off'n your winter blankets.

AGNES. There is no use mincing words. You two have borne false witness against me. You are guilty of a horrible crime . . . the crime of libel! My son, who is a law student at the University, has informed me that I can have you put in jail for sixty days, and heavily fined.

SHINE. Oh, Mrs. Miller, I hope you don't believe I've said

nothin' against you. I don't know who started that lie about me, but you know I never said that you——

AGNES. I'm glad you understand how serious libel is. My duty to society is to have you sent to the penitentiary. My son has urged me to prosecute you to the full extent of the law.

LEONA (*impertinently*). I never heard of that law before.

AGNES. There are a great many things you have never heard of before, Leona, and one of them I regret to say, is the truth. I don't want to cast doubt upon you, but are you sure that you don't know where that beaded buckle is?

LEONA (*stiffening and glaring at* AGNES' *belt*). No'm, I haven't said I didn't know where the buckle was——

SHINE (*taking courage*). She saw you——

JOE. You're a liar!

SHINE. Wal—it's better for me to lie than for you to lose your manners. (AGNES *gives* JOE's *hand an admonishing squeeze*.)

AGNES. I could have you both put in jail to-morrow. But I'm not going to prosecute you. I'm not even going to have my friends boycott you, but I want you to know that I could. I need only speak the word, and no *lady* would ever set foot in your store again.

SHINE. Let's don't have no hard feelin's, ma'am. It's sho' kind of you to do that way arter what Leona said.

LEONA (*insisting*). Well, the buckle was gone.

AGNES. And when I walked in with a similar buckle on my dress you jumped to the conclusion that I had stolen it. Leona, I permitted my son to go to the Public High School. I am not a stickler for caste, but I am forced to speak of it to you. Don't you understand that I am well known in Glendale? That my family for generations has stood for honor and integrity? Don't you see that any one of consequence would laugh at the idea of my stealing a buckle?

LEONA (*weakening*). Well, I couldn't see where it went to.

AGNES. I was terribly hurt that it was you who said these

things, Leona, because you are the only clerk in town who has any taste. I had always felt perfectly safe when I traded with you, but now . . .

LEONA (*showing signs of breaking down*). Well, you know how sometimes when you're worried you . . . s-s-say things. . . .

AGNES (*impulsively*). Yes, dear, I know. But we mustn't let our tongues run away with us. We must always be sure that they are telling the truth.

LEONA (*crying*). I didn't mean . . .

AGNES. I'm glad you're sorry, Leona. Now we can be friends again. I've liked you ever since you were a little girl with such pretty hair—I see you've still got it—and it's all for your own good that I'm saying this. I would hate for you to get into trouble, and the easiest way to do it is to begin talking about people behind their backs and stooping to petty dishonesties——

LEONA (*snivelling*). I wasn't dishonest——

AGNES. Of course you weren't intentionally, but it wasn't right to slander me, Leona. Don't cry, here, take my handkerchief and keep it—to remember me by.

LEONA (*sobbing and blowing her nose*). It smells so sweet!

AGNES. Mr. Shine, I told you that I got this buckle from Raleigh. (*She takes a paper from purse.*) Here is a bill for it. (SHINE *reaches for it.*)

JOE (*rushing toward him*). Can't you take my mother's word? You look at that bill and I'll break your neck! (*The bill slips to the floor.*)

SHINE (*placating*). Naw . . . now, it don't make no difference; and, Mrs. Miller, if any of your friends speaks o' this fool story again, you kin tell 'em thet . . . now's I think about it, I believe I *saw that buckle slip through a hole in the floor!*

LEONA (*relieved*). Yes, there *was* a hole in the floor.

AGNES. Very well, I suppose that's just what happened. I

knew you would explain things to me and that we could be good friends again. Thank you so much for coming. And now—good-by. Good-by, Leona.

SHINE and LEONA (*going*). Good-by.

JOE. Mother, you are the most diabolically clever person! Why, they reacted so to your charm that they left here feeling that you had paid them a compliment.

AGNES (*laughing gaily and sinking down on the sofa, she looks adoringly at* JOE *who is standing by the door*). Well, what's charm good for, if it doesn't get reaction? Oh, dear, I'm so sorry all this happened while you were at home. Come sit down by me and tell me everything. (JOE *starts to obey but stoops to pick up the bill. She raises her hand to detain him, but immediately recovers her composure.* JOE *looks at his mother with an amused chuckle.*)

JOE. Mother, this isn't the bill for the buckle. It's a bill for my new "Tuck!"

AGNES. Is it, dear? I declare . . . I was about to show them the wrong bill! But you saved me. You reacted wonderfully, too!

JOE (*trying to be casual*). But, Mother . . . where *is* the bill for the buckle?

AGNES. The bill for the buckle? (*She laughs merrily.*) There is no bill for the buckle! (JOE *stands looking questioningly at her, then walks away a little.*) What's the matter, dear? Was that very wicked?

JOE. But, Mother . . .

AGNES. Joe, what are you thinking, darling? (JOE *turns to her, takes her face between his hands and looks into her eyes wonderingly.*)

JOE (*smiling whimsically*). When I look at you, Mother, I can't think. I only know that I love you . . . that you are the most adorable woman in the world!

CURTAIN

THE SCUFFLETOWN
OUTLAWS

A Tragedy of the Lowrie Gang

BY

WILLIAM NORMENT COX

211

THE SCUFFLETOWN OUTLAWS

The Scuffletown Outlaws has been a great favorite in The Playmakers' repertory. It concerns the same Lowrie family which Paul Green utilized in the earliest of his plays, *The Last of the Lowries*.[1] The idea came to the author, William Norment Cox, of Robeson County, North Carolina, on one of our annual Playmakers' tours of eastern North Carolina. "Bill" Cox was a member of the company, and he had not yet tried his hand at writing a play.

"Proff," he said to me, "I want to take you out over this Croatan section. There is a great play to be written here."

"Well, Bill," I said, "I guess *you'll* have to write it then."

He took me out into the country to the home of his old Scotch uncle, Frank MacKay, who recounted to us his experiences in the feud between the Scotch settlers and the famous Croatan band. It was a tale of thrilling adventure he had to tell. He still carried five buckshot in his back from the gun of the outlaw chieftain, Henry Berry Lowrie.

"There used to be *six*—but I had one of 'em taken out," he explained dryly.

"Why didn't you have the others taken out too, Uncle Frank?"

"That one was enough—that's why!"

Since his earliest childhood young Cox lived within a stone's throw of Scuffletown Swamp—the mysterious confines of this notorious gang of Indian outlaws. His forefathers were leaders in the campaign to exterminate them. A kinsman of his, Mr. Owen Norment, was shot down from ambush a few feet from his own doorstep, with his wife and children looking on; several other relatives were wounded in defending their homes against the ravages of the Lowrie clan.

[1] See p. 69.

The Croatans have a romantic history. Their forefathers
are thought to have absorbed Sir Walter Raleigh's Lost
Colony—the earliest English settlers in America, who had
disappeared from Fort Raleigh, on Roanoke Island, North
Carolina, by 1590. They migrated to the southwestern part
of what is now Robeson County, and lived in peace with the
Scotch settlers there, assuming many of their characteristics
and adopting their language. This accounts for the Scotch
influences in their speech.

The relations between the Colonists and the Croatans
prior to the War between the States were peaceful and
happy. They rebelled against being conscripted in the Confederate cause, and, under the leadership of the fearless
young Henry Berry Lowrie, for ten years they waged a
bitter warfare with their Scotch neighbors. Large rewards
were offered for the capture of the bandits, fifty thousand
dollars being set on Henry Berry alone—dead or alive.

Such inducements led to many plots for capturing him,
the most famous being that hatched by John Sanders, a
native of Nova Scotia, who won the confidence and affection
of the tribe by two years' residence with them as a missionary. The play centers in the scheme of John Sanders to
assist the Croatans in making their escape by night, in
wagons, to the frontiers of Texas; his attempted betrayal of
them; and his tragic death at the hands of Steve Lowrie,
the meanest of the gang. John Sanders presents the most
tragic figure in all the Lowrie history.

A year later we played Red Springs again, and "Bill"
Cox's tragedy, *The Scuffletown Outlaws*, was included in the
bill. The author himself played the part of the Lowrie chief,
with uncanny sympathy and with grim reality. In the play
he carried a gun which formerly belonged to Henry Berry
Lowrie—given to the young Croatan chief by a deserting
Union soldier, and taken from his dead body in Ashpole
Swamp by the man who shot him, Dan Holcomb, who later
traded it for a fiddle. On the stock of the gun are carved the
initials "S. L." (Steve Lowrie) and "A. S." (Andrew or

"Boss" Strong in the play), and there are three notches recording white men killed.

In the audience at Red Springs were Frank MacKay and others who recalled vividly the terror of the incident portrayed in the drama.

When I saw "Uncle Frank" after the performance I asked him how he liked Bill's play.

"It was fine, all right! But I guess it was too real for me. I could hardly sit through it."

The play really made a sensation, for the tradition of Henry Berry Lowrie is still fresh in the memory of the oldest inhabitants, and is well known throughout North Carolina.

The author has interpreted his materials with remarkable sincerity and with a breadth of sympathy unusual in a young writer. He himself says: "*The Scuffletown Outlaws* was written to throw a true light upon the deplorable condition which existed in Robeson County, North Carolina, immediately after the Civil War. The question is a delicate one and it is well-nigh impossible to present a just picture of the affair. I ask you not to condemn the Croatan Indians too harshly nor to sympathize with the good white people too freely. They were both right. The trouble was kept alive by a pyramiding of circumstances which the settlers as well as the outlaws would gladly have removed if there had been any way to accomplish a mutual settlement. I know the history of these people as well as any one living to-day can be expected to know it. This is my excuse for writing the play."

THE CHARACTERS

As originally produced by The Carolina Playmakers in Memorial Hall, Chapel Hill, North Carolina, December 4 and 5, 1924.

HENRY BERRY LOWRIE, *chief of the Croatan Outlaws,*
William Norment Cox
STEVE LOWRIE, *Henry Berry's brother,*　　　Ted Wilson
RHODY, *Henry Berry's wife,*　　　Louise Sawyer
JUNE, *Henry Berry's niece,*　　　Frances Gray
LUKE LOCKLEAR, *a young Croatan,*　　Lawrence Wallace
JOHN SANDERS, *a white man from Nova Scotia,*
Bob Proctor
JAMES McQUEEN, alias DONAHOE, *a white man of Robeson County,*　　　George Denny

SCENE: John Sanders' shanty, in Scuffletown, the settlement of the Croatan Outlaws. A swampy region of Robeson County, North Carolina.

TIME:
　　Scene 1. The evening of November 19th, 1870—about eight o'clock.
　　Scene 2. The early morning of November 21st.

SCENE I

The scene is JOHN SANDERS' *cabin in Scuffletown Swamp—
the Croatan habitat. There is a barred door in the center of the
rear wall, and to the left of it a small window with a solid board
shutter. To the right, in the corner, is a cot piled with clothing,
a knapsack, and other camp equipment. Down-stage on the
right is a door, also securely barred. On the table in the center
of the room are a Bible, several other books, and two guns.
There are two splint-bottom chairs by the table. On the left down-
stage is a rough fireplace made of sticks and red clay, with a
hand-made bench in front of it. The room has a bare appearance as of hurried preparations for departure.*

The rising curtain reveals HENRY BERRY LOWRIE, STEVE
LOWRIE, *and* JOHN SANDERS. HENRY BERRY *is about twenty-
six years of age and five feet ten inches in height. He is a rugged
man for his years—straight in the back, deep chested, his arms
and shoulders well-set—a well-proportioned figure. His hazel-
gray eyes dilate and flash when he is excited. A smile lights his
face sometimes when he is quiet, but when he is aroused it becomes the smile of a demon. He is the clear-headed young
leader of his tribe. He never betrays to his enemies his real
feelings. His hair is straight and black, characteristic of the
Croatan Indian. He wears calf skin boots, a woolen frock
coat or blouse, breeches of the same material (or Salem or Kentucky jeans) and a wide-brimmed hat. He is seated by the table
leisurely cleaning and wiping his Spencer rifle.*

STEVE LOWRIE *is sitting by the fireplace, carelessly strum-
ming his banjo. He has been drinking heavily and gazes sullenly into the fire.* STEVE LOWRIE *is six feet tall, thirty-four
years of age, and weighs one hundred and seventy pounds. He
has great muscular power and looks the Indian brigand more
than any of the other members of the gang. He has heavy black
hair and a dark thin moustache. The resentment of his race*

lurks in his eyes. He is the robber and the murderer who needs little provocation to kill his man.

JOHN SANDERS *is a native of Nova Scotia. He has lived with the Croatans for two years as a missionary, healer and teacher. In this time he has won their confidence and their affection. He is a tall man, of winning manners, clear-blue, fearless eyes and alert mind—strikingly attractive in his blue homespun shirt, corduory breeches, and calf-skin boots. He is busy packing up his outfit. He appears somewhat nervous and excited, but tries to conceal his anxiety under the show of preparations for the exodus. The room is lighted by the light-wood blaze from the fireplace and a single candle on the table.*

HENRY BERRY. Mon, when first ye come to our swamp-land and begun a-talkin' about movin' to that Texas place, I thought ye a fool.

SANDERS. I reckon you did, Henry, for it did sound foolish at first.

HENRY BERRY. But I sees it now, mon. We can escape by traveling at night an' takin' it easy during the heat of the day. Course I hates to go like this—looks like the Lowries is a-runnin'. That's what them domn whites'll say.

SANDERS. Let them say what they want to, Henry.

HENRY BERRY (*bitterly*). Yes, let 'em. Mon, ye know that it hurts me to go like this. But we are fightin' the whole State now. Outlawed—price on me, ten thousand dollars dead or alive. And a big price set on Steve over thar—on every last one of us. An' I see with ye that this is the way out.

SANDERS (*nervously, tying up a bundle*). Yes, Henry, I believe this will come out all right. And you ain't showing the white feather by leaving like this. Besides, think of where we are going. (*With a show of enthusiasm.*) To a land where we can live as we see fit. A land that is not ruled by court-martial trials.

HENRY BERRY. Court-martial trials! Yeh ho, mon, it were

at a court-martial trial that they murdered my pa for takin' a barrel o' molasses—killed him for takin' a barrel o' sweetenin'. Mon, that sweet killin' ha'e been as bitter as gall-berries to them what done it. Spite of that, we ain't gettin' nowheres. I'm ready to leave it all behind. I feels kind o' happy on my last night in Scuffletown.

STEVE (*breaking in*). Me, too, mon. Hurrah for Texas! Domn Robeson County! (STEVE *has been striking meaningless chords on his banjo. His instrument seems to be out of tune. He strokes it carelessly, not paying much attention to the conversation.*) Kind o' hate to slip off in the night like a domn sheriffs' force though.

HENRY BERRY (*going up to him*). Steve, quit yo' thumpin' that thing. Mon, I believe ye're drunk again. An' this night o' all nights for ye to be a-drinkin'. We need live men for the start, Steve; and you know it. (*He turns to* SANDERS.) Mon, see if ye can fix for him some o' that thar drink ye sober him up with.

SANDERS. Good. There's a little left, I think. (*He mixes a drink. The bottles on the fireplace are easily reached, because they are often used.*) Here you go, Steve, drink it down; it will make you feel better. (STEVE *drains the gourd dipper without changing his expression.*)

STEVE (*dully*). Mon, I'm all right.

HENRY BERRY. That's good. (*To* SANDERS.) Mon, brother Steve owes ye a lot on account o' what ye done for him during his drinkin' spells.

STEVE. Henry, I'm all right, I tell ye. Dunno be all lickered. I was thinkin' how much I'd give for one more shot at that domn Donahoe. Just one more, afore we leave.

HENRY BERRY. It's too late now, Steve. But, mon, let me tell ye, just one more shot at Donahoe, and he'd bleed.

STEVE (*now more mentally and physically alert*). Luck ha'e been agin me with that mon. Everything bein' ready to leave when the moon sets, think I'll strike ye up a tune or two afore we go. (*The meanest and most bloodthirsty of the Lowries is lost for the time being in the plaintive melody of an old ballad.*)

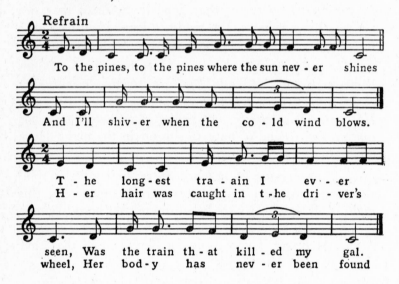

Refrain

To the pines, to the pines where the sun nev - er shines
And I'll shiv - er when the co - ld wind blows.

T - he long - est tra - ain I ev - - er
H - er hair was caught in t - he dri - ver's

seen, Was the train th - at kill - ed my gal.
wheel, Her bod - y has nev - er been found

(HENRY BERRY *and* SANDERS *go on cleaning their guns while* STEVE *is singing. At the conclusion of the song* STEVE *goes to the window, throws open the shutter, and peers out into the swamp.*)

HENRY BERRY (*rebuking him and closing the shutter*). Steve, ye domn fool, shut that thar window. Old Donahoe's rifle will bark out thar in the night and ye won't be a-goin' to Texas.

STEVE (*going back to the fireplace*). An' what'll they be a-sayin' when we do go off to Texas?

HENRY BERRY. Dunno be no help for what they'll say, Steve. Dunno do no good to think about what they'll have to say.

STEVE. Domn 'em! They'll say we run—like women.

SANDERS (*cheerfully*). Oh, it won't matter what they say after we get there. And it won't be long before nine o'clock will be on us. (*To* HENRY BERRY.) And you are sure that everything is ready?

HENRY BERRY. Yes, everything is ready, Sanders.

SANDERS. Have all the wagons been greased?

HENRY BERRY. Yes, every one o' them is fixed right. There's a-plenty o' feed for the mules—everything is ready.

SANDERS. What about my share of the grease for my wagon?

HENRY BERRY. Time Rhody and Luke's here with it now.

SANDERS (*nervously*). Who you got out watching the roads to-night, Henry?

HENRY BERRY. That's all fixed, mon. Don't ye worry about that.

STEVE. We got 'em watched all right. Thar's William Chavis down by the crick bridge, an' George Applewhite is a-watchin' the big road to come this way. Brother Tom's over to Red Banks station to see if some of them domn deputies from Lumberton gits off the train. (*Footsteps are heard outside.* STEVE *and* HENRY BERRY *seize their guns, spring to their feet, and stand ready to fire. A signal of three short whistles is heard.*)

HENRY BERRY. Hit's Rhody and Luke. (HENRY BERRY *answers the signal and* STEVE *opens the door.*)

STEVE. Come in. (RHODY *and* LUKE *enter.* RHODY LOWRIE *is the wife of the robber chief,* HENRY BERRY LOWRIE. *Her figure and countenance mark her as somewhat older than her years. She is dressed poorly, but wears a bright-colored shawl about her shoulders. There is something in her voice which reveals the constant anxiety of her existence and a stoic attitude toward life.*)

RHODY. Everything with us is ready for the start far as I know. (*Turning coldly to* SANDERS.) Here's your grease, mon. (*Going to the fireplace she sits there silently, betraying no emotion.* STEVE *closes the door after* RHODY *and* LUKE, *and bars it.*)

SANDERS. Well, I'd better grease my wagon right now. Can any of you help me?

HENRY BERRY. Come on, Steve, we can holp him.

SANDERS (*to* LUKE). Here, lad. Sit down by the fire with Rhody and rest a bit. (*As they leave* HENRY BERRY *warns them.*)

HENRY BERRY. An' keep that window shut.

RHODY (*darkly*). Hit may be a good thing, but I fear it. Who knows what may happen on the road to Texas, and that mon Sanders a-leadin' o' us. Boy, don't ye never trust a white mon—never, I tell ye.

LUKE. (LUKE LOCKLEAR *is a fearless young outlaw-in-the-making. A handsome tall lad of eighteen, of keen and bright eye and graceful bearing. He is in love with* JUNE LOWRIE, HENRY BERRY'S *niece.*) I ha'e watched him. I ha'e trailed him like a hound-dog, and I aims to keep on his trail. He ain't a-lyin', Aunt Rho'; he means to take us some place far away. Uncle Henry and the rest ain't blind.

RHODY. I dunno be sure, Luke. I dunno know.

LUKE. Hit dunno be the plan, Aunt Rho'. . . . I—I could kill the mon like a moccasin for a-comin' betwixt June and me. But I can't do hit. I can't do hit, 'cause Uncle Henry and Steve and all of 'em don't put no faith in what I think.

RHODY. Boy, I ha'e argued for ye. But June won't listen to me lak she used to. She aims to marry him when we gits to Texas (*doubtfully*)—if we ever git thar. God help 'em. A Lowrie a-marryin' a white mon! (*A low whistle is heard outside.* LUKE *answers the signal.*)

LUKE. Hit's June, Aunt Rho'. (LUKE *goes to the door, unbars it, and lets her in.*)

JUNE. (JUNE LOWRIE *is a Croatan girl. She is well formed and fair to look upon, just turned twenty. Her eyes are dark, her skin is smooth and firm. In the sordid background of a Scuffletown cabin she appears fresh, clear and lovely. She wears a scarlet swamp flower in her hair. There is a wistful quality in her voice which is gentle and low—in marked contrast with the abrupt staccato speech of the men and of her* AUNT RHODY.) We ha'e everything ready to leave over our way and I thought I'd run over and see if I could help John pack some of his things. (*Looking around the room.*) But he's pretty nigh got his house cleaned out.

LUKE. Yes, and he don't need your holp. No white mon does.

JUNE (*fiercely, her eyes shining*). He needs my holp and I'm goin' to he'p him, too.

LUKE. Well, he'p him then if ye want to, and domn ye for it. But it's agin your blood—and him a white mon! (*He goes out, slamming the door.* JUNE *bars it.*)

RHODY. June, thar goes the best boy in Scuffletown—and him a Locklear, too. Luke would be good to ye, lass, and ye dunno do right by throwin' him off.

JUNE. But, Aunt Rho', I love John. He will be good to me, too. But that good part don't make so powerful much difference. I love the mon—here. (*Placing her hand over her heart.*)

RHODY. Lass, ye dunno know white people lak I do.

JUNE. But, Aunt Rho', John is the same as one o' us.

RHODY (*bitterly*). If ye had been with us in that cold and damp jail in Lumberton ye would not be for a-lovin' any white mon. They thought they'd take Steve's wife, and Boss Strong's wife, and me—Henry Berry Lowrie's wife— an' all the wives from Scuffletown, and make our men stop takin' what they wanted and a-killin' them what was a-huntin' of 'em. Hit did no' work. I would ha'e kilt myself if Henry Berry had give up on account of my bein' in jail.—Bless God, no Lowrie has ever touched a white woman!—An' ye go agin your blood, lass, when ye talk o' marryin' this white mon. I dunno trust none of 'em, in spite of what the rest thinks. I dunno forget them nights in that jail, with them cold iron bars a-shadowin' on the wall. An' who knows but what he's a-settin' to ketch us—him a-comin' away down here from that Nova Scotia place.

JUNE (*soothing her*). But, Aunt Rho', ye dunno forget, too, how gentle and kind John has been to all o' us these two years he's been here. He's doctored us for fever, tended the men when they were shot up, and held preachin' for us every Sunday—and all kinds o' things for us he's done. 'Twas a lucky day, I tell ye, for Scuffletown when John Sanders was found out'n his head with swamp-fever, and I brung him back to health. (*She takes up* SANDERS' *coat from the chair and fondles it.*) An' I love him, Aunt Rho'. I love him, I tells ye!

RHODY (*despairing*). I understand what ye say, lass; but the day will come when my words'll sound like buryin' hymns to ye! I dunno be able to trust the mon like ye do. (*She rises.*) I must go home now, so as to be good an' ready for that nine-o'clock leavin' time. There don't seem no sense in a-arguin' with ye.

JUNE (*calling after her*). I'll be along in a little while, Aunt Rho'. (*Alone in the cabin,* JUNE LOWRIE *remains seated by the fireplace. She is gazing intently at the smouldering coals when* JOHN SANDERS *enters. She goes to meet him.*)

SANDERS. Hello, June. I thought you had gone.

JUNE. No, John, that was Aunt Rho'. I just thought I'd stay a little bit longer. You don't care if I do, do ye?

SANDERS. You should be at home resting. Didn't I tell you to get all the rest you could? The road to Texas is hard and treacherous and you should rest now as much as possible.

JUNE. I know that's what ye said, and I love ye John for a-sayin' it; but I couldn't keep from comin' over just for a minute.

SANDERS. Well, young lady, if you love me so much you had

better obey me. (*He goes on with his preparations for the leaving.*) I know what's best for you.

JUNE (*coquettishly*). You dunno be able to make me go right now. Let me stay just a little while, John. I'll no' be in the way.

SANDERS. Oh, all right. Make yourself at home. (SANDERS *goes on with his packing.* JUNE *watches him closely—happy to be near him.*)

JUNE. John, where's Uncle Henry and Steve? Ain't they a-comin', too?

SANDERS. They've gone on down to their wagons to see that everything's ready for the start. (*There is a moment of silence.*)

JUNE. John, we be all by ourselves. . . . Won't you do something for me?

SANDERS. June, you know I would do anything for you.

JUNE. John, tell me more about that wonderful country we be a-goin' to—that country where everything is peaceful and happy, where there will be no more killin' and a-robbin' of folks. Where Uncle Henry and the rest can go to town without fear o' bein' arrested. Where the babes and the chillun can play and laugh knowin' that their pas will come home to the cabin of a night. Oh, John— John! It's good to dream about that country. It makes me believe on that hymn ye taught us to sing on Sundays. "Thar is a happy land, fur, fur away!" Mon, I tell ye one of them miracles is about to happen. Seems jus' lak one o' them you used to preach of.

SANDERS. Yes, June, it is a good country, and a free land. Texas is as big as half a dozen of our states out here. There will be plenty of land for everybody. We can begin at the bottom and build the Croatan nation over again. This trouble will be forgotten in a few years. The sun will shine on us to-morrow—I know it will, June.

JUNE. An', John, ye'll marry me when we get there; an' we can grow old together in that young country.

SANDERS. Yes, June, we'll marry when we get there.

JUNE. John, if ye knew how happy it makes me to hear ye say that, ye wouldn't ever stop sayin' it.

SANDERS. But you must run along home now, June, and try to rest. This escape is mighty serious business, and I must finish the packing right now.

JUNE. I dunno want to go—but I will since ye say to. (*Lightly.*) I'll see ye at Uncle Henry's, John.

SANDERS (*following her to the door,* SANDERS *impetuously draws her to him*). June, I love you, girl. Tell me, would you always love me . . . even if something terrible should happen?

JUNE (*quietly*). Mon, I will love ye forever and ever—it matters not what happens.

SANDERS (*he kisses her*). Go on, child; go on. . . . (JUNE *leaves and* JOHN *is alone. Now he appears tired and worried—unsettled in his mind. A sudden tapping at the side door interrupts his thinking. He listens. Again the tapping. He walks stealthily to the door and gives a signal. It is answered and he opens the door, admitting* DONAHOE. JAMES MC-QUEEN, *alias* DONAHOE, *is a tall, eccentric figure—a gaunt "gawky Scotchman," swift and sure in every movement he makes. Each looks inquiringly at the other.* SANDERS *bolts both doors. Then* DONAHOE *strides to the center of the room and speaks.*)

DONAHOE (*in a repressed voice*). Everything all right, John?

SANDERS. Yes, I think so—not much danger. They all left a few minutes ago. They won't be back soon. Make yourself comfortable. (SANDERS *pours out a glass of whiskey, which* DONAHOE *accepts gratefully.*)

DONAHOE. Thank'ee, lad; that tastes good! This business of crawling through Scuffletown swamp like a snake calls for some kind of a nerve settler.

SANDERS. I don't see how you do it, Donahoe. You must be a ghost. God knows they hate you since you killed Boss Strong. You run in Steve Lowrie's mind all the time.

DONAHOE. An' he runs in mine, the dirty skunk! I'd love to shoot him.—I don't want to see him hung like he will be when we catch 'im. (*A pause.*) Is everything all right, John?

SANDERS. Yes, I reckon so. . . .

DONAHOE. We got our end fixed all right.

SANDERS (*evasively*). Have you?

DONAHOE. Oh, yes. You can count on us. Tell you what we done. We got Wishart's Company, all the sheriff's force from Lumberton, and all the good shots from up Philadelphus way and tried them bridges the other day just to make sure. An' it'll work! You see, some of our men will be under the bridge on scaffolds fixed for it; the rest will be on the dam at both ends; you all drive on the bridge, and we'll close in and catch every damn one of 'em!

SANDERS (*vaguely*). Sounds all right, Donahoe.

DONAHOE. Yes, by God, and it is all right. (*In his enthusiasm his voice rises and* SANDERS *cautions him to speak more quietly.*) We got 'em now (*grimly*)—the rusty swamp-devils. They'll never git away alive if our boys surround 'em. Tell you what you can do, Sanders. Try to call Henry Berry and Steve and the other leaders up to the head wagon for a conference about the time you git to the bridge. They'll be easy to catch up there.

SANDERS (*evasively*). All right. . . .

DONAHOE. I bring ye good news, lad. The Governor has raised them rewards. You stand to clean up nigh on to $52,000.00 on this deal. God knows you deserve every penny of it for what you've been doing here. And I want to shake hands with the bravest man in North Carolina—no—in the United States! (*He offers* SANDERS *his hand, but* SANDERS *does not accept it.*) Oh, come on, John. I mean it, and there ain't no use beatin' 'round the bush.

SANDERS (*slowly, with determination*). Donahoe, I can't shake hands with you on this deal.

DONAHOE. Why, what's the matter, John? Seems to me you ought to be the happiest man in Robeson County.

SANDERS (*walking away from him*). But I'm not happy. I'm miserable. Donahoe, you call me a brave man. I tell you I'd rather be called the biggest coward in the world and have this thing off my hands. (*Resolved.*) I don't believe I can see it through.

DONAHOE (*amazed*). What do you mean about not seein' it through?

SANDERS. Man, you won't be able to understand it when I tell you. For two long years I have lived here with these people. I know the atrocities they have committed. I know things they have done that you will never know. You should go to their cabins as I have done, when their men are away hiding in the Swamp, and see their wives and little ones—wild-eyed, nervous, unable to sleep—listening, eternally listening, for the sound of a gun somewhere far off in the swamps. They can't understand it. The white people tramped on them and they had to strike back in their own way. I've lived with 'em, doctored 'em, taught them—and they have come to put a damning trust in me, in everything.

DONAHOE. John, have you gone crazy? What does this mean?

SANDERS (*firmly*). Donahoe, I mean, that with God as my judge, I swear to you I can't see this thing through. (*He takes from the Bible on the table a faded photograph and observes it intently.*) How could I ever face my wife and children—and me a traitor. . . . Donahoe, man is a queer mixture.—God knows how I can face them anyhow.—What's $50,000.00 for selling the lives of men who trust me as they have never trusted a white man before.

DONAHOE (*facing him*). Sanders, I warn ye not to put any confidence in their trust.

SANDERS. You don't know, Donahoe. Even their suspicious women trust me. There is one girl, June Lowrie—that girl loves me. I began by playing with her so as to make everything run smooth for me in Scuffletown. One little slip and I would have been a dead man. . . . Donahoe, what would you think of me if I told you that I love that girl?

DONAHOE. Good God, man! You are crazy!

SANDERS (*pacing up and down restlessly*). Maybe I am, but I can't help it. I hate to think about it. My two years here make me appreciate affection even from what you call "a damn Croatan."

DONAHOE. Man, don't talk to me about Croatan affection. How much would your trust be worth to Steve Lowrie? I know, and you know, that they would kill you like a dog if they knew what you were doing.

SANDERS. I don't believe they would, Donahoe. They have a keener sense of justice than you give them credit for. I can better stand the wrath and ridicule of North Carolina than to be forever tormented by a guilty conscience. (*Decisively.*) I can't see this thing through.

DONAHOE (*advancing to him*). John, I've listened to all this talk. You must be out of your head. I know it has been a great strain on ye, but try to buck up, mon.

SANDERS (*resolved*). Donahoe, I stand by what I told you, so help me, God!

DONAHOE (*challenging him*). John, have you forgotten the eleven good and honest citizens that these hellions have murdered? Those men they waited on in ambush and blowed their heads off with buckshot? Tell me, have you?

SANDERS. No. . . .

DONAHOE. Have you forgotten so soon Owen Norment, who was shot down in his front yard, with his wife and children looking on and pleading for mercy? Old Sheriff King; they murdered him by his own fireside. Old man Barnes, shot down on his own mill dam. You know all this, Sanders. It's true, isn't it?

SANDERS (*evading him*). Yes, but . . .

DONAHOE. Look at the terrified district—white men can't move from their firesides for fear of bein' shot down. White women and children pray that God Almighty'll take care of them through the night—and you talk like this.

SANDERS. Well. . . .

DONAHOE (*rebuking him*). And the whole country is laughing at us—saying that the people of Robeson County are cowards. You can't pick up a newspaper but has something to say about the cold-footed North Carolina people who let a handful of Indians run wild, murdering and robbing. Well, you know it takes more than talking and even fighting to clean out this gang.—That's the reason we got you, John Sanders.—Tod Caldwell has power as Governor to clean out the gang for us; but he ain't helping any. The Freedmen's Bureau is helping *them;* the Republican troops what was here has helped 'em. You admit this, don't you?

SANDERS (*weakening*). Well, yes. . . .

DONAHOE. Sanders, you've done more by yourself toward ridding the earth of this running sore than all the rest of us put together. Think, man, of the suffering you will rid this country of when your plans go through.—I'm Presbyterian, I am, an' it seems to me that the good Master sent you here to do your work. You've done it well, lad. You deserve—

SANDERS. Don't tell me that again.

DONAHOE. I know how you feel, boy. Brace up. . . . We'll be waitin' for ye.

SANDERS (*resigned*). I'll do what I can.

DONAHOE (*his hand on* SANDERS' *shoulder*). Man, I knowed all the time you was troubled by the strain. You are doing the right thing, and a great thing, for mankind.—We'll be on the bridge. I'll tell the boys that our troubles will soon be over. Guess you'll be along about three o'clock?

SANDERS. If nothing happens. . . .

DONAHOE. Well, good luck, boy; and God guide ye. (*He gives* SANDERS *a warm hand-shake, and slips out by the side door of the shack.* SANDERS *sits down by the table, deeply troubled.* LUKE LOCKLEAR, *who has been spying outside, now opens the shutter softly, and peers in. He watches* SANDERS *take up the photograph, study it intently, and place it in his bosom; then take a sheet of paper from the table, write something hurriedly on it, and leave it by the Bible. Then, with a last look about the walls of the cabin* LUKE *sees him sling a bundle over his shoulder and go out hurriedly by the side door.*

LUKE LOCKLEAR *now slips in at the rear door as stealthily as a cat. He goes swiftly to the table, takes up the written paper—but he cannot make it out. He looks puzzled, places the paper in his shirt and hurries out.*

SCENE 2

The setting is the same. It is early morning of the second day following. HENRY BERRY LOWRIE *is pacing the floor with evident excitement.*

RHODY (*grimly*). I told ye, Henry—many a time I told ye not to trust that white trash. 'Tis a wonder ye ain't cold-dead right now.

HENRY BERRY (*bitterly*). 'Tis the truth, woman, if ye ever spoke it.

RHODY. He fooled ye onct, Henry.

HENRY BERRY. Yes, but domn my hand to the bone (*holding up his hand in front of him*) if ye ever hear o' this mon a-foolin' me twice. A dead mon fools no mon.

RHODY. Ye remember of him a-preachin' to us out'n that book—and him all the time no better'n a stray dog.

HENRY BERRY. Luke and Steve'll get him. They'll get him, I tell ye. They'll run him until he's so tired it'll hurt him to close his domn eyes.—Mon, I kin see ye a-bleedin' on every bush betwixt here an' your stoppin' place— a-bleedin' and a-sweatin' drops o' blood.

RHODY (*sullenly*). I dunno trust no white mon.

HENRY BERRY. I 'tol' Steve to bring him here for me to make up my mind about what to do with him afore I turns him over to the rest of 'em for trial. They ought to be here with 'im by this. (*Outside footsteps, guttural commands, and the clanking of guns are heard.*) They're here, Rhody. (*He goes to the door.*) Woman, ye'll stand over thar (*pointing to the fireplace*) an' dunno move your tongue. (STEVE *and* LUKE *enter with* SANDERS. *He is bound and bleeding, and nearly exhausted. He reels and sinks to the floor.* STEVE *and* LUKE *kick at him viciously, and jerk him to his feet.*)

STEVE. Stand up, ye son-of-a—

HENRY BERRY (*sternly*). Mon, if ye ha'e strength in ye to breathe, ye ha'e strength enough to stand up and hear what I ha'e to tell ye. Stand up!—for Henry Berry Lowrie—afore I nails ye to that wall with hickory pegs. (SANDERS *braces himself with a frantic effort, and stands erect.*) Mon, I got ye! I got ye afore ye could git away with your lyin', dirty scheme. An' till now I ha'e not decided what to do with ye; but I ha'e some notion what it'll be.

STEVE (*casually*). Ye'll remember, Henry, how ol' mon Norment looked when Jack McLaurin blowed his jaw off'n him with them number ten buck-shot. (RHODY *and* LUKE *nod agreement, but* HENRY BERRY *continues calmly.*)

HENRY BERRY. Mon, for two year ha'e I been fooled into trustin' ye. I trusted ye with things that the others'll never know. I thought ye my friend, a-workin' to help me and the rest, when every other domn white mon was a-workin' to kill us. Mon, ye ha'e been brave, but the brave mon most times gits shot.

RHODY. I dunno lak to hear ye speak so, Henry.

HENRY BERRY. Woman, you keep quiet, I tell ye. (*To* SANDERS.) Mon, I hate to see ye there a-whimperin' and a-shiverin' like a cur-dog. Hit's your own doin' though, and I reckon ye kin stand it. What do ye mean o' this? (*He reads the note* SANDERS *had left behind him, studying his face intently as he does so.*) "Good-bye, good friends. Don't follow plans made for to-night and you will be safe from any danger." What do ye mean by that?

SANDERS (*with great effort*). For God's sake, Henry . . . let me tell you. . . .

HENRY BERRY. I tol' ye to speak, mon.

SANDERS (*breathing hard*). I . . . I . . . I came here with a plan for capturing you and the whole Lowrie gang. You know I don't belong to this part of the country . . . and I swear to you that I came all the way from Nova Scotia . . . just for the rewards. I . . . I had you in my power to-night. . . . I could have sold you to the white people of this section . . . for $50,000.00 . . . but I couldn't do it. . . . My two years here with you have made me understand your true feelings so much that on this very night I couldn't see it through . . . Before God, I swear that I'm telling you the truth—I am. . . . (*He is about to sink exhausted to the floor.*)

STEVE (*forcing him to his feet again*). Mon, ye'll stand up, if ye know what's good for ye.

SANDERS. God have mercy. . . .

HENRY BERRY. Don't call on God, mon. Little holp he will ha'e for ye now. 'Tis better you waste your cryin' on me— 'twill do ye more good than a thousand a-prayin' for your soul.

RHODY. Ye speak the truth, Henry.

HENRY BERRY (*speaking calmly and coldly*). Let me tell ye.

One day I went to my fish-box in Drowning Creek to git some fish for Rhody, and one pore little perch had his head all e't away and his fins gone—a jack-fish done it. I can see ye, mon, with your head gone and your body a-bleedin' and a-drippin' lak a stuck hog.—One day, while I was a-watchin' McNeill's dam by myself, I saw a king snake squeeze the life out'n a moccasin. He wropped himself around the other snake and he squeezed, and he squeezed till he mashed the life out'n that mocassin.—Mon, let me tell ye, I could do thot for ye with my own hands and I—(*The door is opened suddenly, and* JUNE *rushes in.*) June, you go home. You—

JUNE (*rushing to* SANDERS *she helps him into the chair*). I know ye tol' me to stay home, Uncle Henry, but I couldn't do it. I had to come. I stayed outside and listened as long as I could stand it; and I tell ye I had to come in. (*Observing* SANDERS' *weakened condition.*) Get me some water quick! (*No one responds. She gets the water herself and lifts the gourd dipper to* JOHN SANDERS' *lips.*) Doesn't that feel better? (SANDERS *can only look at her, gratefully.*)

STEVE. June, why don't you keep your domn mouth shut and go home where you belong?

JUNE (*fiercely*). I hear you, Steve; and I ain't goin'. Can't you see he's too weak to talk for himself. He tried to tell you, but ye wouldn't hear him.

RHODY (*grimly*). He's had too much of a chance already.

JUNE. I'm goin' to speak for him.—You, Steve, what's he done for you? How many times has he saved your life when you were too drunk to move? How many times has he gi'e you medicine to sober you up so you could go to Back Swamp and hide, when the deputies were hot on your trail? How many times, I ask ye?—You, too, Uncle Henry. (*Her voice changes; she speaks with a tone of respect.*) He's been a help to ye; 'cause look how many times he's advised ye about what to do. I know, Uncle Henry, that you are too wise and too brave to ever be caught, but you know what he's done for the rest of the men. (*She turns fiercely now on* LUKE, *with a sneer.*) You, Luke, where'd you be if John Sanders hadn't been here when you broke your leg over at Brown's Grist Mill. Ye'd be walkin' on a wooden peg right now! (*To* RHODY, *reproachingly.*) And you, Aunt Rhody, what did he do for you when you was down with chills and fever? Ye remember how ye tol' us all good-bye, and how ye was ready to die, and John saved you.

RHODY. I dunno trust him in spite of it.

JUNE (*pleading*). I ask all of you to think of the good things he has done for all of us. He has been a guardian angel for Scuffletown for two long years, and now you talk of killin' him.

HENRY BERRY. But I tell ye, he betrayed *me*.

JUNE. But, Uncle Henry, you know that nothing has hurt us for what he has done.

HENRY BERRY. Yes, June . . . that's the truth. But he ain't what we thought he was, and no white man can be. It's just like a great river a-tween us. Them over thar on the one side and us over here on the other. And there ain't no endin' to it but by killin'. (*Gravely.*) An' killin's don't end nothin' neither. (*A pause, then he turns quickly to* SANDERS.) Mon, I gi'e ye six hours to be out'n this territory. If ye're no out by then, and if I ever see ye or hear of ye in Scuffletown again—God help your soul!

SANDERS (*dazed*). You mean . . . I can . . . go? . . . Free? . . . Thanks. . . .

HENRY BERRY (*indicating the door*). Go, go! Don't thank me. Go, I tell ye!

JUNE (*rushing up to* SANDERS). And I'm goin' with ye.

SANDERS. No, no. . . .

JUNE. I am.

HENRY BERRY. Go! Go!

LUKE (*flashing out*). Who you goin' with?

JUNE. You know who I'm goin' with.

LUKE. You wouldn't go if ye knowed what I know. I ain't tol' ye all there is to know, yet.

JUNE. What do you mean?

LUKE (*his eyes flashing*). I mean that he's been a-lyin' and a-foolin' ye. He's been betrayin' ye all along. He tol' ye he loved ye, and he promised to marry ye, jus' so's he could stay on the good side of Uncle Henry.

JUNE (*savagely*). You're a domned liar, Luke Locklear!

LUKE. I ain't neither; I know.

JUNE. How do you know?

LUKE. He's married, and he's got two chilluns—that's how I know!—Last night I crawled up to that thar window just in time to see him a-lookin' at a picture, and a-talkin' to himself.—Wish to God I had knowed it were Donahoe I seed goin' down the path. I thought it was one of our folks.—(*Crossing over to* SANDERS, *he draws out the photograph from his shirt bosom, and hands it to* JUNE.) And here it is for ye to see for yourself! (JUNE *snatches the picture and stares at it fixedly for a moment. Her expression changes. She is puzzled, hurt, afraid. Then she goes slowly over to* SANDERS *and hands the photograph to him.*)

JUNE (*quietly*). Will ye tell them what this is? Whose picture is this? What are they to ye?

LUKE (*savagely*). It belongs to him—they're his wife and chillun. That's what they are.

JUNE (*still very calm*). Is it so? Is this your picture? Does this be your wife and chillun?

SANDERS. (*Erect. He speaks quietly and firmly.*) Yes . . . they are mine . . . my own!

JUNE *is transformed. Her eyes burn with the hate of the diamond-back when he is about to strike. Her face is set, motionless as a mask shadowing a presentiment of tragic fury.*

HENRY BERRY (*grimly*). My word stands; ye can leave, mon.

JUNE (*coldly*). Then, go! Get out of my sight, ye white trash, with your lyin', dirty heart! (*She walks slowly to the table, takes up a large knife she finds there and fondles it distractedly.*) I could cut it out o' ye, mon, just like ye cut the heart of a melon . . . but I don't want to see how filthy it is. . . . I want to kill ye so bad, it makes my heart ache. (*She hesitates a moment, then goes up behind him, and—cuts his bonds.*) Go, you white Judas! (SANDERS *staggers out. There is a pause.*)

HENRY BERRY. I dunno be sure whether I done the right thing or no.

JUNE. Uncle Henry, I pray that God Almighty'll strike him dead, afore he goes a hundred yards! (STEVE *on the instant, takes up the rifle, throws open the shutter and takes aim to shoot.* JUNE, *seeing this, fiercely springs at him and shrieks out.*) No! No!! No!!! (*But* STEVE *has pushed her aside. He takes a careful aim and fires to kill.* JUNE *stands, staring blankly.*)

CURTAIN

THE CROATAN DIALECT

In preparing the text of *The Scuffletown Outlaws* the aim of the Editor has been to preserve the natural speech as far as that is possible. The spelling of the dialect has been simplified as much as is practicable, without destroying the local characteristics of the language.

It is difficult to represent the spoken dialect in print. Below is a list of words, commonly used by the Croatans, which will be of interest to the reader and serve the actor as a guide in the pronunciation.

Man, Can, That, Damn, Land, Swamp, Stand, are pronounced
Mŏn, Cŏn, Thŏt, Dŏmn, Lŏndt, Swŏmp, Stŏnd.
Time, Strike, Right, are pronounced
Toime, Stroike, Roight.
There, Where, Here, are pronounced
Thär, Whär, Hyär.

Do not } Don't know } ....Dunno	Help (noun)...............Hōlp
	Help (verb) present..........Hĕp
Plenty.................Plain-tee	past............Hōlp
Brother.................Bruvver	Wagon..................Waggin
Mean....................Māne	Window.................Winder
Liquor..................Licker	Afraid...................Afeard
Leave....................Lāve	Between................Betwixt
Because.................Becāze	Bring.....................Fetch
Onion...................Inyun	Carry.....................Tote
Creek...................Crĭck	Sack, or Bag.........Wallet (of
("Swamp" is often used)	meal)
Woman..................ōoman	Marry ....Merry
Fire........................Fär	Argue.....................Argy
	Good.....................Goot

JOB'S KINFOLKS

A Play of the Mill People

BY

LORETTO CARROLL BAILEY

JOB'S KINFOLKS

Loretto Carroll Bailey was only twenty years of age when she wrote *Job's Kinfolks*. But she has given us in this play a searching study of a group of mill people from her own neighborhood in her home town of Winston-Salem, North Carolina. She has made use of a crisis in the lives of three generations in the Meadows family. She tells me she tried to make the incident, which forms the plot of her play, a faithful "imitation of life." The lives of these people she regards as not necessarily tragic. They do not, as a class, "hate the mill," but rather cherish it as the heart of their economic and of their social well-being. To her they are not essentially different from the rest of us. They are in search of the things we all pursue—a measure of prosperity and of happiness, which they find in the mill as we find them in other ways. They are our kin.

Job's Kinfolks seems to me a remarkable play for so young a writer. Besides writing the play, the author enacted to the life the chief character, old Kizzie—the querulous, eighty-year-old grandmother of the family. It may be interesting to note, in this connection, that not infrequently do we find that the youthful playwright plays, with uncommon ability, a part in the play he has written.

THE CHARACTERS

As originally produced at The Playmakers Theatre, Chapel Hill, North Carolina, February 10 and 11, 1928.

KIZZIE, *the grandmother,*	Loretto Carroll Bailey
KATE, *the mother,*	Noel Walker
KATHERINE, *the daughter, aged 14,*	Lois Warden
ESTELLE, *a neighbor,*	Helen Dortch
CARL ROGERS, *a mill worker,*	Moore Bryson

SCENE: The living-room of the Meadows' home in the mill section of Winston-Salem, North Carolina.

TIME: Twilight of an evening in early spring.

SCENE

It is thick dusk in the room where old KIZZIE *sits by the window and "moons." A little light, perhaps from the street lamp, outlines her softly against the darkness; her head against the chair-tidy, her body drooping against the deep curves of the rocker, her starched gray skirt billowing out around her feet, her hands spread out stiffly on her white apron. Outside, two feet from the window, which is at the rear of the room, the blank brick wall of the church next door shuts away the street and the light. From somewhere beyond the wall the strains of the first prayer-meeting hymn come faintly—"Pass me not, O Gentle Savior."* KIZZIE *is thinking way back yonder, long before she came to town. It is big-meetin' time. Morning preaching's over and folks are spreading their dinners in the spring lot. The man school-teacher makes lemonade in a wash-tub. The young folks fight over the water bucket. The spring lot is running over with young folks.* KIZZIE *sighs. Young folks don't go to church like they used to—all old'uns singin' next door. Nothin' left to the old folks but trouble.*

The light gleams on the "Rock of Ages" picture to the right of the window—a girl in a flowing white robe, clinging to a cross while a perilous green sea clutches at her. Beneath the picture, the once bright cretonnes of the day-bed seem faded and dull. Behind KIZZIE'S *chair, to the left, the pine bureau, with its sea-shells and gay little bottles, is a dim shape in the corner. The light glances from the surface of the alarm clock somewhere on it. In the center of the room (a little to the right) a round, blue-covered table stands out clearly from the shadows. Its little bunch of crêpe-paper poppies looks dried and dusty.*

A light wind stirs the curtains and the white stockings that are drying in the window. An old calendar flaps against the wall at the right. KIZZIE *nods a little. Sleep comes easier than it used to. Some one raps heavily at the hall door, to the right, and* KIZZIE *sits up with a start.*

KIZZIE. Who is it? (*The door opens, and the figure of a short, stocky, young man comes just inside the room.*)

CARL. I didn't mean to wake you, Mis' Kizzie. Just wanted to ask you if Katherine's come in yet?

KIZZIE (*evidences that she has been crying creep into her voice*). No, she ain't, Mr. Rogers, but I'm a-lookin' for her any time now. Her mother's due to be in from the mill, too. Won't you set awhile? Just turn on the light by the switch there. (CARL *does not turn on the light, but it streams in from the hall.*)

CARL. No, ma'am, I can't stay. I reckon I'll go on upstairs. When Katherine comes, ask her to call me. I'll be up there in my room, an' I want her to go with me to the show.

KIZZIE (*rising*). Better ast her to go with you to church, Mr. Rogers. It's prayer-meetin' night.

CARL (*embarrassed*). Yeah. Reckon I ort—but she wouldn't want to go. They's a Gloria Swanson picture on at the Broadway, and she's crazy about Gloria.

KIZZIE (*sighing*). No. I guess she wouldn't go if you was to ast her. We been livin' here by this church a many a year, and she and her mother has got so they don't hardly set foot in it no more.

CARL. No, ma'am. (*He hesitates.*) I reckon Katherine don't think much more of me than she does of meetin', does she?

KIZZIE. She ain't nothin' but a baby, Mr. Rogers, an' she ain't never had a daddy, nor a brother to he'p her be easy with menfolks.

CARL (*he has come well into the room by this time, and now he turns away, sullenly*). She 'pears to be easy enough with some of 'em. (KIZZIE *is silent.*) Looks like you or her mother could put in a good word for me sometimes, as much money as I've loaned you.

KIZZIE. I do, Mr. Rogers, I do, and that's the Gospel truth. She ain't plumb turned agin you.

CARL. She shore acts like it sometimes. Well, I'll be a-goin' on up to my room.

KIZZIE. All right, Mr. Rogers. I'll tell her when she comes. (*She sits down in the rocker again, her forehead resting against her hand. Once she wipes her eyes. Through the half-open door* CARL *may be heard talking with* KATE.)

CARL. Howdy, Mis' Meadows.

KATE. Hello, Carl.

CARL. I was just askin' Mis' Kizzie for a date with Katherine this evenin'.

KATE. I reckon she'll go with you all right.

CARL. Thank you, ma'am. (KATE *comes in and closes the hall door after her. She is a slender, dark-skinned woman between thirty-five and forty years old. She has been very pretty once, perhaps charming. Now she is a little worn, defeated, and defiant. She is shabbily, but not untastefully, dressed.* KATE *snaps on the light, and the old woman looks up at her and then away.* KATE *stares at her angrily, and when she speaks her voice is petulant.*)

KATE. What are you settin' here in the dark for, a-moonin'? Why don't you turn on the light?

KIZZIE. I wasn't doin' nothin' but settin' here. Every little bit he'ps save. I reckon a body can set without the lights on if she's a mind to.

KATE (*flinging her hat and coat on the couch with a quick, nervous movement*). Mamma, I wish you wouldn't act like that. It sure is hard to work all day as hard as I can tear and then come home and find you snivellin' in the dark. It sure is.

KIZZIE (*getting up*). I'm sorry I can't keep from cryin' when I'm hurt.

KATE. What's the matter with you now?

KIZZIE. Rent man come a-huntin' his money again to-day.

KATE. Well, if I ain't got it, I ain't got it. No use to get upset about that.

KIZZIE. That ain't all. That Welfare Worker woman come here again to-day to see you.

KATE (*angrily*). She did! Did you let her in? I wisht I'd a-been here to slam the door in her rotten face.

KIZZIE. Now you wouldn't a-done no such a thing, Kate, and you know you wouldn't. Of course I treated her kind and polite, and brought her in here. (*She follows* KATE *around the table, pleading with her.* KATE *examines the torn lining of her coat.*)

KATE. I'll bet you just eat her up, and told her everything you know. (*She goes into the kitchen, through the door at the left.*)

KIZZIE (*following her a little way*). Kate, you know I didn't tell her a thing. Just listen to me a minute, will you? Just a minute.

KATE (*coming back with a sewing basket, and sitting down at the table*). The low-down, dirty dog. Sneakin' around, pryin' on people's kids.

KIZZIE. Now, Kate, she meant well. I know she did. She was just as clever and common as she could be. (KATE *tosses her head.*) She come here to tell you she seen Kathern take up with a strange taxi-driver down there on Main Street, near the knittin' mill, and she was worried about her. She says she's seen her take up with several no-count men that just spoke to her 'cause she's pretty; and we got to be careful of her. And it's the truth. I've told you, an' told you so. . . .

KATE. And I guess you told her everything you could think of that Katherine's done that you don't think's right. I reckon you told her Katherine wasn't sick that last time she laid out of school.

KIZZIE (*helplessly*). Kate, you know I didn't do no such thing, I—

KATE. I know you're a fool for lettin' that woman in—that's what I know. I reckon you'll be proud and singin' hymns when you get the child put in a home, or somewheres where she'll be a little drudge, and you won't see her no more till she's eighteen.

KIZZIE. That's hard, Kate. A hard thing for you to say to your mother when she—

KATE. The old buzzard! To come around here tryin' to poke her nose in my business. She made up that tale about the taxi-driver. She come to me with one like that before, an' Katherine said there wasn't a word of truth in it. Of course the child's pretty, and men stare at her, but she's nothin' but a baby. She don't know a thing about men but what she got out of the picture shows.

KIZZIE (*has started to the kitchen, and now she sits down in a chair by the door*). It's a great pity she ain't got no daddy to keep her in order. Seems like a daddy allus has more power over a girl.

KATE. I can't help it that she's got no daddy. Want me to go out and get her one?

KIZZIE. I don't reckon I'd trust another one if I was you, after one man served you such a trick—married you, an' then run off and left you, soon as you got a young'un to take keer of. Kathern shore needs a helpin' hand from some'ers. She shore does.

KATE. She's pretty enough to get by with a lot of things, Mamma. Boys run after her like bees after a honeypot.

KIZZIE. She can't keep her mind on her books with men in her head, and shows in her head. It's shows that's a-ruinin' her. If she'd go to prayer meetin' with Carl Rogers, 'stead of to the show.

KATE. She don't seem to care for Carl Rogers, does she? He's crazy enough about her to marry her any time she'd have him. But he's kind of slow. He don't spend much showin' her a good time.

KIZZIE. He's shore put out some money for us, and I don't know what returns he thinks he's a-goin' to git for it, neither. He ain't a-tryin' to marry her, knowin' how young she is?

KATE. He thinks she's around eighteen. She told him so.

KIZZIE. Kate, she'll be fourteen, come to-morry a week. Why, when I wasn't no older than that, I wasn't a-thinkin' of nothin' but my books and my playthings.

KATE. You wasn't turned loose on these streets to play, neither—and she don't get along in her books. Where is she now?

KIZZIE. Gone, some'ers. I never know where she is, but she's allus gone. She stood there in front of that glass a full hour 'fore she left, an' primped—dobbed herself up shameful with powder and paint. I made her rub off the wust of it 'fore I let her out of the house.

KATE (*rising and going to the bureau*). Let her have her good time as long as I draw my pay. I led the cuttin' room to-day, but it sure took everything out of me. (*She picks up the alarm clock.*) Did you set the clock with the whistle? I was ten minutes late this mornin', and I got docked.

KIZZIE. I set it when I heard the whistle, same as I allus do. (*She gets up stiffly, and goes to the kitchen.*) No tellin' when Kathern'll get home.

KATE. All right, Mamma. I'll help you.

KIZZIE. You go set down and rest yourself. You're plumb wore out, and they ain't so much to do I can't do it. (*KIZZIE goes into the kitchen, and KATE sits at the table, head thrust forward; thinking, rather than resting—tapping the table nervously. The hurried click of high-heeled slippers is heard in the hall, and KATHERINE comes in. She walks straight over to the mirror, and looks at herself casually, taking off her hat, and patting her hair. Her mother watches her appraisingly. KATHERINE might be sixteen, eighteen, or what she is, nearly fourteen. She is extremely pretty; the prettiness shines through her make-up. Her brown hair is becomingly cut, and frames her piquant face charmingly. She is slender and dressed in the appropriate finery that fourteen, abetted by moving pictures and not restrained at home, would choose. Her little slippers are absurdly high-heeled. There is a hint of hardness in her face, and something of defiance lurking in the corners of her mouth. Her mother's face softens with the prettiness of her.)*

KATE. Where have you been?

KATHERINE. To the show.

KATE. Who with?

KATHERINE (*going over to her mother, gaily*). Danny. He's got his new navy uniform on.

KIZZIE (*she has heard them and now she comes in, brandishing a large spoon*). Pretty time of night for you to be comin' in here. You ought to be in before dark, without me or your mother's with you.

KATHERINE. Got anything for supper?

KIZZIE. Got a plenty for them that's not so partic'ler about their eatin's.

KATHERINE. Got any more chocolate cake? (*She starts toward the kitchen, and* KIZZIE *snatches at her arm.*)

KIZZIE. Don't you go in there to that cake again. I'm savin' that for your mother's lunch. (KATHERINE *goes into the kitchen.*) Kate, make her leave that cake alone. She's e't nearly all of it now, an' she won't eat a mouthful of victuals when there's cake in the house.

KATE. Let her have it. I don't want it. Do let the child get enough to eat, Mamma.

KIZZIE. Well, it ain't right for her to act like that, and you know it. (KATHERINE *comes back eating a large, uneven hunk of cake. She makes a little face at* KIZZIE.) Look-a-there at her. She's got the last bit of it. Don't think of nobody but herself. (KATHERINE *laughs and sits down on the edge of the table by her mother.*)

KATHERINE. Mamma, let's me and you go to see Gloria Swanson to-night.

KIZZIE. Kate, it's prayer-meetin' night.

KATE. Oh, Mamma, hush up about prayer-meetin'. You're welcome to go if you want to, but they ain't none of them over there'd stir a step to help you if you fell in your tracks. (KATHERINE *laughs*.)

KIZZIE. You're a-goin' to suck sorrow one of these days, Kate, for talkin' like that. Mark my words if you don't. (*She goes sorrowfully back to the kitchen*.)

KATHERINE. Gran'ma don't know what's what, does she?

KATE. I guess she knows more about raisin' you than I do. (KATHERINE *shakes her head gaily*.) Katherine, have you been takin' up with strange men again?

KATHERINE. No-o-o. . . .

KATE. Yes, you have. That police-woman was around here this evenin', talkin' to your gran'ma, and it's no tellin' what Gran'ma told her.

KATHERINE. She didn't tell her I laid out of school and wasn't sick, did she?

KATE. I don't know. She says she didn't. You had no business to do it, anyway. I'll bet you've done that little thing just one time too many, young lady. I'll bet your goose is cooked this time.

KATHERINE. You can get me out, can't you? You can go to court, like you did before, and swear.

KATE (*wearily*). I got you out twice, but if they get a warrant out for you again, you're done for. I can't do no more for you.

KATHERINE. What'll they do to me, Mamma? I didn't want to go to school. They can't do nothin' just for that.

KATE. They've got the law with them, and they're a dirty bunch. They're gettin' paid for every child they can take away from its mother and put in a home.

KIZZIE (*from the doorway*). That ain't so, Kate. Them Welfare folks is just a-doin' their duty as they see it.

KATE (*savagely*). Why don't you go and join them. You're so crazy about 'em—want to give your own flesh and blood to 'em.

KIZZIE. Now you know, Kate, they ain't a word of that so— ain't a word of it so. (*She goes back into the kitchen.*)

KATE (*quietly, to* KATHERINE). Why don't you be nice to Carl Rogers? You know I borrowed money from him, and he'll give you anything you want. He'd marry you any time you'd have him.

KATHERINE. Aw, I don't like him so much. He's so old. I wouldn't have him. (*Laughing, and kicking her little heels joyously against the table legs.*) I'm gonna marry a good-lookin' millionaire, and have fifteen pairs of shoes and two automobiles, and oodles of money! (*Her mother smiles.*)

KIZZIE (*coming out of the kitchen, and bearing down on the two accusingly*). Just listen to that child, Kate. She's a-goin' to the dogs as fast as she can. Pore child. I shore do pity her. (KATHERINE *laughs.*) If I was you, I would make her treat Carl Rogers decent, if I was a-goin' to keep on borrowin' from him.

KATE. It's so, Katherine. You better had treat him good. I've got to get more out of him to pay some of these pressin' debts, or we'll lose what little we got.

KATHERINE. I can't stand the way he looks at me, and he's always wantin' to put his hands on me, or kiss me, or something. I'm scared of him.

KATE. That's silly, Katherine. He don't mean no harm. But don't let him kiss you—I don't want him to get to thinkin' he's goin' to have you.

KATHERINE. Nobody is gonna have me, lessen I say so.

KIZZIE (*she has been listening attentively*). Just be good and kind to him, and laugh him out of it if he talks too serious. You ain't old enough for that.

KATHERINE. I am, too. But I wouldn't talk about it to him. (*She has finished the cake and now brushes the crumbs from her skirt to the floor.*)

KIZZIE. Kate, do make her stop a-droppin' them crumbs on the floor for me to pick up. She'll not stir a hand to touch 'em.

KATE (*rising*). Come on to supper, Katherine.

KATHERINE (*jumping down from the table, where she has been sitting*). Don't want none.

KIZZIE (*shaking the dish-cloth at* KATE). Looky here. I told you she'd not eat a bite of victuals if she got filled up with cake.

KATE (*going on to the kitchen*). Oh, Mamma, I wish you'd keep that dish-rag out of my face. (KATHERINE *parades up and down the floor before her grandmother, examining her trim, black slippers with pardonable pride.* KIZZIE *finds a new grievance.*)

KIZZIE. Kate, she's got another pair of fine slippers on.

KATHERINE. Hush, up, Gran'ma.

KIZZIE. Where'd you get 'em, and how'd you get 'em?

KATHERINE. I charged 'em at Meyers'.

KIZZIE. Did you hear that, Kate? She charged 'em. As big a bill as we owe there. (*To* KATHERINE.) It's a wonder they let you have 'em. (*There is a knock at the door, and* KATE *silences* KIZZIE *hurriedly.*)

KATE. Hush, Mamma! That's Carl Rogers. Come on in here. (*She disappears in the kitchen, and* KIZZIE *pauses for a final admonition, delivered in a half-whisper.*)

KIZZIE. Now mind what your mamma told you, an' treat Carl Rogers decent. (*She goes out slowly.* CARL ROGERS *knocks again, and* KATHERINE *tosses her head scornfully. She makes him wait while she preens herself before the mirror—dabs her hair and eyebrows and the tips of her ears with perfume, darkens her eyebrows a little, and touches her lips with red. He knocks a third time, and she calls ungracious permission for him to enter.*)

KATHERINE. Come in. (CARL *enters, and stands looking at her admiringly. He is low, and stockily built, with oily hair, and a thick neck that reddens easily. His hands are blunt and roughened by manual labor. His trousers bag a little, and his tie has a large, bright, imitation stick-pin. Altogether he is not a figure to win the admiration, or affection, of a stage-struck child.* KATHERINE'S *mouth tightens with exasperation, and she turns back to the mirror and pats her hair self-consciously.*)

CARL. Your mamma here?

KATHERINE. Yeah. She's eatin' supper. Come on in. Don't stand there holdin' the door open. (*She enjoys his embarrassment, and purposely delays calling her mother for a moment.*) Mamma, Mr. Rogers wants you. (*A chair scrapes the floor in the kitchen and* KATE *comes in.*)

KATE (*cordially*). Come have some supper, won't you?

CARL. I just come to tell you Mis' Bloom says you're wanted on the 'phone.

KATE. All right, thank you. Sit down. (*She goes out.*)

CARL. Thank you. (*He closes the door and goes nearer* KATHERINE, *swaggering a little—trying to be easy with her.*) Swell brand of perfume you're sportin'.

KATHERINE (*holding the little blue atomizer under his nose*). Just smell. Danny gave it to me. It costs about five dollars a thimbleful—but Danny don't care how he spends his money.

CARL. A man don't mind spendin' money on a girl that cares somethin' about him, but nobody wants to waste their money on a girl that gives him the go-by.

KATHERINE. I ain't give you the go-by.

CARL. You broke your last two dates with me. How 'bout Tuesday?

KATHERINE. I forgot I promised Danny.

CARL. How about last night, then?

KATHERINE (*flouncing into the chair by the kitchen*). I was out ridin' and the car broke down. I couldn't help it if the old car broke.

CARL. To hear you tell it, it ain't never your fault you don't want to have a date with me. Your mamma said you'd give me a date to-night.

KATHERINE. My mamma don't fix my dates for me.

CARL. All right. Maybe she don't. I'm not askin' her, now, I'm askin' you. Will you go with me to a show to-night?

KATHERINE. I might got a date with Danny. I don't know.

CARL. I reckon he asked you for it last week, didn't he?

KATHERINE. I don't see it's any of your business.

CARL (*his neck reddens, then his face*). Looky here. You didn't give me no reason to think it wasn't my business. I may be crazy about you, but I don't want no girl that's got half-a-dozen fellers closter to her than I am.

KATHERINE. I reckon you think it makes no matter how many girls you hang out with—no-count girls.

CARL. That ain't got nothin' to do with you and me.

KATHERINE (*stamping her foot at him*). Don't make so much noise or Gran'ma'll hear you, and I don't want her messin' around.

CARL. (*He puts his foot on a chair, takes out a cigarette lighter, and lights a cigarette with heavy nonchalance.* KATHERINE *watches him out of the corner of her eye.*) You know I'm crazy about you, don't you?

KATHERINE. Just so you keep your hands off me. (*Changing the subject.*) That's a cute trick.

CARL. I give it to myself for a present to-day. My bank balance was gettin' kind of heavy.

KATHERINE. Ain't you somethin'. Here, let me see it. (*She goes over to take the lighter from his hand. He holds it out to her, and, at the same time, slyly burns the back of her hand with his cigarette tip.* KATHERINE *lets the lighter fall to the floor with a clatter.*) Oh-h-h! (*Nursing her hand.*) You old fool! (CARL *laughs, and she holds out her burned hand to him indignantly.*) Look-a-there what you done!

CARL. Don't mind a little thing like that. I was just playin'. (*He snatches her hand and tries to kiss it.*) Let me make it well.

KATHERINE. Turn me a-loose.

CARL (*twisting her arm and bringing her face close to his*). Give me a kiss.

KATHERINE. Ouch! Take your old face away or I'll call Gran'ma. (KIZZIE *opens the kitchen door.* KATE'S *footsteps are heard in the hall.*) Here comes mamma anyway. (KATE *opens the door and comes quickly across to her mother. There is something savage and unreasoning in her eyes; the others sense it, and look at her curiously.*)

KATE. Mamma, they got a warrant out for Katherine, an' they're gonna have her up in court to-morrow.

KIZZIE. I knowed it. I knowed it would come to this, with her a-layin' out of school, and cuttin' up like she's done.

KATE. She's gone, Mamma—she's just as good as gone! They've got her away from me like they said they would.

KIZZIE. Ain't there nothin' you can do about it, Kate?

KATHERINE (*she has been watching her mother anxiously*). Mamma, you're goin' to swear for me again, ain't you? They can't get me, can they? I'll run away. (*She tugs at her mother's arm.* KATE *sits down by the table and leans on it heavily.* CARL *looks helplessly embarrassed.*)

KATE. They got you this time, Katherine, sure.

CARL. If they's any way I can help you . . .

KIZZIE. Pore child. I knowed she was a-layin' up misery for herself.

KATE (*fiercely*). That woman thinks she's got me beat, damn her time! She's gettin' paid for takin' Katherine, and she's after all the money she can get. All them Welfarers are in league with the gover'ment, gettin' our children when they can steal a march on us—catchin' a hold on us when we get hard up for help, so's they can strangle us.

KIZZIE. Be careful what you're a-sayin', Kate. You don't know who's a-listenin' to you, nor what'll be done with you for talkin' like that.

KATHERINE. Mamma, take me away somewheres. Don't let them take me to no old home. You can swear for me.

KATE. No, I'll not let 'em have you. I'll fool that old dog. (*Her expression grows cunning. She goes over to the bureau and searches in one of the drawers. The others watch her in amazement.*) Carl, let's you and me and Katherine go to the movies.

KIZZIE. Shorely you're not a-goin' to the shows with such a pack o' trouble on us. Ain't you gonna try to help her at all, Kate?—What are you rummagin' my things for? Leave 'em alone.

KATE. What you say, Carl? Katherine?

CARL. I'm willin', Mis' Meadows, if she is.

KATHERINE. Will they get me, Mamma? You gonna fix it up by swearin'?

KATE (*her voice is hard*). Yes, I'll fix it up. Let's go. (*She turns around suddenly, changing her plans.*) You-all stay here a minute. I got business to 'tend to first. I'll go over to Mis' Bloom's and 'phone; you and Carl stay here and come to meet me in a few minutes.

KATHERINE. Why can't we come on as you do?

KATE (*evasively*). This business can't be 'tended to with nobody listenin'.

KATHERINE. We won't tell.

KIZZIE. What you gonna do, Kate?

KATE. Come on over to Mis' Bloom's in a few minutes. (*She goes to the door, and KIZZIE follows her.*)

KIZZIE. You didn't eat enough supper to keep your legs a-movin', Kate.

KATE. I got enough, Mamma. So long. We'll not be late gettin' back. Estelle will come in an' set with you. (*The door closes after her.* KIZZIE *drops the dish-cloth wearily on the table and looks from one to the other of the two left behind.*)

KIZZIE. I shore wouldn't be at no shows to-night. I shore wouldn't.

KATHERINE. You wouldn't never be at one.

KIZZIE. Well, I ain't a-sufferin' for the lack of them.

CARL. They ain't no real harm in 'em, Mis' Kizzie.

KATHERINE (*jumping up impatiently from her grandmother's rocker*). Come on, let's go find mamma. I want to know what she's up to. (*She goes out, and* CARL *follows.*)

KIZZIE. You better not go. You ain't waited as long as she told you.

KATHERINE. I don't care. (*The door closes after them.*)

KIZZIE. I shore wouldn't be at no shows this evenin'. I shore wouldn't. (*She stoops and picks up the crumbs of cake, and hides them behind the broom in the corner. The second prayer-meeting hymn can be heard distinctly, "Jesus loves me, this I know; For the Bible tells me so—"* KIZZIE *listens a moment to the music. The energy that kept her stirring while her folks were there to be "done for" is gone out of her, and she is again the drooping old woman who sat crying by the window. She gets a large, limp-backed Bible from the table and sits down in her rocker at the window. She reads slowly, spelling the words out to herself, with her finger. Presently the hall door opens, and a comely young woman puts her head in.*)

ESTELLE. Mis' Kizzie?

KIZZIE. Come in, Estelle.

ESTELLE. (ESTELLE *comes in and closes the door softly. She is a large, amiable young woman; red-haired, blue-eyed, dimpled. She is carelessly dressed in a blue gingham wrapper, shapeless bedroom slippers, and stockings with holes. Her hair seems always on the verge of coming down and she is continually taking out hairpins and putting them back with the hope of keeping it up.*) I just nussed the young-un and got him to sleep, if only them prayer-meetin' folks don't wake him. I thought I'd come and set with you awhile and hear the singin'. Your folks is all gone.

KIZZIE. Set down, Estelle.

ESTELLE. Whereabouts was you readin', Mis' Kizzie? Let me read to you awhile; I like to. (*She takes the Bible and sits by the table.*)

KIZZIE. I don't care if you do. Seems like I can understand better through my ears than I can through my eyes.

ESTELLE. Job. I never was so fond of Job myself—too down in the mouth.

KIZZIE. Me an' Job is kinfolks. You knowed I was named for his daughter, didn't you?

ESTELLE. I don't remember hearin' you say, 'cept your name was Keziah. I wouldn't claim kin with Job, Mis' Kizzie.

KIZZIE. Ma used to tell me time and again how she come to call me. Her an' Pa'd had a heap o' trouble—Pa'd been off to the wars—but they thought their troubles was over when I come along. So Ma picked out the likeliest one of Job's daughters that he had after his troubles was over to call me by. She thought she put a good-luck name on me, but Aunt Peeney told her she'd not.

ESTELLE. Lord, Mis' Kizzie, a name don't mean nothin' but somethin' to handle you by.

KIZZIE. Aunt Peeney, one of Ma's niggers, told her it was a bad-luck name. Why, one time, when I wasn't nothin' but a little feller, layin' in my cradle by the kitchen stove, Ma was settin' by me, and Aunt Peeney was fixin' me a sugar-tit, Ma just happened to say that name hadn't proved nothin' but good luck to me yet, when all to onct I reached up and pulled off a hot lamp chimney down on

my face, and burnt me half to death. They never thought
I'd live. Aunt Peeney used to tell me of it when I 'us a
little-un. (*She almost weeps, remembering, pitying herself.*)

ESTELLE. But, Lord, Mis' Kizzie, that don't make you like
Job. You been a lucky woman.

KIZZIE. Whenever I had good luck, bad luck followed it.—
First my man was took from me, and then my home place,
and I reckon I'll end my days in a stranger's house.

ESTELLE. You got friends around you, Mis' Kizzie.

KIZZIE. And look how trouble's come to Kate. She works
so hard and she can't seem to get nowhere. She's the
kind that needed a man, an' she got a worthless man that
was no good to her. (*She feels of the stockings and takes
them down from the window.*) Now Kathern's on the road
to ruin. Seems like the Lord's turned his face from us,
and his light don't shine on us no more.

ESTELLE. Look-a-here, Mis' Kizzie, don't you worry 'bout
Katherine. You're a-gettin' too old to be bothered like
you are. It ain't right. It'll put you in your grave if you
keep at it. (*She eats a little of the cake icing that* KATHERINE
left on the table.)

KIZZIE. I can't help it. Seems like I can't stop. Poor little
Kathern. I pity her so.

ESTELLE. Kate hadn't ought to fight them Welfare folks so
hard.

KIZZIE. I've told her and told her so. (*She puts the stockings
in the bureau drawer and goes back to her chair.*)

ESTELLE. It's dangerous to meddle with the law, much less
to fight it. Course I don't mean Mis' Kate should get
down on her knees and eat 'em up. They's more ways to
kill a dog than choke him with butter.

KIZZIE. I'm so 'feared of what'll happen to Kathern. (*From
the church next door a third hymn is started. It comes to the
two women softened a bit by distance, and they pause to
listen.*)

> *"I was sinking deep in sin,*
> *Far from the peaceful shore,*
> *Very deeply stained within,*
> *Sinking to rise no more.*
> *But the master of the sea,*
> *Heard my despairing cry,*
> *From the waters lifted me,*
> *Now safe am I.*
>
> *"Love lifted me; love lifted me.*
> *When nothing else could help,*
> *Love lifted me.*
> *Love lifted me; love lifted me.*
> *When nothing else could help,*
> *Love lifted me."*

(KIZZIE *turns from the window and her face lights up.*) I do love pretty singin'; I'd rather listen to it than eat when I'm hungry. Seems like a pity to set outside the door listenin'. I reckon a body ought not to let trouble keep 'em from meetin'. It grieves me to think Kate and Kathern's at the show. They can't look for the Good Man to help 'em if they don't set foot in His house.

ESTELLE. Does look like we ought to go, bein' this close, don't it? Sometimes, I wisht we wasn't so close. Seems like this bricked-up wall shuts out the light and air and makes it so dark.

KIZZIE. These church folks ain't so clever and common, somehow, as the folks at Friedburg church was. They're kind o' stand-offish and proud. Don't come a-nigh a body in trouble.

ESTELLE. Lord, I wouldn't want 'em around me. When somethin's wrong with me I want to go off in a hole or a corner, and lick myself, like a dog. I don't want nobody a-pesterin' me.

KIZZIE. You can do that when you're young and strong, Estelle, with your life before you. But when you've knowed what it is to have somethin', and seen it took away from you, and when you get old like I am, you've got to have folks to cling to.

ESTELLE. I reckon so, Mis' Kizzie. (*She blows the dust from the artificial flowers on the table.*)

KIZZIE. I don't know what's to become of us, Estelle. That rent man come here again to-day, an' talked to me so hard I felt like crawlin' off some'ers and hidin'.

ESTELLE. Some folks will never believe you can't get blood out of a turnip till they've had a squeeze at it. (*Several people can be heard coming down the hall, and both women lift their heads to listen.*) Reckon who could that be?

KIZZIE (*rising*). If it's more trouble, I can't stand it, that's all. (*The door opens and* KATE, *followed by* KATHERINE *and* CARL, *comes in.* ESTELLE *gets up and goes to the door. There is an unnatural excitement in* KATE'S *movements and in her face. She has an air of recklessness.* KATHER-INE'S *color is heightened, and she looks at her mother expectantly.* CARL *is as close to* KATHERINE *as he can get.*) You must not have been to the show. You got back so soon.

KATE (*throwing her hat on the bed*). No, we didn't.

ESTELLE. I'll be runnin' along, Mis' Kizzie. You don't need me no more. Did you hear any young-un noises in my bedroom as you passed, Mis' Kate?

KATE. No, I didn't. Thank you for staying with mamma.

ESTELLE (*going out*). You're shore welcome. Mis' Kizzie an' me had a good time listenin' to the singin'.

KIZZIE (*looking from one to the other, suspiciously*). What you been up to, Kate?

KATE. Show your Grandma, Katherine. (KATHERINE *holds up her left hand, which has an old-fashioned wedding ring on the ring finger.* KIZZIE *grabs her hand excitedly.*)

KIZZIE. What's she a-doin' with my weddin' ring? It's mine, ain't it?

KATE. The same thing you done with it. I had to borrow yours, for there wasn't no time for Carl to get her one, and your finger and hers is nearly of a size. Mine wouldn't fit her, an' besides it's got bad luck on it.

KIZZIE. Kate, what have you done?

KATE. I got the best of that woman. She'll not put Katherine in her old reformatory. I've give her to Carl, and he's promised me to take care of her.

KATHERINE. She swore I was eighteen, Grandma.

CARL (*importantly*). We got it fixed up, Mis' Kizzie. They can't put her nowhere as long as she's my wife. (KATHERINE *looks at him timidly*.)

KIZZIE. I knowed it. I knowed she'd be ruint. But for her own folks to ruin her! Better have let her gone where they wanted to put her.

KATE. Mamma!

CARL. You look here. I done you a favor by takin' her like this, even if I did want her, and don't you forget it, neither. (*He turns to* KATHERINE.) Come on, let's go.

KATHERINE (*startled*). I ain't goin' nowhere, am I, Mamma? (KATE *says nothing*.)

CARL. You ain't? (*He turns to* KATE.) So this was just a frame-up on me, was it? I marry her, but I don't get her.

KATE. I didn't say she wouldn't go with you. Try being kind to her.

CARL. Look-a-here, I didn't take no spoiled young-un on my hands. (*To* KATHERINE.) If you ain't enough of a woman, you better act like it, anyhow. (*To* KATE.) I ain't gonna wheedle her along nor baby her none, I can tell you that. Come on.

KATHERINE (*her lips are trembling*). Mamma, don't make me go with him. I'm scared of him. (KIZZIE *looks at* KATE, *whose face has lost its triumph*.)

CARL (*snarling at* KATE, *then at* KIZZIE). You've turned her agin me on purpose, but it'll do you no good. You give her to me when you swore she was eighteen—made her mine, see? If you'd had sense enough to see which side your bread was buttered on you'd have behaved better toward me. (*He takes* KATHERINE'S *hand.*) Come on upstairs with me.

KATE (*her arm around* KATHERINE). Go on with him, Katherine. They ain't nothin' to be afraid of, and you're a married woman now.

KATHERINE (*pausing in the door*). Mamma, don't make me go.

KATE. Go on, Katherine. (*She closes the door after* KATHERINE; *but she has no sooner closed it than* KATHERINE *bursts it open and rushes into her arms.*)

KATHERINE. Mamma, I can't stay with him. You don't know how he is. Honest you don't, Mamma.

KATE. Go on, Katherine. Don't be a baby. He'll be good to you, if you don't cross him now. But it's no tellin' how he'll treat you if you don't do as he says. (*She takes her gently, firmly to the door.*)

KATHERINE. You can't make me go. Nobody can. (*Half sobbing.*) I can do what I please, I guess. I'll run away before I will.

KATE. Katherine!

KATHERINE. Mamma, you take me away somewheres.

KATE. Katherine, who were you running from when you took Carl so quick? You want the law to get you? Had you rather that woman had put you somewhere away from us all than to go upstairs with Carl and stay close to us in the same house? (KATE *speaks to* KATHERINE *as if she were a very small child, afraid of the dark.*)

KATHERINE. No-o-o-o. . . .

KATE. Go on, then. Go on to him, or that woman's waitin' to get you. (*She pushes the girl gently out and shuts the door. She leans limply against it.*)

KIZZIE (*going over to her chair again*). She's gone to him. An' she's got my ring on, too. But she'll never know what I knowed with it. I can see it plain as if 'twas yestiddy— Henry carryin' me over the door sill the night we was married. I was so proud and happy when the door shut on us. (*Somewhere upstairs a door slams faintly. It may not be a door that has anything to do with* KATHERINE, *but it breaks* KATE's *control. She goes to the table, feverishly.*)

KATE (*half whispering*). Did you hear that door slam? On Katherine? I did it. (*She comes to her mother, helplessly.*) I slammed it on my baby. She was all I had. Mamma! (*With her head on her mother's lap she cries, softly.* KIZZIE *pats her shoulder and her hair, with little awkward, comforting movements.*)

KIZZIE. The Lord'll help her, Kate. He don't hold no grudge against nobody. (*She looks out the window.*) Church is dark. I reckon prayer-meetin's out. . . . Don't take on so, Kate. You won't be fit for your work to-morrow. Things goes on. Trouble don't stop nothin'. . . .

CURTAIN

IN DIXON'S KITCHEN

A Comedy of a Country Courtship

BY

WILBUR STOUT

(Written in collaboration with Ellen Lay)

IN DIXON'S KITCHEN

Perhaps the comedy of a country courtship, *In Dixon's Kitchen*, by Wilbur Stout—written by him in the University course in playwriting, English 31, with the assistance of Ellen Lay, another member of the course, will illustrate the friendly spirit of collaboration in our playwriting. This course is conducted informally, the Instructor and the students seated about a long table. The spirit of the group is communal. There is no text-book of dramatic technique to inhibit the young writer's impulse. The approach is frankly empirical. The students come to the meetings of the course with vague ideas of plays-in-the-making. There is much lively discussion, and the unsuspecting novice is often surprised by the reactions of the different members of the group. But no matter how astounding the criticism may be, it is always honest and does present the viewpoint of a potential audience. It challenges the young author, and gives him a new perspective in his work. In this way his conception is tested and enriched by the varying viewpoints of his fellows. Perhaps the following lines, written by one of our young Playmakers in the early days in Dakota, will suggest our method of approach:

> If you can see the world with me
> And I can see the world with you,
> I'm sure that both of us will see
> Things that neither of us do.

In Dixon's Kitchen was Wilbur Stout's first play. The author came from the little town of Burlington, in the Piedmont Section of North Carolina—a prosperous farming community. I remember when he first announced his idea for the play:

"I know about a country boy's courtship which ought to make a play. The old man used to stamp on the floor of his bedroom upstairs as a signal for the boy to go home. One night the boy—we'll call him 'Lem'—conceived the idea of pretending to leave. He called out to the girl a loud 'Good-by,' and banged the outside door. Then after a little he slipped in through the window in his stocking feet to finish saying 'Goodnight.' But the father came in and discovered his trick."

"That's a good one," some one laughs. "But how did the father happen to come in?"

And another pipes up, "I think you ought to make use of the little brother who is always butting in on the courtship."

"That's good," from the prospective playwright. "The girl had two brothers and I can work them both in for some good laughs."

Then a rival suitor is added to complicate the action, and a few days later, when the embryo play comes back to be read to the group, it has the elements of a real plot.

A spirited discussion ensues. "The ending is weak."— "Why not have one of the brothers steal Lem's shoes, so he can't get away?"

"That's bully! I'll do it."

And—with the assistance of Ellen Lay, one of the co-eds in the course, in phrasing the speeches of the girl (which Wilbur declared he could not possibly write down), with much re-shaping of the plot, revising of the characters, recasting of the dialogue, the comedy *In Dixon's Kitchen* finally emerged. Of course it was rewritten again and again before it was ready, at last, for a tryout on the Playmakers' stage. And it underwent still further changes in the lines and in the stage business in the process of rehearsal, before it was finally ready for production.

So the play was really a composite product of all the members of the group, with the experience of the Instructor to guide the instinct of the young playwright in the complex process of building a play.

Wilbur Stout has given us here an authentic comedy of

the country folk of his own neighborhood. Much of the conversation, he tells us, was set down verbatim. The incident, which we suspect—although he has never admitted it—was drawn from his own experience, was somewhat modified for dramatic purposes. And the play is dedicated by the author "to the real Annie Lee, and to all others who have been courting in the country and have contended with the perplexing problem of the Little Brother."

Since leaving the University of North Carolina, Wilbur Stout—now a Ph.D.—has become a "professor" of playwriting in a West Virginia college and his students last year wrote and produced a bill of their own *West Virginia Folk-Plays*.

I cannot refrain from quoting here from a letter Wilbur wrote recently, reminding me of certain offstage rôles he was conscripted to play during his student days at Chapel Hill: "When Shakespeare listed the parts we play in life, he must have forgotten those who speak only in back-stage noises. Neglecting such matters as killing Henry Berry Lowrie [in Paul Green's *The Last of the Lowries*] with G.D. Crawford's army '.45,' my speaking parts have included a jack-ass [Old Bob in the original production of his own play *In Dixon's Kitchen*], a swamp-owl [which hooted in Paul Green's play of the *Lowries*], and a rooster [in Pearl Setzer's comedy *The Black Rooster*]. This fall I narrowly missed having to be a cuckoo. Thank heaven I escaped that!" He is too modest to remind me of the important speaking parts he played here on our Carolina stage—particularly the diverting drollery of his admirable characterization of the big brother Jake in *Dogwood Bushes*,[1] his own charming comedy of a country boy, Bert Perry, who spent his days in writing poetry and in dreaming of going to the big city "to learn to write books."

[1] *Carolina Folk Comedies*, Samuel French, N. Y., 1931.

THE CHARACTERS

As originally produced on The Playmakers' Stage, Chapel Hill, North Carolina, April 29 and 30, 1921.

HIRAM DIXON, *a dour old farmer*,   Le Grand Everett, Jr.

MA DIXON, *his wife*,   Ellen Lay

ANNIE LEE DIXON, *their daughter*,   Mary Yellott

GIL   ⎫
JACK ⎬ *their sons, aged 16 and 12*,   ⎰ Thornton Gholson
    ⎭   ⎱ George Winston

LEMUEL ISLEY, *Annie's "special" friend*,   Lloyd Williams

SCENE: A country district in the Piedmont section of North Carolina. The Dixons' kitchen.

TIME: The present. An evening in June.

270

THE SCENE

*The kitchen of the Dixons' home is a very neat, clean room,
supplied with the furniture ordinarily found in a comfortable
farmhouse. At the rear, left, is a long table set with an abundant
country supper. A kitchen safe is at the right, and a small
cook-table. At the left, front, is the stove, with the usual pots
and pans, a woodbox, and a blue stone jar of cream covered with
a white cloth. At the rear, right, is a window hung with a sash
curtain; the waterbucket is in this corner. A door, at the center,
opens on the side porch, and one at the left leads to the other
part of the house. The unpainted walls of the room are of
yellowish-brown color, presenting a rather attractive appearance
in the glow of the shaded lamp.*

The DIXONS *are sitting at the supper table, all eating heartily.*
LEM ISLEY, *who is "company," sits next to* ANNIE LEE *at the
rear of the table.* MA *is on the right side, with* JACK *close beside
her;* GIL *is opposite her and* PA *is seated with his back to the
audience.*

LEM *is dressed up for the occasion in his Sunday
blue-serge suit, new flowered necktie, and tan oxfords. The
members of the* DIXON *family, with the exception of* ANNIE
LEE, *are in their everyday work-clothes. (*ANNIE LEE *does
not usually wear a pretty white dress when cooking supper,
but to-night she wishes to appear at her best; and* MA *wears a
small white sewing apron over her faded gingham dress.)* JACK
*wears overalls and has already started going barefoot, although
the weather is still a little cool for that. There is hearty laughter
from all the family when the curtain rises.* JACK *has crammed
more chicken into his mouth than he can properly manage,
and* MA DIXON *gives him a reproving yank by the ear, which
calls forth a loud guffaw from* GIL. LEM *cannot refrain from
laughing heartily too. But* MA, *unperturbed, turns sweetly to*
ANNIE LEE'S *"company."*

271

MA. Have another piece of chicken, Lem. You're not eatin' any supper at all.

LEM. Thank you, ma'am. I believe I will. (*By this time* PA *has finished eating and settles himself in a chair by the stove, where he puffs away comfortably at his pipe.*)

GIL. Pass it down this way when you get through with it, Lem. The rest of 'em has quit; I reckon it's up to us to clean out the dish.

ANNIE LEE. You oughtn't to eat so much supper, Gil, if you're going to the candy pullin' over at Carrie's to-night.

GIL. I was about to forget that. (*He eats with renewed energy.*) Annie Lee, it's too much trouble to move that dish. Pitch me one of them cowcumber pickles over here by the tail.

ANNIE LEE. Why, Gil! I never heard such talk! (*She is somewhat embarrassed, but forces a laugh and tosses a pickle across the table to him.* JACK *giggles.*)

GIL. That's the stuff! (*He pushes back his chair, takes the pickle in one hand, reaches with the other halfway across the table for a piece of chocolate layer-cake, crosses to the cook-table and cuts a generous slice from a gooseberry pie which* MA *has left there to cool.*) I'm in a rush! You-all can set and eat as long as you want to; I got somethin' better'n eatin' comin' to me. (*He hurries off to dress up for the party.*)

ANNIE LEE (*with mock formality*). We will excuse you, Gilmer.

GIL (*at the door; with exaggerated politeness*). Thank you, ma'am.

ANNIE LEE. Have another biscuit, Lem. Don't stop eatin' just 'cause Gil did.

LEM (*glancing at his plate and helping himself*). Thank you, Annie Lee.—Did you eat my biscuit, Jack? If you didn't, I'm afraid this makes about six for me.

JACK. Six? Is that the best you can count? You've done e't ten!

LEM (*glancing at* ANNIE LEE). Well, maybe I have, Jack, if you kept count. It's mighty good bread all right.

MA (*smiling*). Yes, Annie Lee is gettin' so she makes right good biscuit.

LEM. Did Annie Lee make these biscuits?

MA. Yes. I had some sewin' to do to-day, so I let Annie Lee do most all the cookin'.

LEM. No wonder I e't so many of 'em. That accounts for me likin' 'em so well.

JACK. You didn't cook enough, Annie Lee. He's hungry yet.

GIL (*from the other room*). What you-all done with my necktie?

MA (*raising her voice*). It's on the foot of your pa's bed, Gil. I pressed it out for you this evenin' when I had the iron on the fire.

JACK. I got a necktie.

LEM. You have?

JACK. Uh-huh. (*Rummaging in his overalls pocket, he produces a bright red one.*) Ed give it to me.

LEM. Who's Ed?

JACK. Ed? Ed Nicholson. He's got red hair and he comes out from town to see Annie Lee sometimes. (ANNIE LEE *knowing* JACK's *propensity for making disconcerting remarks, glances anxiously at* MA.)

LEM (*worried*). Oh, I see. . . . Does he come often?

JACK. Ed was out here the other day in an automobile. Wa'n't he, Pa?

PA. Uh-huh.

JACK. And Annie Lee said she'd rather ride with—(MA *silences* JACK *by putting her hand over his mouth.*)

ANNIE LEE (*flurried*). Do you know Mr. Nicholson, Lem?

LEM (*coldly*). Just know him when I see him. (*There is an awkward pause. Then he pushes back his plate.*) Well, I ain't e't so much supper since old man Simpson's corn-shuckin'. I knowed you was a mighty fine cook, Annie Lee, but I didn't know you could cook like this.

ANNIE LEE (*blushing at* LEM'S *admiring glance*). Oh, I like to cook.

MA (*as they rise from the table*). You-all go in the other room now. I'll wash up the dishes this time.

ANNIE LEE. You better try to get that dress finished, Ma. Lem and me will wash the dishes, if he don't mind.

LEM. I don't mind a bit. I'd like to help you. (MA *takes down the dishpan and pours out the water from the kettle on the stove.* LEM *and* ANNIE LEE *clear the table.*)

MA (*pointedly to* PA, *who is still sitting by the stove, smoking contentedly, absorbed in his own thoughts*). The paper come to-day. It's in yonder on the bed. Don't you want to read it?

PA (*fumbling for his glasses*). Bring me that thar paper, Jack. I'll read a little 'fore I go to bed. (JACK *goes and brings in the newspaper;* PA *settles comfortably to read it.*)

MA. You better go in the other room to read that paper. They'll be washin' the dishes in here. (PA *reluctantly resigns his ease and starts off.* LEM *and* ANNIE LEE *are busy with the dishes but they watch anxiously till* PA *has quit the room.* MA *turns on* JACK *as she goes out.*) Jack, you got your kindlin' to get in for the mornin'.

JACK (*taking a chair at his post of observation, beside the door at the left*). All right, Mom.

PA (*meeting* GIL, *who now returns from the other room*). Gil, you better let the horse git done eatin' 'fore you catch out.

GIL (*pulling at his necktie in an effort to adjust it properly*). He ought to be done eatin' by now. (PA *grunts and goes off.* GIL *begins to rub off his shoes with his handkerchief.*)

JACK (*sniffing the air and crossing to* GIL). Annie Lee, he's been usin' your perfume!

ANNIE LEE. Gilmer Dixon! (*She looks at him severely a moment, and then laughs.*)

LEM (*holding his nose*). You smell like the "Breath-of-Spring" all right; but I think you better take yourself out to walk 'fore you go to the candy-pullin'. How much of it did you use, anyway? (*They all laugh and* GIL *covers his embarrassment by hunting for his hat.*)

GIL. Oh, 'bout a spoonful, I reckon. Some spilled while I was messin' round in there. I wa'n't aimin' to use no perfume. (*He finds his hat on top of the kitchen safe, and starts to leave.*) That horse is done eatin' by now, I know.

PA (*reappearing at the door*). Now, Gil, don't you come blunderin' back in here, 'way late at night, wakin' us all up. Remember the rest of us wants to get a little sleep, even if you don't.

GIL (*in the doorway*). All right, sir. I won't. (LEM *and* ANNIE LEE *have finished clearing off the table and are preparing to wash the dishes on the cook-table which they have moved out into the room.* LEM *takes off his coat and* ANNIE LEE *arrays him in a big pink gingham apron.* JACK *lingers in the room doing nothing in particular.*)

MA (*coming to the door*). Jack! Jack! Come on out of there. I got somethin' I want you to do.

JACK. I'm not botherin' them, Ma. They're not doin' a thing! (*Nevertheless* MA *pulls* JACK *out of the room.* ANNIE LEE *follows them to the door and closes it. She begins washing the dishes, passing them to* LEM *to be dried.* MA *comes back quietly to turn down the lamp which has begun to smoke, beams on them with approving affability, and goes out closing the door softly after her.*)

LEM. I wanted your Ma to get her sewin' done, Annie Lee, but that wasn't the main reason I wanted to help you.

ANNIE LEE. Why, what was the main reason?

LEM (*after a pause*). Oh, . . . just for fun. (*There is another pause.*) Annie Lee, did Ed Nicholson help you wash the dishes when he was out here?

ANNIE LEE. No, he wasn't here for supper. But I reckon he would have helped me.

LEM. Huh! He never had an apron on in his life. He thinks folks wash dishes with a vacuum cleaner.

ANNIE LEE. Now, Lem! You're just runnin' Ed down 'cause he's a city boy. If you knew him like I do, you'd like him fine.

LEM. Oh, I know him well enough. He's just not worth a— much.

ANNIE LEE. I'm sorry you feel that way about him, 'cause I kind o' like Ed.

LEM (*forgetting the dishes and coming close to her side*). How much?

ANNIE LEE (*pushing him away and indicating the unwiped dishes*). Oh, now, Lem. Don't get jealous. Just look how far behind you're getting. (*They work in silence for a time. . . . Shyly.*) I wonder if you'll be willin' to help like this when . . .

LEM (*alert*). When, when?

ANNIE LEE. Oh, you know when . . . when you . . . get . . . married.

LEM. Do you think she'd want me to? (*In taking up a wet dish he fumbles and lets it slip and fall to the floor.*)

ANNIE LEE (*amused*). No, I don't think so. Not if you drop them around like that. (*She picks up the pieces of the broken dish and puts them in the woodbox.*)

JACK (*bursting into the kitchen*). Say, Annie Lee, come on out here! That old cat's got kittens and they ain't got their eyes open yet. Come on out here and see 'em!

ANNIE LEE (*shocked*). Don't bother us, Jack. Can't you see we're busy? (*She goes to the table, gets a plate of scraps, and gives them to him.*) Now you take this to the cat, and you go look at them.

JACK. Aw, you come on, Annie Lee.

ANNIE LEE. Now, run on out, Jack. (*Reluctantly he goes and she closes the door after him.*) I'm much obliged to you, Lem, for helpin' me wash the dishes. I wish I could help you some way.

LEM. Well, if you don't, it won't be because you don't get the chance. (*They continue. When* ANNIE LEE *reaches for the last dish, her face comes temptingly near to* LEM's. *He starts to kiss her, but misses by a few inches.*) Dad gum it! I almost caught myself kissin' you when you leaned over to get that dish.

ANNIE LEE (*carrying a pile of the dishes over to the safe*). That's all right, so long as you don't let me catch you doin' it.

LEM. Um . . . m . . . m. . . . I wish I knew whether . . . whether . . .

ANNIE LEE (*slyly*). What did you say? (PA *enters in his yarn socks—he was warming his feet by the fire in the other room. He says not a word, but crosses the kitchen, gets himself a drink of water at the bucket, turns and walks deliberately back the whole length of the room.* LEM *and* ANNIE LEE *pretend being very busy.* LEM *gets into his coat, preparing to leave.* ANNIE LEE *puts the last of the dishes away in the safe.*)

PA. We all want to get to bed pretty early here to-night; Annie Lee, you know what we got to do to-morrow.

ANNIE LEE (*obediently*). Yes, sir.

PA. And I don't want to hear no such racket as you and Jack was a-makin' last night. I got to get a little sleep sometime.

LEM. Yes, sir. I was just a-thinkin' it was about time for me to be wakin' up old Bob.

PA. Well, I 'spect you better do it then. (*He makes this suggestion half under his breath, and goes off, leaving the door wide open behind them.* ANNIE LEE *hastens to close it.*)

ANNIE LEE. Now, you put the table back in the corner, Lem.

(*He does so while she takes off her apron and hangs it up on a nail. She hesitates a little, then draws a chair toward him.*) Do you want to go in and talk to Ma awhile, or would you just as soon stay out here in the kitchen?

LEM. Naw, I come to talk to you—in the kitchen, or out-doors, or anywhere else. (*They sit down with their chairs not too far apart.*)

ANNIE LEE. Now, don't talk like that, 'cause I know you don't mean it.

LEM. I do mean it, too. I'd swear it on a stack of Bibles a mile high.

ANNIE LEE. You talk like you'd said that before. How many other girls have you said that to in the last month?

LEM. Nobody else. But if I could just say what I'd like to, you'd be surprised.

ANNIE LEE. Say it. I like to be surprised. (*She puts her hand on his arm. He takes it up, impulsively, and kisses it. She breaks away.*) Why, Lem! I wouldn't have thought that of you. I thought you were more of a man than to take advantage of me like that. I'm not that kind of a girl and I thought you knew it.

LEM. But that's nothin' to get red about. (*Rising to go.*) If you're goin' to cloud up and storm . . .

ANNIE LEE. Well, if it's nothin', what was you tryin' to do it for? I don't intend to do anything like that till I'm engaged.

LEM. I'm sorry, Annie Lee. I reckon I did sort o' act the fool. . . . I'm sorry. . . . I'm not that kind of a fellow either. I wouldn't go with a girl that would let anybody kiss her till they was engaged. (*There is a painful silence.*) I feel awful mean about it, Annie Lee. . . . I'll try to do better—next time.

ANNIE LEE (*going to him and putting her hand softly on his arm*). It's not all that bad, Lem. It's just your doin' it without . . .

LEM (*vastly relieved*). Well, let's forget about it and start all over again. (*He takes her impulsively by the hand and leads her back to the chair again.*)

ANNIE LEE (*mischievously, drawing her hand away*). Do you feel any better now?

LEM. Lots better! Folks always feel better after a little spat.

ANNIE LEE. What makes a boy want to kiss a girl for . . . like that, anyway?

LEM. Dad burn it, I don't know! Durn the fellow that invented kissin' anyway. He caused more trouble than anybody else.

ANNIE LEE. Oh, I don't know. It's all right . . . in its place.

LEM. Where is its place?

ANNIE LEE. It's not . . . on the hand.

LEM. Generally speakin', is it—in the kitchen?

ANNIE LEE (*wistfully*). Generally speakin', it's anywhere that a boy and girl . . . love each other. . . .

LEM. I could fill my side of a bargain like that.

ANNIE LEE (*breathlessly*). But you don't love me.

LEM (*boldly now, he puts his arm over the back of her chair*). I do too. I love you, Annie Lee.

ANNIE LEE. No, you don't. You just say you do.

LEM. Maybe that's the way Ed talks. But I mean it. How can I prove it to you?

ANNIE LEE. Not by sayin' so. You just said that . . . to get a chance to . . . kiss me.

LEM. I always thought kissin' was the way to prove it.

ANNIE LEE (*shaking her head*). Nh . . . nh. . . .

LEM. What's the use for me to say it? What do you reckon I rode over here for? To sit around and talk? No! If there's any way to prove it, I'll do it, if it's to swallow old Bob! (*He is down on his knees when* JACK *reappears suddenly at the door.*)

JACK. Annie Lee, get me a drink of water.—What you-all

sayin' your prayers for? (ANNIE LEE *gets him one and holds the dipper for him while he drinks long and thirstily. Then he grins.*) Mamma said I could stay in here a little while, if you-all would let me.

ANNIE LEE (*coldly*). Just a little while, Jack. It's most time for you to be in bed. (*They resume their seats while* JACK *tries to entertain them.*)

JACK. I can stand on my head. . . . Hold my feet up, Lem. Now see if I can stand. (*He stands inverted a moment* LEM *assisting him. A shower of marbles, nails, etc., descends from his pockets to the floor. He makes haste to recover his possessions.* LEM *resumes his chair, but* JACK *persists, following him.*) Wa'n't that good?

LEM (*glumly*). Good a-plenty! (*Now* JACK *climbs up into* LEM'S *lap, and* LEM, *hard-pressed for a way out, scrubs his chin on* JACK'S *face.*)

JACK (*gleefully*). Gee whizz, Annie Lee! Does it hurt you like that?

ANNIE LEE (*at her wit's end*). You'd better go to bed now, Jack.

JACK. No, I'm not sleepy. (*He feels something in* LEM'S *pocket and whispers to* ANNIE LEE.) He's got some candy in his pocket! (LEM *pulls out a paper bag of candy and passes it to* ANNIE LEE. *She offers him some but he refuses; she gives* JACK *a piece and then forces him out of the room.*)

ANNIE LEE (*timidly*). Have you got over your scare yet?

LEM. I wasn't scared. I was just tryin' to convince you. (JACK *has come back for more candy.*)

JACK. I believe I could stand on my head again, if I had another piece of candy. (LEM *is now exasperated—quite.*)

ANNIE LEE (*speaking with authority*). Jack, it's time you were in bed. (*Calling.*) Ma, why don't you put Jack to bed?

MA (*at the door*). Come on out of there, Jack. (JACK *not minding her, she comes into the room after him and leads him out by the ear. He begins to cry and* ANNIE LEE *gives him the rest of the candy to quiet him. Now* PA *appears.*)

PA. Hush up that cryin', Jack. Mind your Ma. (*He directs a meaning glance at* LEM *and retires. In the confusion the door is left open.* ANNIE LEE *slams it to.*)

LEM. Confound it! Every time the signs get right, something has to go and happen.

ANNIE LEE (*they sit down and try again*). Something has happened. I don't know whether to believe what you said awhile ago or not.

LEM. Drat it! I don't believe all the preachers in the world could make you believe that Jonah swallowed the whale. (*There is an awkward pause.* ANNIE LEE *feigns indifference.*) Well, if it's goin' to be like this, I guess I'd better go. (*Starting up.*) You and Ed done got it all fixed up, I reckon. . . . (*He gazes longingly at her.*) I better be goin' on. . . . I got to get up soon in the mornin'. Got to hold the governor cords over the business end of an old jarrhead.[1] (*The mule brays outside.*) There's old Bob callin' me now. He knows when it's time to leave.

ANNIE LEE. 'Tain't worth while to rush off. . . .

LEM. Yeah. . . . I got to be goin' on. . . .

ANNIE LEE (*pursuing him*). No, don't. Set awhile longer.

LEM (*relieved*). Well, if you want me to.

ANNIE LEE. You ought to know I want you to. (*He resumes his seat closer now to* ANNIE LEE *than ever before and takes her hand.* PA *pounds on the floor overhead.*)

LEM. I would like to convince you before I go. (*Before she can reply* PA *pounds the second time.*)

ANNIE LEE. There's Pa again. I reckon you had better go now.

LEM. Yeah, I reckon I had better. . . . (*He is loath to go.* ANNIE LEE *stands looking blankly at him. Then she has a brilliant idea.*)

---

[1] This is the country way of referring to plowing with a mule.

ANNIE LEE. Wait! I've got an idea! Let's . . . (*She takes him by the hand and whispers something in his ear. He seems doubtful at first, glances at the window, then grins broadly, and strides heavily to the door.*)

LEM (*in a loud voice*). Good night, Annie Lee.

ANNIE LEE. Good night, Lem. (*He is heard walking across the porch outside. She closes the door with a bang, goes to the window, raises it, and lets him in that way. He enters noiselessly, in his stocking-feet, carrying his shoes in his hand. They tiptoe back to their chairs.*)

LEM. Well, Annie Lee, I guess we slipped one over on the old man, that time—if that blame mule will just keep his mouth shut. (*With suppressed laughter she picks up the shoes and is about to set them aside. LEM, however, makes for them.*) Better let me get into that pair o' gunboats. I want to be ready to move off from here at about half-a-second's notice.

ANNIE LEE. But Pa might hear you movin' round. Hadn't you better wait?

LEM. Well, I better keep 'em handy, though. (*He puts the shoes to the rear of his chair. They sit very close together now, talking in subdued voices.*)

ANNIE LEE. You never did get it done. . . . (*He is about to kiss her, when GIL bounds up on the porch and breaks in on them. They jump apart.*)

GIL. Howdy, folks! What you-all doin'?

ANNIE LEE. Just talkin'—don't you want an apple?

GIL (*hilarious*). Naw! I ain't got no more appetite than a snake's got tail-feathers. I just e't thirteen in a contest. I couldn't eat no more—that's the reason I came home so early. . . .

ANNIE LEE (*knowingly*). I guess there was some other reason than that.—But don't talk so loud, Gil. Pa said not to wake him up comin' in, and he thinks—

GIL. Say, you-all ought to have been at the candy-pullin'!

We made some molasses candy and it didn't get hard enough, and—

ANNIE LEE. Oh, I guess you didn't boil it long enough.

GIL. Sure, we knew that, but we wanted to get to pullin' it. So Carrie and me, we—

ANNIE LEE. Gil, don't talk so loud! Pa thinks Lem has gone. He called bedtime on us so early to-night, that we decided to play a trick on him. You see (*pointing to the window and the shoes*) Lem said good night and went out with a whole lot of racket, took off his shoes, and—snuck back in again! (*She checks* GIL's *resounding laugh. He sees interesting possibilities in the shoes.*)

GIL. Well, if you-all are goin' to sit up much longer you better punch up the fire. I'm goin' to bed.

LEM. 'Spect we had better, Annie Lee. (*While they are poking the fire,* GIL *gets possession of the shoes, conceals them under his coat, and starts out with them.*)

GIL. Good night, you-all.

ANNIE LEE. Good night.

LEM. Good—(*She checks him by putting her hand over his mouth. He kisses it ardently.* GIL, *with the shoes behind him, chuckles and backs out of the room.*)

LEM (*they are seated together once more*). Gil made a lot of noise in here. Do you reckon your Pa heard?

ANNIE LEE. I hope not. (*But* PA's *heavy footsteps are heard coming down the stairs.*)

LEM. Yes, he did, too!—Where are my shoes? (*A frantic search is made.* LEM *is about to leave without them when* PA, *in his shirtsleeves with one suspender down—apparently having dressed in some haste—appears in the doorway with the shoes in his hand. He has stumbled over them in coming down the stairs.* LEM, *as a last resort, dashes under the table.* ANNIE LEE *covering him.*)

PA (*holding out the shoes*). Who left these here shoes on the staircase? These here ain't Gil's shoes! And what in thunder was you and him raisin' so much Cain about? Didn't I tell you-all to be quiet? Did Gil go to bed?

ANNIE LEE. Yes sir. . . . Gil went to bed. . . . Didn't you meet him just now? . . . I tried to get him to be quiet, but . . .

PA. Well, whose shoes is these?

ANNIE LEE. Why, I guess they're . . . they're . . . they're . . .

LEM (*coming out from under the table*). They're . . . they're mine! I thought Gil hid 'em under the table. . . . I was just lookin' under there.

PA. Well. What the Sam Hill does this mean? I called bedtime long ago. Do you know what time it is? It's time everybody was at home in bed where they belong. I thought you was gone, Lem. What you doin' back here? (GIL *returns, grinning broadly.*)

LEM. Well, you see . . . you see . . . We hadn't quite finished . . . when . . .

PA. Hadn't quite finished! What the fire was you doin', then?

LEM. Yes, sir. You see, I was tryin' to tell Annie Lee—

PA. Well, why didn't you tell her and not take so dad-burn much time about it? (MA *enters with her sewing in her hand.*)

MA (*going to* ANNIE LEE). Now, Pa, don't be so hard on 'em. I knew all the time Lem hadn't gone.

GIL (*appearing on the scene too*). They was waitin' for me to bring 'em some candy. I think they've got a sweet-tooth.

LEM. Yes, sir. I was just about ready to go, when— (JACK *enters, in his nightgown now.*)

JACK (*rubbing his eyes*). Papa, get me a drink of water.

PA (*pushing* JACK *in the direction of the water-bucket*). Well, have you got anything more to say? If you haven't— (*He throws the shoes dangerously near* LEM'S *feet and turns away.* LEM *gets into the shoes as quickly as possible.*)

LEM (*in desperation now*). Yes, I have got something else to say. I've been tryin' to say somethin' to Annie Lee ever since supper, but every time I get ready to say it somebody goes buttin' in. (MA *looks accusingly at* PA.) I I wasn't aimin' to say it to anybody but Annie Lee, but . . . but . . . Well, listen and look! All of you! (*In spite of his determination to get it all said,* LEM *finds that the words still stick in his throat. He gulps, takes* ANNIE LEE *by the hand and makes a final effort.*) Annie Lee . . . I . . . do . . . love you. Will you marry me?

ANNIE LEE (*she looks to* MA *for her approval;* MA, *beaming, nods her head, of course*). Uh . . . huh. . . . (*Then he takes her in his arms and kisses her.* MA *is radiant.* JACK *giggles.* GIL *pretends to be surprised.* PA *says nothing, but grunts and starts out to take up his interrupted sleep. But upon second thought he turns for the final word.*)

PA. Well! That bein' the case, you better come around in the mornin' and . . . slop the hogs!

CURTAIN

A SHOTGUN SPLICIN'

A Mountain Comedy

BY

GERTRUDE WILSON COFFIN

287

A SHOTGUN SPLICIN'

The author of *A Shotgun Splicin'*, Gertrude Wilson Coffin, grew up as a child in the mountain country of western North Carolina, the daughter of a country doctor.

Her play makes an important contribution in preserving the manners and the racy vernacular of a social order which is yielding fast to the forces that beat upon it to break it up. Such a record as this will be invaluable to those who shall come after.

After a tour performance of *A Shotgun Splicin'* in a city in western North Carolina there was a storm of protest from the local Ministerial Association. A resolution challenging the production was sent to the President of the University, and a copy to the Director of The Playmakers, requesting that the play be banned from the repertory of The Carolina Playmakers.

The Resolution held that the members of the Association "do not believe that a young woman should be trained at the state University to play the rôle of an adultress and the mother of a bastard child whose stage father is another student, a young man playing the part of her seducer."

The front page of the local newspaper carried the story under a double column heading: MINISTERS FLAY SPLICIN' DRAMA OF PLAYMAKERS—Girls Should Not Be Trained That Way, They Complain—*University Gets Protest.*

We recall in this connection the case of Mary Magdalene and Jesus' rebuke to his disciples: "Why trouble ye the woman? For she has wrought a good work."

THE CHARACTERS

As originally produced at The Playmakers Theatre, Chapel Hill, North Carolina, March 30 and 31, 1928.

SAIREY-SAM MULL, *the acting postmistress,*
Gertrude Wilson Coffin

FATE GADDY, *the mail carrier,*   Charles T. Lipscomb

PINK GIBSON, *a loafer,*   Walter Spearman

DICEY RADFORD, *a mountain girl,*   Lois Warden

AMOS, *her brother,*   Moore Bryson

SQUIRE BEN HARRISON BAYLES, *an aspirant for the State Legislature,*   Edwin S. Day

SCENE: A roadway in front of the Fargo Post Office, in the mountains of western North Carolina.

TIME: A day in midsummer, 1910.

290

SCENE

*The Fargo Post Office building is cheaply constructed of un-
planed, unpainted planks (of the type known as "box house"
placed vertically with two-inch strips covering the joints. The
gable end faces the narrow, rocky road. At the extreme right of
the front is a batten door, and a batten window is placed high
on the left side. Both the door and the window stand open. The
road is widened in front of the Post Office to allow for the passage
of vehicles. To the left, a low rail fence adjoins the building,
and a cluster of gay zinnias and sunflowers are blooming by it.
Two rails, placed side by side to form the top of the fence, afford
seats for those who arrive ahead of the mail carrier. Between the
door and the window are tacked notices to tax-payers, and tin
signs recommending "Smith's Mule Chewing Tobacco,"
"Sweetbread Tobacco," and "Dutch Snuff." In rather uneven
letters "FARGO, P.O." is crudely lettered on a board above
the doorway. There is a home-made bench beneath the window,
and a splint-bottomed chair is in the doorway.*

*Inside, to the left, is a home-made cabinet containing lettered
pigeon-holes for mail. Shelves line the opposite wall and hold
a small stock of staple groceries, candy, tobacco, and snuff,
supplemented by a few broken bolts of calico and cheap cotton
cloth. To the right of the Post Office is the hitching rack, but it is
not visible to the audience.*

*PINK GIBSON, 28, is a shiftless, good-natured, man-of-the-
neighborhood. His tanned hair and patchy pongee whiskers
match his well-worn tan breeches, which are supported by
"galluses," held in place by eight-penny nails where buttons
are missing. A faded blue shirt echoes the washed-out blueness
of his eyes. His hat, long since deprived of its band, has gone
to seed and is now held to his head by means of a shoe string
slipped through slits in the crown. His sockless feet are enclosed
in brogan shoes.*

SAIREY-SAM, *56 (so named by the neighbors to distinguish her from a sister-in-law named "Sairey"), is the wife of a semi-invalid, Sam Mull, and mother of one daughter, Theodosia (called "Doshy") 16, who is her mother's standard of what every young girl should be. Her small cabin is just beyond the creek, but in view of the Post Office. SAIREY-SAM is decided in her views and caustic in her comments. Her body is thin, work-hardened, and a bit stooped; her streaky grey hair is drawn from a sharp, swarthy face into a knot on top of her head; steel-rimmed spectacles (with one lame side, wrapped with white string) sit on her long, sharp nose. Her dress is a grey calico with a black vine pattern. It is made with a tight basque bodice, joined to a full-gathered skirt, reaching down to her shoes. A black-and-white checked apron ties around her waist. PINK is sprawled out on the bench under the window, his gun and fishing pole stacked against the fence. He is chewing tobacco and whittling on a stick. SAIREY-SAM, unaware of any one's presence, comes to the door and holds up a letter between her eyes and the sun. Her spectacles are set low on her nose and she peers over them, scrutinizingly.*

PINK (*without moving a muscle*). Whar's hit from and who writ it?

SAIREY-SAM (*starting guiltily*). Guess hit's Doshey's. A body never know'd you was here. Whar'd you come a-slinkin' in from?

PINK. Been up th' road a piece. (*Without rising, he turns and stretches his neck so that he can peep inside.*) Whar's Aunt Viney?

SAIREY-SAM. Her ol' neuralgy was so bad, she wasn't able to make it to-day. She axed me to tend the store. How fer up the road was you?

PINK (*indifferently*). Eh? Wasn't so fer.—Got book-larnin' a-plenty to tend mail, hev you?

SAIREY-SAM. Shore, my folks gimme schoolin', an' I's able to larn. Hain't a-measurin' t'other feller's corn in your

half-bushel, air you? Think you're powerful smart, bein'
so shet-mouthed 'bout whar you be'n.

PINK. Squair Ben a-hangin' 'roun' to-day?

SAIREY-SAM. Shore hain't. He's off some'ers a-speakin'
'bout the legislature. 'Lowed he'd a-been here a-fore this.
Whut air you and Ben up to? Some devilment?

PINK. Mebbe. He's done gimme that money. (*Showing it.*)

SAIREY-SAM (*sneering*). Somethin's wrong if Ben's a-throwin'
away money. Le's see how big a piece it was. (PINK *holds
up a dime.*)

PINK. Thar hit is.

SAIREY-SAM. Lordy, onderstood you to say money. Jist a
dime! 'Twas Ben give hit to you shore! Buyin' your vote
ahead of election, air he?

PINK. Hain't nuther. Hit's fer puttin' them air signs up.

SAIREY-SAM. What-uns? Hain't seed nary-un.

PINK. A body never said you had. He was allowin' 'at Fate'd
fetch 'em in the mail to-day—done got his beauty struck.
His picture's goin' to be plumb smack at the head of ever'
sign.

SAIREY-SAM. Lordy, you don't say. Allus was stuck on hisself.
Makin' of him Justice of the Peace p'int-blank ruint him.
(*She starts inside.*)

PINK. Hit hain't.

SAIREY-SAM (*stopping*). Powerful little you know 'bout hit,
Pink Gibson. Hain't I been a-knowin' of him ever sence
he's jist a shirt-tail' boy?

PINK. Got a good chanct o' book-larnin', I reckon.

SAIREY-SAM (*she is sitting in the doorway now sewing*). Jist
enough to bodaciously spile a good field hand. Ef'n he'd
a-been crippled up with white swellin' same as Leander's
Amos, hit'd a-been 'scuse a-plenty to kept from workin'
an' a-bein' a preacher, or a man school-teacher.

PINK. He's a purty good feller.

SAIREY-SAM. Brag on him 'at air dime's wuth. You've sot your head for him. (*Reminiscently.*) 'Tain't ary a grain of use for him to act biggety around whar I'm a-livin', for I've knowed his ol' daddy an' mammy afore him.

PINK. They's as good as . . .

SAIREY-SAM. Spit hit out—as we air. Yeah, an' they hain't no better. Cramped theirselves on victuals so's to give him a heap of schoolin'. A'ter he's got it, hain't done nothin' but run for the legislature.

PINK. Tain't no harm in that.

SAIREY-SAM. Nuther good. Ef he'd ever git thar. Jist a-usin' good tax money for nothin'. Ben's jist too big for his breeches. Ef'n he ever was to git elected, he'd act as big as the President. D'you say 'at he was a-lookin' for that bunch o' signs to come in on this here mail?

PINK. Fate's slow a-fetchin' the mail to-day, hain't he?

SAIREY-SAM (*she turns to look at the clock*). Reckon so. Hain't in no swivet to git back, air you? (*She now resumes her sewing, which she had let fall into her lap during the conversation about* BEN.)

PINK (*still whittling*). That feller 'lowed for me to hurry.

SAIREY-SAM. Plumb lost the little sense you's borned with.— Which feller?

PINK (*ignoring her question*). Talkin' o' the ol' Booger Man shore will scare up his imps. (FATE *outside right,* "*Whoa, Beck.*") Thar's Fate tiein' old Beck to the hitchin' rack right now.

SAIREY-SAM. Yessir, he's jist a shammickin' on in. (FATE *enters and* SAIREY-SAM *lays aside her sewing, ready to take the mail pouch, which he lets slide from his shoulders.* FATE GADDY, *thirty-five, is a long, lank, much tanned and weather-beaten mountaineer. His straight black hair and furtive eyes give him the appearance of an Indian. Two weeks' growth of black beard covers his face. He is dressed in blue denim overalls with a jacket to match, and wears a small, greasy, black felt hat on the back of his head.*)

FATE. Hy, Pink.

PINK. Hy, yourself. Sorter late.

FATE. Yeah.

PINK. Train not a-runnin'?

FATE (*sullenly*). Yeah, hit was a-runnin'. So was 'at air clock 'em devilish Sisk boys axed me to fetch up to their Granny. They gimme a bundle all wropped up, an' jist put hit in my haversack 'thout noticin' hit a-tickin' or nothin'. Pint in the middle of Gyarden Creek, whar ol' Beck was a-drinkin', the blamed ol' 'larm bell sot off and the huzzy wheeled and piled me off 'zactly in the aidge o' the creek. Hit never wet the mail-poke none. A'ter I'd run and ketched 'er, fernent the Company Store, I'se good and mad—and late. (*Ironically.*) Wait'n hain't throwed your craps back none, I reckon.

PINK (*good-naturedly*). No, they hain't a-sufferin'. Whut's the news down in the settlements?

FATE. Never heerd none. Whut you know?

PINK. They's anuther young-un up on Little Hongry.

FATE (*interested*). Whar 'bouts?

PINK. At Mag's and Leander's.

FATE. You're a-lyin', flat-footed, Pink. Their baby crap's done laid by. 'Sides, ef they'd been lookin' out, my mammy 'd a-heered it afore now.

PINK. So holp me God, hit's so. She brung hit in night afore last. Tain't sich a little-un; reckon hit's nigh onto two months ol'. Mam seed hit last night. They 'lowed the young-un had the thrash, an' sent for Mam to blow in hits mouth. Tain't Mag's. Hit's Dicey's!

FATE (*takes hold of* PINK *by the collar and leads him toward the fence so as to be out of ear-shot of* SAIREY-SAM.) Look-a-here, Pink. 'At's powerful low-down talk to be a-handlin'. Furthermore, Dicey hain't been home since last Christmas. She's a-stayin' at her brother Ranz's over in Transylvania, goin' to school.

PINK. Eh? You hain't nary excuse to git so fired up. (PINK *shakes himself free from* FATE's *hold.*) I told you she got in night afore last. Garfield Rogers was in from Transylvania last night, with a load o' licker, and he 'lowed the daddy of hit was from over in here some'ers. Tain't a-steppin' on your toes, air it? Was you a-wantin' of her? Knowed you an' Squair Ben both used to spark her.

FATE (*turning away*). Jist drap sich talk.

PINK (*striving for the last word*). 'Lowed she got fooled.

FATE (*threateningly*). You're the fool. An' a blame, black-guardin' one, to boot. (*He walks toward* PINK, *shaking his fist in his face.*) Keep your blamed mouth shet. Sairey-Sam's mouth's allus a-waterin' for some tale to tell. Now nary nuther word out'n you, or I'll bust your face.

PINK. I hain't a-braggin'. 'Tain't *mine*.

FATE. Cain't allus tell. Hit's a smart daddy 'at can tell his own young-un. (SAIREY-SAM *steps to the door and peeps out, holding a bundle of letters in her hand. She calls to the men.*)

SAIREY-SAM. How come you-uns is a-squanderin' off thar? (*She comes out, and walks toward them.*) Come here, Fate. You can read writin'; holp me put up this mail. (*As* SAIREY-SAM *goes to see why the two men have strayed from the porch,* SQUIRE BEN *comes in at the right.* BEN HARRISON BAYLES *is florid and resounding, approaching thirty. He has not yet settled on any definite work. Farming is too arduous—with pay-days far apart. Paucity of educatian bars him from becoming a man of consequence in the towns of his county. A lawyer is his idea of greatness, largely because he can exchange advice for cash.* BEN *has been very prodigal with advice. He wears dark, baggy trousers and a light, striped shirt. He props his foot on the porch-step, wipes his face with a large handkerchief, smiles broadly, and watches* SAIREY-SAM *round up the men.*)

BEN. How're y'all? Aunt Vine got the mail up?

SAIREY-SAM. Lawsy! She hain't able to tend store to-day. Hit's my job. Jist a'ter Fate to holp me a-puttin' hit up. Step on in. 'At bundle o' your'n is a-layin' a-top o' that pile o' papers.

BEN. So them notices got in? Glad of that. Time they's tacked up over the country so the folks can see what a good-lookin' candidate they've got. (BEN *laughs up-roariously. The others exchange meaning glances.*)

SAIREY-SAM. Ef'n you's as good a hand to hoe, as you air to brag, your'n 'd be the biggest corn crap 'round here. (BEN *goes inside.*) Whew! Hain't hit a miserable hot day. Reckon hit's a-fixin' to rain. Sam's takin' on so all-fired bad 'ith that ol' lame arm o' his'n—'lows hit's a-hurtin' bad as hit done 'never'n them Yankees put the bullet thar.

FATE. They's a ol' Injun "doc" in town to-day, a-sellin' liniment 'at mought cyore 'im.

SAIREY-SAM. Dunno. Powerful juberous o' them peddlars. Them town doctors says nothin'll holp 'ceptin' cuttin' hit off, but Sam 'lows them town fellers is allus studyin' new ways to git a country feller's money. (PINK *is sitting on the fence.*) "Doc" Walton was by our house this mornin', and I axed him to leave some powders to make the ol' man so's he could sleep.

FATE (*quizzically*). How fer up th' road had "Doc" been?

SAIREY-SAM. Up to Leander's.

FATE. Who's sick?

SAIREY-SAM. Ranz's folks come in from Transylvania night afore last, fetchin' a sick young-un. They sent fer "Doc," jist afore day.

FATE. Whose young-un was hit?

SAIREY-SAM. Hain't found out. Ranz's ooman was allus sickly, an' had no young-uns.

PINK. Hit's . . . D—D—D—(*Stammering.* FATE *steps up to him and claps his hand over* PINK's *mouth.*)

FATE. You shet up.

SAIREY-SAM. What'n the world's Pink a-stutterin' about? (PINK *resumes his whittling.*)

FATE. Nothin'. (*He motions her aside.*) Acts as ef he mought a-been a-takin' a dram. Tain't no use to pay no 'tention to him.

SAIREY-SAM (*unconvinced*). Don't 'pear no quairer'n allus to me. En ef hit's licker, some folks is libeller to tell the straight of a thing ef'n they've had a dram 'n ef they's dry as a bone.

FATE. Jist the same, he ort to be left alone. (*He goes into the store, talking as he goes.*) Come on, then. Got to pay me extry for puttin' up the mail, as well as totin' of hit.

SAIREY-SAM (*moving nearer* PINK, *but keeping her eyes on* FATE *as he disappears inside*). I'm a-comin'. (*Crossing to* PINK.) Whut's you a-startin' to say?

PINK (*carelessly*). Eh? Nothin' much.

SAIREY-SAM. You was so, and Fate got so almighty bossy. Know more'n you're a-tellin' 'bout that young-un.

PINK (*shifting his tobacco*). Mebbe. An' you're a-wantin' to larn more'n you're a-hearin'.

SAIREY-SAM (*indignantly*). Keep it to yourself, Mr. Biggety. They's a-plenty as kin git news sides you, and tell hit a sight straighter. (FATE *pokes his head out of the window.*)

FATE. 'Pears as ef your swivet to fix this here letter mail has done wore off. (*He chuckles.*) Ben's jist as happy as a toad under the drip o' the house, a-lookin' at them pictures o' his'n.

SAIREY-SAM. Bet ef he tacks ary'n on the front of the store, hit'll scare the Boogers off. Aunt Vine'll need nary yard-dog. (SAIREY-SAM *goes in.* BEN *brushes against her in the doorway as he comes out with a roll of posters under his left arm. He holds one up for inspection and hands the rest of them to* PINK. *Selecting a most auspicious place, he tacks one of them up on the wall, driving the tacks with the back of his knife. Then he steps back a bit, to see if it is well-placed.*)

BEN. Look all right, Pink?

PINK (*spitting and discarding his tobacco simultaneously*). Cain't read them words. Your picter looks natural enough to eat pie. (SAIREY-SAM *comes out to investigate the hammering.*)

BEN. What's your judgment?

SAIREY-SAM. Never seed the day 'at you looked as good as hit. Rared back like you is the only favorance. (*Looking closely at the reading matter.*) Lordy massy, hit says: "To THEM DIMMICRATS!" Come here, Fate. Jist read them words—"Dimmicrats!" They's Radicals 'round here got four-year-old, and two-year-old young-uns called a'ter him. Ef'n I'se them Radicals, I'd change every last one of 'em to Roozyvelt. Hain't money enough to hire me to name a dog for a turncoat. (*Meanwhile* FATE *has ambled out, with letters in both hands, to inspect the notice.*)

FATE (*turning to* BEN). Them fellers 'at fixed the signs has got it mixed and put your picter top o' the wrong readin', I reckon, Squair. Shore, you hain't quit us.

BEN (*a bit crestfallen*). It's just that-a-way. Studied everything out, Fate, and here's how hit is. The Dimmicrats naturally got us beat for numbers in this county. No way to whip 'em, 'cept to run on their ticket, land in the legislature, put the laws we favored over on 'em.—Good iron bridges, so's you and your mule can cross the river dry-shod! (*He waves his hands becoming oratorical.*) Taxes spent right here at home—not all at the towns down to the lower end o' the county! Too many loopholes in th' law!

FATE. 'At's shore the way of it.

BEN. Big bunch o' meanness goes on. The law's too easy on the evildoers. When my turn comes t' make laws, I intend to make it hard on them 'at's not peaceable and law-abidin'.

FATE. Yeah. Orter work 'at-a-way.

BEN. Now when the law handles a feller, and finds him guilty, he gets off too light. Takes good tax money to put him through the courts, too. Work 'em on the roads, ef'n they cain't pay a fine, is my ticket!

FATE. Squair, ef you'd not a-switched to the Dimmicrats, I believe you'd a-been a good-un to 'lect.

SAIREY-SAM. Heap of us has seed water toted top o' two shoulders afore this. Heap o' book larnin' hain't for doin' a-body no good, 'less'n his principles air right.

BEN. Why, Sairey, they hain't enough schools. When our boys and girls grows up, jist fryin' size, they marries off, 'cause our schools are so short. Some of the smartest ones has to leave home and study. Take that little brown-eyed girl of Leander's—smart as a whip-cracker in school; her folks lacked money to send her off to Asheville—I lent her money myself. Transylvany's schools beats our'n.

FATE. Be keerful 'at you hain't a-braggin' too quick. 'Sides, wheelin' to the other crowd was a pretty lousy trick.

PINK. 'Less'n you could git a passel o' cash for changin'.

FATE. In generally, they's money passes hands.

SAIREY-SAM. Lordy, hain't that the way of it?

BEN (*disgustedly*). Now listen at ye—doubt ef hit's worth the trouble to try to help folks to do better by theirselves. Ef you-all 'd read your papers more, you'd see how I could help you out with schools and taxes. (*To* SAIREY-SAM.) My "Toledo Blade" come in on this mail?

SAIREY-SAM. Yeah, hit's in thar. (BEN *goes in to get his paper. She takes* FATE *by the sleeve and leads him toward the door.*) Let's stick this here passel of letter-mail up and git time to set an' talk. (DICEY *comes in from the left and walks quietly up to* PINK, *surprising him. She is barely seventeen and pretty; demureness is connoted by the rustic simplicity of her dress, yet the toss of her head shows the superiority youth feels for society's laws. Her oval face is framed by dark hair, braided and tied back with a pink ribbon. Roguish eyes look out from beneath a limp Leghorn hat, trimmed with pink roses. Her organdie dress is worn long and has three ruffles at the bottom of the skirt. Dusty white shoes and stockings reveal her imitation of the summer tourists.*)

PINK (*sitting up*). Howdy, Dicey. Like for the world not to a-knowed you.

DICEY. How're you, Pink? Mail in?

PINK. Puttin' hit up.—Well, Dicey, how'd you like hit over in Transylvany?

DICEY. All right, but everything's lookin' mighty purty on this side o' the mountain.

PINK. Hit shore is.

DICEY (*she closes her umbrella*). Sure want to see Aunt Vine. (*Looking inside.*) Where is she?

PINK. Hain't here to-day. Sick. 'Lowed you might a-been a-wantin' to see Fate.

DICEY (*blushing*). Aw, hush. Is she bad sick?

PINK. Reckon she hain't liken to die. Sairey-Sam's a-gittin' her fun out'n the mail and a-seein' what's a-goin' on.

DICEY (*drawing back*). She in there? I don't want to see her. Doshy, too?

PINK (*shaking his head*). Huh-uh. Jist Fate and Sairey-Sam a-puttin' the mail up. Orter be 'bout done. Squair Ben sulled up and tuk hisself in thar to read.

DICEY (*wistfully*). Wisht I had time to run out to the house and see Doshy, but I got to hurry on back. (FATE *comes out of the door, cramming some small packages into his coat pocket, and producing some cheese and crackers.*)

FATE. C'm on, Pink. Let's go. Nary a grain o' need a-settin' a-mutterin' to yourself.

PINK. Hain't a-mutterin'. Purty company.

FATE (*glancing up quickly and seeing* DICEY). Blessed ef

hit hain't— Howdy, Dicey. (*Extending his hand;* DICEY *takes it.*)

DICEY. Howdy. She ready to wait on me?

FATE. Yeah. Step right in. (DICEY *goes to enter the store, but meets* SAIREY-SAM *bustling out.*)

SAIREY-SAM. Lord, hit's Dicey. Heerd you-uns was in.— You're lookin' awful peak-ed.—Whose young-un was hit that "Doc" was a-tendin' on? Ramsay's tuk a young-un to raise? How come you hain't answered me? Cat's got your tongue?

PINK. Two-legged cat! (BEN *comes out, reading his newspaper.*)

SAIREY-SAM. Looky, Ben, here's Dicey.

BEN (*overdoing the welcome*). Hit's a fact. How are you, little girl? Lookin' fine! (*He extends a pudgy, moist hand, which she is slow to accept.*)

DICEY. Miss Sairey, I'm in a hurry; could you wait on me?

SAIREY-SAM. Shore. 'At's what I'm here for. What's your hurry? Hain't a-borrowin' a chunk o' fire on a hot day as this'n, air you?

DICEY. No, ma'am. (*The two go inside.* FATE *starts toward his mule.* PINK *rises and brushes the whittlings off himself, as if he, too, might consider leaving.* BEN *takes* PINK'S *seat on the bench, burying himself in his newspaper.*)

PINK (*to* BEN). 'Peared as ef she wasn't overly proud to see you.

FATE (*eating cheese and crackers as he goes*). Reckon I mought as well rack on towards home. Le's go, Pink.

PINK (*sitting down on the steps*). Eh, what's your hurry?

FATE (*glancing toward the western sky*). Hit's a-comin' a plumb gully-washer ef'n them black clouds ain't a-sidlin' around Cole Mountain, and I hain't a-cravin' two wettin's the same day.

PINK. Ye hain't salt, nuther sugar. Ol' widder-men's allus a-thinkin' how sweet and purty they air, hain't they?

FATE. With some folks hit's a sight easier to git the secont ooman than to git the fust un.

PINK. Them as I want I cain't git, and them as I can git the Devil wouldn't hev. Gimme a chaw of sun-cyored?

FATE (*shakes his head, and dives deep into his pockets*). Plumb out. Got some store terbaccer. (*He reaches into his coat pocket.*) Hain't, nuther. Jist a seegar one of them town fellers gimme. Bite ye a chaw off the end of hit. (*He extends the cigar toward* PINK *who waves it aside.*)

PINK. Uh-uh. Hit's as dry as rabbit terbaccer.

FATE. Hain't ye a-goin' with me?

PINK. My tradin' hain't done, yet. (*Insinuating.*) 'Lowed as how Dicey mought walk a piece o' the way with me. (SAIREY-SAM *and* DICEY *reappear in the doorway.* DICEY *is carrying a small package wrapped in very yellow paper.*)

DICEY. Doshy at home? I'd sure love to see her.

SAIREY-SAM. Yeah. Doshy's a-settin' right thar a-piecin' quilts. She can imitate every quilt pattern she's seed, clean down to them picters in the papers. Whar you was so smart in your books, she was good to work. Proud you can drap by to see her.

DICEY. Thank you. (*She walks on toward the right.* FATE *hesitates a moment, then joins her. The two stroll off together, leaving* PINK *pop-eyed and* SAIREY-SAM *astounded.*)

PINK (*extending his dime to* SAIREY-SAM). Gimme a nickel's wuth of store terbaccer and a nickel's wuth o' Franch mixture candy.

SAIREY-SAM (*she takes the dime absentmindedly, her eyes still following the two retreating figures*). Hain't that the beatinest sight! I knowed Fate was a-lookin' out for a secont wife! Jist the same as t'other-uns. He'll git tuk in with a purty face and figger and pay nary speck o' 'tention to a gal smart to work.

PINK. Reckon they's a-sparkin'?

SAIREY-SAM. Yeah. And her a-lettin' on that the young-un

was a-needin' 'at air Castoria so bad. Nary a grain o' sati'faction 'd she gimme 'bout that young-un.

PINK (*cryptically*). Hit's *her'n!*

SAIREY-SAM (*drawing in her breath sharply*). You hain't a-tellin' hit! Well, hain't she fixed herself?—Allus a-takin' on about 'er bein' so smart for book-larnin'.—Who'd she lay hit to? The brazen piece, walkin' in to see my Doshy! I'm goin' straight atter 'em! (*She reaches for her bonnet and starts off.*)

PINK. Come back here with 'at dime o' mine. 'Sides, you cain't git away from the store. 'Pears as ef I seed a feller a-comin'.

SAIREY-SAM. A-ridin' or a-walkin'? Ben could tend the store tel I git back. (BEN *has been shading his face and pretending to read.*)

PINK (*to* BEN). Reckin you'd heerd 'bout the young-un?

BEN. Folks can be put in the penitentiary for slander; Fate's mighty foolish about her.

SAIREY-SAM. What air *you* so 'mazin' techous about?

PINK (*looking off left*). Hoppin' Amos is a-bilin' down the road a-foot.

SAIREY-SAM (*shading her eyes with her hand*). He shore air a-single-footin'.

PINK. Yeah. He's a-kiverin' ground. (*To* SAIREY-SAM.) Gonna gimme my terbaccer and candy?

SAIREY-SAM. Take your ol' dime ontil I git back in the store. (*She hands it to him.*) Act as ef you're awful rich, a-spendin' for candy and store 'baccer.

PINK. Hoppin' Amos was scan'lous mad about Dicey's young-un. Wantin' to marry 'er off. He was a-takin' on wuss ner Leander and Mag. Reckon hit's becase he's a preacher.

SAIREY-SAM. Who's he a-splicin' 'er to? Amos ort to see that his own blood sister acts right, or his preachin' ain't wuth nothin'. (AMOS *enters as fast as he can. He is twenty-five, but appears much older. His hatchet face is sallow, with deep-set eyes. When he walks he sways to the right because his right leg is smaller and much shorter than his left. He is dressed in a blue work-shirt and corduroy pants, tucked into the tops of his teamster's boots—a well-worn rush hat is set on the side of his head. As he draws up and rests his crippled leg on the bench, he wipes the perspiration from his face with first one sleeve and then the other. He takes off his battered hat to fan himself with it. After catching his breath he speaks haltingly.)*

AMOS. 'S awful warm.

SAIREY-SAM. Lord, who wouldn't be sich a swultry day as this, ef he had two good legs stid of one and a piece lak your'n, and a-hittin' the grit like you was. Startin' off some'ers to hold a meetin' an' skeer the ol' Booger Man?

PINK. Bet Amos could out-run him.

AMOS. I hain't got to hunt the Booger Man—'cause Hell's bust loose up at our house!

SAIREY-SAM. Whut ye a-runnin' for? Wouldn't a-been much hotter to a-stayed thar than you got a-tearin' off from hit. Hit's a Lord's blessin' that ye air one o' them as c'n slide from grace stid of them as is allus stuck *in* grace, Amos. Here ye go, put' nigh a-cussin' never'n you've been made a jack-leg preacher.

AMOS (*gasping*). Sairey, hit wasn't intended for cussin'.

SAIREY-SAM (*dubiously*). Hit wasn't? Boys, hit 'peared pow'ful as ef ye was a-ticklin' the ol' Booger Man in the ribs, didn't hit? Some preachers air made of awful warpy timber.

AMOS. Ary un seed Dicey?

SAIREY-SAM. Yeah. Dicey's been here for Castoria. Stid of tearin' on back home, her and Fate traipsed off towards my place, 'lowin' she was a-wantin' to see Doshy. Ef that talk that's a-goin' around here is the straight of hit, she ort to be spliced to Fate, and no time lost.

BEN (*laying aside his paper and showing interest for the first time*). Sairey is exactly right. That's another law that ought to be stricter. Ef you had the license I could perform the ceremony right here to-day.

AMOS (*pulling a packet from his pocket*). Got them papers! 'Spicioned Fate of hit. Borrowed Jake's ol' fast-steppin' bay mule and rid to town for this very pair of licenses yisterd'y. 'Lowed I'd find you-uns all here 'bout mail time. Sent Pink here to hold you.

BEN. Ef we had more good citizens like you, this country would need fewer laws.

SAIREY-SAM. Ben's that buttery-mouthed hit might-nigh makes me sick at the stummick. Course he's a-wantin' your vote. Don't differ ef you're a Dimmicrat or a Radical, he'll take ary vote he c'n git, and he'll need 'em all to git to the legislature. Hurry on, Amos, an' fetch 'em back.

PINK (*drawling*). I'm a-needin' of that terbaccer and candy.

SAIREY-SAM (*to* BEN). Go in thar and weight out half of this here in candy, and t'other half in terbaccer. (BEN *goes into the store.*)

AMOS. Gimme your squirrel rifle, Pink, so's I c'n git the drap on him ef he shows fight. (*He takes up the gun and hops off down the road to the right.*)

SAIREY-SAM. Travelin' is so slow for Amos. You'd ort to went stid o' him, Pink. Cain't you holp him go quicker?

PINK (*slyly*). Dunno. Mought sick my ol' dog, Sank, on him. (*He whistles, as if setting a dog on him.*)

SAIREY-SAM. Idyot! That hain't a-goin' to cyore his short breath.

PINK. Ef that's a-pesterin' you, there's longer-winded ones ne'r me a-standin' their tracks.

SAIREY-SAM. Hit's a sight pitifuller to be crippled in the head 'n to be lame in the legs.

PINK. Aunt Sairey, you put me in mind of a ol' rattlesnake in a coil[1] jist a-wantin' to strike everything a-passin'.

SAIREY-SAM. Quit a-auntin' me, Pink Gibson. I ain't no kin o' your'n. Reckon Amos hain't a-goin' to run a-foul o' no trouble gittin' 'em headed this-a-way sence he tuk your rifle? Fate's pow'ful muley 'never he sets 'is head agin a thing. He'll shore argy 'bout hit.

PINK. Hit's nary use a-argyin' ef t'other feller's a-totin' ammynition. Amos was het up bad 'nough to a-fetched 'em by main stren'th and awk'ardness.—Yander they air. Bound to a-met 'em, for they hain't been left long enough to miss 'em.

SAIREY-SAM. Lordy, hit's so. Amos' dander's up. He's sot for a weddin'. Ben, fetch yourself and Pink's sweetenin' on out here. (BEN *comes out and hands the bag of candy and a slim slice of plug tobacco to* PINK. *He appears nervous, brushing imaginary specks of dust from his clothes, and clasping and unclasping his hands.*)

BEN (*to* SAIREY-SAM). Where's the best place for 'em to stand?

SAIREY-SAM. Better leave the say-so to Amos. He's the law. (*The wedding procession enters, with* DICEY *plainly rebellious and* FATE *sullen.* AMOS *is enjoying his armed determination.*)

AMOS (*crossing down to the left and keeping the gun leveled at the middle of* FATE'S *back*). Pink, step around here and git the papers from my hip-pocket, and pass 'em over to Ben.

PINK (*he is now eating his candy vociferously*). Busy. Let Sairey git 'em. (SAIREY-SAM *gets the papers with alacrity, and hands them to* BEN, *who takes his place before the two intimidated ones and begins the ceremony. Suddenly* DICEY *breaks ranks.*)

DICEY. Take that gun off of Fate, Amos. Guess I'm in

[1] Pronounced kwīle.

trouble for the rest o' my life, but I won't lie. (*She points at* SQUIRE BEN.) It's *him!*

PINK (*gulping down the last pieces of candy*). Gimme back my gun, Amos. I'd love to turn hit loose on Ben, myself. (*He acts quickly, strangely for him, and pushes* BEN *into the bridegroom's place, freeing* FATE.)

SAIREY-SAM (*snatching the license from* BEN's *hands and thrusting it at* AMOS). You're a pore chanct for a preacher —mighty nigh a-cussin'. But mebbe you c'n tie a knot that won't slip.

DICEY (*resolved*). I won't have him!

AMOS (*the license shaking in his hand*). Whut you got to say about hit?

DICEY (*conscious of victory*). Ever'thing. (*Quavering.*) I love Fate.

SAIREY-SAM (*explosively*). Eh, Lordy! Hain't that jist like a ooman!—Jist the same, that pair o' licenses was allus Fate's. Nary a grain a good for Ben.

FATE (*relishing his release at first but warming toward* DICEY *appreciably after her declaration in his favor, he sidles awkwardly up to her side*). Sence you hain't *a-makin'* me git spliced, I want you-uns to know that Dicey's jist the one I been a-lovin'. I allus have craved to marry 'er. Glad to git 'er, ef she'll have me—but I hain't a-goin' to raise Ben's young-un!

AMOS (*exuberantly*). That's all right. Me and Pa and Ma'll be proud to keep the little-un. (*He goes up to the sign bearing* BEN's *picture, spits on it, tears it down, and tramples on it. Then, laconically*): 'Druther have a bastard in the fam'ly than a damn' legislater!

CURTAIN

LIGHTED CANDLES

A Tragedy of the Carolina Highlands

BY

MARGARET BLAND

(Written in collaboration with Louisa Duls)

LIGHTED CANDLES

Here is a play drawn from the tragic life of a mountain girl of Mitchell County some thirty years ago. The scene is a remote valley of the Carolina highlands, and the author, Margaret Bland of Charlotte, has given us a genre picture of a family well known to her.

The tale which forms the basis of *Lighted Candles*, she heard by the fireside of a lonely old woman, who often invited her "to set a spell" to visit.

It is a strange tale of a young husband who, growing tired of hoeing his corn and of trying to wrest a scant living for his family from the rocky mountain slopes, had gone off to the West, "leavin' his wife an' young-uns" behind. Much of the conversation the author has remembered and cherished for us in this play.

Lighted Candles is a favorite with the people of the mountain neighborhood in which the incident occurred. It has been presented there from time to time by the people themselves. On one occasion Preacher Wakecaster of the play was enacted with great gusto by the original mountain man after whom the character was drawn. Miss Lucy Morgan of Penland [1] tells me that the title of the play, *Lighted Candles*, has already found a place in the folklore and vernacular of the community. At Spruce Pine, not long ago, she heard the phrase applied to a similar case: "It's just another *Lighted Candles*."

[1] Founder and Director of The Penland School of Handicrafts, Inc. Penland, North Carolina.

THE CHARACTERS

As originally produced at The Playmakers Theatre, Chapel Hill, North Carolina, February 10 and 11, 1927.

EFFIE, *a young mountain woman,*	Enita Nicks
MAME, *her mother,*	Josephine Sharkey
ZEENIE, *her aunt,*	Anita Darling
MOTE, *her lover,*	Charles T. Lipscomb
BROTHER WAKECASTER, *a mountain preacher,*	Hubert Heffner

SCENE: A mountain cabin in a remote valley of western North Carolina.

TIME: The present. An evening late in November.

SCENE

The scene is a remote valley of western North Carolina—the plain room of a mountain cabin, which serves as both living room and kitchen. On the left is a huge fireplace in which a hickory back-log is smouldering. There is an old-time clock on the chimney place. A pile of logs is on the floor near by. There is no furniture other than a table in the center of the room and several splint-bottom chairs. A tall curtained box at the right serves as a cupboard. There is a liquor jug on the cupboard, and two candles set in pottery candlesticks. An unlighted oil lamp is on the table. The cooking pots and pans hang on nails in the wall. The only picture in the room are several "Prominent Society Women" (cut out of the weekly newspaper) and a framed motto, gilt-edged and blue-flowered— "GOD BLESS OUR HOME."

The outside door is in the rear wall at the right, and there is a single window, unshaded, at the left. A door on the right side leads into the only other room of the cabin—the bedroom.

MAME and AUNT ZEENIE are sitting before the fire, smoking their short clay pipes with evident satisfaction. They are typical middle-aged mountain women, fair of complexion but rather faded looking, somewhat bent by hard work, stolid, and conspicuously unanimated. AUNT ZEENIE is taller than her sister, slightly more prosperous in appearance, and of more commanding manner.

AUNT ZEENIE. Law, Mame! You an' me a-settin' here jes' like common, an' hit's Effie's weddin' day.

MAME. I hain't quite able to believe hit yit.

AUNT ZEENIE. She did hol' out agin Mote powerful long. What made her give in d' you reckon?

MAME. I dunno. Hit was the young-un dyin' maybe. She

313

might a-felt like she didn't have no more claim onto Jake, and him not comin' nor a-writin' her a line in five year. Then the craps was a-gittin' poorer. . . . We couldn't a-got on much longer without a man.

AUNT ZEENIE. Is she still got a notion Jake ain't dead?

MAME. I couldn't say for certain. She's been so quare about him—settin' up evenin's waitin' for him, and puttin' candles in the window nights, so as he could see to come up the path ef he was a-comin' home.

AUNT ZEENIE. Suppose'n Jake'd come now after she's married Mote!

MAME. Ef he hain't showed up in five year, he hain't likely to show up now. He's dead, or he would have come back long ago.

AUNT ZEENIE. Hit allus did puzzle me what got into Jake to go way out West, him with a ooman like Effie and a young-un not more'n a few months old.

MAME. I never did put no trust in that man Jake. He was allus that restless. I wasn't wantin' Effie to marry him to begin with, but, law, she didn't have no eyes for Mote or nobody else, as long as Jake was here.

AUNT ZEENIE. Mote's steadier'n Jake. He'll make you-uns good craps; Billy Burnett says thar hain't a better worker in Mitchell County'n Mote.

MAME. I'm hopin' things'll be easier for us now, and that Effie'll brighten up a bit.

AUNT ZEENIE. Is she still takin' on 'bout that young-un?

MAME. Not no more. She took on powerful when hit died. Went down to the graveyard and talked to hit same as hit was livin'. I got sort o' scared she was gittin'—(*she indicates her head with a knowing look*)—teched. But she don't do no more wild talkin' now, jes' works without never sayin' nothin' nor smilin' nuther. (MAME *goes to the bedroom door.*) What's keepin' Effie so long, I wonder? Law, she hain't put her dress on yit—she's jes' a-settin' thar moonin', lookin' out'n the window.

AUNT ZEENIE. Mote'll make her perter than common. Gittin' a man allus sets a ooman up.

MAME. Mote do set a store by Effie. He's been askin' her steady now for nigh onto three year with her a-hol'in' out agin him all the time, till yestiddy. She took a notion sudden yestiddy, and said she'd have him.

AUNT ZEENIE (*looking at the clock on the chimney place*). What time did Mote 'low he'd git here this evenin'?

MAME. Long 'bout five or after. Preacher Wakecaster wouldn't come no sooner. Said he couldn't be marryin' folks in the daylight, and his corn a-needin' hoein.' (*Calling* EFFIE.) Come on out, Effie, and I'll button your dress. (EFFIE *comes into the room. She is a frail young woman of twenty-three with soft brown hair and blue eyes. There is a strange remote look in her eyes. Her sensitive face registers expressions of varying emotion, in contrast to the unchanging stolidity of her mother's.*)

AUNT ZEENIE. Howdy, Effie.

EFFIE. Howdy, Aunt Zeenie. Didn't know you was comin'. (EFFIE *comes slowly over to her mother, who gets up to fasten her dress.*)

AUNT ZEENIE. Yes, Brother Wakecaster don't like to do no marryin' less thar's two witnesses anyway. So I 'lowed I'd come over. Thought I'd take your Ma home with me for the night after hit's over, so as you an' Mote kin have the first evenin' to yerselves.

EFFIE (*dully*). We'll be havin' years and years of evenin's to ourselves.

MAME (*pulling at* EFFIE). Stan' round this way to the light so as I kin see to button you straight.

AUNT ZEENIE (EFFIE *is facing the fireplace now*). Law, you're lookin' purty, Effie—purty as you did t'other time you married.

EFFIE (*quietly*). Twa'n't no other time. I only jes' dreamed hit. Twa'n't no Jake; I only jes' dreamed him too. Twa'n't no young-un neither, no little Jake to hol' in my arms an' talk to 'bout his pa in the West. He ain't dead 'cause he hain't never been. I was only jes' dreamin' him too. (MAME *crosses to her chair by the fire.* EFFIE *goes away to the right.*)

MAME. Now, look here, Zeenie. Don't go a-talkin' to Effie 'bout the las' time she was married. Hit upsets her, that's what hit does. Hit's time for her to forgit what's gone and to think about what's comin'.

EFFIE. I've forgot hit, Ma. Thar hain't no past. Thar's jes' the now. Jes' the meadows as has to be mowed, and the animals as has to be fed, and the craps as has to be planted. Thar hain't no Jake no more, or no little Jake; jes' you an' me.

MAME. And Mote.

EFFIE. And Mote. . . .

AUNT ZEENIE. Mote's a powerful good man, Effie.

EFFIE. He hain't Jake.

MAME. Now, look here, Effie. Don't be a-talkin' that way.

AUNT ZEENIE. Jake's gone, and he's dead more'n likely. And you're gittin' up in your twenties. When a ooman gits up in years, any man's better'n no man.

MAME. Mote'll be kind to you, Effie.

EFFIE. Yes, he'll be kind to us, and he's a good worker.

AUNT ZEENIE (*standing now before the fire*). Course he's sort o' slow but he's a powerful man once he gits het up.

PREACHER WAKECASTER (*outside*). Whoa! Lazarus! (AUNT ZEENIE *goes to look out of the window.*)

AUNT ZEENIE. Law, Mame, ef'n hit hain't Mote and the Preacher.

MAME (*hovering over* EFFIE). Pull yer ha'r out a bit more fluffy-like, Effie. And go back in t'other room, Effie.

Hit's bad luck for the groom to see you 'fore time for the weddin' to begin. (EFFIE *goes back into the bedroom.*)

AUNT ZEENIE. Have you got a drink o' licker for Brother Wakecaster?

MAME. Hit's in the cupboard along with the weddin' supper I done cooked up for 'em. (*A knock sounds at the door, and she crosses over to the fireplace.*) Pull the latch and push the door! (PREACHER WAKECASTER *and* MOTE *enter. The Preacher is a man of fifty or more, huge of stature, with a bald head, and with bristling moustache. He is unkempt in appearance, but he has a kindly air toward every one, and a genial smile. On Sunday, he strikes terror to the hearts of his congregation by his eloquent descriptions of Hell-fire and Damnation, but on Monday, he would hesitate to frighten a chipmunk in his field. Beside him,* MOTE *appears to be a man of much less force. He is powerful of body. His face bespeaks slowness of thought and of emotion, once aroused. He speaks little. The greetings are cordial at their entrance.* PREACHER WAKECASTER *enters first;* MOTE *hangs back a little awkwardly.* MAME *puts another log of wood on the fire.*)

AUNT ZEENIE (*shaking hands with him*). Howdy, Brother Wakecaster. How air ye?

PREACHER WAKECASTER. Stout as common, stout as common, thank ye, Zeenie! But when a man is gittin' old like me thar hain't much for him to do but pray the good Lord to make his last days easy.—Howdy, Mame, air you purty pert? (MAME *steps forward, wiping her hands on her apron, and shakes hands with the Preacher.*)

MAME (*nudging him and chuckling*). Only jes' middlin', Brother Wakecaster, only jes' middlin'.

AUNT ZEENIE. Howdy, Mote, an' wishes for your happiness. You're gittin' a fine ooman.

MOTE. Howdy, Aunt Zeenie. Howdy, Aunt Mame.

MAME. Howdy, Mote. Hit's time you was callin' me Ma

now 'stead of Aunt Mame. I'm powerful proud to have you for a son-in-law.

PREACHER WAKECASTER. But whar's the bride? Too modest to come out—waitin' like a Lily o' the Field till she's sent for? Go bring your daughter out, Mame. Bring her out to this here joyful occasion!

MAME. She's 'bout ready, I reckon. I'll go see. (*She goes into the other room.*)

AUNT ZEENIE. Why don't you-uns set? We-uns'll be back in no time. (*She follows* MAME.)

PREACHER WAKECASTER (*seating himself by the fire*). Well, I reckon settin's cheap as standin'. They might keep us waitin', them oomans. (PREACHER WAKECASTER *puts his satchel on the floor, draws out his Bible, and stretches himself comfortably.* MOTE *continues to stand, awkwardly staring into the fire, warming his hands.*) Hain't you goin' to set, Mote?

MOTE. Reckon I'm not.

PREACHER WAKECASTER. Did you git the license?

MOTE. Uh-huh. . . .

PREACHER WAKECASTER. You got hit with you?

MOTE (*feeling in his pocket*). Uh-huh. . . .

PREACHER WAKECASTER. You're joyful, hain't you?

MOTE. Uh-huh. . . .

PREACHER WAKECASTER. Cain't you say nothin' 'cept "uh-huh"? I hain't never seed such a cheerless bridegroom. Man, this here hain't no funeral. Hit's a weddin', and hit's your'n. (*Pointing to the other room.*) Thar's a Rose o' Sharon waitin' for you in yander. Did you know hit?

MOTE. Uh-huh. . . .

PREACHER WAKECASTER. Lord, Lord, Mote! I believe ye're gittin' narvous, hain't you?

MOTE (*shaking his head*). Nuh. . . .

PREACHER WAKECASTER. Not jes' a little bit narvous? Not jes' a bit shaky in the knees?

MOTE. No, I tell you! I hain't narvous. . . . I'm damned scared!

PREACHER WAKECASTER. Courage, man, courage! Jes' one word and she's your'n. That Lily of the Valley; that apple tree among trees of the wood; that Rose o' Sharon—her that's got lips like a thread o' scarlet; her that's like a young roe on the mountains of Bethel!—That's in the Bible, did you know hit, Mote? (*He spits in the fireplace.*)

MOTE. Nuh. . . .

PREACHER WAKECASTER (*resuming his seat*). 'Tis. All about ol' man Solomon when he got married to his wife—to his wives! Lord! He knowed how to make love, ol' man Solomon did; but he was a wise 'un, he was a wise 'un was ol' man Solomon. (MAME, ZEENIE *and* EFFIE *now return.*) Thar she is, lookin' purttier'n a picture. Thar she is—a Rose o' Sharon, I tell you. Lord, Lord, ef'n I was as young as you, Mote, you wouldn't a-had a chanct. Don't tell the ol' ooman on me, but I can't help sayin' a compliment to a beautiful young lady. (PREACHER WAKECASTER *goes to meet her.*) Blessin's on you, my dear; blessin's on you! You're gittin' yer a fine man this day, a fine man, I'll tell you!

EFFIE (*staring at him intently*). Brother Wakecaster, do you believe . . . do you believe Jake's dead?

AUNT ZEENIE. Law, Effie, be quiet! Don't start that.

MAME. I might a-knowed somethin' 'd go wrong at the last minute. Don't ask him nothin' like that, Effie.

PREACHER WAKECASTER. Hit's all right, Zeenie. Hit's all right, Mame. The child wants to be right in her own min' that she hain't goin' ag'in' the will of the Lord. Why, the Good Book says that ef'n any man can show just cause why they should not be lawfully j'ined together, let him speak now or forever after hol' his peace. An' she wants to be right in her own min', don't you, Effie, child?

EFFIE (*softly*). Yes, Preacher Wakecaster.

PREACHER WAKECASTER. Effie, he ain't been nigh you in five year, an' he hain't wrote you in five year, an' he hain't never sent you no money; so, Effie, in the eyes of the law you're as free as a widow.

MOTE (*drawling*). I asked the sheriff. He said 'twas all right; an' the clerk sol' me the license, he said 'twas all right.

EFFIE. But, Brother Wakecaster, do you believe he's dead?

PREACHER WAKECASTER. Of course, of course! Ef'n he warn't dead he'd a-been back long ago. Are you ready to begin the ceremony? (PREACHER WAKECASTER *puts down his Bible on the table.* EFFIE *picks it up and holds it out to him.*)

EFFIE. Brother Wakecaster, you say he'd a-been back ef'n he hain't been dead. Will you swear to me on this Book that you believe hit's true?

PREACHER WAKECASTER. Thar, thar, now, Effie. I don't min' sayin' hit's true, 'cause I believe hit's true; but I'll be blamed ef'n I want to say hit's damned true!

EFFIE (*going over to* MOTE *at the fireside*). Mote, do you believe he's dead? Mote, would you solemnly swear to me on this Book that you believe he's dead?

MOTE. Effie, do you reckon I'd want to take you for my ooman, a-thinkin' all the time he was a-livin'?

EFFIE (*resigned*). I reckon not.

MOTE. Are you satisfied?

EFFIE. Yes, Mote. (*She gives the Bible to the Preacher, who holds the Book open before him during the ceremony.*)

PREACHER WAKECASTER. Let's get on with this thing. Let's get on with this thing before hit turns dark. Mame, are you ready? Zeenie, are you ready?

MAME AND ZEENIE. Yes, Brother Wakecaster.

PREACHER WAKECASTER. Well, let the wedding party take their places. Take your places everybody. The bride ought to be on my right, and the bridegroom on my left, an' a witness on each side. You stand right here, Effie; Mote, you thar. (*In taking their places,* ZEENIE *goes to the Preacher's right by* EFFIE, *and* MAME *goes to his left with* MOTE.)

MAME. Law, I want to be standin' by my own gal! You come over on this side, Effie.

AUNT ZEENIE. Let Effie stay whar she be. You change with me, Mame. (MAME *and* ZEENIE *exchange places.*)

PREACHER WAKECASTER. Everythin's sot, everythin's sot. The ceremony will now begin.—The Good Book says that God created ooman to be a helpmate to man. (*Reading from the Bible.*) "Therefore, shall a man leave his father and his mother, and shall cleave unto his wife." Mote, wilt thou have this ooman to be thy lawfully wedded wife, to live together after God's ordinance in the holy estate of matrimony? Answer, "I will."

MOTE. I will.

PREACHER WAKECASTER. Effie, wilt thou have this man to be thy lawfully wedded husband to live together after God's ordinance in the holy estate of matrimony? Answer, "I will."

EFFIE. I . . . I will. . . .

PREACHER WAKECASTER. J'in your right hands. (*They do so.*) Those whom God hath j'ined together, let no man put asunder. For as much as Mote and Effie have consented together in holy wedlock, and have witnessed the same before this here company, I pronounce them man and wife. (*During the ceremony* PREACHER WAKECASTER *pronounces each word slowly and distinctly, accenting the long words on the last syllable. During the prayer, all bow reverently.*)

PREACHER WAKECASTER (*with his hands uplifted*). Oh, Lord, pour forth thy blessin's on this man and this ooman. Let

the light of the countenance be upon them as they go
through this life together. Keep them in health and
prosperity, and make them long to live for the doin' o'
thy will. Amen. (*There is silence for a moment.* MAME
and AUNT ZEENIE *wipe their eyes furtively.*)

PREACHER WAKECASTER (*cheerfully*). Kiss the Preacher first,
Effie! (*He kisses her loudly, then shakes hands with* MOTE.
Then PREACHER WAKECASTER *crosses over to* MOTE *by the
fireplace.*) Congratulations, Mote! Congratulations! I'm
'feared you've sort o' out-married yourself; but try to live
up to her, man; try to live up to her. (MAME *and* ZEENIE
kiss EFFIE *and go to shake hands with* MOTE.)

AUNT ZEENIE. Law, Mame, ef'n you hain't forgettin' Brother
Wakecaster's licker! (EFFIE *is now seated at the right of the
table, and* ZEENIE *is comforting her.*)

MAME. Law, Brother Wakecaster, 'scuse me, but I'm that
excited. Mote, would you keer for a drap yourself?

MOTE. Don't keer ef'n I do. (MAME *hurries to the cupboard,
pours out two glasses of corn liquor, and gives one to each of
the men.* MOTE *gulps his down nervously, but* PREACHER
WAKECASTER *surveys his glass, smacking his lips, and
wiping his mouth with due ceremony.*)

PREACHER WAKECASTER. I hain't averse to hit! I hain't
averse to hit! The Good Book says that wine maketh glad
the heart. Don't forgit to sign the license, witnesses. We
want to git these young-uns hitched up proper!

MOTE (*pulling the license from his pocket*). Here's the license.

AUNT ZEENIE. I'll do the signin', Mame. Your mark and
mine. You git your things quick and mebbe Brother Wakecaster'll give us a lift as far as the holler. (ZEENIE *takes
the license from* MOTE *and goes to the table to sign it.*)

PREACHER WAKECASTER. Sure, Mame, come along with me.
Come along with me. Me and my ol' mule Lazarus'll be
plumb proud to have you both. (*Examining the license and
directing* ZEENIE.) Right here, Zeenie, right under my

name. (*Raising his re-filled glass.*) I drinks to your health, my children. (MAME *goes into the other room and returns almost immediately, with her hat on, and a package in her hand. She goes to* EFFIE *and kisses her affectionately.*)

MAME. Good-bye, Effie. Good-bye, my little gal. (EFFIE *is frightened and clings to her mother.*) You know your weddin' supper's in the cupboard and I'll be back in time to git breakfast for you in the mornin'.—Good-bye, Mote.

AUNT ZEENIE (*at the door*). Good-bye, Effie. Good-bye, Mote.—Come along, Mame, don't let's keep the Preacher waitin'!

PREACHER WAKECASTER. Good-bye, my chil'ren, good-bye. I was plumb tickled to hitch you-uns up; and I'll be right on the spot ef'n thar is any baptizin' to be done! (*He laughs heartily and follows* MAME *and* ZEENIE *out.* EFFIE *is still sitting at the table, staring into the fire.* MOTE *stands awkwardly by the door for a time, then closes it.*)

MOTE. Hit's gittin' dark, Effie.

EFFIE (*without looking up*). So 'tis.

MOTE. Whar's the matches, Effie? I'll make a light.

EFFIE. On the chimney place. (MOTE *crosses to the fireplace, finds the matches and lights the lamp. He stands close to* EFFIE, *waiting for her to speak; but she does not turn. He tries to speak gently to her.* EFFIE *glances at the window.*)

MOTE. Effie, you hain't kissed me yit.

EFFIE. No, not yit. . . . (*He bends over her, and she lifts her face slightly. He kisses her with reverence, almost fearfully— as if she were a crucifix.*)

MOTE (*gently*). You are my ooman now, Effie. . . . You'll be happy with me, won't you, Effie?

EFFIE (*in a dead voice*). Yes. . . . (MOTE *crosses to the fireplace and sits there in silence.*)

MOTE. Effie, would you keer ef'n I took off my shoes?

EFFIE. No. . . .

MOTE (*proudly, as he unties the shoes*). Them's new shoes—new shoes I bought in Spruce Pine this mornin'—special for the weddin'. (*He stretches his stocking feet out before the fire.*) But I hain't used to weddin' shoes. They kind o' pinches. (*He continues to warm his feet at the fire, glancing furtively at* EFFIE *from time to time. She is silent.*) Hain't you kind o' hungry, Effie? I am.

EFFIE (*rousing herself*). Law, Mote, 'scuse me. I hain't give a thought to fixin' you no supper. I'll git hit now. (*She gets up, a trifle dazed, and goes to the cupboard to get the supper her mother has prepared for them.*)

MOTE. Tain't no matter, Effie. I'll have more appetite when hit is ready.

EFFIE. Ma left the milk in the spring-house. Would you git hit, Mote, while I fix the table?

MOTE (*pulling on his shoes*). Whar's the pitcher?

EFFIE (*she brings the pitcher to the table and hands it to* MOTE). Here 'tis.

MOTE (*going to the door*). Spring-house locked?

EFFIE. No, hit's open. (*He goes out, carrying the pitcher.* EFFIE *sets the liquor jug on the floor. She takes down the two candles from the cupboard and places them on the table. She lights them, holds them up a moment. Radiant, she takes them to the window and stands looking out into the dark. She cries out, "Jake, Jake!" lifting the candles high. Then she puts them down on the window sill and remains a moment in silence, looking off.* MOTE *is heard returning, and she hurries back to the table and goes on with the preparations for supper.*)

MOTE (*with the pitcher of milk*). Here 'tis, Effie. (*He puts it down on the table and goes back to the fireplace. Then he sees the candles burning in the window.*) We don't need them candles, Effie—the lamp's enough.

EFFIE. They're purty.

MOTE. Law, yes, but hit's wasteful.

EFFIE. They don't burn down much in one evenin', an' . . . an' I likes lighted candles.

Mote. Well, so long as hit's our weddin' day, we can afford to be festive, I reckon. But so long as we've got 'em lighted we ought to have 'em on the table, 'stead of in the window —'cause that's whar we'll be a-settin'. (*He starts to get them from the window.*)

Effie. Let 'em be, Mote! Let 'em be!

Mote. They'd look jes' as purty on the table, Effie, and they'd be a sight more useful. (Mote *moves a step nearer the window.* Effie *stands between him and the candles.*)

Effie. Don't, Mote! Don't!

Mote. What's got into you, Effie? I don't like your damned candles burnin' in the window. You seem to have some creepy notion about 'em. Why don't you want 'em moved? (Effie *is silent.*) Well, if'n you hain't got no reason you can tell, I don't know no reason. (*He takes the candles from the window and places them on the table.*)

Effie (*pleading*). Don't, Mote! Don't! (*She takes up the candles gently, places them back in the window, and stands between them and* Mote *as if to protect them.*)

Mote. Well, why hain't I to move 'em?

Effie. Mote, hit's jes' a notion o' mine.

Mote (*suspicious*). Is that notion o' your'n 'bout . . . Jake? (*She does not answer.*) Effie, are them candles burnin' for Jake? (*She nods reluctantly.*) I hain't goin' to have no candles burnin' in my windows for Jake. Hit's time for you to forgit Jake. You're my ooman now. (*He seizes one of the candles and blows it out.* Effie *shrieks and replaces it.*)

Effie. Don't, Mote! Don't! I don't mean no harm. Hit's jes' that I've been a-doin' hit for five year now—havin' a bit of a light in the window so as he could see to git home ef'n he was comin' up the path.

Mote. I hain't goin' to have no candles burnin' in my windows to light a dead man home to a ooman that's mine. (*Fully determined now, he goes to get them.*)

EFFIE (*screaming and pushing him away*). Don't you blow out them candles. Don't you *dast!*

MOTE. I hain't a-goin' to have them candles burnin', I— (*He is about to extinguish them.*)

EFFIE. Don't you blow hit out, Mote. Hit's all I got—jes' one little notion—that's all that's left me o' Jake.

MOTE. I don't want you to have nothin' left you of Jake— not even a notion. You're married to me, now, to *me!*

EFFIE. Ef'n you blow out them candles I'll leave you, Mote —I swear I'll leave you. I'll leave you to-night. I'll leave you now!

MOTE (*he pushes* EFFIE *violently away and blows out the candles*). You can't leave me. You're mine. (EFFIE *begins setting the table again.* MOTE *strides sullenly down to the fireplace.*) You needn't fool with no plates. You've riled me so, I hain't a-wantin' to eat now. (*He stalks to the door, bolts it and comes down to the bedroom.*) Come on, Effie, you hear me?

EFFIE. Yes, Mote. . . .

MOTE. Hain't you comin'? (*There is a silence.*)

EFFIE. I . . . reckon. . . . (*He goes in, glancing back at* EFFIE, *and closing the door after him.*) EFFIE *picks up a dish from the table, absentmindedly, but it falls from her hand with a dull thud. . . . She looks toward the bedroom, hesitates, then strikes a match and lights one of the candles. . . . She realizes what she has done. . . . With a fixed determination she lights the other candle. . . . Then she places them again on the window ledge. . . . She takes her shawl and wraps it about her shoulders, and starts to leave. . . . She hesitates at the door, then comes down in the direction of the bedroom. . . . But shudders and turns away. . . . She goes back to the chair by the table and drops down into it helplessly, staring before her. . . . Then her face becomes luminous. . . . The candles are still burning in the window.*

CURTAIN

QUARE MEDICINE
A Country Comedy of a Quack Doctor

BY

PAUL GREEN

327

QUARE MEDICINE

Quare Medicine was Paul Green's first comedy. It was written for the occasion of the dedication of The Playmakers Theatre building, the week of November 23, 1925. I have written of him in a foreword to his first published book, *The Lord's Will and Other Carolina Plays*. Born on a farm in Harnett County in eastern Carolina, Paul Green is as much a part of North Carolina as the soil from which he springs. His plays are as indigenous as the pine tree to his sand-hills. Like the tree his roots strike deep. And from the raw materials of the land he draws forth the life itself.—After a performance of *Old Wash Lucas* (originally *The Miser*) on one of our Playmakers' tours, a man in the audience said to me, "I know every member of that family; it's all *true.*"

I remember when young Green returned from the war to his studies—in the fall of 1919. The war had made a deep impression on him, and the first play he wrote in the University playwriting course was a transcript of his own experience in the trenches of France. Then came the first play to be produced by our Carolina Playmakers—*The Last of the Lowries*. Here, we knew, was a sound artist—a new playwright of tragic power and poetic insight. There is a lyric note intrinsic in all of Green's dramatic writing. Even in the homely comedy of *Quare Medicine* there is in the doggerel chanting of Doctor Immanuel a rare feeling for the imagery and the melody of the simple country folk he knows so well—his own people.

In this play, Paul Green recalls a familiar figure from his boyhood days in the little town of Lillington, North Carolina. To those acquainted with the rural life of eastern Carolina as it was a few years ago, the patent-medicine vendor or quack doctor is not unknown. Formerly this species of cure-all could be met with frequently enough as he plied his trade among the country people with considerable profit to himself. Of late years, though, his tribe has more and more decreased before the inroads of science and sanitary methods. And in our complex civilization he will soon be lost altogether. The so-called doctor pictured in this play is by no means a true representative of the type. He does, however, resemble a loud-mouthed, lonely fellow, the author tells me, who used to dare to sell his wares before the courthouse in Lillington during "court." The situation which Doctor Immanuel untangles, is by no means a usual one. But it is true that these doctors often exercised among their clientele both a veterinary and a spiritual influence hard to conceive of now.

I recall in the early days of the Playwriting course, when we gathered around a long seminar table in an upper room of the old Library Building here, Paul Green asking me one afternoon a question which was really a challenge: "'Proff,' where is this thing going to lead us to, anyhow?" I have thought about his question many times, and I am still thinking about it. Of one thing I am certain, however—we would do well to encourage the young playwright in expressing the life he knows, and we can help him by providing a stage for him. Perhaps he may be able to help us on our way.

Only the other day Paul brought to me a copy of his latest volume *In the Valley and Other Carolina Plays*, and on the fly-leaf he wrote these lines:

> *Who are these walking in November—*
> *the trees bare, the birds singing no more?*
> *These are the sisters, these are the brethren*
> *marching to Canaan Land.*

For are we not all sisters and brethren marching to Canaan Land?

Chapel Hill, North Carolina.
February, 1941.

THE CHARACTERS

As originally produced at The Playmakers Theatre, Chapel Hill, North Carolina, November 23, 24, 25 and 26, 1925, on the occasion of the Dedication of the Theatre.

OLD MAN JERNIGAN,   Claudius Mintz
HENRY JERNIGAN, *his son*,   E. R. Patterson
MATTIE JERNIGAN, *Henry's wife*, Helen Leatherwood
DOCTOR IMMANUEL, *a patent-medicine vendor and cure-all*,
                 Charlie Gold

SCENE: The sitting-room of the Jernigan farmhouse in eastern North Carolina.
TIME: Several years ago, at the close of a winter day.

SCENE

The scene is the combined sitting-room and bedroom of the JERNI-
GAN *house, with a fireplace to the left, a sewing-machine to the
right and a table in the center of the room. The floor is carpeted
with bright straw matting, and everything bristles with tidy prim-
ness. A door is at the center back and one at the left rear. The
window at the right center, neatly curtained, shows a streak of
sombre autumn fields filling up with the blue dusk of a fading
winter day. From another part of the house the voice of a woman
can be heard shrilly singing "Rescue the perishing, care for the
dying." The elder* JERNIGAN, *walking with a stick, comes carefully in at the rear door shivering with cold and carrying a mug-
cup in his hand. Below a mass of white hair his face shines out
like a ruddy apple, and his whole person suggests the toughness
and durability of a dried hickory root. Half-way across the room
he stops and listens to the singing.*

JERNIGAN (*sharply imitating*). "Rescue the perishing, care
for the dying!" (*He moves over to the fire and sets his mug to
warm; after which he takes a bottle from the mantel, pours out
some medicine in a spoon and swallows it. He sits down and
stretches his hands to the blaze with a grunt of satisfaction.
In a moment he feels the cup and takes a long drink. The
woman's voice calls from off the right.*)

VOICE. Father!

JERNIGAN (*starting*). Ah-hanh! What is it?

VOICE (*nearer*). Father—fath-er!

JERNIGAN (*moving towards the door at the left*). What is it,
Mattie?

VOICE. Supper's 'bout ready. Where's Henry? (*The singing
begins again, fading towards the kitchen.*)

JERNIGAN (*calling futilely after her*). He's feeding up and'll

331

be here in a minnit. (*He listens awhile and then reseats himself thoughtfully before the fire. Presently there is a heavy scraping of feet on the steps outside and* HENRY JERNIGAN *comes timidly in at the rear. He is a big awkward farmer of thirty or more, hesitating and shy. He takes his seat silently and wearily in a rocking chair, being careful not to touch the whitewashed hearth with his feet. The old man looks at him closely.*) Tired out, ain't you? Hyuh, try some o' this 'simmon beer, I jest dreaned the barrel.

HENRY (*in a slow, fumbling voice*). I don't want none o' that, I believe.

JERNIGAN. Unh-hunh. (*They both lapse into silence, staring before them. Soon the elder* JERNIGAN *peers through the window at the winter sunset.*) Gonna be cold, Henry, cold. Robins been flying towards the south all day. (HENRY *says nothing.*) You're tireder'n common, ain't you, Henry?

HENRY. Yeh. (*Lifelessly.*) Wore out, wore out.

JERNIGAN (*taking his bottle from the mantel*). Hyuh, take this last dost of Doctor 'Manuel's tonic. (HENRY *shakes his head.*) Well, I will then. (*He pours out the last drop and swallows it.*) Doctor said he'd be by to-day. 'Bout night and he ain't hyuh yit. You better git him to give you something, ye better, Henry, you're looking thin, thin.

HENRY. He ain't no doctor, he's a humbug.

JERNIGAN. Lard help my life!

HENRY. Wonder that mess don't kill you—old branch water and chemicals he's mixed up, I betcha. (*He sighs heavily, listening to the song in the kitchen.*) That old man's crazy with poetry and talking and medicine!

JERNIGAN. Hunh, not hardly. (*Solemnly.*) 'Tain't body tired what ails ye, Henry, is it? (*After a moment he jerks his thumb in the direction of the song.*) Still singing, Henry. There it is.

HENRY. Yeh, I know.

JERNIGAN. Ah-hah, but folks will marry jest the same. She's

worse'n ever, Henry. Good she is, religious good. Cooking and sewing and scrubbing and all fixed up fer to-night. Look over there on the machine at what she's got finished fer them there Hindoos or whatever they are. There's my coat I bought in Dunn five years back at Old Man Ransome Taylor's sale!

HENRY (*his eyes travelling heavily about the room*). What's she got on fer to-night?

JERNIGAN. Another one o' them there meetings. Old Mis' Pate and her gang's coming hyuh to sew fer the heathen and them that's starving over in the Old World. (*Staring at him intently.*) This religious mess is gonna kill Mattie off ef you don't git up manhood enough to stop it. Sing and talk, sing and talk, Lard, I cain't stand it no more.

HENRY. I—I cain't—I ain't gonna put my authority on nobody. She's her own boss.

JERNIGAN. Own boss! She's her own boss and our'n too. Well, ef you're scared of her, all right. They ain't no help fer it. (*He turns towards the fire, patting his foot forlornly on the floor.*) But, Henry, ye ain't gittin' no fun out'n living, and right now's the time ye ort.—And as fer me—I been wanting to talk—(*hitching up his chair*)—to you 'bout this. Why in the name o' Old Scratch you don't up and putt down yer foot I cain't see. (HENRY *says nothing.*) But ye won't. (*Half to himself.*) He ain't got no backbone, lets everybody run over him. (*He reaches for his cup and drains down the last of his beer in an angry gulp.*) Ye didn't git that from yer mammy ner from me, Henry. (*He mocks the singing in the kitchen*): "Rescue the perishing—"

HENRY (*suddenly standing up*). I cain't have no row with nobody, not with her nohow, I tell you. (*At the door.*) I got to go part the cow and calf. (*He slams the door behind him and the old man jumps in astonishment.*)

JERNIGAN. Dinged ef he didn't slam the door—hee, hee, hee. Good fer you, Henry, good fer you! (MATTIE, *a fair-faced young woman, comes in from the left, singing and carrying a stone churn in her arms. Despite her housewifely certainty of action, there is an indefinite femimine frailty about her.*)

MATTIE. What's good for Henry?

JERNIGAN (*hurrying in confusion to his chair*). Nothing, Mattie, nothing at all. (*She looks sharply at him a moment and then sets the churn by the hearth.*)

MATTIE. I'm putting the milk here to turn. I wisht you'd look at it every now and then and stir it with the dasher.

JERNIGAN. All right, Mattie, all right.

MATTIE. And mind, don't you spill none o' that old beer on the hearth.

JERNIGAN. I won't, Mattie, I won't.

MATTIE. What'd Henry go out for?

JERNIGAN. To git the calf away from the cow.

MATTIE (*the words piling out*). I bet he didn't wipe his feet when he come in. And did you? (*Staring at the floor and following* HENRY's *trail.*) No, he didn't—just look at the dirt, just look at it. (*She hurries into the room at the left and returns with a broom sedge broom.*) Here, sweep it up, Father. (*She pushes the broom into his hand.*) I've got to go back to my batter. (*She sticks her head out of the door at the rear and calls.*) Henry—Hen-ry! Supper! (*She turns back into the room and old* JERNIGAN *falls to sweeping.*) Sweep it towards the hearth, towards the hearth, Father, and mind the milk, don't git it full of dust. (*She goes out singing, beginning where she left off*)—"from sin and the grave—"

JERNIGAN (*sweeping*). Lard, Lard A'mighty, was ever martel man so persecuted! (*Leaning on his broom and musing.*) There he is—(*nodding his head to the right*)—pore soul, not at peace in his own household, going about like a man with the mulligrubs, cain't eat, cain't sleep, worried, worried down to the ground. And there she is—(*nodding to the left*)—reading the "Christian Herald" and hearing about dirt and disease and famine over in Azhy till she ain't fit to live with. Listen to her, listen to her, will you? What's to become of me, Old Moster only knows. What, to come to this, to this in my old age and me—(*thumping on his chest*)—yeh, me, old and with a crippled leg from marching in Furginny! (*He wipes his sleeve across his eyes and goes back to sweeping. Presently he stops and begins to muse again.*) Putts me to sweeping, she does, and churning and gitting up the eggs, and following old setting hens around. And she's had me at the wash-tub like an old woman, she has. Damn it! (*His voice sags over the oath.*) I ain't no woman. If Henry ain't got the grit to say something, I have. It's "Father do this, Father do that, Father —Father—Father!" But ding it all, she's a good girl. It's that drot'n old bellcow of a Bella Pate and her gang what's got her worse'n she ever has been. I wisht a starm would come up and blow the whole shooting-match of 'em clean to Roosia or wherever it is. Then they'd git enough o' them there heathen, I reckon. But they ain't got no right to interfere with me, not a bit. (*He puts a hand into his pocket and holds up a small tin box in his left hand and a plug of tobacco in his right.*) Here they come and set 'pon me about my tobacco. Chew chewing-gum, chewing-gum, they say, to save fer the heathen and to pertect my health. (*He rattles the tin box.*) And I've chewed that wad o' stuff till I cain't git rid of it in my sleep. Cain't wear it out, cain't by no means. I'm done of it, I am. Have to slip off and hide to chew my tobacco, and all in a land of freedom. (*He stands thinking, then goes to the door at the left and calls.*) Mattie, air ye busy?

MATTIE. Yes, I've got my hands in the dough!

JERNIGAN. All right. (*He stealthily bites off a chew from his plug, drops his tin box in his pocket and spits in the fire with grim happiness. Just as he is leaning to spit a second time, the door opens suddenly at the left rear, and* MATTIE *comes in with a cloth.* OLD JERNIGAN *draws back, and begins*

sweeping in a fury of embarrassment. He calls out testily.)
Thought you was busy. Ain't I doing all right?

MATTIE. Sweep it clean, Father. I forgot this cloth for the churn. (*She raises the lid from the churn and stirs the contents around with the dasher.*) It's all right and ready, lacking just a bit for churning. Don't you let it slosh on anything while you're a-churning it. (*She wraps the cloth around the handle of the dasher. The old man is sweeping and watching her out of the corner of his eye. While she is bent over she sees something on the hearth that attracts her attention. She rises up to her height and with a sharp note in her voice turns upon him.*) Mr. Jernigan—

JERNIGAN. Nah, nah, Mattie.

MATTIE. Signs don't lie, and there's signs of it there on my hearth. (*Working around the room and watching him furtively.*) Right here in my front room! Ain't you got your mouth full of tobacco right this minute? (*He shakes his head.*) Yes, you have, yes, you have. (*She stands looking at him as he sweeps.*) Father, why don't you say something, cain't you talk? (*He makes little movements of agony and finally chokes.*) Yes, yes, you are chewing right now. Spit it out, spit it out! Don't stand there and swallow that juice, it'll kill you. (*In desperation he runs to the fireplace and explodes into the fire, and stands coughing with a nauseated look on his face.*) I'll get you some water! (*She hurries out and reappears immediately with a glass of water and a battered wash-basin full of claying material.*) Here, drink it, and take this pan and rag and clay the hearth over. (*After drinking the water, he ruefully gets down on his knees and begins work. She goes to the machine.*) Hurry and get it done, I got supper nearly cooked. (*She sits down and begins singing, "How firm a foundation—"*)

JERNIGAN (*indicating the garments*). Air they fer the heathen?

MATTIE. They are that.

JERNIGAN (*timidly*). 'Course you know best, I reckon. But how do you know they wear britches over there?

MATTIE (*staring at him in amazement*). Who ever heard of folks not wearing britches! You know they'd put 'em in jail for such, if they didn't.

JERNIGAN (*venturing*). I hearn they don't wear nothing over there but a string around their waist to tell where the middle is.

MATTIE (*pedaling furiously*). You men don't care, of course, care 'bout nothing but your farming and your crops. Why, it's in the "Christian Herald" where the little children just go through the woods in big droves gnawing the bark off of the trees they're so hungry. We've decided to give up our breakfast and send the cost of it to them.

JERNIGAN. That's why you didn't eat breakfast this morning. Well—you e't a whole lot more fer dinner to make up fer it, didn't ye?

MATTIE (*sharply and with a nervous note in her voice as she gets suddenly up from the machine*). Father, take all this mess out when you get done—that old 'simmon beer cup, and that old 'Manuel patent medicine bottle, and don't forget to carry the clay pan out. (*She goes out at the left. Her song is heard rising in the distance.* OLD JERNIGAN *continues claying the hearth, muttering to himself.* HENRY *comes in at the rear.*)

HENRY (*stretching his legs carefully towards the fire*). What's the matter with the hearth *now*?

JERNIGAN (*setting the pan in the corner by the wood-box*). Nothing, nothing, Henry. She thought she saw a speck on it somewhere.

HENRY. You must a-been chewing tobacco ag'in.

JERNIGAN. Well, why shouldn't I chew?

HENRY. Yeh, yeh, I wisht you could in peace.

JERNIGAN. You'd be better off ef you'd go back to chewing.

HENRY. I know. But I promised her I'd quit and I have.

JERNIGAN. I used to chew it 'fore it quit raining in Africky or wherever it is and 'fore old Bella Pate brung her sanctified self around here, I did, and they was some joy in having a far then, and some reason for having a farplace too. (*Tapping on the andiron with his stick.*) That's what it's made fer—to spet in.

HENRY (*timidly and somewhat hopefully*). Why don't you talk it out with Mattie? (*Earnestly*). I wisht you would.

JERNIGAN. Durned ef I didn't come purty nigh telling her something a while ago. (*He catches* HENRY *by the arm.*) Now look-a-here, Henry, you'n me's got to do something. The thing for you to do is to walk down the road to-night and meet Mis' Pate and them folks and tell 'em they cain't come up here to carry on no prayer-meeting and sewing business. Tell 'em to go som'r's else. Tell 'em to go to—hell!

HENRY (*shrinking away*). I cain't do that, I cain't. Lord, you're near 'bout gone to cussing.

JERNIGAN. And tell 'em yer wife ain't gonna have nothing else to do with sich.

HENRY (*quickly*). I tell you what, you do it.

JERNIGAN. I would in a minnit, Henry, but you're the head of the house and you better. It's yer place to. (HENRY *turns himself about before the fire.*)

HENRY. Mebbe they won't come to-night, and before they meet another time mebbe we can figger on something to do.

JERNIGAN. Hunh, they'll be hyuh, all right.

HENRY (*staring off*). I hear they's mad dogs about. One bit Dick Ryall's child this evening.

JERNIGAN (*studying*). Well, that may break up the meeting, but I won't believe it till I see it, not me. Take more'n mad dogs to stop religion. You stand up to Mattie, I tell you, putt the britches on and wear 'em yourself. Lard, I cain't understand you. Why you let her impose on me in my old age the way you do I cain't see. (*He turns away and sits down in his armchair.* MATTIE *comes in with a tin bucket in her hand.*)

MATTIE. I've got to go across the field to Mis' Ragland's a bit. (*Suddenly stopping.*) Henry, go right back out that door and wipe off your feet.

HENRY (*mumbling*). I thought I cleaned my feet. (*He goes outside and is heard scraping his shoes on the edge of the porch.*)

MATTIE. Sweep it up, Father. (*He gets the broom and sweeps.*) I got to borrow some soda from Mis' Ragland and she wanted me to bring her a jar o' jam.

HENRY (*coming back into the room*). I'll go over there for you, Mattie.

MATTIE. No, I'll go, and you-all go on and git your supper. I've put the biscuits in the stove, and they'll be ready by the time you wash and get to the table. Now, Henry, don't let them biscuits burn. (*She goes out.*)

JERNIGAN (*scornfully*). Jest look at her—didn't have a bit o' business over there, jest wants to go over and see what old Nonie Ragland's got made up for the heathen. Henry, you got to lay down the law, I tell you.

HENRY. Yeh, yeh.

JERNIGAN. Now, I'm gonna talk straight to you. Women is like mules and all dumb brutes, Henry, you got to break 'em 'fore they'll work.

HENRY. Nah, nah, I cain't do that. (*There is a knock on the porch.*)

JERNIGAN. Who kin that be? (*Happily.*) That's my doctor, I betcha. (*The knock is repeated at the door.*)

HENRY (*raising his voice in sudden irritability*). Go on away! Go way!

JERNIGAN (*staring at him*). What—Come in, come in! (DOCTOR IMMANUEL *comes in.*) I knowed it was you, Doctor. I knowed it was you. (*The* DOCTOR *is a man of medium height, about fifty years old, dressed in a cheap threadbare dark suit, celluloid collar and dark tie. His coat hangs low and nearly to the knees, clerical-like. Despite his cheap dress there is an indefinable air of distinction about him; some-thing scholarly, something forlorn in his pale clean-cut face and dark piercing eyes. He carries a well-worn medicine case in his hand. As he enters the door, he pulls off his derby hat, disclosing a huge mop of long black hair streaked with gray and resting like a bolster on his neck and shoulders.)*

DOCTOR (*in a deep level voice*). Masters of this house, friends—

JERNIGAN (*pushing up a chair*). Come right in, come right in and make yourself at home. (*The* DOCTOR *lays his hat on the bed at the right and puts his case in a chair. He moves in a sort of dream-like, mask-like manner, intent upon his business and paying little attention to the two men.*)

DOCTOR (*his voice moving in a level chant, half-singing as he opens the case*). What can I do for you to-night? What can I do for you to-night? (*He takes out bottle after bottle, shakes it, squints at it towards the light, and replaces it, chanting as he does so.*)

> As you all know, wherever I go,
> My name is Immanuel,
> I treat you well, I make you well,
> Sound as the sweet church bell.

(*He turns suddenly on* OLD JERNIGAN *who starts back in surprise.*) Now what is it, brother? What can I do for you?

JERNIGAN (*fetching the bottle*). Another bottle. I just drunk the last.

HENRY (*growling*). Another bottle of stump water, dish water, rain water.

DOCTOR (*holding up the bottle*). Doctor Immanuel's Universal Remedy! Right it is and very fit. Distilled from secret weeds and herbs by mystic processes. Cures internal ailments, cuts, burns, bruises, is an antidote for poisons, can be taken internally or externally. For swelling in the joints, leg sores, sore throat, convulsions, dizziness, fits, and general disorders. (*The words roll from him in a flood. He turns towards* OLD JERNIGAN, *fixes him with his eyes, and suddenly sings out.*) What is your trouble, brother? Are you healed, better or—It's cold to-night, cold to-night, and ice on the pools in the lane.

JERNIGAN. In my knee, you remember, in my knee. (*He slaps his hand to it.*) I'm getting better, doctor, slowly, slowly.

DOCTOR (*holding his hand up in assurance*). Slowly but surely, certainly, absolutely. Another bottle and you walk straight as any man.

> As you all know, wherever I go,
> My name is Immanuel,
> I always make you well,
> As any man will tell. . . .

(*His voice drops to a whisper and he hums under his breath, the while he is putting away the empty bottle and getting out another. He hands the bottle to* OLD JERNIGAN.) The price is one and a quarter now, brother. Prices have gone up, prices are going up. The demand exceeds the supply. (*Again he chants.*)

> I travel from morning till night
> Curing and fixing things right.
> From night until day
> I'm on a-my way—

(*He begins placing his bottle back in his case.*)

> Seeking the saddened sight—

(*Again he whirls upon the old man.*) Is the knee all that troubles you? Have you other troubles, diseases of the body or the soul?

JERNIGAN (*shaking his head quickly*). Nanh, nanh, I'm all right saving my knee.

DOCTOR (*picking up a small bottle and holding it lovingly before him*). Now here is a remedy, *the* remedy, the heart and soul of the matter, the help for the world's evils. Down in Egypt, the country of darkness, it was discovered. Dug out of the tombs of the powers of evil. Hid away they had it, but my agent discovered it, sent it to me, here it is. (*Reading.*) Dr. Immanuel's Egyptian Tonic. (*Suddenly barking like an auctioneer, as* HENRY *jumps in his chair.*)

> Two dollars a bottle, two dollars,
> Going at two dollars.
> Are you weak and heavy laden,
> Sore distressed, sad distressed?
> It will cleanse of evil passion,
> Restore you bowels of compassion,
> Accidents, diseases chronic—

(*Shouting.*)

> The marvelous Egyptian Tonic.

(*He sticks it out at* OLD JERNIGAN.)

> Two dollars once, two dollars twice—
> Going at two—

JERNIGAN (*backing away from him as he fumbles in his pocket-book for his money*). Nanh, nanh, this bottle's enough. Here's your dollar and a quarter. (*The* DOCTOR *takes the money impersonally.*) Come up to the fire and warm yourself.

HENRY (*looking at* OLD JERNIGAN *significantly*). Anh-hanh, what'd I tell you? (*The* DOCTOR *closes his case and goes to the bed for his hat.* HENRY *calls to him bitterly.*) You better look out down in that creek for mad dogs.

DOCTOR (*turning back quietly but with dignity*). Mad dogs?

HENRY. Yeh, dogs that are mad. Mad dogs. One of 'em bite you and you'll be madder'n you are now.

JERNIGAN. Yeh, you git bit and you'll foam at the mouth and gnaw bedposts and cut up terrible like Sarah Williams done 'fore she died. She run out in the yard and screamed, and they tried to ketch her but she run off and lay down by the hedgerow and died biting her legs and arms and barking like a dog.

DOCTOR (*quickly taking a tiny package from his case*). Doctor Immanuel's Mad Stone, good for all bites and poisons. Bring it near the afflicted spot and it seizes upon it— (*Clapping it to the top of his hand*)—and sucks out the poison. Five dollars apiece, five dollars. (*Gazing at it in cold fondness.*) This mysterious stone was taken from the belly of a bewitched deer, killed by the old prophet of the Cape Fear. (*Barking again.*) Five dollars apiece, five dollars, going at five dollars. (*He pushes the stone quickly out at* OLD JERNIGAN.)

JERNIGAN. Nanh, nanh, I ain't run mad.

DOCTOR. Five dollars—Five dollars once, five dollars twice— five dollars—(*Suddenly he stops and stares at* HENRY *as if perceiving something remarkable and strange about him. He mechanically wraps up the stone and drops it back in the case, never taking his eyes from the young man. He moves toward him and walks obliquely around him.* OLD JERNIGAN *watches him with open mouth. As the* DOCTOR *approaches him,* HENRY *turns and follows him suspiciously with his eyes.*)

HENRY. Hyuh, hyuh, what you up to? (*The* DOCTOR *continues to stalk him. He draws back dramatically and points a sharp finger at* HENRY.)

DOCTOR (*grotesquely*). Trouble.

JERNIGAN (*jumping and giggling nervously*). Trouble, hee, hee!

HENRY (*staring at him*). Trouble?

DOCTOR (*his words again beginning to pour out in a roll*). I see upon that brow suffering. My name is Immanuel. I am

needed, needed here and now. (*Looking at him in anguish.*)
You are weak and heavy laden. Tell me. Speak forth your
heart. I am come that ye might have rest from your suffering. Speak forth, thou unbeliever.

HENRY. Hhuy, hyuh, I ain't gonna have no monkey shines.
(*With a touch of entreaty in his voice.*) Stop it now.

DOCTOR (*shaking his head mournfully*). I must help you. I feel
the call of pain. Speak forth your heart.

HENRY (*turning towards* OLD JERNIGAN). What's he up to
nohow?

JERNIGAN. Now, now, you needn't ax me. (*There is a long
silence while the* DOCTOR *stares fixedly at* HENRY.)

HENRY (*looking anxiously about the room and presently bursting out*). I tell you to stop looking at me thataway!

DOCTOR. Trouble, trouble, suffering in the countenance of
that face! (*Imploringly.*) Speak, speak, I have remedy for
suffering. I can help and aid thee. (*He clasps his hands and
waits.* HENRY *stirs uneasily in his chair and* OLD JERNIGAN
*teeters nervously on his feet, beating his thighs with the back
of his hands. At last* OLD JERNIGAN *explodes.*)

JERNIGAN. Well, you air in trouble, Henry!—In a way ye're
in the deepest sort of trouble. (*Muttering.*) Me, too, and
me too.

DOCTOR (*triumphantly*). Ah-hah! Speak, speak!

HENRY (*half in wrath and half in perplexed fear*). Well, what'n
the name of Old Scratch you want?

DOCTOR. Speak forth the evil that is possessing thee.

HENRY (*twisting about*). You tell him, Pa, if they's any evil
to be told.

JERNIGAN. Him and me's been seeing a right smart o' worry
lately. We was talking about it before you come.

DOCTOR. I know, I perceive it.

JERNIGAN (*going on haltingly*). As the scripture putts it, he's
married to a wife. (*He stops.*)

DOCTOR. One had his land, one had his yoke of oxen, another had his wife and could not come. As set forth in the gospel according to Luke.

JERNIGAN (*eagerly*). That's it, Doctor, his wife's tuk possession of everything hyuh.

HENRY. Now, now.

JERNIGAN. Well, she has. And that there doctor kin help you, I done told you he could. (*He steps nimbly out into the room and sweeps it with his arms.*) Look a-here, will you? Look at that there h'a'th. Clean as a sheet. And the floor and everything. A speck o' dirt got no home hyuh and we ain't nuther. (*Pointing to the sewing-machine.*) And look over there at that there sewing. My good coat and britches gone fer good, all fer the heathen over the water.

HENRY. You mought stop trying to tell everything.

JERNIGAN. Well, you tell it then.

HENRY. Go on then and say what you wush.

JERNIGAN. All right and I will as shore as you're born. That's just it, doctor, she's plumb tuk with religion and sweeping and talking.

DOCTOR. Where is the lady of the house?

JERNIGAN. Off, off.

DOCTOR. A common case, a common case. The man must stand up and be the master. The scripture tells as much.

JERNIGAN (*jubilantly*). There you air, Henry, there you air. (*Jerking his thumb at* HENRY.) But he won't, he won't, not him. He sets lak a wedge in the rain and takes it every bit. Big as a house he is and ain't got no backbone in him more'n a sack.

DOCTOR. Timid? Afraid? Lacking in manly courage?

HENRY (*wrathfully*). Go on and have it your way!

DOCTOR. Doctor Immanuel will provide. He can cure.

JERNIGAN. You cure 'em both and I'll pay you. Fix it so's I

kin chew my tobacco in peace and here's a five-dollar bill fer ye. (*He pulls out his pocketbook.*)

DOCTOR. I shall cure them, I must cure them, I will cure them. Amen!

JERNIGAN. Do that and this here's your'n. (*He flaps a bill in his hands. The* DOCTOR *begins to pace up and down the room, pushing back his hair and mumbling to himself.*)

DOCTOR (*snapping*). When will the lady of this house return?

HENRY. She just stepped across the field. But you needn't be planning none of your mess, I ain't gonna take no part in it.

DOCTOR. Mess! Mess! (*He resumes his walk.*)

JERNIGAN (*becoming excited*). I dunno what you gonna do, Doctor, but I jest betcha you do it. (*Gleefully.*) I bet he does, Henry. Yeh, she'll be right back.

DOCTOR. No sooner said than done. (*Whirling upon* HENRY.) I can cure you both. I can bring peace and order into this distracted home. I can make a man of might out of you. I can make you a mighty man in Israel, both in deed and in word. I can bring back humility and love to the erring woman's heart. Yea (*Lifting up his voice*) I can prepare a proper helpmeet for you in your distress. (*Thundering and glaring.*) But—but—have you faith in my powers?

HENRY. I dunno—I dunno—Hah, crazy!

JERNIGAN (*ecstatically*). Try to raise up yer faith, Henry. (*Grinding his hands in excitement.*) Hurry up, Henry, hurry up, she's gonna be back in a minute.

HENRY (*shaking his head weakly*). I'm scared of all this business. How I know he won't kill me or something or hurt her?

DOCTOR. Kill! Hurt! (*His jaw falling open in amazement.*) Alas, young man, your words are wild, wild and full of poison to my kindly heart. (*His tone suddenly changes to anger.*) Take your own benighted way then. I offer you peace, you choose strife. So be it. (JERNIGAN *grasps* HENRY'S *arms in supplication.*)

JERNIGAN. Henry, Henry, try it, try it, boy!

DOCTOR (*raising a warning hand*). But listen, before I depart over the creek—(*To himself.*) A mule there swelled with the colic—Behold salvation is at hand and you refuse it.

JERNIGAN. Air ye crazy, Henry? There he is now going off.

HENRY (*beginning to show an unwilling interest under the* DOCTOR'S *spell*). Well—

DOCTOR (*picking up his hat*). I shall say no more.

JERNIGAN. Henry, Henry, don't let him go off like that there! (*The* DOCTOR *picks up his case and moves towards the door.*)

HENRY. Well, if you're shore you won't hurt me ner her, I mought—

DOCTOR (*apparently no longer interested in him*). Well, good night and may you endure your punishment as befits a sufferer so blind. (*He grasps the door knob.*)

JERNIGAN. Henry, Henry!

HENRY. Are you shore you won't hurt me?

DOCTOR. Faith! Have you faith?

HENRY (*standing up with sudden decision*). Well, I'll try it then, by God! Where's your medicine? Bring it on. (*With an amazingly agile bound the doctor springs back into the room.*)

DOCTOR. Saved! Saved! (*He opens his case and searches in its depths. Extracting two tiny bottles, he holds them up in his hands.* HENRY *sits down again watching him with open mouth.*) Ah, here they are, Doctor Immanuel's Cure for the Unhappy Soul. The one is red, the other gray. The red is for the rich blood of manhood. Drink it and you become masterful, fearless, a tamer of the weaker sex. They will bow down to you, worship you, feed upon your words of wisdom as upon honey-dew. Let the woman drink the gray and the man the red. He becomes the lord of his house and his goods. She becomes the meek and lowly helpmeet. There she sits by the fire silent, gentle and sweet. There he sits her master, her lord.

JERNIGAN (*his eyes shining*). Listen at him, Henry, listen at him talk.

DOCTOR (*lifting up the red vial*). I remember, I remember. I see in the past. It is a night of storm. The moon is sick and pale and wasting in the west.

> The pale moon doth rain,
> The pale moon doth blow,
> It bringeth water in its beak.
> The white moon doth neither rain nor snow.

I rise up in my dreams. Doctor Immanuel comes forth from his couch at the midnight hour, for now it is the time to seek for the cure of the unhappy souls. Silently I go through the forest towards the appointed place. The rain and the wind they comfort me on my journey. I go forth alone in the forest, under the watchful heavens. The signs are right in the sky, it is the time of the bull, and the bull means life and more abundant life. (*He waves his hands before his face and treads up and down the room acting out his journey.* HENRY *and* OLD JERNIGAN *stare at him as if mesmerized.*) I go by the elder bush in the pathless swamp, I touch the sorrel tree, and place my hand upon the bark of the smooth bay tree. I mount the hill and taste of the sweet sassafras and a bit of the bitter pine, and I, Doctor Immanuel, as the cocks begin to crow, come to the place of the silent old man and he waits for me. He has had his dream. Together we go far to the east, he with six dried sticks of the bloody mulberry and I with six of the nameless bush under our arms. We come where the young strong man died for love and his rich red blood ran into the ground. There we set the pot and build the fire. (*His voice takes on a hypnotic monotone and he moves back and forth in the room with the queer unreal steps of a jumping-jack.*) And into the pot Doctor Immanuel casts his one and two and three. And likewise the silent one casts his one and two and three which shall not be named till time is done. The bottles are brought forth and filled. The silent old one to his home again which none but two can find. And Doctor Immanuel forth into the world to heal the distressed. (*His voice dies away and he hums to himself.*)

HENRY (*breaking from the spell*). Ain't he crazy right?

DOCTOR (*picking up the gray vial and throwing up his hand*). And hark! (*He stands with his hand uplifted, and they wait.*) It is night, a night of peace. The farmer sleeps his toil away, and the stock rest in the stall. The seeds wait in the earth, in the warm ground. The poor bird sits in the hedgerow and the snake goes not forth to prey. And now the old moon sleeps in the new moon's arms, hanging in the heavens above the three dark pines. (*Again he falls to striding up and down the floor.*) Doctor Immanuel is forth from his couch. The signs are right. The virgin walks in the sky. He comes to the three dark pines and waits in prayer. And the three maids of the deep swamp minister unto him, they minister unto him. Out of the darkness they come with song and with dancing, their heads hanging low and their rings shining and their garments flashing silver with the flames of gold. (*He turns and stares at* HENRY *who watches him groggily.*) From the mud of the turtle and the scaly snake they come, rising out of the deep night time, out of the mire and swampy slime, where the owl and the bat and the fever are. They rise, bringing the cure, the gray cure, the draught of humility, of peace. (*He stares at the gray vial and stands lost in thought. Presently he turns, his voice humming.*) Drink the red and be filled with life and power; drink the gray, become the meek and gentle of the earth. Doctor Immanuel has said his say! (*He begins walking back and forth across the room.* HENRY *and* OLD JERNIGAN *stare at him as if fascinated. Far off a woman's voice is heard in song. It draws nearer, and* MATTIE *passes around the house, singing "Rescue the Perishing" and goes into the kitchen.*)

HENRY (*swallowing hard*). Hyuh, they's something quare!

JERNIGAN. He's gonna cure you, Henry. He is! Sink yer trust in him, Henry!

DOCTOR. Come, drink the drink! (*He closes his case and sets the two bottles on top of it.*) Call the lady of the house. She shall have the gray.

HENRY (*starting from his dream, sidling up to the bottles, and staring at them suspiciously*). Mought be something in it, mought not. (*A queer unreal smile breaks over his face and he comes up to the* DOCTOR *and stares at him intently.*) All right, dinged if I don't do it. Dinged if I don't! (MATTIE'S *sharp insistent voice is heard in the kitchen.*)

MATTIE. Father! Fathe-er-r! Henry! Henr-y!

JERNIGAN. Drink it, swallow it down, Henry! Can't be no worse'n. (*He turns and mocks* MATTIE.) Father! Henry! and (*singing*): "Rescue the Perishing—" Go on, Henry. (HENRY *picks up the red vial, uncorks it and smells it and sets it down, then takes up the gray one and does likewise.*)

HENRY. Why, it don't smell like nothing a-tall.

DOCTOR (*stopping in his walk and looking at him piercingly*). Bid the lady of the house come in.

HENRY (*throwing his head about and beating himself as if trying to fight off the* DOCTOR'S *influence*). You call her, Pa. (*The door flies open at the left and* MATTIE *springs in with a pan of burnt biscuits in her hands.*)

MATTIE (*in a shrill, nervous voice*). Look what you've done, both of you. I told you not to let the biscuits burn. (JERNIGAN *looks at* HENRY *and* HENRY *looks at him.*)

JERNIGAN (*finally*). I thought Henry was looking after them biscuits.

HENRY (*fumbling*). I didn't even think of 'em, Mattie.

MATTIE. I know. I know. That's just the way it is. That's just the way it is. That's always the way it is.

DOCTOR. Madam, lady of the house!

MATTIE (*starting back*). Oh, I didn't see you, Doctor 'Manuel. Put some wood on the fire, Father. When'd you come, Doctor 'Manuel?

DOCTOR. Madam, when you appeared in the door we were in the midst of a most momentous question.

MATTIE. What'n the world is all this to-do about? You'll have to tell it quick, I've got to hurry and get supper. We are sewing here to-night—(*with a weary, defiant look towards* HENRY *and* OLD JERNIGAN)—sewing for the heathen.

DOCTOR. Madam, after to-night you will not bother about the heathen. You have enough trouble in your own household. We are solving that momentous question.

MATTIE. What in the world is all this to-do about, I ask you?

DOCTOR (*with high dignity*). Madam, behold the two bottles there. The one is red, the other gray. The red is for your husband, the gray for you.

MATTIE. Needn't think I'll drink any of your crazy mess.

DOCTOR. The husband will drink the red and take charge of his household. You will drink the gray and obey him in what he says hereafter.

MATTIE. The Lord help my life! (*Turning to* HENRY.) Have you gone out'n your head same as him, to be taking on to such stuff?

HENRY (*timidly*). Try and drink a little bit, Mattie. It won't hurt you! He says it's good for you.

MATTIE. The dog's foot!

HENRY (*with a hint of determination in his voice*). He's done said if I drink that stuff you won't know me for another man. (*Decisively.*) And I've said I'll drink it.

DOCTOR. He's going to drink his and you're going to drink yours.

MATTIE. That I'm not. I've never heard of such. Henry Jernigan, you must be crazy to fool with him.

HENRY. Yes, I'm gonna do it. I'm plumb tired of sich a mess of things. I'm gonna change it or die a-trying. (*With a lunge he grabs one of the bottles and throws the contents down his throat.*)

MATTIE (*screaming*). Henry, it'll poison you! (HENRY *stands tasting with his lips and tongue. A foolish smile breaks over his face.*)

HENRY. Why, it ain't no more'n—(*The* DOCTOR *brings his hand down on* HENRY'S *shoulder with a whack and stares significantly at him.* HENRY'S *eyes gradually narrow in comprehension and he turns and walks back and forth across the room thinking. The* DOCTOR *moves around as if unconcerned. Suddenly* HENRY *springs into the air with a yell.* OLD JERNIGAN *starts back and falls over a chair.*)

JERNIGAN. Lard, Lard a-mercy!

MATTIE (*running up to* HENRY). Henry, Henry, honey, what is it?

HENRY (*tearing wildly around the room and shrieking*). I'm pizened, pizened! Help, water, I'm afar inside. (*He doubles over in pain.* MATTIE *pursues him wringing her hands. All the while the* DOCTOR *walks ecstatically and yet unconcernedly around the room, carrying on his automaton-like actions and his monologue.*)

DOCTOR (*chanting*).

> As you all know, wherever I go,
> My name is Immanuel.
> I treat you well, I make you well,
> As sound as the sweet church bell.
> Down the road I travel,
> Going in rain or shine,
> Helping the sick and afflicted,
> No medicine like unto mine.
> This I tell who comes like Immanuel.

HENRY (*falling into a chair and slobbering heavily at the mouth as he gasps*). Pizened! Pizened! Help, water! (MATTIE *throws her arms around his neck.*)

MATTIE. Run, Father, run and bring the bucket of water. (*The old man shoots into the kitchen and back like a streak. All the while* MATTIE *is crooning over* HENRY *and rubbing his face and forehead feverishly.*) Oh, darling, honey. What can I do? (*She breaks into wild sobs.*)

JERNIGAN. Hyuh, hyuh, drink some water, Henry. (HENRY *springs out of his chair, knocking* MATTIE *from him. He souses his head in the bucket and drinks, spits out great mouthfuls of water on the floor and empties the bucket over his head. Then he stamps the bucket to pieces, shrieking and yelling*): Hooah! I'm a-dying!

MATTIE. Run for the doctor, run for the doctor!

DOCTOR. I am Doctor Immanuel at your service, madam. (MATTIE *turns and glares at him a moment and slaps him in the face.* HENRY *snatches up the broom and begins chasing the* DOCTOR *around the room beating him. The* DOCTOR *makes an effort to get his case and hat as he is pursued, calling out*): This is wrong! Ye do not understand. (*He opens the door and flees into the night.* HENRY *falls into a chair and rocks back and forth, groaning and moaning.* MATTIE *comes up to him, sobbing.*)

HENRY (*whirling and seizing* MATTIE *by the throat*). Who are you? I know: Mattie. You sew for the heathen and worry your husband's life out about dirt. Now in the grave they'll be plenty of dirt. And you sing, and you sing; and you talk, and you talk. (*He grabs the remaining bottle and uncorks it.*) Drink this here bottle o' stuff.

MATTIE (*clenching her teeth and fighting back*). I won't, I won't! It'll poison me, it'll kill me!

HENRY. (*Pulling open her mouth and pouring the contents in.*) Nunh-unh, I reckin it won't! (*She swallows and coughs and strangles, then drops to the floor crying.* HENRY *strides about the room kicking the furniture to pieces and throwing out his shoulders and shouting*): I'm a new man, a man o' might, a he-man in Israel! (*Turning upon* MATTIE.) And you have drunk the drink. You gonna be humbled down, a helpmate. (*He drops back in his chair in a dying posture.*)

MATTIE. Oh, Henry, Henry, baby!

HENRY. When I'm gone, take care of Pa. Let him live in peace. Let him have his tobacco and spet in the far. (MATTIE *crawls on her knees before him and lays her head in his lap, weeping.*)

MATTIE. Get the doctor, Father. Hitch up and go for the doctor. (OLD JERNIGAN *starts for the door.* HENRY *jumps up and snatches him back.*)

HENRY. You ain't, you ain't. Let me die in peace. (*There is the sound of a medley of voices outside. Women gabbling in excitement.* MATTIE *climbs up to her feet and runs to the door.*)

MATTIE. Is that you, Mis' Bella? Come here, come here, quick! Henry's poisoned and he's a-dying. (*The gabble and excitement outside increases. A voice replies from the yard.*)

VOICE. I'm coming, Mattie, I'm coming. (*She is heard coming up on the steps.* HENRY *gets up from his chair and begins to bark like a dog, blubbering and growling.*)

HENRY (*shrieking again*). I been bit by a mad dog. (*He barks.*)

VOICE. Lord a-mercy, he's run mad! (*A low murmur of horror rises from the women outside, followed by shrieks and then the sound of running feet.* HENRY *rushes out of the door barking and pursuing them.*)

MATTIE (*looking at* OLD JERNIGAN *through her tears*). He ain't been bit by no mad dog!

JERNIGAN (*stuttering with excitement*). Mabbe that's the way pizen works. That doctor said he got it a quare way in the middle of the night and a storm on and a' old man helping him.

MATTIE. He's crazy. (*Wringing her hands.*) Why'd you let him give Henry that stuff? The mess I took wa'n't nothing —weak as water! (*She goes to the door calling piteously.*)

Henry! Henry! (OLD JERNIGAN *comes up to the bottle she has dropped and looks at it.*)

JERNIGAN (*with a shout*). He's tuk the wrong medicine, Mattie! He tuk that there gray stuff and you tuk the red!

MATTIE (*at the door*). Henry! Henry! (HENRY *comes back on the porch and gives a farewell bark.* MATTIE *runs out and throws her arms around him. He flings her from him and strides into the room. His shoes are covered with mud. He goes to the fireplace and stamps it off on the hearth.*)

JERNIGAN (*running up to him excitedly*). Hyuh, hyuh, you tuk that gray stuff. Look, look!

HENRY (*waving him off*). It don't make no difference. 'Twon't nothing but water. (MATTIE *comes in and stares at him as he casually cleans his boot on the hearth.*)

MATTIE (*whimpering*). What's happened, Henry? You seem—

HENRY. I been cured, that's what. The medicine done it. (*He gets up, looks around the room, goes over to the machine, gathers up the clothes for the heathen, picks out a coat and trousers and throws them at the old man.*) Here, there's your Ransome Taylor coat and your britches. The heathen ain't gonna git 'em. (*He wipes his shoes with the other garments and then calmly goes to his chair and sits down.* MATTIE *has been looking on a moment and then with a glad cry of comprehension falls on her knees by him and lays her head sobbing in his lap.*)

JERNIGAN (*dropping in his chair thunderstruck*). Well, I be durned if I ever seed the beat! (*He thinks a moment and then breaks out in a low musical chuckle. His face spreads into a grin that breaks in a thousand wrinkles. He cuts a caper on the floor, stopping now and then trying to comprehend what has happened.* HENRY *sits solemnly stroking* MATTIE'S *head. The door is cracked open at the rear and* DOCTOR IMMANUEL *pokes his head in.*)

DOCTOR. Masters of this house—

HENRY (*turning and snarling*). Hanh—Scat! (*He barks and*

the DOCTOR *slams the door. After a moment* HENRY *calls* OLD JERNIGAN.) Pa, go and tell him to come in and get his hat and case. (MATTIE'S *sobs gradually die away.*) Yeh, I know, poor child, I did scare you, didn't I? (*Only a whimper from* MATTIE *and hugging of* HENRY'S *knees answer him.*)

JERNIGAN (*at the door*). Come on in, Doctor, and get yer stuff. He ain't gonna hurt you. (*The* DOCTOR *comes gravely in and gets his case and hat.*)

HENRY. Pa, give him that five dollars.

JERNIGAN (*his sides shaking with enjoyment*). Hyuh, hyuh, it is. You done it, Doc, same as you said you would.

HENRY. And you needn't come back. I don't need you! (*He lifts his head with decision written on his face.*) Lemme have a look at the plug of tobacco, Pa.

DOCTOR (*at the door*). Remember that I am always at your service. Peace abide with you and this house always. I am on my way now to another patient.

HENRY. That's all right, Doctor. You needn't bother about us. We ain't gonna need you no more. Are we, Mattie? (MATTIE *shakes her head.*)

DOCTOR (*going out*).

As you all know, wherever I go,
My name is Immanuel.

(*He closes the door and his chant dies away in the night.*)

HENRY. I said, Pa, I'd like to have a look at that tobacco.

MATTIE (*raising her head*). Don't you spit on—

HENRY (*crushing her back to the floor*). Nanh, nanh, I tell you I been cured. I'm boss. (*Breaking into a loud roaring laugh.*) Hooray! Hooray! I'm another man, I'm cured, I'm boss. Gimme that 'backer. (*The old man hands it to him eagerly.* HENRY *bites off an enormous chew and hands the plug back.* OLD JERNIGAN *hesitates a moment and then also bites off a mouthful. A look of deep content comes over him. He snuggles into his chair and chews.* HENRY *chews. They look across at each other.* HENRY *signifies to the old man with a motion of his hand that he spit first.* OLD JERNIGAN *with a vast gesture refuses.* HENRY *spits profusely and loudly in the direction of the fire.* OLD JERNIGAN *does likewise.*)

JERNIGAN (*eyeing* HENRY *slyly, as he rolls his tobacco sweetly in his mouth*). Hee-hee! (MATTIE *sits hugging* HENRY's *knees.*)

HENRY (*nodding happily and wisely*). Unh-hunh-yeh. (*They sit saying nothing. Presently* HENRY *looks over at the old man and laughs suddenly and deeply.*)

JERNIGAN. What?

HENRY. I run them there women right into the mudhole out there.

JERNIGAN (*beating his thigh gleefully*). Hee-hee! Hee-hee!

HENRY. I shore did. (*They lapse into silence. By this time* MATTIE *has raised her head and is staring contemplatively by* HENRY's *shin into the fire.*)

JERNIGAN (*shivering a bit and stirring the fire*). Gonna be cold, Henry, cold.

HENRY. Yeh.

JERNIGAN. Robins been flying towards the south all day. (*They both lean towards the fire and spit with great gusto.*)

CURTAIN

APPENDIX I

September 1, 1918 to January 1, 1941

I. ORIGINAL PLAYS PRODUCED

1. FULL-LENGTH PLAYS

Job's Kinfolks, a play of the mill people, in three acts, by Loretto Carroll Bailey, November 7–8–9, 1929.

Strike Song, a new play of Southern mill people, by Loretto Carroll Bailey, December 10–11–12, 1931.

Sad Words to Gay Music, a new comedy in three acts, by Alvin Kerr, February 23–24–25, 1933.

Shroud My Body Down, a folk dream, by Paul Green, December 7–8, 1934.

The Enchanted Maze, by Paul Green, December 6–7 and 9, 1935.

Singing Valley, a comedy of Mexican village life, by Josephina Niggli, July 15, 1936.

The Fair-God (Malinche), a new play of Maximilian of Mexico, by Josephina Niggli, December 3–4–5, 1936.

Sharecropper, a new Negro drama in five scenes, by Fred Howard, February 24–25–26, 1938.

Smoky Mountain Road, a comedy of the Carolina Highlands, by Fred Koch, Jr., July 11–12–13 (matinee and night), 1940.

2. ONE-ACT PLAYS

FIRST BILL, MARCH 14–15, 1919.

When Witches Ride, a play of folk superstition, by Elizabeth A. Lay.

The Return of Buck Gavin, a tragedy of a mountain outlaw, by Thomas Clayton Wolfe.

What Will Barbara Say?, a romance of Chapel Hill, by Minnie Shepherd Sparrow.

SECOND BILL, MAY 30–31, 1919.

Peggy, a tragedy of the tenant farmer, by Harold Williamson.

The Fighting Corporal, a Negro comedy, by Louisa Reid.

THIRD BILL, DECEMBER 12–13, 1919.

Who Pays?, a tragedy of industrial conflict, by Minnie Shepherd Sparrow.

The Third Night, a ghost play of the Carolina Mountains, by Thomas Clayton Wolfe.

The Hag, a comedy of folk superstition, by Elizabeth A. Lay.

FOURTH BILL, APRIL 30 AND MAY 1, 1920.

Off Nag's Head, a tragedy of the Carolina coast, by Dougald MacMillan.

The Last of the Lowries, a play of the Croatan outlaws, by Paul Green.

"Dod Gast Ye Both!", a comedy of mountain moonshiners, by Hubert Heffner.

FIFTH BILL, FEBRUARY 11–12, 1921.

The Miser, a farm tragedy, by Paul Green.

The Vamp, a comedy of university life, by William Royall.

The Old Man of Edenton, a melodrama of colonial Carolina, by Paul Green.

SIXTH BILL, APRIL 29–30, 1921.

The Chatham Rabbit, a comedy of college life, by Legette Blythe.

The Reaping, a play of social problems, by John Terry.

In Dixon's Kitchen, a comedy of a country courtship, by Wilbur Stout and Ellen Lay.

SEVENTH BILL, DECEMBER 2–3, 1921.

Reward Offered, a comedy of mountain characters, by Jane Toy.

Trista, a play of colonial superstition, by Elizabeth A. Lay.

Waffles For Breakfast, a comedy of newly-married life, by Mary Yellott.

EIGHTH BILL, MARCH 10–11, 1922.

The Lord's Will, a tragedy of a country preacher, by Paul Green.

Dogwood Bushes, a romance of the Carolina country, by Wilbur Stout.

Blackbeard, Pirate of the Carolina Coast, by Paul Green and Elizabeth A. Lay.

NINTH BILL, JANUARY 26–27, 1923.

Wrack P'int, a melodrama of the Carolina coast, by Paul Green.

Agatha, a romance of the old South, by Jane Toy.

Wilbur's Cousin, a comedy of college life, by Ernest Thompson.

TENTH BILL, APRIL 13–14, 1923.

John Lane's Wife, a tragedy of the farm, by Mack Gorham.

The Berry Pickers, a Colorado folk comedy, by Russell Potter.

Mamma, a comedy of modern manners, by Ernest Thompson.

ELEVENTH BILL, NOVEMBER 16–17, 1923.

The Black Rooster, a comedy of country folk, by Pearl Setzer.

Nat Macon's Game, the romance of a revolutionary patriot, by Osler Bailey.

Gaius and Gaius, Jr., a comedy of plantation days, by Lucy M. Cobb.

TWELFTH BILL, FEBRUARY 8–9, 1924.

Servants of God, a play of a small-town preacher, by Robert S. Pickens.

The Beaded Buckle, a comedy of present day aristocracy, by Frances Gray.

Fixin's, a tragedy of a tenant farm woman, by Erma and Paul Green.

THIRTEENTH BILL, APRIL 4–5, 1924.

The Younger, a comedy of the present day flapper, by Sue Byrd Thompson.

The Wheel, the evolution of a college boy, by Ernest Thompson.

FOURTEENTH BILL, DECEMBER 4–5, 1924.

The Honor of Bonava, a chapter from reconstruction days, by Robert Watson Winston.

Politicin' in Horse Cove, a comedy of mountain folk, by Martha Boswell.

The Scuffletown Outlaws, a tragedy of the Lowrie gang, by William Norment Cox.

FIFTEENTH BILL, MAY 8–9, 1925.

Old Imes, a comedy of the village store, by Ray Heffner.

The Thrice Promised Bride, a Chinese folk play, by Cheng-Chin Hsiung.

The Scuffletown Outlaws, a tragedy of the Lowrie gang, by William Norment Cox.

SIXTEENTH BILL (DEDICATION OF THE PLAYMAKERS THEATRE), NOVEMBER 23–24–25–26, 1925.

Out of the Past, a romance of college life at Carolina in '61, by Frances Gray.

Yon Side O' Sunk Creek, a tragedy of mountain folk, by Martha Boswell.

Quare Medicine, a country comedy of a quack doctor, by Paul Green.

SEVENTEENTH BILL, MARCH 12–13, 1926.

A Carolina Pierrot, a play of Pierrot on the university campus, by William J. Macmillan.

Clay, a play of the farm, by David Reid Hodgin.

The New Moon, a whimsical folk fantasy, by Telfair Peet.

EIGHTEENTH BILL, FEBRUARY 10–11, 1927.

In Dixon's Kitchen, a comedy of a country courtship, by Wilbur Stout and Ellen Lay.

Lighted Candles, a tragedy of the Carolina Highlands, by Margaret Bland.

The Muse and the Movies, a comedy of Greenwich village, by Alice Rodewald.

NINETEENTH BILL, MAY 5–6, 1927.

Mr. Perry Writes a Play, a burlesque of folk play writing, by William DeCatur Perry.

Quare Medicine, a country comedy of a quack doctor, by Paul Green.

The Marvelous Romance of Wen Chun-Chin, a Chinese folk play, by Cheng-Chin Hsiung.

TWENTIETH BILL, FEBRUARY 10–11, 1928.

Mountain Magic, a California folk play, by Edith Daseking.

Job's Kinfolks, a tragedy of the mill people, by Loretto Carroll Bailey.

The Queen Has Her Face Lifted, a fantastic satire, by Alvin M. Kahn.

TWENTY-FIRST BILL, MARCH 30–31, 1928.

The New Eve, an expressionistic play of the future, by Mary Dirnberger.

Day's End, a California folk play, by Alice Pieratt.

A Shot Gun Splicin', a mountain comedy, by Gertrude Wilson Coffin.

TWENTY-SECOND BILL, FEBRUARY 8–9, 1929.

The Family, an episode of the American home, by Catherine Wilson Nolen.

Graveyard Shift, a play of California factory workers, by Edith Daseking.

O Promise Me, a modern romance cycle, by Curtis Benjamin.

TWENTY-THIRD BILL, APRIL 5–6, 1929.

The Lie, a play of Revolutionary Carolina, by Wilkeson O'Connell.

Black Water, a sequel to *Job's Kinfolks*, by Loretto Carroll Bailey.

Companion-Mate Maggie, a Negro comedy, by Helen Dortch.

TWENTY-FOURTH BILL, OCTOBER 24–25–26, 1929.

The No 'Count Boy, a comedy of Negro life, by Paul Green.

Magnolia's Man, a comedy of the mountain people, by Gertrude Wilson Coffin.

Being Married, a domestic comedy, by Catherine Wilson Nolen.

TWENTY-FIFTH BILL, NOVEMBER 7–8–9, 1929.

Job's Kinfolks, a new play of the mill people, in three acts, by Loretto Carroll Bailey.

TWENTY-SIXTH BILL, MARCH 6–7–8, 1930.

For Auntie's Sake, a comedy of college life, by John Patric.

Hollyhocks, a play of New England village folk, by Joseph Philip Fox.

Suspended Animation, a comedy of playmaking, by Kent Creuser.

Death Valley Scotty, a play of the California Desert, by James Milton Wood.

TWENTY-SEVENTH BILL, NOVEMBER 6–7–8, 1930.

Samuel Hinkle, Fireman, a comedy of New England village life, by Joseph Philip Fox.

Cloey, a play of Winston-Salem folk, by Loretto Carroll Bailey.

Git Up An' Bar The Door, a farce of Mississippi folk life, by Arthur Palmer Hudson.

TWENTY-EIGHTH BILL, APRIL 9–10–11, 1931.

Ever' Snitch, a comedy of Carolina fisherfolk, by Irene Fussler.

The Blue Remembered Hills, a play of college life, by Theodore Herman.

A Very Pale Pink Angel, a whimsical satire, by Ellen Stewart.

Always A Bettin' Man, a comedy of Maryland folk, by Tom Loy.

TWENTY-NINTH BILL, DECEMBER 10–11–12, 1931.

Strike Song, a new play of Southern mill people, in three acts, by Loretto Carroll Bailey.

THIRTIETH BILL, MARCH 3–4–5, 1932.

Bloomers, a comedy of family life, by Jo Norwood.

The Common Gift, a tragedy of working women, by Elwyn de Graffenried.

The Loyal Venture, a drama of Colonial Carolina, by Wilkeson O'Connell.

THIRTY-FIRST BILL, DECEMBER 8–9–10, 1932.

Creek Swamp Nigger, a Carolina Negro tragedy, by Harry W. Coble.

Davy Crockett, half horse, half alligator, by John Philip Milhous.

Four on a Heath, a grotesque, by Foster Fitz-Simons.

Stumbling in Dreams, a folk comedy of Tin Pan Alley, by George Brown.

THIRTY-SECOND BILL, MAY 11, 1933.

Judgment Comes to Daniel, a folk comedy of eastern North Carolina, by Bernice Kelly Harris.

A Little Boat to India, a springtime farce, by Foster Fitz-Simons.

THIRTY-THIRD BILL, MAY 12, 1933.

Comedy at Five, an American comedy, by Martha Matthews Hatton.

Eternal Spring, a tragedy of prejudice, by Robert Barnett.

Blow Me Down, a comedy of Long Island sailor folk, by William Bonyun.

THIRTY-FOURTH BILL, MAY 13, 1933.

The Queen Was in the Kitchen, a persistent comedy, by Ellen Stewart.

Etowah Plantation, a legend of the land, 1846–1864, by Eugenia Rawls.

Comedy at Five, an American comedy, by Martha Matthews Hatton.

THIRTY-FIFTH BILL, DECEMBER 7–8–9, 1933.

Everglades, an episode in the life of Andrew Jackson, by John F. Alexander.

The Head-Ax of Ingfell, a tragedy of the Igorote Hill folk of the Philippines, by Anne B. Walters.

Shadows of Industry, a drama of the financial world, by Vermont C. Royster.

Sing Your Own Song, a comedy—we hope!, by Nat Farnworth.

THIRTY-SIXTH BILL, MAY 10, 1934.

The Girl With the White Sweater, a fantasy of the Carolina mountains, by Margaret Siceloff.

Third Verse, a comedy of a small-town newspaper, by Wilbur Dorsett.

Tomorrow, a play of a lodging house, by Douglas Hume.

THIRTY-SEVENTH BILL, MAY 11, 1934.

Third Verse, a comedy of a small-town newspaper, by Wilbur Dorsett.

Where There Is Faith, a sophisticated play of an unsophisticated girl, by Kathleen Krahenbuhl.

THIRTY-EIGHTH BILL, MAY 12, 1934.

Release, a play of courage, by Jean Smith Cantrell.

Where There Is Faith, a sophisticated play of an unsophisticated girl, by Kathleen Krahenbuhl.

THIRTY-NINTH BILL, MAY 14, 1934.

Concealed Aim, a drama of a small-town bank, by Carl W. Dennis.

New Rasthenia, a nervous break-down, by Herman Fussler.

FORTIETH BILL, FEBRUARY 28 AND MARCH 1–2, 1935.

Ancient Heritage, a drama of a New England family, by Philip Goddard Parker.

Cottie Mourns, a comedy of Carolina fisherfolk, by Patricia McMullan.

Yours and Mine, a comedy of domestic difficulties, by Ella Mae Daniel.

FORTY-FIRST BILL, APRIL 25, 1935.

Goldie, a comedy of a Negro Saturday night, by Wilbur Dorsett.

Hunger, a tragedy of Carolina farm folk, by Ella Mae Daniel.

Spare Ribs, a comic drama of the sea, by Donald B. Pope.

FORTY-SECOND BILL, APRIL 26–27, 1935.

April 26: *Ca'line*, a Carolina folk comedy, by Bernice Kelly Harris.

Metropolitan Feodor, a romantic drama of seventeenth-century Russia, by Philip Goddard Parker.

New Nigger, a tragedy of the tobacco country, by Fred Howard.

April 27: *Back Page*, a newspaper melodrama, by Don Shoemaker.

Ca'line, a Carolina folk comedy, by Bernice Kelly Harris.

New Nigger, a tragedy of the tobacco country, by Fred Howard.

FORTY-THIRD BILL, APRIL 30, 1935.

Clam Digger, a play of Maine sea-folk, by Jean Ashe.

The Devil's Trampin' Ground, a tragedy of mixed blood, by Sara Seawell.

New Anarchy, a play of the banking crisis, by Philip Goddard Parker.

Pretty Plump Angel, a play of youth, by Cecilia Allen.

FORTY-FOURTH BILL, FEBRUARY 27–28–29, 1936.

Election, a play of politics in a small Texas town, by Mary Delaney.

Prairie Dust, a play of the Dakota drought, by Gerd Bernhardt.

Soldadera (Soldier-Woman), a play of the Mexican revolution, by Josephina Niggli.

FORTY-FIFTH BILL, APRIL 23, 1936.

Awakening, a play of disillusionment, by Eleanor Barker.

An Orchid to You, a comedy of sorority life, by Jean Walker.

Raise a Tune, Sister, a play of Carolina fisherfolk, by Patricia McMullan.

FORTY-SIXTH BILL, APRIL 24, 1936.

The Eternal Comedy, a play of adolescence, by Mary Delaney.

Hangman's Noose, a play of character conflict, by Charles A. Poe.

Hjemlengsel (Home Longing), a Norwegian folk play, by Gerd Bernhardt.

FORTY-SEVENTH BILL, APRIL 25, 1936.

Azteca, a tragedy of pre-Conquest Mexico, by Josephina Niggli.

The Cry of Dolores, the story of Mexican independence, by Josephina Niggli.

The Red Velvet Goat, a tragedy of laughter and a comedy of tears, by Josephina Niggli.

Sunday Costs Five Pesos, a Mexican folk comedy, by Josephina Niggli.

FORTY-EIGHTH BILL, FEBRUARY 25–26–27, 1937.

Sleep On, Lemuel, a Carolina Negro comedy, by John W. Parker.

Leavin's (Nancy Hanks, Bondwoman), a legend of the Carolina mountains, by Janie Malloy Britt.

Fire of the Lord, a play of religious fanatics, by Frank Durham.

Funeral Flowers for the Bride, a comedy of the Blue Ridge Mountains, by Beverley DuBose Hamer.

FORTY-NINTH BILL, APRIL 22, 1937.

Drought, a tragedy of rural South Carolina, by Walter Spearman.

The Sun Sets Early, a play of a small college, by William Peery.

Fightin' Time, a comedy of Southern Indiana, by Kate May Rutherford.

FIFTIETH BILL, APRIL 24, 1937.

Toujours Gai, a modern tragedy, by Virginia La Rochelle.

Barge Incident, a play of the New York water-front, by Herb Meadow.

Naughty Boy, a New York suburban comedy, by William T. Chichester.

FIFTY-FIRST BILL, APRIL 26, 1937.

Cockle Doody Doo, a play of Carolina fisherfolk, by Patricia McMullen.

The Good-bye, by Paul Green.

Lighted Candles, a tragedy of the Carolina highlands, by Margaret Bland.

Abide With Me, a comedy of rural South Carolina, by Walter Spearman.

FIFTY-SECOND BILL, APRIL 20–21, 1938.

Pair of Quilts, a folk comedy of eastern North Carolina, by Bernice Kelly Harris.

While Reporters Watched, a Christmas Eve newspaper mystery, by Rose Peagler.

Mary Marge, a comedy of Carolina fisherfolk, by Ellen Deppe.

One Man's House, a play of a Canadian reformer, by Gwen Pharis.

FIFTY-THIRD BILL, APRIL 22–23, 1938.

The Worm Turns, a comedy of adolescent love, by Jean Brabham.

Murder in the Snow, a drama of old Montana, by Betty Smith and Robert Finch.

Three Foolish Virgins, a Carolina folk comedy, by Bernice Kelly Harris.

This Is Villa, a portrait of a Mexican general, by Josephina Niggli.

FIFTY-FOURTH BILL, MARCH 2–3–4, 1939.

Twilight Song, a play of religious superstition, by Donald Muller.

Kid Sister, a comedy of adolescence, by Wieder Sievers.

Pasque Flower, a play of the Canadian prairie, by Gwen Pharis.

3. OCCASIONAL PERFORMANCES
One-Act Plays

FIRST PERFORMANCE OUT-OF-TOWN, MUNICIPAL THEATRE, GREENSBORO, NORTH CAROLINA, MAY 7, 1920:
Off Nag's Head, by Dougald MacMillan; The Last of the Lowries, by Paul Green; "Dod Gast Ye Both!", by Hubert Heffner.

DEDICATION OF THE HIGH POINT MUNICIPAL THEATRE, HIGH POINT, NORTH CAROLINA, OCTOBER 25, 1923:
When Witches Ride, by Elizabeth A. Lay; Wilbur's Cousin, by Ernest Thompson.

NORTH CAROLINA TEACHERS ASSOCIATION, RALEIGH, NORTH CAROLINA, MARCH 14, 1924:
The Black Rooster, by Pearl Setzer; Fixin's, by Erma and Paul Green; Gaius and Gaius, Jr., by Lucy M. Cobb.

GREENSBORO, NORTH CAROLINA, MAY 4, 1923:
Agatha, by Jane Toy; Peggy, by Harold Williamson; Mamma, by Ernest Thompson.

GREENSBORO, NORTH CAROLINA, MAY 2, 1924:
The Beaded Buckle, by Frances Gray; Fixin's, by Erma and Paul Green; Gaius and Gaius, Jr., by Lucy M. Cobb.

SUMMER PERFORMANCES, CHAPEL HILL, NORTH CAROLINA, JULY 21–22, 1919:
When Witches Ride, by Elizabeth A. Lay; Peggy, by Harold Williamson. July 22–23, 1920: The Last of the Lowries, by Paul Green; Off Nag's Head, by Dougald MacMillan; "Dod Gast Ye Both!", by Hubert Heffner. July 18–19, 1921: In Dixon's Kitchen, by Wilbur Stout; The Miser, by Paul Green; The Vamp, by William Royall.

THE CAROLINA DRAMATIC ASSOCIATION, CHAPEL HILL, NORTH CAROLINA, MAY 8, 1925:
Old Imes, by Ray Heffner; The Scuffletown Outlaws, by William Norment Cox; The Thrice Promised Bride, by Cheng-Chin Hsiung.

THE NATIONAL RECREATION CONGRESS, ASHEVILLE, NORTH
CAROLINA, OCTOBER 6, 1925:
Gaius and Gaius, Jr., by Lucy M. Cobb; *Old Wash Lucas*,
by Paul Green.

FOR FRESHMEN, CHAPEL HILL, NORTH CAROLINA, OCTOBER 8,
1925:
Gaius and Gaius, Jr., by Lucy M. Cobb; *Old Wash Lucas*,
by Paul Green.

THE NORTH CAROLINA LIBRARIANS ASSOCIATION, CHAPEL
HILL, NORTH CAROLINA, NOVEMBER 19, 1925:
Out of the Past, by Frances Gray.

THE STATE LITERARY AND HISTORICAL ASSOCIATION OF
NORTH CAROLINA, RALEIGH, NORTH CAROLINA, DECEM-
BER 9, 1925:
Out of the Past, by Frances Gray; *Yon Side O' Sunk Creek*,
by Martha Boswell; *Quare Medicine*, by Paul Green.

THE NORTH CAROLINA PRESS ASSOCIATION, CHAPEL HILL,
NORTH CAROLINA, JANUARY 14, 1926:
Quare Medicine, by Paul Green.

SPECIAL TOUR: FAYETTEVILLE AND RED SPRINGS, NORTH CARO-
LINA, MARCH 4–5, 1926:
The First Year, by Frank Craven.

THE DRAMATIC INSTITUTE (CAROLINA DRAMATIC ASSOCIATION),
CHAPEL HILL, NORTH CAROLINA, MARCH 25, 1926:
Quare Medicine, by Paul Green; *Clay*, by David Reid
Hodgin.

SPECIAL TOUR: SILER CITY AND PITTSBORO, NORTH CAROLINA,
MARCH 26–27, 1926:
Quare Medicine, by Paul Green; *Clay*, by David Reid
Hodgin; *Gaius and Gaius, Jr.*, by Lucy M. Cobb.

THE ROTARY CLUB CONVENTION, DURHAM, NORTH CAROLINA,
APRIL 20, 1926:
Gaius and Gaius, Jr., by Lucy M. Cobb.

SPECIAL TOUR: PITTSBORO, NORTH CAROLINA, FEBRUARY 12,
1927:

In Dixon's Kitchen, by Wilbur Stout and Ellen Lay; *Lighted Candles*, by Margaret Bland; *The Muse and the Movies*, by Alice Rodewald.

REPERTORY REVIVAL, CHAPEL HILL, NORTH CAROLINA, MARCH 12, 1927:
Trista, by Elizabeth Lay; *Old Wash Lucas*, by Paul Green; *Old English Folk Dances*, directed by Josephine Sharkey.

THE NATIONAL ASSOCIATION OF DIRECTORS OF UNIVERSITY EXTENSION, CHAPEL HILL, NORTH CAROLINA, APRIL 26, 1927:
Quare Medicine, by Paul Green; *Old English Folk Dances*, directed by Josephine Sharkey.

THE NATIONAL ASSOCIATION OF ALUMNI SECRETARIES, CHAPEL HILL, NORTH CAROLINA, APRIL 28, 1927:
Quare Medicine, by Paul Green; *Old English Folk Dances*, directed by Josephine Sharkey.

SUMMER PERFORMANCES, CHAPEL HILL, NORTH CAROLINA, AUGUST 18–19, 1927:
The Scuffletown Outlaws, by William Norment Cox; *In Dixon's Kitchen*, by Wilbur Stout and Ellen Lay.

FOR FRESHMEN, CHAPEL HILL, NORTH CAROLINA, NOVEMBER 5, 1927:
The Scuffletown Outlaws, by William Norment Cox; *Lighted Candles*, by Margaret Bland; *On Dixon's Porch*, by Wilbur Stout and Ellen Lay.

THE ANNUAL NEWSPAPER INSTITUTE, CHAPEL HILL, NORTH CAROLINA, JANUARY 12, 1928:
Ten Nights In A Bar-Room, by William W. Pratt.

THE CHAPEL HILL SCHOOL, CHAPEL HILL, NORTH CAROLINA, FEBRUARY 16, 1928:
The Marvelous Romance of Wen Chun-Chin, by Cheng-Chin Hsiung.

THE SOUTHERN REGIONAL CONFERENCE ON THE DRAMA, CHAPEL HILL, NORTH CAROLINA, APRIL 5, 1928:
Lighted Candles, by Margaret Bland; *Job's Kinfolks*, by

Loretto Carroll Bailey; *A Shot-Gun Splicin'*, by Gertrude Wilson Coffin.

THE SOUTHERN CONFERENCE ON EDUCATION, CHAPEL HILL, NORTH CAROLINA, NOVEMBER 15, 1928:
Job's Kinfolks, by Loretto Carroll Bailey; *Quare Medicine*, by Paul Green.

NATIONAL RADIO PERFORMANCE, STATION WABC, NEW YORK CITY, COLUMBIA BROADCASTING SYSTEM; NATIONAL HOOK-UP OF TWENTY-ONE STATIONS, NOVEMBER 25, 1928, 10:30 P.M.:
Quare Medicine, by Paul Green.

THE CAROLINA DRAMATIC ASSOCIATION (THE DIRECTOR'S CONFERENCE), CHAPEL HILL, NORTH CAROLINA, JANUARY 12, 1929:
The Man Who Died At Twelve O'Clock, by Paul Green.

THE SIXTH DRAMATIC FESTIVAL (THE CAROLINA DRAMATIC ASSOCIATION). CHAPEL HILL, NORTH CAROLINA, MAY 4, 1929:
Black Water, by Loretto Carroll Bailey.

THE AMERICAN ASSOCIATION FOR ADULT EDUCATION (FOURTH ANNUAL MEETING), CHAPEL HILL, NORTH CAROLINA, MAY 22, 1929:
Job's Kinfolks, by Loretto Carroll Bailey; *Quare Medicine*, by Paul Green.

THE SOUTHERN CONFERENCE ON EDUCATION, CHAPEL HILL, NORTH CAROLINA, OCTOBER 23, 1929:
The No 'Count Boy, by Paul Green; *Magnolia's Man*, by Gertrude Wilson Coffin; *Being Married*, by Catherine Wilson Nolen.

THE SEVENTH DRAMATIC FESTIVAL (THE CAROLINA DRAMATIC ASSOCIATION), CHAPEL HILL, NORTH CAROLINA, APRIL 11, 1930:
Magnolia's Man, by Gertrude Wilson Coffin.

THE SOUTHERN CONFERENCE ON EDUCATION, CHAPEL HILL, NORTH CAROLINA, NOVEMBER 1, 1930:

Cloey, by Loretto Carroll Bailey; *Git Up an' Bar the Door*, by Arthur Palmer Hudson.

THE ASSOCIATION OF GOVERNING BOARDS OF STATE UNIVERSI-
TIES AND ALLIED INSTITUTIONS, CHAPEL HILL, NORTH
CAROLINA, NOVEMBER 13, 1930:
Cloey, by Loretto Carroll Bailey; *Git Up an' Bar the Door*, by Arthur Palmer Hudson.

THE SEVENTH ANNUAL NEWSPAPER INSTITUTE, CHAPEL HILL,
NORTH CAROLINA, JANUARY 15, 1931:
Cloey, by Loretto Carroll Bailey; *Git Up an' Bar the Door*, by Arthur Palmer Hudson.

THE ASSOCIATION OF AMERICAN UNIVERSITIES (ANNUAL MEET-
ING), CHAPEL HILL, NORTH CAROLINA, NOVEMBER 13,
1931:
Job's Kinfolks, by Loretto Carroll Bailey; *Magnolia's Man*, by Gertrude Wilson Coffin.

THE GOETHE CENTENARY, CHAPEL HILL, NORTH CAROLINA,
APRIL 19, 1932:
The Masterpieces of Goethe.

THE SHAW-HENDERSON FESTIVAL, CHAPEL HILL, NORTH CARO-
LINA, FEBRUARY 2–3–4, 1933:
You Never Can Tell, by George Bernard Shaw.

THE DOGWOOD FESTIVAL (FIRST ANNUAL), CHAPEL HILL,
NORTH CAROLINA, APRIL 29, 1933:
Ali Baba and the Forty Thieves, by Harry Davis.

A FIFTEENTH CENTURY NATIVITY PLAY (IN GERMAN), ADAPTED
BY MENO SPANN, CHAPEL HILL, NORTH CAROLINA, DECEM-
BER 10, 1933.

THE DOGWOOD FESTIVAL (SECOND ANNUAL) CHAPEL HILL,
NORTH CAROLINA, APRIL 14, 1934:
Magnolia's Man, by Gertrude Wilson Coffin; *The Man Who Died at Twelve O'clock*, by Paul Green.

THE UNITED DAUGHTERS OF CONFEDERACY (38TH CONVEN-
TION), CHAPEL HILL, NORTH CAROLINA, OCTOBER 10, 1934:
Agatha, by Jane Toy.

A FIFTEENTH CENTURY NATIVITY PLAY (IN GERMAN), ADAPTED
BY MENO SPANN, CHAPEL HILL, NORTH CAROLINA, DECEM-
BER 9, 1934.

THE DOGWOOD FESTIVAL (THIRD ANNUAL), CHAPEL HILL,
NORTH CAROLINA, APRIL 25–26–27, 1935:
Goldie, by Wilbur Dorsett; *Hunger*, by Ella Mae Daniel;
Spare Ribs, by Donald Pope; *Ca'line*, by Bernice Kelly
Harris; *Metropolitan Feodor*, by Philip Goddard Parker;
New Nigger, by Fred Howard; *Back Page*, by Don Shoe-
maker.

THE SOUTHEASTERN ARTS ASSOCIATION, CHAPEL HILL, NORTH
CAROLINA, APRIL 8, 1937:
Leavin's (*Nancy Hanks, Bondwoman*), by Janie Malloy
Britt.

THE NINETY-THIRD MEETING OF THE AMERICAN CHEMICAL
SOCIETY, CHAPEL HILL, NORTH CAROLINA, APRIL 12,
1937:
Leavin's (*Nancy Hanks, Bondwoman*), by Janie Malloy
Britt; *Funeral Flowers for the Bride*, by Beverley Du-
Bose Hamer.

DRAMA IN THE SOUTH, CHAPEL HILL, NORTH CAROLINA, APRIL
1–6, 1940:
The Field God, by Paul Green, April 5, 1940.

ANNUAL TWELFTH NIGHT REVELS
The First, January 6, 1928.
The Second, January 12, 1929.
The Third, January 11, 1930.
The Fourth, January 10, 1931.
The Fifth, January 9, 1932.
The Sixth, January 7, 1933.
The Seventh, January 6, 1934.
The Eighth, January 12, 1935.
The Ninth, January 11, 1936.
The Tenth, January 9, 1937.
The Eleventh, January 8, 1938.
The Twelfth, January 6, 1940.

ANNUAL CAPERS
  The First, October 24, 1919.
  The Second, October 15, 1920.
  The Third, May 28, 1927.
  The Fourth, May 26, 1928.
  The Fifth, June 1, 1929.
  The Sixth, May 24, 1930.
  The Seventh, May 30, 1931.
  The Eighth, May 28, 1932.
  The Ninth, May 27, 1933.
  The Tenth, June 2, 1934.
  The Eleventh, June 1, 1935.
  The Twelfth, May 30, 1936.
  The Thirteenth, May 29, 1937.
  The Fourteenth, May 28, 1938.
  The Fifteenth, May 27, 1939.
  The Sixteenth, June 1, 1940.

ANNUAL COMMENCEMENT PERFORMANCES
  The First, June 17, 1919: *What Will Barbara Say?*, by
    Minnie Shepherd Sparrow; *Peggy*, by Harold William-
    son.
  The Second, June 15, 1920: *"Dod Gast Ye Both!"*, by
    Hubert Heffner; *The Last of the Lowries*, by Paul Green.
  The Third, June 14, 1921: *When Witches Ride*, by Eliza-
    beth A. Lay; *In Dixon's Kitchen*, by Wilbur Stout.
  The Fourth, June 13, 1922: *The Miser*, by Paul Green;
    Dogwood Bushes, by Wilbur Stout.
  The Fifth, June 12, 1923: *Agatha*, by Jane Toy; *Mamma*,
    by Ernest Thompson.
  The Sixth, June 10, 1924: *Fixin's*, by Erma and Paul Green;
    The Wheel, by Ernest Thompson.
  The Seventh, June 9, 1925: *The Rivals*, by Richard Brins-
    ley Sheridan.
  The Eighth, June 4, 1932: *The Butter and Egg Man*, by
    George S. Kaufman.
  The Ninth, June 5, 1933: *Henna Rinse*, by Marion Tatum;

Davy Crockett, by John Philip Milhous; *Good-bye to Alice*, by Foster Fitz-Simons.

The Tenth, June 11, 1934: *Third Verse*, by Wilbur Dorsett; *Where There Is Faith*, by Kathleen Krahembuhl; *Art for Spite's Sake*, by Walter Terry.

The Eleventh, June 10, 1935: *Yours and Mine*, by Ella Mae Daniel; *Ancient Heritage*, by Philip Goddard Parker; *Goldie*, by Wilbur Dorsett.

The Twelfth, June 8, 1936: *Texas Calls*, by Paul Green; *Sunday Costs Five Pesos*, by Josephina Niggli.

The Thirteenth, June 7, 1937: *Leavin's*, by Janie Malloy Britt; *Funeral Flowers For the Bride*, by Beverley Du-Bose Hamer.

The Fourteenth, June 6, 1938: *Still Stands the House*, by Gwen Pharis; *Sunday Costs Five Pesos*, by Josephina Niggli.

The Fifteenth, June 5, 1939: *Pasque Flower*, by Gwen Pharis; *These Doggone Elections*, by Fred Koch, Jr.

The Sixteenth, June 10, 1940: *Swamp Outlaw*, by Clare Johnson Marley; *Wash Carver's Mousetrap*, by Fred Koch, Jr.

4. STUDIO PRODUCTIONS
One-Act Plays

MAY 28, 1928.

The Impertinence of the Creature, by Cosmo Gordon-Lennox.

Cocaine, by Pendleton King.

Brothers in Arms, by Merrill Dennison.

MAY 29, 1928.

Françoise' Luck, by Georges de Porte-Riche.

The Mirror, by Catherine M. Roof.

The Constant Lover, by St. John Hankin.

DECEMBER 9, 1929.

Blood, a folk melodrama, by Herbert T. Browne.

Hollyhocks, a New England folk play, by Joseph Philip Fox.

MAY 28, 1930.

Git Up an' Bar the Door, a farce of Mississippi folk life, by Arthur Palmer Hudson.

NOVEMBER 25, 1930.

ver' Snitch, a comedy of Carolina fisherfolk, by Irene Fussler.

DECEMBER 8, 1930.

In the Shadow of the Desert, a comedy of Death Valley, by Laurabelle Dietrick.

The White Senorita, a romance of Southern California, by Laurabelle Dietrick.

DECEMBER 9, 1930.

Saturday Market, a Carolina mountain comedy, by Louise Perry.

DECEMBER 10, 1930.

Lonely Hearts, a comedy of the Alabama Backwoods, by Philip Milhous.

She's Perfectly Innocent, a comedy of college girls, by Ann Wishart Braddy.

JANUARY 21, 1931.

Walnut Boards, a folk comedy of Eastern Carolina, by William Long.

JANUARY 22, 1931.

Doses of Life, a modern comedy, by Tom Loy.

FEBRUARY 13, 1931.

The Blue Remembered Hills, a play of college life, by Theodore Herman.

MARCH 5, 1931.

Penny For Your Thoughts, a stylized bit of life in the subjective, by Tom Loy.

There's a Nigger For You, a tragedy of Negro life, by Mary Griffith.

Always a Bettin' Man, a comedy of Maryland folk, by Tom Loy.

My Business and My Wife, a domestic comedy, by John
    Edwards.

MARCH 9, 1931.
Immoral Holly, a college comedy, by Closs Peace.

APRIL 22, 1931.
The Stray Bullet, an incident in the Chinese War, by
    Robert Barnett.

MAY 6, 1931.
Herbs of Love, a folk comedy of Eastern North Carolina,
    by William Long.
Spice Cake, a play of old romance, by Malcolm Seawell.

MAY 14–15–16, 1931.
Love An' Likker, a play of pioneer days in Dakota, by
    Irene Fussler.
The Stray Bullet, an incident in the Chinese War, by
    Robert Barnett.
Glenhurst, a play of a Maryland family, by Tom Loy.
Pleasantly Purple, a modern satire, by Ellen Stewart.

MAY 18, 1931.
A Village Tragedy, a play of Maine folk, by Charlotte
    Hammond.
Lonely Hearts, a comedy of the Alabama Backwoods, by
    Philip Milhous.
The House of Grief, a poetic fantasy, by Margaret Vale.

5. EXPERIMENTAL PRODUCTIONS

University of North Carolina

FULL-LENGTH PLAYS

Playthings, a comedy of illusion in three acts, by Anthony
    Buttitta, February 28, 1931.
Rest For My Soul, a play in three acts, by Ann Wishart
    Braddy, May 28, 1931.
Snow White, a children's play in two acts, by Sallie M. Ewing,
    May 26, 1932.

A House Divided, a comedy-drama in three acts, by Frederica Frederick, May 8, 1934.

Water, a play of pioneer settlement in California, by Alton Williams, April 13, 1935.

ONE-ACT PLAYS

FIRST SERIES, DECEMBER 14, 1931.

A Vision of Eugenics, a very modern extravaganza, by Maurice Ferber.

Old Aus Ramsey, a comedy of Carolina mountain folk, by Charles Elledge.

The Mandarin Coat, a very foolish comedy, by Olive Newell.

Those Children, a modern comedy, by Osmond Molarsky.

Whispering Shadows, a tragedy of the blind, by Vernon B. Crook.

Patches, a comedy of family life, by Jo Norwood.

SECOND SERIES, FEBRUARY 23, 1932.

The Last Two Shots, a mountain tragedy, by Irene Fussler.

Treasures, by Irene Fussler.

King, Queen, and Joker, a drama of royalty, by Irene Fussler.

THIRD SERIES, MARCH 7, 1932.

Birds of a Feather, a domestic comedy, by Jo Norwood.

Granny, a domestic tragedy, by Jack Riley.

The Golden Lioness, a phantasy of Paris in 1750, by Reuben Young Ellison.

Proof, a play about love, by Osmond Molarsky.

FOURTH SERIES, MAY 12, 1932.

Boardin' Out, a mountain folk comedy, by Charles Elledge and Malcolm Seawell.

Proof, a play about love, by Osmond Molarsky.

Sleep On, Lemuel, a Carolina Negro comedy, by John W. Parker.

Granny, a tragedy of North Carolina farm folk, by Jack Riley, May 23, 1932.

FIFTH SERIES, MAY 25, 1932.

Neighbors of the Dead, a tragedy of heredity (first act of a full-length play), by Vernon Crook.

Ol' Honeycutt's Boy, a play about a country boy, by Jack Riley.

The Boss of the House, a Carolina country comedy, by Lubin Leggette.

Chicken Money, a play of Iowa farm life, by Winifred Tuttle.

The Battle of Shaw's Mill, a Carolina country comedy, by Charles Elledge and Malcolm Seawell.

SIXTH SERIES, JULY 15, 1932 (AFTERNOON AND EVENING).

Election Returns, a social tragedy (Act I of a full-length play), by Alonzo Hoyle.

Freights, a drama of the side-lines, by Marjorie Craig.

A Revolt in the Nineties, a romance, by Anne Wilson.

Playing with Fire, a tragedy of country life, by Thea W. Whitefield.

A Little Cajun, a play of Louisiana folk, by Peg Williamson.

It's Just Too Bad, a tragedy of college youth, by James Alfred Stanley.

Blessed Assurance, a Carolina country comedy, by Evelyn McCall.

SEVENTH SERIES, NOVEMBER 12, 1932 (AFTERNOON AND EVENING).

Old Ninety-Seven, a tragedy of railroad life, by Wilbur Dorsett.

Nothing Ever Happens, a modern domestic tragi-comedy, by Elmer R. Oettinger, Jr.

Gateway, an interlude, by Eugenia Rawls.

Four on a Heath, a grotesque, by Foster Fitz-Simons.

Sour Fodder, a play of Iowa small-town folk, by Burdette Kindig.

Creek Swamp Nigger, a Carolina Negro tragedy, by Harry W. Coble.

Hell Bent for Honolulu, a college comedy, by William Bonyun.

And They Lived Happily, a domestic comedy, by Marion Tatum.

Stumbling in Dreams, a comedy of Tin Pan Alley, by George Brown.

Davy Crockett, half horse, half alligator, by John Philip Milhous.

EIGHTH SERIES, DECEMBER 14, 1932 (AFTERNOON AND EVENING).

Coal, a play of West Virginia mine folk, by Marguerite McGinnis.

The State Rests, a play of a small-town court, by Peggy Ann Harris.

In His Hand, a play of village folk, by Betty Bolton.

The Elders Play, a problem play of youth, by Sue Roberson.

Honora Wade, a play of Georgia folk, by Eugenia Rawls.

Back Door, a Carolina folk comedy, by Wilbur Dorsett.

NINTH SERIES, MARCH 1, 1933 (AFTERNOON AND EVENING).

Fool's Justice, a Negro tragedy, by Harry W. Coble.

A Little Boat to India, a springtime farce, by Foster Fitz-Simons.

Heart Trouble, a comedy of Georgia village folk, by Bradford White.

Mumsey, a drama of Long Island folk, by Sarah M. W. Huntley.

One Every Minute, a modern comedy, by Everett Jess.

Malone, an Irish folk tragedy, by Marion Tatum.

TENTH SERIES, MARCH 3, 1933 (AFTERNOON AND EVENING).

The Last Skirmish, a play of West Virginia mountain people, by Marguerite McGinnis.

Second Edition, a psychological drama, by Robert W. Barnett.

Lights in the Sky, an American comedy, by William Bonyun.

Design for Justice, a social commentary, by Elmer R. Oettinger, Jr.

Comedy at Five, an American comedy, by Martha Matthews Hatton.

Mihalusek's Wagner, a drama of Polish military life, by Edward V. Conrad.

ELEVENTH SERIES, APRIL 13, 1933 (AFTERNOON AND EVENING).

Discontent, a play of industrial strife, by J. M. Ledbetter, Jr.

Blow Me Down, a comedy of sailor folk, by William Bonyun.

And the Poet Laughed, a modern comedy drama, by Burdette Kindig.

Etowah Plantation, a legend of the land, 1846–1864, by Eugenia Rawls.

Tintagil, a dream play, by Martha Matthews Hatton.

Farewell to Glamour, a modern American comedy, by James P. McConnaughey.

My Son, a tragedy of a Southwest trapper, by Frank McIntosh.

The Salted Pup, a comedy of the time of sap and smalle fooles, by John Philip Milhous.

TWELFTH SERIES, MAY 25, 1933 (AFTERNOON).

The Moon Turns, the conclusion of a youthful romance, by Elmer R. Oettinger, Jr.

Beer on Ice, the burp of a nation, by Harry W. Coble.

Bull Session, an ironic comedy of college life, by George Brown.

For Poland, a tragedy of the Great War, by Ed Conrad.

THIRTEENTH SERIES, MAY 25, 1933 (EVENING).

No Word from the Wise, a little comedy of small-town people, by Wilbur Dorsett.

A Mocking Bird Singing, a romance of the South, by Foster Fitz-Simons.

Burgundy for Breakfast, an effervescent farce, by Martha Matthews Hatton.

Three Muggy Rooms in the Bronx, a play of father and son, by George Brown.

Henna Rinse, a play of "Ye Venus Beauty Shoppe," by Marion Tatum.

FOURTEENTH SERIES, NOVEMBER 7, 1933 (AFTERNOON).

Showing at Eight, a play of a small-town moving picture theatre, by Leonard Rapport.

O Woman, a modern comedy of an ancient tragedy, by Carl G. Thompson.

November Night, a play of a Pennsylvania mining town, by Margaret Belle McCauley.

FIFTEENTH SERIES, NOVEMBER 7, 1933 (EVENING).

Hell's Dreams, a play of modern life, by Frederica Frederick.

Diana, a moonlight chase, by Kathleen Krahenbuhl.

Shadows of Industry, a drama of the financial world, by Vermont C. Royster.

Sing Your Own Song, a comedy—we hope!, by Nat Farnworth.

Flight Unending, a tragedy of youth, by Robert W. Barnett.

Everglades and Hickory, an episode in the life of Andrew Jackson, by John F. Alexander.

SIXTEENTH SERIES, DECEMBER 13, 1933 (AFTERNOON AND EVENING).

Grand Slam, a satiric comedy, by James Thompson.

Copper Penny, a modern domestic drama, by Douglas Hume.

Bought with the Vittles, a dude ranch comedy, by Alton Williams.

Opposite Poles, a play of the divorce problem, by Margaret Siceloff.

New Rasthenia, a nervous break-down, by Herman Fussler.

Driftwood, a tragedy of the fisherfolk of eastern Carolina, by Patricia McMullan.

La Capilla (The Chapel), a legendary romance of Spanish California, by Frederica Frederick.

SEVENTEENTH SERIES, FEBRUARY 7, 1934 (AFTERNOON AND EVENING).

Over the Doorsill, a play of small-town life, by Harry W. Coble.

Another Journey, a modern tragedy, by Virgil Lee.

Borrowed of the Night, a tragedy of youth, by Kathleen Krahenbuhl.

Moon in the Hawthorne Tree, a Georgia farm tragedy, by Foster Fitz-Simons.

Prelude, a story of youth, by Vermont C. Royster.

The Stars Are Fire, a comedy of earnest youth, by Nat Farnworth.

John Brown, an episode in his campaign in "Bleeding Kansas," by John F. Alexander.

Oh, Hell, a very modern political satire, by Margaret McCauley.

Shipmates, a play of the water-front, by Donald Pope.

EIGHTEENTH SERIES, MARCH 9, 1934 (AFTERNOON AND EVENING).

Cottie Mourns, a comedy of sea island folk, by Patricia McMullan.

Tomorrow, a play of a lodging-house, by Douglas Hume.

The Lo Fan Joss, a subtle thing, by Herman Fussler.

Pretty, Plump Angel, a play of youth, by Cecilia Allen.

Never a Second Time, a romantic interlude, by Leonard Rapport.

Release, a play of courage, by Jean Smith Cantrell.

Third Verse, a comedy of a small-town newspaper, by Wilbur Dorsett.

Unto the Hills, a play of faiths, by Leonard Rapport.

Strange Interlaken, a vignette, by Robert Barnett.

Lifeguards and Fish, a modern comedy of errors, by Margaret Siceloff.

NINETEENTH SERIES, MARCH 22, 1934.

Back Page, a newspaper melodrama, by Don Shoemaker.

The Golden Wedding, a romantic comedy, by Alton Williams.

Rich Man! Poor Man!, a Marxian romance, by Cecilia Allen.

When Floosies Meet, a comedy of pseudo-artists, by Walter Terry.

TWENTIETH SERIES, MAY 30, 1934 (AFTERNOON).

The Suicide, a modern interpretation of hell, by Sara Seawell.

A Beating of Wings, a poetic tragedy, by Foster Fitz-Simons.

Beginners, a belligerent satire, by Bradford White.

Belle, a small-town tragedy, by Patricia McMullan.

TWENTY-FIRST SERIES, MAY 30, 1934 (EVENING).

When Doctors Fail, a comedy of faith healing, by W. A. Sigmon.

The Skeleton Rattles His Bones, a modern domestic comedy drama, by Douglas Hume.

Spare-Ribs, a comedy of nautical cookery, by Donald Pope.

Crash, a story of "The Street," by Milton Kalb.

TWENTY-SECOND SERIES, NOVEMBER I, 1934 (AFTERNOON).

Sea Psalm, a tragedy of Carolina sea-folk, by Charles Edward Eaton.

New Anarchy, a play of the banking crisis, by Philip Goddard Parker.

TWENTY-THIRD SERIES, NOVEMBER I, 1934 (EVENING).

New Nigger, a tragedy of the tobacco country, by Fred Howard.

Clam Digger, a play of Maine sea-folk, by Jean Ashe.

Hunger, a tragedy of North Carolina farm folk, by Ella Mae Daniel.

TWENTY-FOURTH SERIES, NOVEMBER 15, 1934 (AFTERNOON).

Traficante, a play of Spanish Florida, by Maxeda von Hesse.

TWENTY-FIFTH SERIES, DECEMBER 11, 1934 (AFTERNOON AND
EVENING).

The Passer-By, a play of Carolina village folk, by Ralph
Lyerly.

Ancient Heritage, a drama of a New England family, by
Philip Goddard Parker.

Octagon Soap, a Carolina country comedy, by Nancy
Lawlor.

Damned Idealist, a college drama, by Charles A. Poe.

Rations, a mountain folk comedy, by Catherine Threlkeld.

Confidentially Speaking, a satire on true-story writing, by
Wilbur Dorsett.

TWENTY-SIXTH SERIES, FEBRUARY 5, 1935 (AFTERNOON).

Muddy Jordan Waters, a tragedy of the Carolina mountains, by Mildred Moore.

The Villain Gets the Girl, a modern satire in the old style,
by Charles A. Poe.

TWENTY-SEVENTH SERIES, FEBRUARY 5, 1935 (EVENING).

Pensioner, a play of contemporary social conditions, by
Alice A. Truslow.

The Devil's Trampin' Ground, a tragedy of mixed blood,
by Sara Seawell.

Yours and Mine, a comedy of domestic difficulties, by
Ella Mae Daniel.

TWENTY-EIGHTH SERIES, MARCH 7, 1935 (AFTERNOON).

I Sing Forever, a tragedy of the North Carolina mountains, by Mildred Moore.

The Settin' Up, a country wake, by Sara Seawell.

Tsalagi, an historical drama of the Cherokee Indians, by
Billy Greet.

TWENTY-NINTH SERIES, MARCH 7, 1935 (EVENING).

And So They Grow, a play of little ladies, by Ellen Deppe.

Wait a While, the first act of a full-length domestic drama,
by Kenneth Bartlett.

Goldie, a comedy of a Negro Saturday night, by Wilbur
Dorsett.

Crazy-Patch Quilt, a play of the Carolina tobacco country, by Anne Hyman Moore.

THIRTIETH SERIES, MAY 13, 1935.

So It Will Last, an eighteenth-century romance, by William Howard Wang.

The Best Butter, a modern tea-room comedy, by Joseph Lee Brown.

Virtue, a satiric interlude, by Leonard Rapport.

Hangman's Noose, a tragedy, by Charles A. Poe.

Bathroom Echoes, or *The Tale of a Tub*, a slightly ribald farce of character, by Walter Terry.

THIRTY-FIRST SERIES, MAY 29, 1935 (AFTERNOON).

Dark Journey, a drama of a farm family, by Virgil Jackson Lee.

There Ain't No Escape, a comedy of arrested courtship, by Ella Mae Daniel.

Thou Thief!, a play of small-town complacency, by Ralph Lyerly.

Barn Trash, a mountain mystery-comedy, by Mildred Moore.

THIRTY-SECOND SERIES, MAY 29, 1935 (EVENING).

Penny-Wise, a drama of misunderstanding, by Ellen Deppe.

Queer New World, a Negro comedy-comment, by Wilbur Dorsett.

Debtor's Hell, an historical incident of Colonial Massachusetts, by Jean Ashe.

THIRTY-THIRD SERIES, OCTOBER 31, 1935 (AFTERNOON).

The School Teacher, a play of character conflict, by Kenneth E. Bartlett.

The Jew, a poetic drama of the Inquisition, by William Howard Wang.

THIRTY-FOURTH SERIES, OCTOBER 31, 1935 (EVENING).

Across the Tracks, a play of Southern slums, by Frank Durham.

Cockle Doody Doo, a play of Carolina fisherfolk, by Patricia McMullan.

Hjemlengsel (*Home Longing*), a Norwegian folk play, by Gerd Bernhart.

The Red Velvet Goat, a tragedy of laughter and a comedy of tears, by Josephina Niggli.

THIRTY-FIFTH SERIES, DECEMBER 12, 1935 (AFTERNOON).

Take Your Choice, a play of college liberalism, by George Starks.

Black Sheep, a tragedy of the color line, by Marjorie Usher.

THIRTY-SIXTH SERIES, DECEMBER 12, 1935 (EVENING).

Election, a play of politics in a small Texas town, by Mary Delaney.

The Other Way, a tragedy of indecision, by Lawrence Wismer.

A Most Lamentable Comedy, a true story, by Barbara A. Hilton.

Horses and Mice, a tragi-comedy of musical playmakers, by Joseph Lee Brown.

THIRTY-SEVENTH SERIES, FEBRUARY 4, 1936 (AFTERNOON).

With Onions, an illogical play of social protest, by Frank Durham.

There Is No Guilt, a play of a pacifist who died, by William Howard Wang.

THIRTY-EIGHTH SERIES, FEBRUARY 4, 1936 (EVENING).

Transient, a play of homeless men, by Walter Spearman.

The Eternal Comedy, a play of adolescence, by Mary Delaney.

Prairie Dust, a play of the Dakota drought, by Gerd Bernhart.

Raise a Tune, Sister, a play of Carolina fisherfolk, by Patricia McMullan.

THIRTY-NINTH SERIES, MARCH 5, 1936 (AFTERNOON).

Grandma's Bonnet, a comedy of age, by June Hogan.

Brownstone Front, a modern domestic tragedy, by William Chichester.

FORTIETH SERIES, MARCH 5, 1935 (EVENING).

Cat Alley, a college comedy, by Kenneth Bartlett.

An Active's Pledge, a play of college fraternity life, by William A. Barwick.

Frame-Up, a play of social protest, by Jane Henle.

An Orchid to You, a comedy of sorority life, by Jean Walker.

FORTY-FIRST SERIES, MAY 12, 1936.

Country Sunday, a play of white justice, by Walter Spearman.

Mob-Tide, an anti-lynching play, by John Walker.

Strike-Breaker, a play of protest, by George Starks.

So Spin the Norns, a play of Norse gods, by Gerd Bernhart.

Fire of the Lord, a play of religious fanatics, by Frank Durham.

FORTY-SECOND SERIES, MAY 27, 1936.

Ocean Harvest, a tragedy of Maine sea-folk, by Jean Ashe.

FORTY-THIRD SERIES, OCTOBER 30, 1936.

Ugly Hands, a tragedy of factory women, by Kate May Rutherford.

And Things Happen, a play of post-war shadows, by Don Watters.

Waitin', a drama of the Southwest Virginia mountains, by William Peery.

The Barren Year, a tragedy of a South Carolina farm woman, by David Beaty.

FORTY-FOURTH SERIES, DECEMBER 11, 1936 (AFTERNOON).

Tidal Wave, a tragedy of the South Carolina low country, by Evelyn Snider.

Cause Unknown, a tragedy of modern youth, by John Walker.

Who's Boss?, a comedy of Negro farm life, by Lubin Leggette.

FORTY-FIFTH SERIES, DECEMBER 11, 1936 (EVENING).

Widening the Channel, a play of piedmont Virginia, by Sally Wills Holland.

Six Dollars, a tragedy of youth, by Virginia Peyatt.

Leavin's, a legend of the Carolina mountains, by Janie Malloy Britt.

In the Jungle, a drama of the "Milk and Honey Route," by William Peery.

FORTY-SIXTH SERIES, FEBRUARY 2, 1937.

The Steep Road, by Joseph Feldman.

Funeral Flowers for the Bride, a comedy of the Blue Ridge Mountains, by Beverley DuBose Hamer.

Mrs. Juliet, an ironic essay, by David Beaty.

Rosemary's for Remembrance, a play from the legends of Old Lynnhaven, by Sally Wills Holland.

Abide With Me, a comedy of rural South Carolina, by Walter Spearman.

FORTY-SEVENTH SERIES, MARCH 4, 1937.

The Sun Sets Early, a play of a small college, by William Peery.

Near a Spring, a play of southern Indiana, by Kate May Rutherford.

FORTY-EIGHTH SERIES, MAY 7, 1937.

Thank Rotary, a play of the Big Brother movement, by William Peery.

Penguin Soup, a Second Avenue nightmare, by Jean Ashe.

Shattered Glass, a play of a woman's frustration, by Marion Hartshorn.

Long Sweetenin', a comedy of the hill folk, by Janie Malloy Britt.

FORTY-NINTH SERIES, MAY 27, 1937 (AFTERNOON AND EVENING).

Courtship at Eight, a play of children's love triangles, by Charlotte Wright.

By Any Other Name, a racial tragedy, by Marion Hartshorn.

From Sullen Earth, a play of rural South Carolina, by Frank Durham.

Earth Treading Stars, a Travelers Aid incident, by Manuel Korn.

The White Doe, a legend of North Carolina Indians, by William Peery.

FIFTIETH SERIES, JULY 19, 1937.

Seventy Times Seven, a Carolina folk play, by William Ivey Long.

"*A-Pinin' and A-Dyin'*," a mountain comedy, by Emily Polk Crow.

The Ivory Shawl, a folk play of South Alabama, by Kate Porter Lewis.

FIFTY-FIRST SERIES, NOVEMBER 4, 1937.

The Cross of Cannair, a social drama of New York in 1887, by Lynette Heldman.

Uncle Smelicue, a Carolina mountain comedy, by Lois Latham.

This Side Jordan, a play of farm life in the Middle West, by Lynn Gault.

It Don't Make No Difference, a folk play of Tin Pan Alley, by Joseph Lee Brown.

FIFTY-SECOND SERIES, DECEMBER 9, 1937.

Hello, Hanging Dawg, a Carolina mountain comedy, by Lois Latham.

Kunstbeflisener (Student of Art), a play of an artist's conflict, by Thad Jones.

Pennies for Their Thoughts, a domestic comedy of an author, by Noel Houston.

Washed in De Blood, a symphonic play of Negro life, by Rietta Winn Bailey.

FIFTY-THIRD SERIES, FEBRUARY 2, 1938.

Hit's Man's Business, a Carolina mountain play, by Lois Latham.

And Darling, Do Be Tactful, a domestic comedy, by Rose Peagler.

The Last Christmas, a drama of death row, by Noel Houston.

His Boon Companions, a temperance comedy, by Lynn Gault.

FIFTY-FOURTH SERIES, MARCH 3, 1938.

Where the Wind Blows Free, a play of the Texas range, by Emily Polk Crow.

Hidden Heart, a comedy of Armenian-American folk, by Howard Richardson.

Still Stands the House, a drama of the Canadian frontier, by Gwen Pharis.

Wings to Fly Away, a Negro ritual drama, by Rietta Winn Bailey.

FIFTY-FIFTH SERIES, MAY 26, 1938.

Last Refuge, an outlaw comes home, by Noel Houston.

Chris Axelson, Blacksmith, a folk comedy of western Canada, by Gwen Pharis.

West from the Panhandle, a tragedy of the Dust Bowl, by Clemon White and Betty Smith.

Let the Chips Fall, a comedy of domestic intrigue, by Emily Polk Crow.

FIFTY-SIXTH SERIES, JULY 20, 1938 (AFTERNOON AND EVENING).

Fresh Widder, a play of Colington Island fisherfolk, by Lacy Anderson.

Stick 'Em Up, a comedy of frontier New Mexico, by Gordon Clouser.

Me an' De Lawd, a Negro play of eastern North Carolina, by Jameson Bunn Dowdy.

Montana Night, a drama of the Old West, by Robert Finch and Betty Smith.

Triflin' Ways, a comedy of the Missouri Ozarks, by Lealon N. Jones.

FIFTY-SEVENTH SERIES, JANUARY 11, 1939.

Uncle Spence Goes Modern, a play of the North Carolina Highlands, by William Wolff.

The Long Ago, a nostalgic Oklahoma comedy, by Noel Houston.

Bad Yankees, a boarding school comedy of Mississippi, by Antoinette Sparks.

Wash Carver's Mouse Trap, a Carolina mountain comedy, by Fred Koch, Jr.

FIFTY-EIGHTH SERIES, JANUARY 27, 1939.

Swappin' Fever, a comedy of Missouri Ozarks, by Lealon N. Jones.

Runaway, a play of a reform school boy, by Dorothy Lewis.

Design for Stella, a comedy of Manhattan, by Sanford Stein.

FIFTY-NINTH SERIES, APRIL 17, 1939 (AFTERNOON AND EVENING).

Old Man Taterbug, a play for children, by Mary Louise Boylston.

The Reticule, a comedy of the reconstruction period, by Katherine Moran.

According to Law, a drama of an Oklahoma court, by Noel Houston.

SIXTIETH SERIES, MAY 24, 1939.

Out from New Bedford, a play of the whaling days in old New Bedford, by Frederick G. Walsh.

These Doggone Elections, a comedy of the Great Smoky Mountains, by Fred Koch, Jr.

Texas Forever, a play of the revolt against Mexico, by Emily Polk Crow.

SIXTY-FIRST SERIES, JULY 15, 1939.

Lipstick, a comedy of college life, by Mary Hyde.

Swamp Outlaw, a drama of Henry Berry Lowry, by Clare Marley.

Store-Bought Teeth, a comedy of the Kentucky mountains, by Marie Haass.

SIXTY-SECOND SERIES, NOVEMBER 7, 1939.

Squaw Winter, a play of a family in Maine, by Frances Langsdorf Fox.

Got No Sorrow, a Negro ritual drama of the Carolina Low Country, by Caroline Hart Crum.

Strong Hands for Hurting, a tragedy of Piedmont North Carolina, by Edward Post.

SIXTY-THIRD SERIES, DECEMBER 9, 1939.

New Britches, a comedy of western North Carolina, by Evelyn Dawn Matthews.

Winter Parade, a play of changing America, by Adrian Spies.

Black Tassels, a play of South Carolina Negro life, by Frank Guess.

SIXTY-FOURTH SERIES, FEBRUARY 20, 1940 (AFTERNOON AND EVENING).

Whipplesnout, a frog fantasy for children, by Mary Louise Boylston.

Mist in the Hills, a play of the Carolina Highlands, by Evelyn Dawn Matthews.

Torch in the Wind, a drama of "Billy the Kid," by Chase Webb.

Banked Fires, a play of an apartment house janitor, by Constance Smith.

SIXTY-FIFTH SERIES, MARCH 7, 1940.

The Devil's Bread, a morality play, by Edward Post.

SIXTY-SIXTH SERIES, MARCH 9, 1940 (AFTERNOON AND EVENING).

Patches, a play for children, by Mary Louise Boylston.

Outside De Gate, a Negro graveyard fantasy, by William Long.

Mi Amigo, a comedy of "Billy the Kid," by Chase Webb.

SIXTY-SEVENTH SERIES, MAY 6, 1940 (AFTERNOON AND EVENING).

Taffy, the Tiger, a play for children, by Mary Louise Boylston.

Come Spring, a play of old age and relief, by William Long.

The Woman from Merry River, a folk fantasy with music, by Chase Webb.

The Scarlet Petticoat, a folk comedy of the Black Belt, by Kate Porter Lewis.

SIXTY-EIGHTH SERIES, MAY 30, 1940.

Truth or Consequences, a play of spring in New York City, by Constance Smith.

Billy, The Kid, by Chase Webb.

Watermelon Time, a folk comedy of the Black Belt, by Kate Porter Lewis.

SIXTY-NINTH SERIES, JULY 2, 1940.

Three Links O' Chain, a comedy of the Alabama Black Belt, by Kate Porter Lewis.

Party Dress, a tragedy of the Alabama Backwoods, by Kate Porter Lewis.

The House in Avondale, a comedy of Birmingham Aristocracy, by Kate Porter Lewis.

SEVENTIETH SERIES, JULY 16, 1940.

June Bug, a play about an ordinary family, by Lucy Crenshaw.

Dark Bayou, a play of Louisiana farm folk, by Laurraine Goreau.

August Angel, a play of "Big Meetin' Time," by Neil Hartley.

SEVENTY-FIRST SERIES, JULY 18, 1940 (JUNIOR PLAYMAKERS).

Cozy Corners, a farce of a women's hotel, by Katherine Hill.

A Daughter to Marry, a comedy of the Pennsylvania Amish, by Caryl Bashore.

Sho' Nuff Dead, a Negro comedy, by Herbert Lee.

SEVENTY-SECOND SERIES, NOVEMBER 5, 1940.

Night Run, a play of a bus trip, by Emilie Johnson.

Sarah Baske, a play of the Maine Coast, by Merle McKay.

The Bridegroom Waits, a comedy of the country, by Frank Guess.

SEVENTY-THIRD SERIES, DECEMBER 10, 1940.

Sermon On a Monday, a play of the democratic ideal, by Joseph D. Feldman.

Nine-Hour Shift, a play of the importance of reason, by Marian Maschin.

Swing You Sinner, a Negro play with music, by Tom Avera, Jr.

6. Experimental Productions

Other Universities

COLUMBIA UNIVERSITY

August 10, 1926.

Circumventin' Saandy, a play of Nova Scotia village folk, by Zillah K. Macdonald.

Saturday Afternoon, a play of the Chicago West Side, by Katherine Prosser.

The Muse of the Unpublished Writer, a play of Greenwich village characters, by Alice Rodewald.

August 12, 1935 (Authors' reading of new plays).

Idy Stover, a play of prairie folk, by Margaret Radcliffe.

Good Old War, a play of Oklahoma folk, by Ben Henneke.

Chorale, an episode in convent life, by Eva Wolas.

The Day Coach, an incident on "The Blue Bonnet Special," by Ben Henneke.

UNIVERSITY OF CALIFORNIA, BERKELEY

July 29, 1927.

Mountain Magic, a romance of early California, by Edith Daseking.

Schoolin', a play of the Mission District of San Francisco, by Edith Daseking.

Puttin' It Over, a cross section of college life, by Eloise Sterling.

August 7, 1928 (Authors' reading of new plays).

Calla Lilies, by Patience Paschall.

The Beard of Moses, by Alice Holdship Ware.

Graveyard Shift, by Edith Daseking.

UNIVERSITY OF SOUTHERN CALIFORNIA

July 22, 1931.

Conchita, an Arizona folk play, by Rosemary Shirley DeCamp.

Stoves (*Spring Storm*), a Utah farm comedy, by Mary C. Hatch.

Casting Office, a farcial treatment of Hollywood, by Harold Herson.

August 26, 1931.

Weather-beaten, a Montana folk play, by Phyliss Judith Pierson.

Object—Matrimony, a Wyoming folk comedy, by Coza Clausen.

The Fatted Calf, a Dakota folk play, by Charles Upham Patmore.

UNIVERSITY OF COLORADO

July 12, 1933.

Vanity, Vanity, a folk comedy of Dakota, by Anne B. Walters (a reading).

Bosewell's 'Dobe, a folk play of Oklahoma ranch life, by Josephine McGinnis.

Perfect Understanding, a comedy of a sorority kitchen, by Nat Farnworth.

July 14, 1933.

Mountain Storm, a tragedy of the Colorado Rockies, by Will Easton and Robert Morrison.

Strange Inner-Tube, or *A Punctured Romance*, by Nat Farnworth.

Seven Chords, an incident in a girls' boarding school in the South, by June West.

August 16, 1933.

Sigrid, a tragedy of Norwegian pioneer life in the Dakotas, by Margaret Radcliffe.

Wind Through the Cottonwood Trees, a poetic play, by Jean Wilson Stafford.

Reno Romance, a comedy of marital meandering, by Elizabeth Nixon.

Tenderfoot Gold, a comedy of old Central City, Colorado, by Eugene Ivey.

August 18, 1933.

Gold Fever, an incident of the early Colorado mining days, by La Verne F. Mock.

Granite Gulch, a play of Colorado mountain folk, by Elizabeth Nixon.

The Head-Ax of Ingfell, a tragedy of the Igorote Hill folk of the Philippines, by Anne B. Walters.

November 8–9–10, 1933 (Written in Professor Koch's Playwriting courses).

Water, a portrayal of a Colorado irrigation feud, by Adrienne Roucolle Wormington.

The Bluffers, a comedy of love in the West, by Thora Wiseman.

NORTHWESTERN UNIVERSITY

August 14, 1934.

Traficante, a play of Spanish Florida, by Maxeda von Hesse.

Black Religion, a Negro folk tragedy, by Homer Hamilton.

Bulldog Edition, a Chicago newspaper comedy, by Albert R. Crews.

UNIVERSITY OF ALBERTA

The Banff School of Fine Arts
Banff, Alberta, Canada

FIRST SERIES, AUGUST 26, 1937.

Thunderbird, a tragedy of the fisherfolk of West Vancouver Island, by Elsie MacCleave.

On to Ottawa, a play of the unemployed, by Mary Ellen Burgess.

The Last Race, a drama of the race track, by Cecil Young.

Rolling Logs, a play of the mining industry in Western Canada, by Jessie M. Robertson.

SECOND SERIES, AUGUST 24, 1938.

Sterner Stuff, a comedy of a country schoolteacher, by Wesley Oke.

You Got to Do Somethin', a comedy of the Peace River country, by Jack Cheal.

Their Love, a modern romance, by Betty Sue Snelson.

Mute Company, a comedy of Maine folks, by Helen Brown.

THIRD SERIES, AUGUST 26, 1938.

On to Ottawa, a play of the unemployed, by Mary Ellen Burgess.

For Naught, a tragedy of an Alberta farm family, by Milwyn Adams-Davies.

Chris Axelson, Blacksmith, a Canadian folk comedy, by Gwen Pharis.

Catalogue Brides, a comedy of Montana ranch life, by Olive M. Scholz.

FOURTH SERIES, AUGUST 24, 1939.

Milka-Noups of Inkameep (Young Eagle), a play of the Okanagan Indians, by Anthony Walsh.

Chinook Wind, a tragedy of the Peace River country, by Magdalena Polley.

The Best Laid Plans, a folk comedy of southern Illinois, by L. Louise Stephens.

Down North, a drama of aviation in the Yellow Knife District, by John McLaren.

Red Tape, a play of a Canadian National Park, by T. H. Lonsdale.

Billi Be Damned, a comedy of modern youth, by Betty Sue Snelson.

FIFTH SERIES, AUGUST 28, 1940.

Chipmunk and The Owl-Woman, a legend of the Okanagan Indians, by Elizabeth Renyi.

When The Geese Fly, a comedy of village life, by T. H. Lonsdale.

Shafts of Light, a play of a small-town family, by Billy Carr.

Final Edition, a comedy of a small-town editor, by John A. MacNaughton.

Harvest Heat, a play of Alberta wheat fields, by N. Alice Frick.

Double Dare, a play of boys' life, by Stuart Carson.

II. THE PLAYMAKERS' TOURS

FIRST TOUR, NORTH CAROLINA, MAY 7–14, 1921.
The Miser, by Paul Green.
When Witches Ride, by Elizabeth A. Lay.
In Dixon's Kitchen, by Wilbur Stout and Ellen Lay.

SECOND TOUR, NORTH CAROLINA, JANUARY 16–24, 1922.
The Miser, by Paul Green.
In Dixon's Kitchen, by Wilbur Stout and Ellen Lay.
Trista, by Elizabeth A. Lay.

THIRD TOUR, NORTH CAROLINA, MAY 1–27, 1922.
The Lord's Will, by Paul Green.
Dogwood Bushes, by Wilbur Stout.
In Dixon's Kitchen, by Wilbur Stout and Ellen Lay.
Trista, by Elizabeth A. Lay.

FOURTH TOUR, NORTH CAROLINA, FEBRUARY 5–14, 1923.
Agatha, by Jane Toy.
Off Nag's Head, by Dougald MacMillan.
Wilbur's Cousin, by Ernest Thompson.

FIFTH TOUR, NORTH CAROLINA, APRIL 16–28, 1923.
Agatha, by Jane Toy.
Peggy, by Harold Williamson.
Mamma, by Ernest Thompson.

SIXTH TOUR, NORTH CAROLINA, NOVEMBER 19–DECEMBER 7, 1923.
Nat Macon's Game, by Osler Bailey.
The Black Rooster, by Pearl Setzer.
Gaius and Gaius, Jr., by Lucy M. Cobb.

SEVENTH TOUR, NORTH CAROLINA, FEBRUARY 13–21, 1924.
The Black Rooster, by Pearl Setzer.
Fixin's, by Erma and Paul Green.
Gaius and Gaius, Jr., by Lucy M. Cobb.

EIGHTH TOUR, NORTH CAROLINA, APRIL 9–17, 1924.
The Beaded Buckle, by Frances Gray.
Fixin's, by Erma and Paul Green.
Gaius and Gaius, Jr., by Lucy M. Cobb.

NINTH TOUR, NORTH CAROLINA, NOVEMBER 12–26, 1924.
The Honor of Bonava, by Robert Watson Winston.
Politicin' in Horse Cove, by Martha Boswell.
The Scuffletown Outlaws, by William Norment Cox.

TENTH TOUR, NORTH CAROLINA, SOUTH CAROLINA, GEORGIA,
    JANUARY 23—FEBRUARY 2, 1925.
Gaius and Gaius, Jr., by Lucy M. Cobb.
Fixin's, by Paul and Erma Green.
When Witches Ride, by Elizabeth A. Lay.

ELEVENTH TOUR, WESTERN NORTH CAROLINA, APRIL 24–MAY
    9, 1925.
Old Imes, by Ray Heffner.
The Thrice Promised Bride, by Cheng-Chin Hsiung.
The Scuffletown Outlaws, by William Norment Cox.

TWELFTH TOUR, NORTH CAROLINA, VIRGINIA, DECEMBER 11–14,
    1925.
Quare Medicine, by Paul Green.
Fixin's, by Paul and Erma Green.
Gaius and Gaius, Jr., by Lucy M. Cobb.

THIRTEENTH TOUR, NORTH CAROLINA, VIRGINIA, MARYLAND,
    DISTRICT OF COLUMBIA, FEBRUARY 5–20, 1926.
Quare Medicine, by Paul Green.
Fixin's, by Paul and Erma Green.
Gaius and Gaius, Jr., by Lucy M. Cobb.

FOURTEENTH TOUR, NORTH CAROLINA, APRIL 5–12, 1926.
The First Year, by Frank Craven.

FIFTEENTH TOUR, NORTH CAROLINA, APRIL 30–MAY 12, 1926.
The First Year, by Frank Craven.

SIXTEENTH TOUR, NORTH CAROLINA, NOVEMBER 11–22, 1926.
She Stoops to Conquer, by Oliver Goldsmith.

SEVENTEENTH TOUR, NORTH CAROLINA, VIRGINIA, SOUTH
    CAROLINA, GEORGIA, FEBRUARY 22–MARCH 19, 1927.
Trista, by Elizabeth A. Lay.
Old Wash Lucas or *The Miser*, by Paul Green.
In Dixon's Kitchen, by Wilbur Stout and Ellen Lay.

EIGHTEENTH TOUR, NORTH CAROLINA, VIRGINIA, MAY 7–19, 1927.

Quare Medicine, by Paul Green.

Lighted Candles, by Margaret Bland.

The Marvelous Romance of Wen Chun-Chin, by Cheng-Chin Hsiung.

NINETEENTH TOUR, NORTH CAROLINA, VIRGINIA, MARYLAND, PENNSYLVANIA, NEW YORK, NOVEMBER 5–25, 1927.

The Scuffletown Outlaws, by William Norment Cox.

Fixin's, by Paul and Erma Green.

Lighted Candles, by Margaret Bland.

On Dixon's Porch, by Wilbur Stout and Ellen Lay.

TWENTIETH TOUR, NORTH CAROLINA, FEBRUARY 17–29, 1928.

Lighted Candles, by Margaret Bland.

Mountain Magic, by Edith Daseking.

The Marvelous Romance of Wen Chun-Chin, by Cheng-Chin Hsiung.

TWENTY-FIRST TOUR, NORTH CAROLINA, TENNESSEE, MAY 4–15, 1928.

Mountain Magic, by Edith Daseking.

Job's Kinfolks, by Loretto Carroll Bailey.

A Shotgun Splicin', by Gertrude Wilson Coffin.

TWENTY-SECOND TOUR, NORTH CAROLINA, VIRGINIA, MARYLAND, PENNSYLVANIA, NEW JERSEY, CONNECTICUT, NEW YORK, NOVEMBER 13–DECEMBER 1, 1928.

The Man Who Died at Twelve O'clock, by Paul Green.

Job's Kinfolks, by Loretto Carroll Bailey.

Quare Medicine, by Paul Green.

TWENTY-THIRD TOUR, EASTERN NORTH CAROLINA AND SOUTH CAROLINA, FEBRUARY 15–27, 1929.

The Man Who Died at Twelve O'clock, by Paul Green.

Job's Kinfolks, by Loretto Carroll Bailey.

Quare Medicine, by Paul Green.

TWENTY-FOURTH TOUR, EASTERN NORTH CAROLINA, MARCH 20–23, 1929.

The Man Who Died at Twelve O'clock, by Paul Green.

Job's Kinfolks, by Loretto Carroll Bailey.
Quare Medicine, by Paul Green.

TWENTY-FIFTH TOUR, WESTERN NORTH CAROLINA AND TEN-
NESSEE, APRIL 15–26, 1929.

The Lie, by Wilkeson O'Connell.
Old Wash Lucas (*The Miser*), by Paul Green.
Quare Medicine, by Paul Green.
The Man Who Died at Twelve O'clock, by Paul Green.

TWENTY-SIXTH TOUR, NORTH CAROLINA, VIRGINIA, MARYLAND,
PENNSYLVANIA, NEW JERSEY, NEW YORK, MASSACHU-
SETTS, AND CONNECTICUT, NOVEMBER 16–30, 1929.

The No 'Count Boy, by Paul Green.
Job's Kinfolks, by Loretto Carroll Bailey.
Black Water, by Loretto Carroll Bailey.
Magnolia's Man, by Gertrude Wilson Coffin.

TWENTY-SEVENTH TOUR, NORTH CAROLINA, SOUTH CAROLINA,
GEORGIA, FEBRUARY 14–26, 1930.

The No 'Count Boy, by Paul Green.
Job's Kinfolks, by Loretto Carroll Bailey.
Black Water, by Loretto Carroll Bailey.
Magnolia's Man, by Gertrude Wilson Coffin.

TWENTY-EIGHTH TOUR, WESTERN NORTH CAROLINA, SOUTH
CAROLINA, APRIL 18–30, 1930.

The No 'Count Boy, by Paul Green.
Job's Kinfolks, by Loretto Carroll Bailey.
Black Water, by Loretto Carroll Bailey.
Magnolia's Man, by Gertrude Wilson Coffin.

TWENTY-NINTH TOUR, EASTERN NORTH CAROLINA, FEBRUARY,
26–28, 1933.

Davy Crockett, by John Philip Milhous.
Four On a Heath, by Foster Fitz-Simons.
Stumbling in Dreams, by George Brown.

THIRTIETH TOUR, WESTERN AND EASTERN NORTH CAROLINA,
MARCH 22–25, 1933.

Davy Crockett, by John Philip Milhous.
Four On a Heath, by Foster Fitz-Simons.
Stumbling in Dreams, by George Brown.

THIRTY-FIRST TOUR, NORTH CAROLINA, KENTUCKY, MISSOURI,
    APRIL 24–MAY 2, 1934.
On Dixon's Porch, by Wilbur Stout.
Job's Kinfolks, by Loretto Carroll Bailey.
Quare Medicine, by Paul Green.

THIRTY-SECOND TOUR, EASTERN NORTH CAROLINA, VIRGINIA,
    MARYLAND, NOVEMBER 19–27, 1934.
The Loyal Venture, by Wilkeson O'Connell.
Fixin's, by Paul Green.
Quare Medicine, by Paul Green.

THIRTY-THIRD TOUR, EASTERN NORTH CAROLINA, VIRGINIA,
    NOVEMBER 13–26, 1935.
Cottie Mourns, by Patricia McMullan.
New Nigger, by Fred Howard.
Tooth or Shave, by Josephina Niggli.

THIRTY-FOURTH TOUR, NORTH CAROLINA, NEW JERSEY,
    NEW YORK, NOVEMBER 13–20, 1936.
Quare Medicine, by Paul Green.
New Nigger, by Fred Howard.
Tooth or Shave, by Josephina Niggli.

THIRTY-FIFTH TOUR, NORTH CAROLINA, VIRGINIA, MARYLAND,
    NOVEMBER 22–DECEMBER 4, 1937.
Funeral Flowers for the Bride, by Beverley DuBose Hamer.
Leavin's, by Janie Malloy Britt.
Sunday Costs Five Pesos, by Josephina Niggli.

THIRTY-SIXTH TOUR, NORTH CAROLINA, VIRGINIA, NEW YORK,
    NOVEMBER 10–23, 1938.
Three Foolish Virgins, by Bernice Kelly Harris.
Soldadera (Soldier-Woman), by Josephina Niggli.
Magnolia's Man, by Gertrude Wilson Coffin.

THIRTY-SEVENTH TOUR, NORTH CAROLINA, SOUTH CAROLINA,
    VIRGINIA, NOVEMBER 11–23, 1940.
The House of Connelly, by Paul Green.

III. PROFESSIONAL PLAYS PRODUCED

1. FULL-LENGTH PLAYS

The Importance of Being Earnest, by Oscar Wilde, March 1–2, 1920.

Seventeen, by Booth Tarkington, November 10–11, 1922.

The Torch-Bearers, by George Kelly, March 10–11, 1925.

Le Malade Imaginaire, by Molière, May 21–22, 1926 (in French).

A Thousand Years Ago, by Percy MacKaye, October 15–16, 1926.

She Stoops to Conquer, by Oliver Goldsmith, December 3–4, 1926.

Le Barbier De Seville, by Beaumarchais, March 30–31, 1927 (in French).

Ten Nights in a Bar-Room, by William W. Pratt, December 9–10, 1927.

You and I, by Philip Barry, July 19–20–21, 1928.

The Dover Road, by A. A. Milne, July 12–13, 1929.

The Show-Off, by George Kelly, January 30–31–February 1, 1930.

The Crocodile Chuckles, by Elmer Greensfelder, July 15–16, 1930.

The Importance of Being Earnest, by Oscar Wilde, December 11–12–13, 1930.

East Lynn, by Mrs. Henry Wood, February 5–6–7, 1931.

The Perfect Alibi, by A. A. Milne, May 23, 1931.

The Taming of the Shrew, by William Shakespeare (done in the modern manner), July 13 and 15, 1931.

Saturday's Children, by Maxwell Anderson, October 22–23–24, 1931.

A Doll's House, by Henrik Ibsen, February 4–5–6, 1932.

Cinderella, by Harry Davis, April 8–9, 1932 (Junior Playmakers).

The Butter and Egg Man, by George S. Kaufman, May 19–20–21, and June 4, 1932.

Uncle Tom's Cabin, dramatized by George L. Aiken, November 3–4–5, 1932.

You Never Can Tell, by George Bernard Shaw, February 2–3–4, 1933.

Ali Baba and the Forty Thieves, by Harry Davis, April 28–29, June 21–22, 1933 (Junior Playmakers).

The House of Connelly, by Paul Green, November 2–3–4, 1933. (Also Greensboro, North Carolina, November 8, 1933.)

Princess Ida, by Gilbert and Sullivan, February 2–3, 1934. (Also Greensboro, North Carolina, February 14, 1934.)

The Witching Hour, by Augustus Thomas, March 1–2–3, 1934.

Wappin Wharf, by Charles S. Brooks, April 21, 1934. (Junior Playmakers).

Topaze (in French), by M. Marcel Pagnol, April 28, 1934.

Hay Fever, by Noel Coward, May 25–26, 1934.

The Cradle Song, by G. Martinez Sierra, July 18, 1934.

R. U. R., by Karel Capek, October 25–26–27, 1934.

The Young Idea, by Noel Coward, January 31 and February 1–2, 1935.

Three Cornered Moon, by Gertrude Tonkonogy, October 24–25–26, 1935.

Paths of Glory, by Sidney Howard, January 31 and February 1, 1936.

La Porteuse de Pain (in French), by Montepin and Donnay, May 14, 1936.

The Drunkard, by W. H. Smith and A Gentleman, October 22–23–24, 1936.

The Pirates of Penzance, by Gilbert and Sullivan, January 29–30–31, 1937.

Monsieur de Pourceaugnac, by Molière, May 15, 1937.

Personal Appearance, by Lawrence Riley, July 15, 1937.

Johnny Johnson, by Paul Green, October 29–30 and November 2, 1937.

Boy Meets Girl, by Bella and Samuel Spewack, January 27–28–29 and 31, 1938.

La Tour de Nelse, by Alexander Dumas *père* et Frederic Gaillardet, May 16, 1938.

Laburnum Grove, by J. B. Priestly, July 14, 1938.

The Blue Bird, by Maurice Maeterlinck, July 18, 1938 (Junior Playmakers).

Room Service, by John Murray and Allen Boretz, October 21–22, 1938.

The Sorcerer, by Gilbert and Sullivan, February 6–8, 1939.

Our Town, by Thornton Wilder, April 11, 13–15, 1939.

Mr. Pim Passes By, by A. A. Milne, July 12, 1939.

No More Peace, by Ernst Toller, October 18–21, 1939.

The Highland Call, by Paul Green, December 5–6, 1939. (Also Fayetteville, North Carolina, November 20–24, 1939.)

H M S Pinafore, by Gilbert and Sullivan, February 2–3, 1940.

Kiss the Boys Good-bye, by Clare Booth, February 28–29, March 1–2 and 4, 1940.

The Field God, by Paul Green, April 5 and 8, 1940.

Ah, Wilderness!, by Eugene O'Neill, May 23–24–25, 1940.

Love's Old Sweet Song, by William Saroyan, October 23–24–25–26, 1940.

The House of Connelly, by Paul Green, November 11–12, 1940.

2. ONE-ACT PLAYS

Suppressed Desires, by Susan Glaspell and George Cram Cook, October 28–29, 1921.

How He Lied to Her Husband, by Bernard Shaw, October 28–29, 1921.

Joe, by Jane Dransfield, December 6, 1929.

The Angel Intrudes, by Floyd Dell, December 6, 1929.

The Stronger, by August Strindberg, December 6, 1929.

Modesty, by Paul Hervieu, December 6, 1929.

The Man in the Bowler Hat, by A. A. Milne, April 4–5, 1930.

The Open Door, by Alfred Sutro, April 4–5, 1930.

The Man on the Kerb, by Alfred Sutro, April 4–5, 1930.

The Mayor and the Manicure, by George Ade, April 4–5, 1930.

Enter the Hero, by Theresa Helburn, April 4–5, 1930.

Dawn, by Percival Wilde, April 4–5, 1930.

Suppressed Desires, by Susan Glaspell and George Cram Cook, April 4–5, 1930.

The Constant Lover, by St. John Hankin, March 6, 1931.

Mansions, by Hildegard Flanner, March 6, 1931.

Fancy Free, by Stanley Houghton, March 6, 1931.

The Rising of the Moon, by Lady Gregory, March 7, 1931.

Cocaine, by Pendleton King, March 7, 1931.

Suppressed Desires, by Susan Glaspell and George Cram Cook, March 7, 1931.

A Proposal under Difficulties, by John Kendrick Bangs, March 9, 1931.

The Chased Lady, by Ruth Welty, March 9, 1931.

The Boor, by Anton Chekhov, March 9, 1931.

Helena's Husband, by Philip Moeller, March 9, 1931.

The Hand of Siva, by Ben Hecht and Kenneth Sawyer Goodman, May 13, 1932.

The Man on the Kerb, by Alfred Sutro, May 13, 1932.

Words and Music, by Kenyon Nicholson, May 13, 1932.

In the Morgue, by Sada Cowan, May 14, 1932.

The Open Door, by Alfred Sutro, May 14, 1932.

Things Is That-A-Way, by E. P. Conkle, May 14, 1932.

Rosalie, by Max Maurey, May 14, 1932.

The Man in the Stalls, by Alfred Sutro, May 23, 1932.

Tomorrow and Tomorrow (Act II, Scene I), by Philip Barry, May 23, 1932.

The Constant Lover, by St. John Hankin, May 23, 1932.

The Stronger, by August Strindberg, May 11, 1933.

The Proposal, by Anton Chekhov, May 11, 1934.

Rosalie, by Max Maurey, May 12, 1934.

Einer Muss Heiraten (in German) by Alexander Wilhelmi, May 17, 1934.

The House Across the Way, by Katherine Kavanaugh, May 14, 1934.

Modesty, by Paul Hervieu, May 14, 1934.

Le Crime d'un Cerveau Malade, adapted by Walter Creech, May 16, 1935.

The Twelve Pound Look, by J. M. Barrie, March 2, 1937.

The Flattering Word, by George Kelly, February 12, 1937.

The Boor, by Anton Chekhov, March 3, 1937.

Fin d'Apres-Midi d'automne, adapted by Walter Creech, May 15, 1937.

Funiculi Funicula, by Rita Wellman, May 15, 1939.

Dance of Death, by W. H. Auden, May 15, 1939.

Air Raid, by Archibald MacLeish, March 7, 1940.

Bury the Dead, by Irwin Shaw, May 14, 1940.

Salome, by Oscar Wilde, May 16, 1940.

L'Anglais Tel Qu'On Le Parle, by Tristan Bernard, May 16, 1940.

IV. OUTDOOR PRODUCTIONS

Professional Plays

1. FOREST THEATRE PRODUCTIONS

The Taming of the Shrew, by William Shakespeare, July 31, 1919.

Twelfth Night, by William Shakespeare, July 29, 1920.

Much Ado About Nothing, by William Shakespeare, July 29, 1921.

As You Like It, by William Shakespeare, July 29, 1922.

The Comedy of Errors, by William Shakespeare, August 28, 1923.

The Taming of the Shrew (Tercentenary Production), by William Shakespeare, October 12, 1923.

Prunella, by Laurence Housman, and Granville Barker, May 30 and August 26, 1924.

The Rivals (Sesquicentennial Revival), by Richard Brinsley Sheridan, May 29–30, 1925.

The Poor Little Rich Girl, by Eleanor Gates, August 21, 1925.

The Romancers, by Edmond Rostand, May 28–29, 1926.

A Thousand Years Ago, by Percy MacKaye, August 24, 1926.

The Tempest, by William Shakespeare, April 30 and May 1, 1928 (Benefit Shakespeare Memorial Theatre Fund).

Rip Van Winkle, as played by Joseph Jefferson, May 24–25, 1929.

Romeo and Juliet, by William Shakespeare, May 16–17, 1930.

A Midsummer Night's Dream, by William Shakespeare, May 19–20, 1933.

The Women Have Their Way, by Joaquin and Serafin Alvarez Quintero, July 7, 1933.

Hamlet, by William Shakespeare, May 25 and 27, 1935.

Lysistrata, by Aristophanes (Gilbert Seldes' Modern Version), May 22–23, 1936.

Androcles and the Lion, by George Bernard Shaw, May 21–22, 1937.

The Merry Wives of Windsor, by William Shakespeare, May 20–21 and 28, 1938.

Noah, by Andre Obey, May 18–20, 1939.

The Cradle Song, by G. Martinez Sierra, July 8, 1939 (Junior Playmakers).

2. KENAN STADIUM PRODUCTIONS

Agamemnon, by Aeschylus, July 17, 1929.

Alcestis, by Euripides, July 11–12, 1932.

Iphigenia in Tauris, by Euripides, July 16 and 19, 1935.

APPENDIX II

THE CAROLINA PLAYMAKERS: A SELECTED BIBLIOGRAPHY

September 1, 1918 to January 1, 1941

I. PUBLICATIONS OF THE CAROLINA PLAYMAKERS

1. PUBLISHED PLAYS: VOLUMES

Carolina Folk Plays, First Series, edited with an introduction, "Folk-Play Making," by Frederick H. Koch, containing five one-act plays by native authors. Five full-page illustrations from the original productions. (New York, Henry Holt and Company, 1922.)

Carolina Folk Plays, Second Series, edited with an introduction, "Making a Folk Theatre," by Frederick H. Koch, containing five one-act plays by native authors. Seven full-page illustrations from the original productions. (New York, Henry Holt and Company, 1924.)

Lord's Will and Other Plays, The, by Paul Green, with an introduction by Frederick H. Koch. Illustrated from the original productions. (New York, Henry Holt and Company, 1925.)

Lonesome Road, by Paul Green. A volume of Negro plays. (New York, Robert McBride and Company, 1926.)

Carolina Folk Plays, Third Series, edited with an introduction, "The Carolina Playmaker," by Frederick H. Koch. Foreword by Paul Green. Containing six one-act plays by native authors. Six full-page illustrations from the original productions. (New York, Henry Holt and Company, 1928.)

Carolina Folk Comedies, edited with an introduction, "Adventures in Playmaking," by Frederick H. Koch. Foreword by Archibald Henderson. Containing eight one-act plays by native authors. Eight full-page illustrations from the original productions. (New York, Samuel French, 1931.)

American Folk Plays, edited with an introduction, "American Folk Drama in the Making," by Frederick H. Koch. Foreword by Archibald Henderson. Containing twenty one-act plays by native authors from various states. Fifteen full-page illustrations from the original productions. (New York, D. Appleton-Century Company, 1939.)

Mexican Folk Plays, by Josephina Niggli. (The Carolina Playmakers Series.) Edited with an introduction, "Playmaker of Mexico," by Frederick H. Koch. Foreword by Rodolfo Usigli. Containing five one-act plays and seven full-page illustrations from the original productions.

(Chapel Hill, University of North Carolina Press, 1938.)

Folk Plays of Eastern Carolina, by Bernice Kelly Harris. (The Carolina Playmakers Series.) Edited with an introduction, "Plays of a Country Neighborhood," by Frederick H. Koch. Containing seven one-act plays and nineteen full-page illustrations. (Chapel Hill, University of North Carolina Press, 1940.)

2. PLAYS PUBLISHED SEPARATELY

According to Law, by Noel Houston, *One-Act Play Magazine*, January, 1940. (Boston, Massachusetts.) Also in *Best One Act Plays of 1940*, edited by Margaret Mayorga. New York: Dodd, Mead and Company, 1941.

Agatha, a play of the Old South, by Jane Toy, *The Southern Ruralist*, April 15, 1924. (Atlanta, Georgia.)

Alice Markham, Spinster, by Sara Duncan, *The Carolina Magazine*, February, 1924. (Chapel Hill, North Carolina.)

And Cling to Thee, by Lealon N. Jones. Chicago: T. S. Denison and Company, 1940.

Another Night Has Gone, by Lealon N. Jones. Chicago: T. S. Denison and Company, 1940.

Aunt Mahaly's Cabin, a Negro folk play, by Paul Green, *The Reviewer*, April, 1924. (Richmond, Virginia.)

Barge Incident, a play of the New York water front, by Herb Meadow, *The Players Magazine*, November–December, 1938. (Peru, Nebraska.)

Bayou Harlequinade, a folk fantasy of the Bayou country of Louisiana, by Clemon White and Betty Smith, in *Twenty Short Plays on a Royalty Holiday* (Second Series), edited by Margaret Mayorga. New York: Samuel French, 1940.

Black Rooster, The, a comedy of country life, by Pearl Setzer, *The Southern Ruralist*, April 1, 1924. (Atlanta, Georgia.)

Black Water, a sequel to *Job's Kinfolks*, by Loretto Carroll Bailey, *The Carolina Play-Book*, March, 1929. (Chapel Hill, North Carolina.)

Ca'line, a Carolina Folk comedy, by Bernice Kelly Harris, *The Carolina Play-Book*, September, 1932. (Chapel Hill, North Carolina.)

Chinese Usurer In His Village, The, a drama in three acts, by George Kuhung, adapted by Scott Farnworth. New York: Samuel French, 1938.

Cloey, a play of Winston-Salem folk, by Loretto Carroll Bailey, *The Carolina Play-Book*, March, 1931 (Chapel Hill, North Carolina). Illustrated. Also in *A Player's Handbook*, by Samuel Selden. New York: F. S. Crofts, 1934.

Common Ground, a drama of a small town boy in Iowa, by Betty Smith and Jay G. Sigmund. Evanston, Illinois: Row, Peterson and Company, 1938. Also in *The Sixth Yearbook of Short Plays*, edited by Lee Owen Snook. Evanston, Illinois: Row, Peterson and Company, 1940.

Companion-Mate Maggie, a Negro comedy, by Helen Dortch, *The Carolina Play-Book*, September, 1929. Illustrated. (Chapel Hill, North Carolina.)

Conchita, a romance of a copper mining town, by Rosemary Shirley DeCamp, *The Carolina Play-Book*, September, 1931. Illustrated. (Chapel Hill, North Carolina.)

Copper Bracelet, The, a romance of old Carolina, by Betty Smith and Robert Finch. Syracuse, New York: Willis Bugbee, 1938.

Cottie Mourns, a comedy of sea island folk, by Patricia McMullan, *The Carolina Play-Book*, March, 1935. Illustrated. (Chapel Hill, North Carolina.)

Country Sunday, a play of white justice, by Walter Spearman. Atlanta, Georgia: The Association of Southern Women for the Prevention of Lynching, 1936.

Darkness, by Chase Howard Webb, in *The Fifth Yearbook of Short Plays*, edited by Lee Owen Snook. Evanston, Illinois: Row, Peterson and Company, 1940. Reprinted in pamphlet form, Evanston, Illinois: Row, Peterson and Company, 1940.

Darkness at the Window, an Iowa folk play, by Betty Smith and Jay G. Sigmund. Chicago: Dramatic Publishing Company, 1938.

Davy Crockett, half horse, half alligator, by John Philip Milhous, *The Carolina Play-Book*, March, 1933. Illustrated. (Chapel Hill, North Carolina.)

Day's End, a California folk play, by Alice Pieratt. In *The American Scene, an Anthology of American Plays*, edited by Barrett H. Clark, and Kenyon Nicholson. New York: D. Appleton-Century Company, 1930.

Death Comes to Sonia, a play of the Russian Revolution, by Esther Roush, *The Carolina Play-Book*, March, 1930. Illustrated. (Chapel Hill, North Carolina.)

Death Valley Scotty, a California folk play, by James Milton Wood, *The Carolina Play-Book*, March, 1930. Illustrated. (Chapel Hill, North Carolina.)

Deferred Payment, a play of the North Carolina mountains, by Thomas Clayton Wolfe, *The Magazine*, June, 1919. (Chapel Hill, North Carolina.)

Desert Shall Rejoice, The, a play of the Nevada Desert, by Robert Finch. New York: Samuel French, 1940.

Door Mats, a folk play of the Ozarks, by Stella Dunaway Whipkey, *Poet Lore*, Spring Number, 1930. (Boston, Massachusetts.)

Early Worm, The, by Anne Walters, in *The Sixth Yearbook of Short Plays*, edited by Lee Owen Snook, Evanston, Illinois: Row, Peterson and Company, 1940.

Elemental Man, a play of the mountain people, by Williard Goforth, *The Magazine*, June, 1919. (Chapel Hill, North Carolina.)

Ever' Snitch, a comedy of the Carolina fisherfolk, by Irene Fussler, *The Carolina Play-Book*, June, 1931. Illustrated. (Chapel Hill, North Carolina.)

Enchanted Maze, The, a play of a modern university, by Paul

Green, *The Carolina Play-Book*, December, 1935 (Scene 7). (Chapel Hill, North Carolina.)

Fair-God, The (*Malinche*), a new play of Maximilian of Mexico, by Josephina Niggli, *The Carolina Play-Book*, December, 1936. (An excerpt from the final scene.) (Chapel Hill, North Carolina.)

Fire of the Lord, a play of religious fanatics, by Frank Durham, in *Twenty Short Plays on a Royalty Holiday* (First Series). New York: Samuel French, 1937. Reprinted in pamphlet form, New York: Samuel French, 1937.

Fixin's, a tragedy of a tenant farm woman, by Erma and Paul Green. New York: Samuel French, 1934. Reprinted in pamphlet form from *Carolina Folk Plays, Second Series*, New York: Henry Holt, 1924.

Folk Stuff, a folk comedy of Iowa, by Betty Smith and Jay G. Sigmund. New York: Samuel French, 1937.

Four on a Heath, a grotesque, by Foster Fitz-Simons, in *The Gateway Series of Tested Plays*. Evanston, Illinois: Row, Peterson and Company, 1935.

Frontier Night, a drama of Old New Mexico, by Chase Webb. Evanston, Illinois: Row, Peterson and Company, 1938.

Fun After Supper, a drama of New York City, by Betty Smith, in *Twenty Short Plays on a Royalty Holiday* (Second Series), edited by Margaret Mayorga. New York: Samuel French, 1940.

Funeral Flowers for the Bride, a comedy of the Blue Ridge Mountains, by Beverley DuBose Hamer, *The Carolina Play-Book*, September, 1937. (Chapel Hill, North Carolina.)

Gaius and Gaius, Jr., a play of plantation times, by Lucy M. Cobb, *The Carolina Magazine*, November, 1923. (Chapel Hill, North Carolina.)

Git Up An' Bar The Door, a farce of Mississippi folk life, by Arthur Palmer Hudson, *The Carolina Play-Book*, December, 1930. Illustrated. (Chapel Hill, North Carolina.)

Glendale Plantation, a play of a Maryland family, by Tom

Loy, *The Carolina Play-Book*, December, 1931. (Chapel Hill, North Carolina.)

Got No Sorrow, a Negro ritual drama of the Carolina low country, by Caroline Hart Crum, *The Southern Literary Messenger*, April, 1940. (Richmond, Virginia.)

Granny Boling, a play of Negro life, by Paul Green, *The Drama*, August–September, 1921. (Chicago, Illinois.)

Heroes Just Happen, by Betty Smith and Robert Finch. New York: Samuel French, 1940.

Highland Call, The, a symphonic drama of American history, by Paul Green, *The Carolina Play-Book*, December, 1939. Illustrated. (An excerpt from Scene I.) (Chapel Hill, North Carolina.)

His Last Skirmish, an historical folk comedy of North Carolina, by Betty Smith and Robert Finch. New York: Samuel French, 1937.

Hit's Man's Business, by Lois Latham. Illustrated. Evanston, Illinois: Row, Peterson and Company, 1940.

Hollyhocks, a play of New England village folk, by Joseph Philip Fox, *The Carolina Play-Book*, September, 1930. Illustrated. (Chapel Hill, North Carolina.)

Hunger, a tragedy of North Carolina farm folk, by Ella Mae Daniel. Published in pamphlet form by Encyclopaedia Britannica, Inc., Atlanta, Georgia, 1935. Also published by the Northwestern Press, Minneapolis, Minnesota, 1938.

In Dixon's Kitchen, by Wilbur Stout, *The Southern Ruralist*, January 15, 1925. Illustrated. (Atlanta, Georgia.)

Job's Kinfolks, a play of the mill people, by Loretto Carroll Bailey, *The Carolina Play-Book*, June, 1928. (Chapel Hill, North Carolina.) [One-act version.] Three-act version published by Walter H. Baker Company, Boston, 1931.

Joe, a comedy in three acts, by Robert Finch and Betty Smith. New York: Samuel French, 1940.

John Brown of Pottawattomie, a play of "Bleeding Kansas," by John F. Alexander, *The Carolina Play-Book*, March, 1934. (Chapel Hill, North Carolina.)

Judgment Comes to Daniel, a folk comedy of eastern North Carolina, by Bernice Kelly Harris, *The Carolina Play-Book*, September, 1933. (Chapel Hill, North Carolina.)

Jumpin' The Broom, a Carolina country comedy, by Caro Mae Green, *The Carolina Magazine*, January, 1926. (Chapel Hill, North Carolina.) Also in *One-Act Plays for Stage and Study*, Fifth Series. New York: Samuel French, 1929.

Keynote for Christmas, a Christmas play, by Anne Walters. Minneapolis, Minnesota: The Northwestern Press, 1939.

Kiss the Star, a comedy, by Josephine Victor and Scott Farnworth. New York: Samuel French, 1937.

Lacquer and Jade, by Frances L. Fox, in *Twenty Short Plays on a Royalty Holiday* (Second Series), edited by Margaret Mayorga. New York: Samuel French, 1940.

Last of the Lowries, The, a play of the Croatan outlaws, by Paul Green, in *More One-Act Plays by Modern Authors*, edited by Helen Louise Cohen. New York: Harcourt, Brace and Company, 1927. Also in *In Search of America* by Lucy Lockwood Hazard. New York: Thomas Y. Crowell, Company, 1930. Reprinted in pamphlet form, New York: Samuel French, 1934, from *Carolina Folk Plays*, *First Series*. New York: Henry Holt and Company, 1922. Also in *Regional America—Prose and Poetry of Today*, edited by Harriet M. Lucas. Syracuse, New York: L. W. Singer Company, 1941.

Lawyer Lincoln, a comedy in one act, by Chase Webb and Betty Smith. New York: Dramatists Play Service, Inc., 1940.

Leavin's, a legend of the Carolina mountains, by Janie Malloy Britt, *The Carolina Play-Book*, March, 1937. (Chapel Hill, North Carolina.) [Later published under the title of *Nancy Hanks, Bondwoman* in *American Folk Plays*. New York: D. Appleton-Century Company, 1939.]

Lie, The, a play of Revolutionary Carolina, by Wilkeson O'Connell, *The Carolina Play-Book,* June, 1929. Illustrated. (Chapel Hill, North Carolina.)

Light and Shadow, a tragedy of North Carolina Negroes, by Jameson Bunn Dowdy. (Chicago: T. S. Denison and Company, 1940.)

Lighted Candles, a tragedy of the Carolina Highlands, by Margaret Bland, *The Carolina Play-Book,* September, 1928. Illustrated. (Chapel Hill, North Carolina.)

Lion and the Second Fiddle, The, a comedy of university life, by Betty Smith and Robert Finch. Chicago: Dramatic Publishing Company, 1938.

Little Chipmunk and the Owl Woman, a legend of the Okanagan Indians, by Elizabeth Renyi, *The Carolina Play-Book,* December, 1940. Illustrated. (Chapel Hill, North Carolina.)

Lord's Will, The, a tragedy of a country preacher, by Paul Green, *Poet Lore,* Autumn, 1922. (Boston, Massachusetts.) Reprinted in pamphlet form, New York: Samuel French, 1934, from *The Lord's Will and Other Plays.* New York: Henry Holt and Company, 1925.

Loyal Venture, The, a drama of Colonial Carolina, by Wilkeson O'Connell, *The Carolina Play-Book,* March, 1932. Illustrated. (Chapel Hill, North Carolina.)

Magnolia's Man, a mountain comedy, by Gertrude Wilson Coffin, *The Carolina Play-Book,* December, 1929. Illustrated. (Chapel Hill, North Carolina.)

Manana Bandits, a play of the old Southwest, by Betty Smith and Chase Webb, in *The Best One-Act Plays of 1938,* edited by Margaret Mayorga. New York: Dodd, Mead and Company, 1939.

Mannequin's Maid, a tragedy of New York City by Betty Smith. Chicago: T. S. Denison and Company, 1939.

Marvelous Romance of Wen Chun-Chin, The, a Chinese folk play, by Cheng-Chin Hsiung, *Poet Lore,* Autumn, 1924. (Boston, Massachusetts.)

Mary Finds a Mother, by Phoebe Hoffman, in *Twenty Short*

Plays on a Royalty Holiday (Second Series), edited by Margaret Mayorga. New York: Samuel French, 1940.

Muley, a comedy of North Carolina, by Chase Webb. Evanston, Illinois: Row, Peterson and Company, 1937.

Murder in the Snow, a drama of old Montana, by Betty Smith and Robert Finch. New York: Samuel French, 1938.

Naked Angel, a folk comedy of Lake Ronkonkoma, New York, by Betty Smith and Robert Finch. New York: Samuel French, 1937.

Near Closing Time, a mystery drama of a small Montana town, by Betty Smith and Robert Finch. Chicago: T. S. Denison and Company, 1939.

New Nigger, a tragedy of the tobacco country, by Fred Howard, *The Carolina Play-Book*, September, 1936. (Chapel Hill, North Carolina.)

Night in the Country, A, a folk comedy of Lake Ronkonkoma, New York, by Betty Smith and Robert Finch. Evanston, Illinois: Row, Peterson and Company, 1938.

No 'Count Boy, The, a Negro comedy, by Paul Green, *Theatre Arts Monthly*, November, 1924. (New York.) Reprinted in pamphlet form, New York: Samuel French, 1934, from *The Lord's Will and Other Plays*. New York: Henry Holt and Company, 1925. Also in *50 One-Act Plays*, Second Series, selected by Constance M. Martin. London: Victor Gollancz, 1940.

Off Nag's Head, by Dougald MacMillan, in *Modern Plays*, edited by Frederick H. Law. New York: The Century Company, 1924. (Illustrated.)

Old Man Taterbug, a play for children, by Mary Louise Boylston. New York: Samuel French, 1939.

Pasque Flower, a play of the Canadian Prairie, by Gwen Pharis, *The Carolina Play-Book*, March, 1939. Illustrated. (Chapel Hill, North Carolina.)

Pageant of the Lower Cape Fear, A, a communal historical

drama, written under the direction of Frederick H. Koch. Wilmington, North Carolina: The Wilmington Printing Company, 1921.

Peggy, a tragedy of a tenant farmer, by Harold Williamson, in *An Introduction to Drama* by Hubbel and Beaty. New York: MacMillan Company, June, 1927. Also in *Readings in Contemporary Literature* by Hanes and McCoy. New York: The MacMillan Company, 1928.

Pensioner, a play of contemporary social conditions, by Alice Truslow, published in pamphlet form by Encyclopaedia Britannica, Inc., Atlanta, Georgia, 1935.

Popecastle Inn, a pirate legend of old Carolina, by Betty Smith and Robert Finch. New York: Samuel French, 1937.

Raleigh, the Shepherd of the Ocean, a tercentenary drama by Frederick H. Koch. Raleigh, North Carolina: Edwards and Broughton, 1920. Illustrated. Excerpts reprinted in *The Carolina Play-Book*, June, 1937. (Chapel Hill, North Carolina.)

Red Velvet Goat, The, a tragedy of laughter and a comedy of tears, by Josephina Niggli, *One Act Play Magazine*, July, 1937. (New York.) Also in *50 One Act Plays*, Second Series, London: Gollancz, 1940.

Released, a poetic drama of biblical times, by Betty Smith and Jay G. Sigmund. Franklin, Ohio: Eldridge Entertainment House, 1938.

Ridin' the Goat, a Negro comedy, by May Miller (Negro), in *Plays and Pageants From the Life of the Negro*, by Willis Richardson. Washington, D. C.: The Associated Publishers, Inc., 1930.

Road Into the Sun, a play in one act, by Foster Fitz-Simons. Chicago: Dramatic Publishing Company, 1939.

Room For a King, by Betty Smith. Franklin, Ohio: Eldridge Entertainment House, 1940.

Saints Get Together, The, a modern morality play of Iowa, by Betty Smith and Jay G. Sigmund. Chicago: T. S. Denison and Company, 1937.

Sam Tucker, a Negro tragedy, by Paul Green, *Poet Lore*, Summer, 1923. (Boston, Massachusetts.)

Saturday Market, a Carolina mountain comedy, by Louise Sublette Perry, in *The Year Book of Short Plays*. Evanston, Illinois: Row, Peterson and Company, 1931.

Schoolin', a play of the San Francisco "mission district," by Edith Daseking. San Francisco: The Banner Play Bureau, 1933.

Scuffletown Outlaws, The, a tragedy of the Lowrie Gang, by William Norment Cox, *The Southwest Review*, April 1926. (Dallas, Texas.) Also in *The Scholastic*, Part I, May 11, 1929; Part II, May 25, 1929. Illustrated. (New York.)

Shakespeare, the Playmaker, a tercentenary masque, by Frederick H. Koch and twenty student-playwrights of The Dakota Playmakers at the University of North Dakota, *The Quarterly Journal* of the University of North Dakota, July, 1916. Reprinted in *Plays For Graduation Days*, compiled and edited by A. P. Sanford. New York: Dodd, Mead and Company, 1930.

Shroud My Body Down, a folk dream, by Paul Green, *The Carolina Play-Book*, December, 1934. (First episode, Scene I.) (Chapel Hill, North Carolina.)

Sigrid, farm woman of the prairie, by Margaret Radcliffe, *The Carolina Play-Book*, September, 1934. (Chapel Hill, North Carolina.)

Silvered Rope, The, a biblical poetic drama, by Betty Smith and Jay G. Sigmund. Chicago: T. S. Denison and Company, 1937.

Singing Piedmont, a choral drama of the tobacco fields of North Carolina, by Anthony Buttitta, *One-Act Play Magazine*, August, 1937. (New York.) Reprinted by Contemporary Play Publications, New York, 1938.

Singing Valley, a Mexican village comedy, by Josephina Niggli, *The Carolina Play-Book*, December, 1936 (Excerpts from Act II). (Chapel Hill, North Carolina.)

Skin Deep, a drama of the Negro problem, by Wieder Sievers, *The Carolina Magazine*, June, 1939. (Chapel Hill, North Carolina.)

Sleep On, Lemuel, a Carolina Negro comedy, by John W. Parker, *The Carolina Play-Book*, December, 1932. (Chapel Hill, North Carolina.)

So Early in the Morning, a folk comedy of North Carolina, by Jameson Bunn Dowdy. New York: Samuel French, 1939.

So Gracious is the Time, a drama of today, by Betty Smith, *One Act Play Magazine*, June–July, 1938. (New York.)

Soldadera (*Soldier-Woman*), a play of the Mexican Revolution, by Josephina Niggli, in *The Best One-Act Plays of 1937*, edited by Margaret Mayorga. New York: Dodd, Mead and Company, 1938.

Still Stands the House, a drama of the Canadian frontier, by Gwen Pharis, *The Carolina Play-Book*, June, 1938. (Chapel Hill, North Carolina.)

Summer Comes to the Diamond O, a play of the mountains of Montana, by Robert Finch and Betty Smith. New York: Dramatists Play Service, 1940. Also in *Best One Act Plays of 1940*, edited by Margaret Mayorga. New York: Dodd, Mead and Company, 1941.

Sunday Costs Five Pesos, a Mexican folk comedy, by Josephina Niggli, *One-Act Play Magazine*, January, 1938. (New York.) Also in *The Best One-Act Plays of 1938*. London: George G. Harrap and Company, 1939. In pamphlet form by Samuel French of London, 1939.

Swamp Outlaw, a drama of the Croatan rebellion, by Clare Johnson Marley, *The Carolina Play-Book*, March, 1940. (Chapel Hill, North Carolina.)

These Doggone Elections, a comedy of the Great Smoky Mountains, by Fred Koch, Jr., *The Carolina Play-Book*, September, 1939. Illustrated. (Chapel Hill, North Carolina.) Also in *Player's Magazine*, January, 1940. Illustrated. (Peru, Nebraska.)

Third Night, The, a play of the Carolina mountains by

Thomas Clayton Wolfe, *The Carolina Play-Book*, September, 1938. (Chapel Hill, North Carolina.)

This Bull Ate Nutmeg, a Mexican folk comedy, by Josephina Niggli, in *Contemporary One-Act Plays*. New York: Charles Scribner's Sons, 1938.

This Confusion, a modern psychological play, by Shirley Carter, *The Carolina Magazine*, December, 1930. (Chapel Hill, North Carolina.)

This Is Villa, a portrait of a Mexican general, by Josephina Niggli, in *The Best One-Act Plays of 1938*, edited by Margaret Mayorga. New York: Dodd, Mead and Company, 1939. Also in *One-Act Play Magazine*, January, 1939. (New York.)

Thrice Promised Bride, The, a Chinese folk play, by Cheng-Chin Hsiung, in *Theatre Arts Magazine*, October, 1923. (New York.) Also in *The Carolina Magazine*, October, 1923 (Chapel Hill, North Carolina); *Twenty-Five Short Plays: International*, edited by Frank Shay. New York: D. Appleton and Company, 1925; *The Golden Book*, August, 1925 (New York); *One-Act Plays*, edited by George A. Goldstone. New York: Allyn and Bacon, 1926. Illustrated; *The Carolina Play-Book*, December, 1928. Illustrated. (Chapel Hill, North Carolina.) *Typical Plays* by Webber and Webber. New York: Houghton Mifflin Company, 1929; *The Magazine World*, January, 1931. Illustrated. (Concord, New Hampshire.) In pamphlet form, by Thomas Nelson and Sons, Ltd. of London. Illustrated. 1932.

Tower, by Edward Post, *One Act Play Magazine*, July-August, 1940. (Boston, Massachusetts.)

Transient, a play of homeless men, by Walter Spearman. Charlotte, North Carolina; The Herald Press, 1936.

Trees of His Father, The, a tragedy of Iowa farm life, by Betty Smith and Jay G. Sigmund. New York: Samuel French, 1937.

Vine Leaves, a small town comedy of Iowa, by Betty Smith and Jay G. Sigmund. New York: Samuel French, 1937.

Wash Carver's Mousetrap, a Carolina mountain comedy, by Fred Koch, Jr., *The Carolina Play-Book*, December, 1938. Illustrated. (Chapel Hill, North Carolina.)

Washed in de Blood, a Negro ritual drama of rural Georgia, by Rietta Winn Bailey, *The Carolina Play-Book*, March, 1938. (Chapel Hill, North Carolina.)

West From the Panhandle, a tragedy of the Texas Dust Bowl, by Clemon White and Betty Smith, *One-Act Play Magazine*, February, 1939. (New York.)

Western Ghost Town, a drama of a Montana ghost town, by Betty Smith and Robert Finch. Chicago: T. S. Denison and Company, 1939.

Western Night, a poetic drama of Montana cowboys, by Betty Smith and Robert Finch. New York: Dramatists Play Service, 1938.

When Witches Ride, a Carolina folk play, by Elizabeth A. Lay, *The Magazine*, April, 1919. (Chapel Hill, North Carolina.)

White Dresses, a tragedy of Negro life, by Paul Green, in *Contemporary One-Act Plays*. New York: Charles Scribner's Sons, 1922.

Why The Ant's Waist is Small, an Okanagan Indian folk legend, by Isabel Christie and Elizabeth Tenyi, *The Carolina Play-Book*, December, 1939. (Chapel Hill, North Carolina.)

Why The Chipmunk's Coat is Striped, an Okanagan Indian folk tale, by Isabel Christie and Elizabeth Tenyi, *The Carolina Play-Book*, December, 1939. (Chapel Hill, North Carolina.)

Yours and Mine, a comedy of domestic difficulties, by Ella Mae Daniel, published in pamphlet form by Encyclopaedia Britannica, Inc., Atlanta, Georgia, 1935. Also included in *The Fifth Yearbook of Short Plays*, edited by Lee Owen Snook. Evanston, Illinois: Row, Peterson and Company, 1939.

Youth Takes Over, a comedy of high school days in three acts, by Betty Smith and Robert Finch. New York: Samuel French, 1939.

3. THE CAROLINA PLAY-BOOK [1]

ARTICLES

"Actor—A Definition, The," by Samuel Selden, June, 1934.

"Actor's Presence, The," by Samuel Selden, December, 1932.

"*Alcestis* in the Greek Stadium," by Rebecca Cushman, December, 1932.

"American Culture," by Franklin Roosevelt, September, 1939.

"American Folk Theatre," by Thomas Brahan, June, 1940.

"*American Folk Plays*," by John Selby, September, 1939.

"*American Folk Plays*," by Robert Finch, December, 1938.

"American Theatre—A Radio Interview," by Paul Green, June, 1938.

"And So It Began," by Bernice Kelly Harris, December, 1937.

"*Androcles and the Lion*," by Archibald Henderson, June, 1937.

"Anniversary Letters," edited by Archibald Henderson, September, 1935.

"Another Note On the Theatre," by Paul Green, September, 1930.

"Apropos Questions Concerning the Cinema," by Paul Green, September, 1933.

"Art of the Theatre, The," by Elmer Hall, June, 1929.

"Arts Section, The,—The North Carolina Education Association," by Nettina Strobach, September, 1929.

"Author's Foreword, An," by Wilkeson O'Connell, March, 1932.

"Ballad Hunting," by Maud Minish Sutton, June, 1928.

"Bernard Shaw as a World Power," by Archibald Henderson, June, 1933.

"By the Roadside," by William Butler Yeats, December, 1934.

---

[1] Edited by Frederick H. Koch, and published by The Carolina Playmakers, Inc., Chapel Hill, North Carolina. Plays included in *The Play-Book* are listed under I., 1., "Published Plays."

"Carolina Dramatic Association, The," by Louise Perry, September, 1930.

"Carolina Dramatic Association, The." by Louise Perry, December, 1930.

"Carolina Dramatic Festival," by Rebecca Cushman, June, 1933.

"Carolina Drama," by Gerald Johnson, March, 1937.

"Carolina Playmakers Define Drama, The," by Ralph Westerman, September, 1930.

"Carolina Playmakers in New York, The," by Roland Holt, March, 1928.

"Coming of Age," by Samuel Selden, March, 1940.

"Comment from London," by Robert W. Madry, March, 1940.

"Creative Dramatic Experimentalism," by Archibald Henderson, September, 1931.

"Color in Stage Lighting," by Samuel Selden, December, 1931.

"Cut Is The Branch That Might Have Grown Full Straight," by Maxwell Anderson, December, 1937.

"Dakota Dialect, The," by Margaret Radcliffe, September, 1934.

"Defense on the Main Front," by Paul Green, December, 1940.

"Democratic Man," by Paul Green, September, 1940.

"Directors Meet, The," by Nettina Strobach, March, 1928.

"Directors Meet, The," by Nettina Strobach, March, 1930.

"Directors Meet, The," by Irene Fussler, March, 1933.

"Drama in the High School Curriculum," by W. Robert Wunsch, March, 1928.

"Drama and the New Deal," by N. W. Walker, December, 1934.

"Drama Festival," by Bernice Kelly Harris, March, 1937.

"Drama Festival," by Bernice Kelly Harris, September, 1939.

"Drama in the Open," by Gwen Pharis, June, 1939.

"Drama of Bali, The," by George Koch, December, 1940.

"Dramatic Festival, The," by Nettina Strobach, June, 1929.

"Dramatic South, The," by Paul Green, March, 1939.

"Education and Economy," by John Dewey, December, 1935.

"Eleventh Dramatic Festival, The," by Alton Williams, June, 1934.

"Elsinore in Battle Park," by Nell Battle Lewis, September, 1935.

"Elizabethan—and Modern," by Elmer Hall, June, 1930.

"Empathy," by Samuel Selden, December, 1936.

"European Stages Before the War," by Samuel Selden, December, 1940.

"Experimental Production," by Noel Houston, March, 1938.

"Eyes Toward the Altar," by Montrose J. Moses, September, 1932.

"Festival, The (Eleventh)," by Irene Fussler, March, 1934.

"Festival, The (Twelfth)," by John W. Parker, December, 1934; March, 1935.

"Festival, The (Thirteenth)," by John W. Parker, June, 1936.

"Festival, The (Fourteenth)," by Robert Finch, March, 1937.

"First Carolina Players, The," by Archibald Henderson, March, 1931.

"First National Folk Festival, The," by Carl Thompson, June, 1934.

"Fisherman All," by Paul Green, March, 1928; June, 1933.

"Folk Drama Defined," by Paul Green, December, 1932.

"Folk Drama Festival," by Rebecca Cushman, June, 1932.

"Folk Theatre, A," by Albert Shaw, December, 1933; September, 1938.

"For the Theatre and the Drama," by Percy MacKaye, June, 1933.

"Forest Theatre Scenery," by Samuel Selden, September, 1938.

"Foreword to *Shroud My Body Down*," by Paul Green, December, 1934.

"Founding Fathers," by Brooks Atkinson, December, 1937.

"Freddy Folkplay," by Archibald Henderson, June, 1940.

"From Coast to Coast," by Earl Wynn, March, 1940.

"Georgia Scene," by Rietta Bailey, March, 1938.

"Greetings and Tributes," (selected) by Archibald Henderson, June, 1940.

"Good Plays," by Arthur Hobson Quinn, June, 1940.

"Greetings From Einstein," by Albert Einstein, June, 1933.

"*Hamlet*, in the Forest," by Samuel Selden, June, 1935.

"Inky Cloak Is Touched With Crimson, The," by Samuel Selden, September, 1935.

"Johnny Q Sees *The Lost Colony*," by Bernice Kelly Harris, September, 1937.

"Junior Theatre, A," by Harry Davis, December, 1931.

"Junior Playmakers," by Frank Guess, March, 1940.

"Kenan Professorship, The," by Robert B. House, March, 1932.

"King of Death Valley, The," by James Milton Wood, March, 1930.

"Koch," by Archibald Henderson, September, 1935.

"Little Theatre in the South, The," by William Dean, March, 1929.

"Log of the Show-Bus," by Josephina Niggli, December, 1935.

"London Stage, The," by Paul Green, December, 1929.

"*Lost Colony*, and the Greeks, The," by Samuel Selden, June, 1939.

"*Lysistrata* and the Greeks," by W. S. Bernard, June, 1936.

"*Lysistrata*—1936," by Herb Meadow, June, 1936.

"MacKaye," by Archibald Henderson, June, 1934.

"Making of *Strike Song*, The," by Loretto Carroll and J. O. Bailey, June, 1932.

"Make-Up," by Hubert Heffner, March, 1928.

"Man and Play-Man," by Percy MacKaye, June, 1934.

"Merry Wives of Windsor, The," by Betty Smith, September, 1938.

"Mildred Seydell Says," by Mildred Seydell, March, 1937.

"Miracle at Manteo," by Anthony F. Merrill, June, 1939.

"Mister Punch Turns Propagandist," by Fred Koch, Jr., June, 1936.

"Modern Shakespeare," by Elmer Hall, September, 1931.

"Movies and the Stage, The," by Paul Green, March, 1934.

"Mr. Partridge and the Actor," by Samuel Selden, December, 1933.

"Music in the Theatre," by Paul Green, September, 1937.

"Native American Theatre, A," by Paul Green, September, 1931.

"Native Theatre, The," by Stephen Vincent Benét, September, 1939.

"Natural Theatre, The," by Barrett H. Clark, June, 1932.

"Negro Drama in the South," by Randolph Edmonds, June, 1940.

"Negro Dramatic Tournament," by Loretto Carroll Bailey, June, 1935.

"New Controlboard, The," by Harry Davis. December, 1940.

"New Department of Dramatic Art, The," by Frank Durham, June, 1936.

"New Mexican Play, A," by Josephina Niggli, December, 1936.

"New Theatre in the New South, The," by Joseph Mitchell, June, 1928.

"*Noah* and the Night," by Betty Smith, June, 1939.

"Note on Mexican Pronunciation," by Josephina Niggli, March, 1936.

"O Pioneers," by Herb Meadow, June, 1936.

"On Mounting Shakespeare's Comedies," by Samuel Selden, March, 1928.

"On the Lap of the Gods," by Harry Davis, June, 1934.

"On Speech," by Howard Bailey, December, 1937.

"On the Presentation of the Duse Bust," by Katherine Pendleton Arrington, March, 1938.

"One Act Play Magazine," by William Kozlenko, December, 1938.

"Opening the Season," by Hubert Heffner, June, 1929.

"Our American Folk Arts, by Franklin D. Roosevelt, June, 1934.

"Our Troupers to the North," by J. Milton Wood, December, 1929.

"Out of the Past," by John M. Booker, June, 1940.

"Palmy Days," by George McFarland McKie, March, 1932.

"Play in the Audience, The," by Samuel Selden, December, 1937.

"Playmakers in *Hamlet*, The," by Phillips Russell, September, 1935.

"Playwright's Credo, A," by Clifford Odets, June, 1940.

"Poor Player, The," by Walter Prichard Eaton, June, 1928.

"Proff Goes to Heaven," a biography by Barrett H. Clark, June, 1940.

"Radio Debate," by Earl Wynn, June, 1940.

"Receives the Palm," by Archibald Henderson, September, 1935.

"Repertory Groups," by Shepperd Strudwick, December, 1940.

"Rockefeller Grant, The," by Alton Williams, June, 1934.

"Roland Holt Theatre Collection, The," by Harry Davis, June, 1936.

"Russian Theatre Under the Soviet, The," by Ella Rush Murray, December, 1928.

"Scenery, An Environment," by Samuel Selden, September, 1929.

"Scenery for the Little Theatre," by Roland Holt, December, 1928.

"School Called Broadway, The," by George Vernon Denny, March, 1930.

"School Drama, The," by Milton Smith, September, 1929.

"Scientist's Comment, A," by G. J. K., March, 1940.

"Scratchata of our Dixie, A," by Arthur Palmer Hudson, June, 1930.

"Seventh Dramatic Festival, The," by Nettina Strobach, June, 1930.

"Shakespeare à la Mode and Mood," by Montrose J. Moses, September, 1928.

"Shaw in the Forest," by Phillips Russell, June, 1937.

"Sixteenth Festival, The," by John W. Parker, March, 1939.

"South of Times Square," by J. Brooks Atkinson, September, 1928.

"Stadia and Night," by Phillips Russell, March, 1937.

"Stage Lighting," by Samuel Selden, September, 1930.

"Staging of *Hamlet*, The," by Samuel Selden, September, 1935.

"State Dramatic Tournament, The," by Irene Fussler, March, 1932.

"State Is Our Campus, The," by John W. Parker, June, 1935.

"State Directors' Conference," by Frank Durham, December, 1935.

"State Tournament, The," by Irene Fussler, March, 1931.

"Strolling Players in North Carolina," by Richard G. Walser, December, 1937.

"Summer Repertory," by Harry E. Davis, September, 1937.

"Texas Calls," by Walter Spearman, December, 1936.

"Thalian Association, The," by Archibald Henderson, March, 1930.

"Theatre, The," by Belford Forrest, December, 1935.

"Theatre Collections," by George Freedley, June, 1940.

"Theatre Gossip from Germany," by Paul Green, June, 1929.

"Theatre Festival," by Archibald Henderson, December, 1939.

"Theatre Rededicated," by Gwen Pharis, December, 1938.

"Thomas Godfrey," by Archibald Henderson, March, 1928.

"Thomas Jefferson and Democracy," September, 1940.

"Till We Meet Again," by Betty Smith, June, 1940.

"*Tobacco Road* in Chapel Hill," by Noel Houston, December, 1938.

"Tombs of the Tar Heels," by Howard Mumford Jones, June, 1928.

"Touring Equipment of The Carolina Playmakers," by Harry Davis, June, 1937.

"Trouping to the North," by Gwen Pharis, December, 1938.

"Twelfth Night Revels," by Elizabeth Farrar, March, 1929.

"Universal Southerner, The," by F. Meredith Dietz, September, 1940.

"Voice for the Actor," by Earl Wynn, June, 1939.

"When People Say Folk Drama," by Lynn Riggs, June, 1931.

"World and the Village, The," by Frank Porter Graham, June, 1933.

"Youth and the Theatre," by Maxwell Anderson, December, 1940.

EDITORIALS

"American Drama in the Making," September, 1935.

"American National Theatre, An," December, 1936.

"American Regional Drama," June, 1932.

"Announcing Elmer Hall," September, 1929.

"Announcing Harry Davis," September, 1931.

"Announcing Miss Morris," September, 1928.

"Arizona Folk Play, An," September, 1931.

"Back to the Stage," March, 1934.

"*Black Water*," March, 1929.

"Bureau of Community Drama, The," September, 1928.

"California Folk-Play, A," March, 1930.

"Canadian Frontier Theatre," December, 1940.

"Canadian Prairie Play," March, 1939.

"Canadian Indian Folk Drama," December, 1939.

"Caper," June, 1930.

"Carolina Dramatic Association Conference, The," March, 1928.

"Carolina Dramatic Association, The," March, 1928.

"Carolina Dramatic Association, The," June, 1928

"Carolina Dramatic Association, The," September, 1928.

"Carolina Dramatic Association, The," December, 1928.

"Carolina Dramatic Association, The," March, 1929.

"Carolina Dramatic Association, The," September, 1929.
"Carolina Dramatic Association, The," March, 1930.
"Carolina Dramatic Association, The," June, 1931.
"Carolina Dramatic Association, The," September, 1931.
"*Carolina Folk Comedies*," September, 1931.
"Carolina Playmakers' Tenth Season, The," March, 1928.
"Carolina Negro Theatre," June, 1935.
"Celebrare Domestica Facta," September, 1929.
"Christmas Carol, A," December, 1933.
"Comedy in the Smokies," December, 1938.
"Comedy of the Earthquake, A," September, 1933.
"Coming Festival, The," March, 1933.
"Communal Playmaking," September, 1936.
"*Companion-Mate Maggie*," September, 1929.
"Country Neighborhood, A," September, 1939.
"Croatan Drama," March, 1940.
"Curtain Falls and Rises, The," September, 1928.
"Davy Crockett, The Yellowest Flower of the Forest,"
    March, 1933.
"Dickens as an Actor," December, 1932.
"Directors Meet, The," March, 1931.
"Dogwood Festival," June, 1933.
"Dogwood Festival Plays, The," June, 1934.
"Drama in the South," June, 1940.
"Drama of Roanoke, The," June, 1937.
"Drama of the Scotch Settlement, A," December, 1939.
"Drama Up-To-Date," March, 1929.
"Dramatic Festival of the Carolina Dramatic Association,
    The," June, 1928.
"Dramatic Instrument, The," June, 1936.
"Eighteenth Season," December, 1936.
"*Ever' Snitch*," June, 1931.
"Extending the Drama, An Announcement," September,
    1934.
"Federal Theatre," December, 1935.
"Festival Exhibit," June, 1940.
"Fifteenth Festival, The," June, 1938.

"Fifteenth Season, The," September, 1933.
"First American Playwright, The," March, 1928.
"Folk Drama Defined," September, 1939.
"Follow the Star," September, 1940.
"Foreword to *Ca'line*, A," September, 1932.
"Henrik Ibsen, Viking," December, 1928.
"Hopi Indians at Carolina," September, 1928.
"I Can't Write a Play," September, 1937.
"I Remember," March, 1940.
"Igorote Plan, An," December, 1933.
"Immortal Duse," March, 1938.
"Interesting Experiments," March, 1931.
"Introducing Howard Bailey," December, 1937.
"Job's Kinfolks," June, 1928.
"*Job's Kinfolks*—How the One-Act Play Became a Full-Length Play," March, 1930.
"*Lie, The*, A Play of Revolutionary Carolina," June, 1928.
"*Lighted Candles*," September, 1928.
"Log-Cabin Theatre, A," September, 1932.
"Loretto Bailey's New Play," March, 1931.
"*Lost Colony, The*," June, 1939.
"*Magnolia's Man*," December, 1929.
"Maryland Playmaker, A," December, 1931.
"*Mexican Folk Plays*," December, 1938.
"Nancy Hanks," March, 1937.
"Negro Ritual Drama," March, 1938.
"Negro Sharecropper Play, A," September, 1936.
"Negro Theatre Advancing, The," December, 1933.
"New Book of Carolina Plays, The," December, 1928.
"New Negro Play," December, 1932.
"New Personnel," December, 1938.
"New Playwrights, The," March, 1933.
"New Season, The," September, 1931.
"Nineteenth Season, The," December, 1937.
"Ocracoke Island Folk," March, 1935.
"Okanagan Folk Play," December, 1940.
"Our Chinese Playmaker," December, 1928.

"Our Cover Design," March, 1928.
"Our Fourteenth Season," June, 1932.
"Our New State Representative," December, 1928.
"Our Next Issue," June, 1928.
"Our Way of Playwriting," June, 1939.
"Paul Green," September, 1931.
"Paul Green's New Play," December, 1935.
"Paul Green and Symphonic Drama," December, 1934.
"Play of Bleeding Kansas, A," March, 1934.
"Play-Acting," September, 1937.
"Play-Book, The," March, 1928.
"Playboy of Oklahoma," June, 1931.
"Playmaking at Banff," September, 1937.
"Playmaker from Mississippi, A," December, 1930.
"Playmakers in the West," September, 1933.
"Playwright of Mexico," March, 1936.
"Politicin' in the Smokies," September, 1939.
"Prairie Folk-Play, A," September, 1934.
"Richard B. Harrison," March, 1935.
"Roanoke Island Celebration, The," December, 1931.
"Scenery and Lighting," September, 1929.
"School and Play," March, 1929.
"Scottish Festival Play," September, 1940.
"Seventeenth Season, 1918–1935, The," December, 1935.
"Shakespeare in the Forest Theatre," September, 1933.
"Shakespeare Memorial Theatre Fund, The," June, 1928.
"Shaw-Henderson Festival, The," March, 1933.
"Shaw-Henderson Festival," June, 1933.
"Sixteen Years, 1918–1934," September, 1934.
"Southern Regional Conference, The," June, 1928.
"*Stage in Action, The*," December, 1940.
"Stage Lighting," March, 1929.
"*Strike Song*," June, 1932.
"*Strike Song* in New York," December, 1934.
"Summer Courses in Dramatics," March, 1929.
"Summer Playmaking," September, 1934.
"Teaching Playwriting," March, 1929.

ILLUSTRATIONS

Harrison, Richard B., March, 1935.

Hamlet, The setting (A drawing), by Lena Alice Tuttle, June, 1935.

Hamlet, The setting, September, 1935.

Hamlet, A scene from, September, 1935.

Hang the Directors, March, 1934.

Head-Ax of Ingfell, The, A scene from, December, 1933.

Helen Dortch in the title role of her own play, *Companion-Mate Maggie*, September, 1929.

Highland Call, The, A scene from, December, 1939; September, 1940.

Hollyhocks, A scene from, September, 1930.

Hopi Indians at Carolina, September, 1928.

House of Connelly, The (3 sketches), by Bradford White, March, 1934.

Hubert Heffner as Uncle January Evans in Paul Green's *The Man Who Died at Twelve O'clock*, March, 1929.

Indian Madonna and Papoose (A woodcut), December, 1939.

Iphigenia in Tauris, The setting (A drawing), by Lena Alice Tuttle, December, 1935.

Johnny Johnson, A scene from, December, 1937.

Junior Carolina Playmakers, June, 1939.

Leavin's, Scenes from, March, 1937.

Lie, The, A scene from, June, 1929.

Lighted Candles, A scene from, March, 1928.

Little Chipmunk and the Owl Woman, A scene from (A drawing), December, 1940.

Log Cabin Theatre and Its Founders, The, September, 1932.

Lost Colony, The (Author, Actors, Directors), June, 1937.

Lost Colony, The, A scene from, September, 1937.

Loyal Venture, The, A scene from, March, 1932.

Lysistrata, The setting and a scene from, June, 1936.

Lysistrata, The setting (A drawing), by Lena Alice Tuttle, June, 1936.

Marvelous Romance of Wen Chun-Chin, The, A scene from, March, 1928.

Rip Van Winkle, Program design (A drawing), by Elizabeth Cameron, June, 1929.

Roanoke Island Outdoor Theatre, Selecting the site for, December, 1931.

Robinson, Lennox, December, 1933.

Roland Holt Collection Bookplate (A woodcut), by Julius J. Lankes, June, 1936.

Romeo and Juliet, The setting (A drawing), by Elmer Hall, June, 1930.

Sharecropper, A scene from (A drawing), by Dan Nachtmann and John Roughton, March, 1938.

Shaw and Henderson, June, 1933.

Shroud My Body Down, Scenes from, December, 1934.

Soldadera (Soldier-Woman), A scene from, March, 1936.

Speakers at the Shaw-Henderson Festival, June, 1933.

Still Stands the House, A scene from, June, 1938.

Strike Song, A scene from, June, 1932.

Swamp Outlaw, A scene from, March, 1940.

Ten Nights in a Barroom (A drawing), March, 1928.

These Doggone Elections, A scene from, September, 1939.

Third Night, The, A scene from, June, 1935.

Third Night, The, A scene from, September, 1938.

Three Carolina Playwrights: Fred Howard, Patsy McMullan, Josephina Niggli, September, 1936.

Three Carolina Playwrights: Don Muller, Gwen Pharis, Wieder Sievers, March, 1939.

Thurman, Bedford, as Maximilan in *The Fair God*, December, 1937.

Troupers to St. Louis, June, 1934.

Twelfth Night, the Revel Scene (A drawing), by Wautell Selden, September, 1940.

Uncle Tom's Cabin (A drawing), by Mary Dirnberger, December, 1932.

Visitors at The Playmakers Theatre: Sir Philip Ben Greet, Percy MacKaye, Archibald Henderson, September, 1931.

Wash Carver's Mousetrap, A scene from, December, 1938.

Washed in de Blood, A scene from, March, 1938.

Why the Ant's Waist Is Small, A scene from, (A drawing), by Frank Stalkia, December, 1939.

Why the Chipmunk's Coat Is Striped, A scene from (A drawing), by Johnnie Stalkia, December, 1939.

Winning Dogwood Design (Linoleum block), by Ruth Valentine, June, 1934.

Wolfe, Thomas, in the title role of his own play, *The Return of Buck Gavin,* June, 1935.

Women Have Their Way, The, A scene from, September, 1934.

POETRY

Chapel Hill, by Josephina Niggli, June, 1936.

Dogwood, by Ethel Stephens Arnett, June, 1933.

Dogwood Speaks, The, by Lucy Philips Russell, June, 1934.

Festival of Youth, by Marjorie Craig, December, 1936.

Gran'daddy Brant, by Rebecca Cushman, June, 1935.

Heritage, The, by Elizabeth A. Lay, September, 1930.

House of Connelly, The, by Robert Leeper, March, 1934.

Mexico, My Beloved, by Josephina Niggli, March, 1936.

Niver-Stills, The, by Abby Crawford Milton, June, 1933.

Prologue for "The Drunkard," A, by Josephina Niggli, September, 1936.

Sandy, by Gwen Pharis, December, 1937.

Sea Chantey, by Paul Green, September, 1934.

Song of the Prairies, A, by F. H. K., September, 1935.

Sower of Dreams, The, by Joy Kime Benton, September, 1935.

Who Are These? by Paul Green, September, 1928.

1908–1935, For F. H. Koch, by Maxwell Anderson, September, 1935.

4. EXTENSION BULLETINS

Scenery and Lighting for School and Little Theatre Stages, by Samuel Selden. Chapel Hill, North Carolina: University of North Carolina Extension Division, 1928. (Illustrated.)

Play Producing for School and Little Theatre Stages, by Frederick H. Koch and Staff Members of The Carolina

Playmakers. Chapel Hill, North Carolina: University of North Carolina Extension Division, 1935. (Illustrated.)

Plays for Schools and Little Theatres, by Frederick H. Koch and Nettina Strobach. Chapel Hill, North Carolina: University of North Carolina Extension Division, 1930. Revised by Frederick H. Koch, Betty Smith and Robert Finch, 1936.

Play Direction (First Principles), by Samuel Selden. Chapel Hill, North Carolina: University of North Carolina Extension Division, 1937. (Illustrated.)

II. REFERENCES IN BOOKS

ANDERSON, JOHN, *The American Theatre*. Illustrations: The Carolina Playmakers' Forest Theatre, scene from "Peggy," a tragedy of the tenant farmer, by Harold Williamson. New York: The Dial Press, 1938.

BAILEY, LORETTO CARROLL, *Job's Kinfolks*. Boston: Walter H. Baker Company, 1930.

BAKER, BLANCHE M., *Dramatic Bibliography*. New York: The H. W. Wilson Company, 1933.

Bulletin of the Dramatist's Assembly. "Carolina Playmaking," by William Peery and "Contemporary American Theatre" by Hubert Heffner. Issued by Dramatist's Alliance of Stanford University, 1939.

BOTKIN, E. A., Ed., *Folk-Say*. Norman, Oklahoma: The University of Oklahoma Press, 1930.

BELLINGER, MARTHA F., *A Short History of the Drama*. New York: Henry Holt and Company, 1927.

BRANSON, E. C., *Farm Life Abroad*. Chapel Hill, North Carolina: University of North Carolina Press, 1924.

BROWN, JOHN MASON, *Upstage*. New York: W. W. Norton Company, 1930.

BROWN, JOHN MASON, *Broadway in Review*. New York: W. W. Norton and Company, 1940.

BROWN, ROLLO WALTER, *The Creative Spirit*. New York: Harper and Brothers, 1925.

Bookshelf of Brander Matthews, The. New York: Columbia University Press, 1931.

BURLEIGH, LOUISE, *The Little Theatre in the Community.* Boston: Little, Brown and Company, 1917.

CALVERTON, V. F., *The Liberation of American Literature.* New York: Charles Scribner's Sons, 1932.

CARTER, JEAN and OGDEN, JESS, *Everyman's Drama.* New York: American Association for Adult Education, 1938.

CASH, W. J., *The Mind of the South.* New York: Alfred A. Knopf, 1941.

CHANDLER, FRANK W., and CORDELL, RICHARD A., *Twentieth Century Plays.* New York: Thomas Nelson and Sons, 1934.

CHENEY, SHELDON, *The Art Theatre.* New York: Alfred A. Knopf, 1925.

CLARK, BARRETT H., *Paul Green.* New York: Robert M. McBride and Company, 1928.

CLARK, BARRETT H., *Speak the Speech.* Seattle, Washington: University of Washington Book Store, 1930.

CLARK, BARRETT H., *Maxwell Anderson, the Man and His Plays.* New York: Samuel French, 1933.

CLARK, BARRETT H., *An Hour of American Drama.* Philadelphia: J. B. Lippincott Company, 1930.

CLARK, EMILY, *Innocence Abroad.* New York: Alfred A. Knopf, 1931.

CONNOR, R. D. W., *The History of North Carolina.* Chicago and New York: American Historical Society, Inc., 1928.

COUCH, W. T., Ed., *Culture in the South.* Chapel Hill, North Carolina: University of North Carolina Press, 1934.

COURSES OF STUDY FOR THE HIGH SCHOOLS OF NORTH CAROLINA. Raleigh, North Carolina: State Superintendent of Public Instruction, 1930.

DICKINSON, THOMAS H., *Playwrights of the New American Theatre.* New York: The Macmillan Company, 1925.

DOLMAN, JOHN JR., *The Art of Play Production.* New York: Harper and Brothers, 1928.

EATON, WALTER PRICHARD, *The Drama in English*. New York: Charles Scribner's Sons, 1930.

ENCYCLOPAEDIA BRITANNICA, *College Theatre and Workshops*, by Edith J. R. Isaacs. Atlanta, Georgia; Encyclopaedia Britannica, 1929.

FUCHS, THEODORE, *Stage Lighting*. Boston: Little, Brown and Company, 1929. (Illustrated.)

FEDERAL WRITERS' PROJECT, North Carolina: *A Guide to the Old North State*. A summary of the work of The Carolina Playmakers is found on pp. 112–113, 151–156, other references are on pp. 129, 156. Illustrations: The Playmakers Theatre and performance in The Forest Theatre. Chapel Hill, North Carolina: The University of North Carolina Press, 1939.

FINCH, ROBERT, *Folk Playmaking in North Carolina, 1918–1941*,[1] with a Foreword, "Early Drama in North Carolina," by Archibald Henderson, 1941.

FLANAGAN, HALLIE, *Arena*. New York: Duell, Sloan and Pearce, 1940.

FREEDLEY, GEORGE, and REEVES, JOHN A., *A History of the Theatre*. (Dedicated to Frederick H. Koch.) New York: Crown Publishers, 1940.

GASSNER, JOHN, *Masters of the Drama*. New York: Random House, 1940.

GILDER, ROSAMOND, and FREEDLEY, GEORGE, *Theatre Collections*. New York: Theatre Arts, Inc., 1936.

GORELIK, MORDECAI, *New Theatres For Old*. New York: Samuel French, 1940.

GREEN, PAUL, *Lonesome Road*. Introduction by Barrett

---

[1] A brief account of the beginnings of folk playmaking in North Dakota (1905–06 to 1917–18) and a comprehensive study of the development of native drama in North Carolina from 1918 to 1941 with a detailed history of The Carolina Playmakers, the state-wide Carolina Dramatic Association and other Extension activities of The Carolina Playmakers. The Foreword by Archibald Henderson describes early theatrical activities in North Carolina. Multigraphed copies available in the library of The Rockefeller Foundation (New York City), and in the library of the University of North Carolina (Chapel Hill, North Carolina). 309 pp.

Clark. New York: Robert M. McBride and Company, 1926.

GREEN, PAUL, "Folk Drama" in *The National Encyclopaedia*. New York: P. F. Collier and Son, 1935.

GREGOR, JOSEPH, *Das Amerikanische Theatre*. Zurich, Leipzig, Wien: Amalthea-Verlag, 1931.

HAINES, HELEN E., *Living with Books*. New York: Columbia University Press, 1935.

HANEY, JOHN LOUIS, *The Story of our Literature*. New York: Charles Scribner's Sons, 1923.

HARTMAN, GERTRUDE, and SCHUMACHER, ANN, Eds., *Creative Expression*. New York: John Day Company, 1932.

HAZARD, LUCY LOCKWOOD, *The Frontier in American Literature*. New York: Thomas Y. Crowell Company, 1927.

HAZARD, LUCY LOCKWOOD, *In Search of America*. New York: Thomas Y. Crowell Company, 1930.

HEFFNER, HUBERT, SELDEN, SAMUEL, and SELLMAN, HUNTON D., *Modern Theatre Practice*. New York: F. S. Crofts, 1935.

HINSDELL, OLIVER, *Making the Little Theatre Pay*. New York: Samuel French, 1925.

HUBBELL and BEATY, *An Introduction to Drama*. New York: The Macmillan Company, 1927.

HUGHES, GLENN, *The Story of the Theatre*. New York: Samuel French, 1928.

ISAACS, EDITH J. R., *The American Theatre in Social and Educational Life*. New York: National Theatre Conference, 1932.

ISRAEL, HENRY and LANDIS, B. Y., *The Handbook of Rural Social Resources*. Chicago: University of Chicago Press, 1926.

KEPPEL, FREDERICK PAUL, *Education for Adults*. New York: Columbia University Press, 1926.

KOCH, FREDERICK H., and STROBACH, NETTINA, *Plays for Schools and Little Theatres*. Chapel Hill, North Carolina: The University of North Carolina Extension Division,

1930. Revised by Frederick H. Koch, Betty Smith and Robert Finch, 1936.

KOCH, FREDERICK H., and STAFF MEMBERS OF THE CAROLINA PLAYMAKERS, *Play Producing for School and Little Theatre Stages*. Chapel Hill, North Carolina: The University of North Carolina Extension Division, 1935. (Illustrated.)

KOCH, FREDERICK H., *The Lost Colony* by Paul Green. (Souvenir Program Book. Illustrated.) Manteo, North Carolina: Roanoke Colony Memorial Association. *The Drama of Roanoke*, 1937 edition; *Drama in the Open*, 1938 edition; *The Drama of Roanoke Island*, 1939 edition; *Paul Green and American Historical Drama*, 1940 edition. (Also articles by Paul Green and others.)

KOCH, FREDERICK H., *The Highland Call* by Paul Green. (Souvenir Program Book. Illustrated.) Fayetteville, North Carolina: The Cape Fear Valley Scottish Festival. *The Drama of Fayetteville*, 1939 edition; *Towards An American People's Theatre*, 1940 edition. (Also articles by Paul Green and others.)

KOZLENKO, WILLIAM, *The One-Act Play Today*. New York: Harcourt, Brace and Company, 1938.

LANDIS, BENSON Y., and WILLIARD, JOHN D., *Rural Adult Education*. New York: The Macmillan Company, 1933.

MACGOWAN, KENNETH, *Footlights Across America*. New York: Harcourt, Brace and Company, 1929. (Illustrated.)

MCWILLIAMS, CAREY, *The New Regionalism in American Literature*. Seattle, Washington: The University of Washington Book Store, 1930.

MCCLEERY, ALBERT, and GLICK, CARL, *Curtains Going Up*. New York: Pitman Publishing Company, 1939.

MANTLE, BURNS, *American Playwright of Today*. New York: Dodd, Mead and Company, 1929.

MANLY and RICKERT, *Contemporary American Literature*. New York: Harcourt, Brace and Company, 1929.

MAYORGA, MARGARET, *Best One-Act Plays of 1937*. New York: Dodd, Mead and Company, 1938.

MAYORGA, MARGARET, *Best One-Act Plays of 1938*. New York: Dodd, Mead and Company, 1939.

MAYORGA, MARGARET, *Best One-Act Plays of 1939*. New York: Dodd, Mead and Company, 1940.

MEYER, HAROLD D., *Handbook of Extra-Curricula Activities in the High School*. New York: A. S. Barnes and Company, 1926.

MIMS, EDWIN, *The Advancing South*. New York: Doubleday, Page and Company, 1926.

MIMS, EDWIN, *Adventurous America*. New York: Charles Scribner's Sons, 1929.

MOSES, MONTROSE J., *Representative American Dramas, National and Local*. New York: Little, Brown and Company, 1925.

MOSES, MONTROSE J., *The American Dramatist*. New York: Little, Brown and Company, 1925.

MODERWELL, HIRAM K., *The Theatre of Today*. New York: Dodd, Mead and Company, 1928.

National Cyclopaedia of American Biography, Biography of Frederick H. Koch. Current Volume A. New York: James T. White and Company, 1930.

National Encyclopaedia, "Theatre Schools." New York: P. F. Collier and Sons, 1935.

National Encyclopaedia, "The Little Theatre Movement in America," by Kenneth Macgowan. New York: P. F. Collier and Sons, 1935.

NEWSOME, A. R. and LEFLER, HUGH T., *The Growth of North Carolina*. New York: World Book Company, 1940. (Illustrated.)

OVERSTREET, HARRY, *About Ourselves*. New York: W. W. Norton Company, 1927.

PATTEN, MARJORIE, *The Arts Workshop of Rural America*. New York: Columbia University Press, 1937.

PENCE, RAYMOND WOODBURY, *Dramas by Present-Day Writers*. New York: Charles Scribner's Sons, 1927.

PERRY, CLARENCE ARTHUR, *The Work of the Little Theatres*. New York: Russell Sage Foundation, 1933.

PLESSOW, GUSTAV L., *Das Amerikanische Kurzschauspiel Zwischen 1910 und 1930*. Halle Salle, Germany: Max Niemeyer Verlag, 1933.

QUINN, ARTHUR HOBSON, *A History of the American Drama*, Vol. II. New York: Harper and Brothers, 1927.

QUINN, ARTHUR HOBSON, *Representative American Plays*. New York: The Century Company, 1925. Fifth edition, 1930.

ROCKWELL, ETHEL THEODORA, *A Study Course in American One-Act Plays*. Chapel Hill, North Carolina: The University of North Carolina Press, 1929.

ROCKWELL, ETHEL THEODORA, *American Life as Represented in Native One-Act Plays*. Madison: University of Wisconsin, 1931.

ROWE, NELLIE M., *Discovering North Carolina*. Chapel Hill, North Carolina: The University of North Carolina Press, 1933.

ROWE, KENNETH THROPE, *University of Michigan Plays*. Ann Arbor, Michigan: George Wahr, 1932.

ROWE, KENNETH THORPE, *Write That Play*. New York: Funk and Wagnalls Company, 1939.

SELDEN, SAMUEL, *Scenery and Lighting*. Chapel Hill, North Carolina: The University of North Carolina Extension Division, 1928. (Illustrated.)

SELDEN, SAMUEL, SELLMAN, HUNTON D., *Stage Scenery and Lighting*. New York: F. S. Crofts and Company, 1930. (Illustrated.)

SELDEN, SAMUEL, *A Player's Handbook*. New York: F. S. Crofts and Company, 1934.

SELDEN, SAMUEL, *Play Direction* (First Principles). Chapel Hill, North Carolina: The University of North Carolina Extension Division, 1937. (Illustrated.)

SELDEN, SAMUEL, *The Stage in Action*. New York: F. S. Crofts, 1941. (Illustrated.)

SOBEL, BERNARD, *Theatre Handbook and Digest of Plays*. New York: Crown Publishers, 1940.

STEENE, WILLIAM, *Six Etchings of the University of North*

Carolina, "The Playmakers Theatre." Chapel Hill, North Carolina: The University of North Carolina Press, 1930.

STRATTON, CLARENCE, *Theatron*, an illustrated record. New York: Henry Holt and Company, 1928.

TAYLOR, CARL C., *Rural Sociology*. New York: Harper and Brothers, 1933.

TILLETT, NETTIE S., and YARBOROUGH, MINNIE CLARE, *Image and Incident*. New York: F. S. Crofts, 1933.

TUCKER, S. MARION, *Modern American and British Plays*. New York: Harper and Brothers, 1931.

TUCKER, S. MARION, *Twenty-Five Modern Plays*. New York: Harper and Brothers, 1931.

TUFTS, JAMES H., *Education and Training for Social Work*. New York: Russell Sage Foundation, 1923.

WAGNER, CHARLES, *Seeing Stars*. New York: Putnam's Sons, 1940.

WAUGH, FRANK A., *Outdoor Theatres*. Boston: Richard G. Badger, 1917.

WHITMAN, CHARLES HUNTINGTON, *Representative Modern Dramas*. New York: The Macmillan Company, 1936.

WHITMAN, WILSON, *Bread and Circuses*. New York: Oxford University Press, 1937.

WOLFE, THOMAS, *Story of A Novel*. New York: Charles Scribner's Sons, 1936.

WOLFE, THOMAS, *Of Time and the River*. New York: Charles Scribner's Sons, 1935.

III. PERIODICAL REFERENCES TO THE CAROLINA PLAYMAKERS

Associated Press: a syndicated article published in many American newspapers. "The Blue-Jeans Circuit" concerning The Carolina Playmakers' Southern Regional Festival by John Selby, Arts Editor, Associated Press. April 14, 1940.

Alumni Review (Chapel Hill, North Carolina).
"Playmaker Alumni Invited back for Festival," editorial. Illustration: "Proff" Koch, March, 1940.

American Magazine of Art (Washington, D. C.).
"A New Art Interest in our College," by Rose Henderson, November, 1926.
"The Carolina Playmakers: Their Contribution to American Art," by Edith J. R. Isaacs. Illustrated. September, 1930.

American Review of Reviews, The (New York).
"The Carolina Playmakers," editorial. Illustrated. September, 1919.
"The Little Theatre," by Montrose J. Moses. Illustrated. January, 1927.

Atlanta Journal Magazine, The (Atlanta, Georgia).
"Folk Drama of North Carolina," by Frederick H. Koch. Illustrated. January 5, 1930.

Baltimore Sun, The (Baltimore, Maryland).
"State Owned Theatre for Native Drama," syndicated article by Robert Madry. Illustrated. December 6, 1925.
"Drama in the Sticks," by Gerald W. Johnson, December 29, 1925.

Billboard, The (New York).
"The Carolina Playmakers," by George V. Denny. Illustrated. December 16, 1922.
"The Irresistible Theatre and the Amateurs," by George V. Denny, December 11, 1926.
"The Carolina Playmakers visit the 'Big Town,'" by Elita Miller Lenz, December 3, 1927.
"Carolina Playmakers Visit New York," by Elita Miller Lenz, December 8, 1928.
"Native Drama in the Little Theatre," editorial, November 29, 1930.

Banta's Greek Exchange (Menasha, Wisconsin).
"The Carolina Playmakers are Famous," by E. C. Daniel, Jr. Illustrated. July, 1930.

Birmingham News (Birmingham, Alabama).

"The Wanderer," by Lewis Follett, January 31, 1939.

"The South Owes Much to This Group—Carolina Play-makers Bring Pleasure to Wide Area," by William Peery, February 5, 1939. Illustrations: Scenes from *Quare Medicine, On Dixon's Porch,* and *Job's Kinfolks;* also, "Proff" Koch, Playmakers Theatre, Playmakers Loading Bus and Playmakers Making Scenery. (This syndicated article appeared in other Southern newspapers.)

Bookman, The (New York).

"Paul Green," by Julian R. Meade, January–February, 1932.

Boston Transcript, The (Boston, Massachusetts).

"Theatre of the Folk," editorial, October 4, 1924.

Bridgeport Life (Bridgeport, Connecticut).

"College Dramatics," by Carl Glick, February 4, 1933.

Bulletin of the American Library Association, The (Chicago).

Illustrations of The Forest Theatre and The Playmakers Theatre, University of North Carolina, July, 1932.

"Making a Regional Drama," by Frederick H. Koch, August, 1932.

Carolina Magazine (Chapel Hill, North Carolina).

"Life Comes to the Local Stage," by Adrian Spies, May, 1940.

"Bigger Is Reborn: Paul Green and Richard Wright collaborate on what may be one of America's great plays—told by their secretary," by Ouida Campbell, October, 1940.

Calgary Herald, The (Banff, Alberta, Canada).

"School of Fine Arts Has Continent-Wide Reputation," by F. M. Ferguson, August 26, 1939.

Charlotte Observer, The (Charlotte, North Carolina).

"North Carolina Has Contributed Much to the Stage," by Jo Holt Harden. Illustrated. April 19, 1931.

"Lost Colony Becomes American Oberammergau," by Bill Rhodes Weaver. Illustrations: Scenes from *The Lost Colony* and a photograph of Paul Green, the author, November 30, 1939.

"Great Names Scintillate on Roster of Playmakers," by Bill Rhodes Weaver.

Illustrations: The Playmakers Theatre, setting for *The Merry Wives of Windsor* in The Forest Theatre, and Frederick H. Koch, November 30, 1939.

"First Play Produced in America written in North Carolina," by Gertrude S. Carraway. Illustrated. November 30, 1939.

Christian Science Monitor, The (Boston, Massachusetts).

"Raleigh, a Tercentenary Pageant-Drama," by Elizabeth A. Lay. Illustrated. January 7, 1921.

"The Carolina Playmakers," by Rose Henderson, January 19, 1925.

"The Carolina Playmakers, 1924–1925," editorial. Illustrated. July 28, 1925.

"The Carolina Playmakers," by George B. Lay. Illustrated. July 12, 1930.

"*Sing Your Own Song*," by Rebecca Cushman. Illustrated. August 22, 1931.

"Think the Thought," biography of Shepperd Strudwick, by L. A. Sloper, June 25, 1932.

"The Carolina Playmakers," by Rebecca Cushman, August 20, 1932.

"A Carolina Folk Theatre," by Rebecca Cushman, September 3, 1932.

"Shaw's 'Boswell' Honored at North Carolina Festival," March 2, 1933.

"The Carolina Playmakers," by Rebecca Cushman, July 31, 1933.

"Tiny Tim's Message Once More Rings Out Its Good Will to Men to Firesides All Over the World," by Rebecca Cushman, December 22, 1933.

"Days of Elizabethan Period Revived by Carolina

'Twelfth Night' Revels," by Rebecca Cushman, January 18, 1934.

"American Folk Drama," September 26, 1934.

College English (Ann Arbor, Michigan).

"Playwriting in the Liberal-Arts Curriculum," by Kenneth Thorpe Rowe, December, 1939.

Current History (New York).

"The American Note in Drama," by Montrose J. Moses, October, 1933.

Dearborn Independent, The (Dearborn, Michigan).

"American Drama Which comes from the Heart," by J. Olin Howe. Illustrated. November 17, 1923.

Delphian Quarterly, The (Chicago, Illinois).

"Thomas Wolfe's Apprenticeship," by Carlos Baker. Illustration: Thomas Wolfe in the title rôle of his own play, *The Return of Buck Gavin*, January, 1940.

Delta of Sigma Nu Fraternity, The (Indianapolis, Indiana).

"Shaw-Henderson Festival," May, 1933.

Drama, The (Chicago, Illinois).

"The Challenge of the Theatre Today," by Frederick H. Koch, November, 1919.

"Raleigh, the Shepherd of the Ocean," Illustrated. April, 1921.

"The Acted Drama in our Colleges and Universities," by Frederick H. Koch, October–November, 1921.

"Folk-Play Making in North Carolina," by Frederick H. Koch. Illustrated. November, 1922.

Illustration of The Forest Theatre, April, 1923.

"The Thrice Promised Bride," editorial, November, 1925.

"The Carolina Playmakers Theatre and The Playmakers Tour," editorial. Illustrated. May, 1926.

"The Carolina Playmakers in New York," by Roland Holt, January, 1928.

Drama, The (London, W. C.).

"Footlight Trails, The Little Theatre Movement in the South," by Lois Upshaw. Illustrated. October, 1928.

"Needed! A Native American Theatre," by Paul Green. Illustrated. October, 1930.

Scene from *The Thrice Promised Bride*, as performed at the National Festival of Community Drama at The Globe Theatre, Monday, April 20, by the Liverpool Playgoers' Club, May, 1931.

A Photograph of Paul Green, Barrett Clark, and Lynn Riggs on the Portico of The Playmakers Theatre, April, 1931.

Durham Herald-Sun, The (Durham, North Carolina).

"Thomas Wolfe's Simple Autobiographical Sketch," September 18, 1938.

"Wolfe's Discouragements Are Outlined by Professor," by R. W. Madry. Illustration: Thomas Wolfe as Buck Gavin in his own play, *The Return of Buck Gavin*, September 25, 1938.

"Barnstorming in Dixie," by William Peery. Illustrations: Scenes from *Quare Medicine, On Dixon's Porch* and *Job's Kinfolks;* also "Proff" Koch, Playmakers Theatre, Playmakers Loading Bus and Playmakers Making Scenery, January 15, 1939.

"A North State Novel—Bernice Kelly Harris Writes an Interesting Tale With an Eastern Carolina Locale," by A. W. S., May 7, 1939. Illustrated.

"Dr. Frederick Koch to Give Famous Reading on Tuesday." (Announcing Dr. F. H. Koch's reading of Dickens' *A Christmas Carol* in Page Auditorium, Duke University, Durham, North Carolina.) December 17, 1939.

"Carolina Playmaker goes to the Top: Eugenia Rawls Playing Beside Miss Bankhead," by Anthony Buttitta. Illustration: Eugenia Rawls and Tallulah Bankhead in *The Little Foxes*, January 28, 1940.

"Fifteen States Will Take Part in Full University of North Carolina Drama Week," by Walter Spearman, March 31, 1940.

"First State Theatre Celebrating 21st Birthday," by Robert W. Madry. Illustrations: Elmer Rice, Du-

Bose Heyward, George Freedley, Arthur Hobson Quinn, Barrett Clark, Proff Koch, Playmakers Theatre, March 31, 1940.

Duse Art Review, The (Philadelphia).
"Koch's Carolina Playmakers," by Roland Holt. Illustrated. April, 1929.

Dublin Magazine, The (Dublin).
"An American Folk-Dramatist, Paul Green," by Andrew E. Malone, April–June, 1929.

Emerson Quarterly, The (Boston, Massachusetts).
"Lighting a Forest Theatre Stage by Telephone," by Elmer Hall. Illustrated. May, 1931.
"A Unit Set for *The Taming of the Shrew*," by Elmer Hall, March, 1932.

English Journal, The (Chicago).
"*The Carolina Play-Book*," March, 1933.
"The Creative Impulse and Playmaking," by Frederick H. Koch, May, 1920.

Equity Magazine (New York).
" 'Dr. Dixie' Is With Us No More," February, 1931.

Farmer's Wife, The (New York).
"The Carolina Playmakers," by Leonore Dunnigan. Illustrated. August, 1925.

Forum and Century (New York).
"Town Meeting's on the Air Again," by Earl Sparling, October, 1939.

Freeman, The (New York).
"Towards a New Theatre," by Walter Prichard Eaton, July 12, 1922.

Greensboro (*North Carolina*) *Daily News, The* (Greensboro, North Carolina).
"Koch, The Playmaker," by Gerald W. Johnson, May 6, 1923.
"Thomas Wolfe Made Fine Record at the University of North Carolina," by R. W. Madry.

Illustration: Thomas Wolfe as Buck Gavin in his own play, *The Return of Buck Gavin*, September 25, 1938.

"Bernice Kelly Harris Got Real Encouragement to Write Novels," by Raymond Lowery, May 28, 1939.

High School Thespian, The (Cincinnati, Ohio).

"Paul Green," by Joseph Mersand. Illustration: Cover photograph of Paul Green. March, 1940.

Hollands, The Magazine of the South (Dallas, Texas).

"Footlight Trails, The Little Theatre Movement in the South," by Lois Upshaw. Illustrated. September, 1928.

"Dixie Plays on Broadway," by Julia Morrow Church. Illustrated. May, 1929.

"The Carolina Playmakers," by Mary H. Phifer. Illustrated. February, 1930.

"Southern Personalities—Paul Green—Philosopher and Playwright," by Mary H. Phifer, October, 1931.

"Southern Personalities—Frederick H. Koch," by Winifred Camp, July, 1936.

"*The Lost Colony* Is Found," by Anthony Buttitta. Illustrated. June, 1940.

Institute Magazine, The (Columbia University, New York).

"Towards An American Folk Drama," by Frederick H. Koch. Illustrated. November, 1929.

La Renaissance D'Occident (Brussels).

"Un Ecrivain Pour Le Théâtre Nègre En Amérique," editorial, November, 1926.

Landmark, The (London).

"Sixty Weeks of Shakespeare in the United States," by Sir Philip Ben Greet, August, 1932.

"The Folk Theatre of the South-Eastern United States," by Phillip Cummings, January, 1938.

Liberty Magazine (New York).

"To the Ladies!" (Interview with Frederick H. Koch), by Princess Alexandra Kropotkin, September 17, 1932.

"He Makes Democracy Think! Success Story! Here's How Radio's Most Remarkable Ringmaster (George V.

Denny) Rose to Fame," by Frederick L. Collins, December 9, 1939.

Life (New York).

"College Theatres Do Fine Plays on $1,000,000 Stages," Illustrations: The Playmakers Theatre at Night, Professor Koch and his dog, scenes from *Funeral Flowers for the Bride*, *Soldadera*, and *Sharecropper*, May 29, 1939.

"Lost Colony Play Is Carolina Hit." Illustrations: Four scenes from the play, July 31, 1939.

Literary Digest, The (New York).

"A Revolt Against Broadway," by Walter Prichard Eaton, December 26, 1925.

"The Work of the Carolina Playmakers," by David Carb, April 14, 1934.

Little Theatre Monthly, The (New York).

"Trouping with The Carolina Playmakers," by Frederick H. Koch. Illustrated. April, 1925.

Magazine of Art (Washington, D. C.).

"Experiment with Music: The Lost Colony," by Huntington Cairns. Illustrations: Two views of the Waterside Theatre and four scenes from the production, December, 1938

Magazine World, The (New York).

"A Chinese Playmaker," by Frederick H. Koch. Illustrated. January, 1931.

Momento (Monterrey, Mexico).

"Josefina Niggli," July, 1937.

National Theatre Conference, "*Quarterly Bulletin*" (Cleveland, Ohio).

"Field Notes," October, 1939.

"Drama in the South," by Frederick H. Koch, Volume II, No. 1, April, 1940.

"Defense on the Main Front," by Paul Green, Volume II, No. 2, December 1940.

News and Observer, The (Raleigh, North Carolina).

"State University Pioneer in Developing North Carolina

Community Drama Centers," by Lucy M. Cobb, March 20, 1927.

"Paul Green Is Native North Carolina Dramatist Who Found His Inspiration and Achieved Success at Home," by Nell Battle Lewis. Illustrated. March 20, 1927.

"Tar Heels Score in Native Drama," by George V. Denny. Illustrated. December 18, 1927.

"A Cracker Box Poet Grows Up," by Bernice Kelly Harris, April 23, 1939.

"Capacity Crowd Hears Koch Here," December 18, 1939.

"Koch's Reading Becomes Expected Yule Feature," by Gladys Best Tripp, December 17, 1939.

"Mayflower Cup Winner Maps Extensive Program of Writing," by Edith Harbour. Illustrated. December 10, 1939.

"Carolina Playmakers Pave Way to Broadway for Eugenia Rawls," by Roy Wilder, Jr., February 11, 1940.

New Masses (New York).

"Thomas Wolfe," by Robert Forsythe, September 27, 1938.

New Student, The (New York).

"Pulitzer Prize," editorial, May 11, 1927.

New Theatre Magazine (New York).

"Drama in Dixie," by Molly Day Thatcher, October, 1934.

"Negro Players in Southern Theatres," by J. O. Bailey, July, 1935.

New York Review, The (New York).

"Augustus Thomas on the National Theater," by Colgate Baker, December 23, 1922.

New York Sun, The (New York).

"Paul Green Has a Stage Dream—Great American Theatre Is Coming, He Says." May 28, 1940.

New York Times, The (New York).

"Carolina Playmakers Give Mill Drama," by H. I. Brock,

November 24, 1929. Illustration: A scene from Paul Green's *The Lost Colony*, July 30, 1939.

New York Times Magazine, The (New York).

"The Carolina Playmakers." Illustrated. December 31, 1922.

"State Owned Theatre for Native Drama," Syndicated article, by Robert W. Madry. Illustrated. December 27, 1925.

"Non-Metropolitan Drama," editorial, April 6, 1928.

"Professor George P. Baker and Professor Frederick H. Koch at The Playmakers Theatre." Illustration. (Pictorial Section.) April 15, 1928.

"South of Times Square" (The Southern Regional Conference), by J. Brooks Atkinson, April 15, 1928.

"Ought We to Found a National Theatre," by Brooks Atkinson. Illustrated. March 24, 1940.

New York Herald Tribune, The (New York).

"State Owned Theatre for Native Drama," syndicated article, by Robert Madry. Illustrated. December 13, 1925.

"College Courses Called Hope of Stage," by George V. Denny, Jr. Illustrated. July 13, 1930.

"There's Life in the Old Road Yet," by Walter Prichard Eaton. Illustrated. July 12, 1931.

New York World, The (New York).

"State Owned Theatre for Native Drama," syndicated article, by Robert Madry. Illustrated. December 13, 1925.

North American Review, The (New York).

"The Social Significance of Little Theatres," by Montrose J. Moses, March, April, May, 1927.

"Cobwebs of Antiquity: A Plea for Folk Basis in American Drama," by Montrose J. Moses, January, 1931.

North Carolina Education (Raleigh, North Carolina).

"Centennial Pageant Making," by Frederick H. Koch, November, 1936.

"A Festival of Youth," by Frederick H. Koch, April, 1937.

Nya Dagligt Allehanda (American-Swedish News Exchange, New York).
"Moderna Amerikanska Dramatiker: Paul Green," June 1, 1940.

Ohio Wesleyan Magazine, The (Delaware, Ohio).
"A Biographical Sketch of Frederick H. Koch." Illustrated. May, 1931.

Opportunity (Washington, D. C.).
"The Carolina Playmakers," by Montgomery Gregory, December, 1925.

Our World Weekly (Camden, New Jersey).
"Native American Drama," editorial. Illustrated. March 30, 1925.

Philadelphia Forum Magazine (Philadelphia).
"The Carolina Playmakers," by George V. Denny, December, 1925.
"The Carolina Playmakers," by George V. Denny. Illustrated. November, 1927.

Pine and Thistle, The (Flora Macdonald College, Red Springs, North Carolina).
"A Drama of the Scotch Settlement in North Carolina," by Frederick H. Koch, March, 1940.

Play-Actin'—1938–1939 (Cape Girardeau, Missouri). Edited by Lealon N. Jones.
"An Ideal Drama of the People," by Lealon N. Jones.
"The Negro 'Gits Religion,'" by John G. Rousseau.
"America's Own Passion Play," by Gordon Clouser.
"Sea Island Folk of North Carolina," by Lacy Anderson.
"Dunkard Farm," by Phoebe Bashore.
"Brooklyn Folk Plays," by Betty Smith.
Illustrations: A scene from *Triflin' Ways*, a Missouri folk play, by Lealon N. Jones.

Playground, The (New York).
"Folk Play Making in Dakota and in Carolina," by Frederick H. Koch, January, 1925.

Players Magazine (Peru, Nebraska).

"The Carolina Playmakers Feature *The Taming of the Shrew.*" Illustrated. November–December, 1931.

"Carolina Playmakers Open Fourteenth Season," by Ora Mae Davis, January–February, 1932.

"*Alcestis* in the Greek Stadium," by Rebecca Cushman. Illustrated. January–February, 1933.

"Shakespeare in the Forest Theatre," November–December, 1933.

"Carolina Playmakers Complete Fifteenth Season," by Frederick H. Koch, January–February, 1934.

"Politicin' in the Smokies," by Frederick H. Koch, February, 1940.

"*The Lost Colony* on Roanoke Island," by Frederick H. Koch. Illustrated. April, 1940.

Popular Educator, The (New York).

"Community, Summer, and Amateur Theatres," by Walter Prichard Eaton. Illustrations: Interior of The Playmakers Theatre, The Forest Theatre, Lighting Equipment on the Stage of The Playmakers Theatre, November 28, 1938.

Progressive Education (Washington, D. C.).

"The Carolina Playmakers," by Ralph Westerman, January, 1931.

Publishers' Weekly, The (New York).

"Thomas Wolfe," September 24, 1938.

Quarterly Journal, The (University of North Dakota).

"Towards a New Folk Theatre," by Frederick H. Koch, May, 1930.

Readers Digest (Pleasantville, New York).

"Town Meeting's on the Air Again," by Earl Spalding, October, 1939.

Saturday Review of Literature, The (New York).

"The Reader's Guide," by May Lamberton Becker, May 27, 1933.

"Thomas Wolfe," by Ann Preston Bridgers, April 6, 1935.

"Native Theatre, The," by Stephen Vincent Benét, July 1, 1939.

"Literature and the South," by W. J. Cash, December 28, 1940.

Scholastic (Pittsburgh).

"Folk Playmaking," by Frederick H. Koch. Illustrated. April 13, 1929.

"How *The Scuffletown Outlaws* Came to Be Written," by Frederick H. Koch. Illustrated. May 11, 1929.

"Folk Chronicler of Carolina (Paul Green)." Illustrated. February 18, 1933.

Scribner's Magazine (New York).

"The Real Revolt in our Theatre," by Walter Prichard Eaton. Illustrated. November, 1922.

"Playboys of the College World," by Frederick P. Keppell. Illustrated. January, 1926.

Shadowland (New York).

"Amateurs and the Future," by Walter Prichard Eaton. Illustrated. September, 1921.

Southerner, The (Atlanta).

"Little Theatres in the South," by Mary Martin Remage. Illustrated. December, 1930.

Southern California Trojan (Los Angeles).

"Experimenting in Playmaking," by Quentin Reger. July 27, 1931.

"Original Mexican Folk Plays Shown in Quaint Theatre," by Quentin Reger. August 18, 1931.

Southern Folklore Quarterly (Gainesville, Florida).

"Making a Native Folk Drama," by Frederick H. Koch, September, 1937.

Southern Literary Messenger (Richmond, Virginia).

"Pride of the South," by F. Meredith Dietz, June, 1938.

"A Gullah Negro Drama," by Frederick H. Koch, April, 1940.

"More Recent Development," by F. Meredith Dietz, April, 1940.

"Drama in North Carolina," by Lucy M. Cobb, April, 1940.

Southern Magazine, The (Nashville, Tennessee).

"Write and Act Your Own Drama," by W. O. Saunders. Illustrated. May, 1924.

Springfield Republican, The (Springfield, Massachusetts).

"Playmakers Plan Coming-of-Age Drama Festival," by Carl Glick, January 28, 1940.

Stage, The (London, England).

"Job's Kinfolks" (New York Performance), by J. Fletcher Smith, December 12, 1929.

State, The (Raleigh, North Carolina).

"The Man Who Made North Carolina Drama Conscious," by Majel Ivey Seay. July 7, 1934.

"The Festival of Youth," by Majel Ivey Seay, April 3, 1937.

Illustration: Scene from Paul Green's *The Lost Colony*, August 5, 1939.

"George V. Denny," by Hoyt McAfee. Illustrated. December 23, 1939.

Theatre Arts Monthly (New York).

"A Folk Theatre in the Making," by Frederick H. Koch. September, 1924.

"Little Theatre Foregrounds," by Walter Prichard Eaton, September, 1925.

"The Forest Theatre of The Carolina Playmakers." Illustrated. November, 1925.

"The Great World Theatre," editorial, February, 1926.

Two full page illustrations (Interior of The Playmakers Theatre, Playmakers on Tour), and scene from *The Thrice Promised Bride*, September, 1926.

Scenes from *Lighted Candles* and *The Marvelous Romance of Wen Chun-Chin*, September, 1927.

"The Tributary Theatre," editorial, January, 1928.

Illustrations: Portrait study of Hubert Heffner as Uncle January Evans in Paul Green's *The Man Who Died At Twelve O'Clock*, scene from Helen Dortch's Negro comedy, *Companion-Mate Maggie*, July, 1929.

"Teaching Theatre," by Kenneth Macgowan, October, 1929.

Scene from *Death Valley Scotty*, by James Milton Wood, July, 1930.

Scene from *Git Up An' Bar the Door*, by Arthur Palmer Hudson, July, 1931.

"American Plays" (with illustrations from *Git Up An' Bar the Door* and Paul Green's *The Field God*), July, 1931.

"Adventures in Playmaking," by Carl Carmer, July, 1932.

Strike Song (photograph), July, 1932.

"Paul Green, the Making of an American Dramatist," by Carl Carmer, December, 1932.

"Frederick H. Koch as 'Death' in *Alcestis*" (a photograph), December, 1932.

"Drama and the Weather," by Paul Green, August, 1934.

"Paul Green's *Shroud My Body Down*" (photograph), April, 1935.

"History Repeats Itself," by Edith J. R. Isaacs (two photographs from *Shroud My Body Down*), July, 1935.

"Paul Green's *The Enchanted Maze*" (photograph), July, 1936.

"Josephina Niggli's *The Red Velvet Goat*" (photograph), July, 1937.

"The Carolina Playmakers' Touring Equipment," by Harry E. Davis, July, 1937.

"Paul Green's *The Lost Colony*" (photograph), July, 1938.

"Paul Green's *Johnny Johnson*" (two photographs), July, 1938.

"Making Canadian Drama," by Edith J. R. Isaacs, December, 1938.

"A Young Man of Promise," February, 1939.

"Where Do We Go From Here?" by Edith J. R. Isaacs, July, 1939.

"The Next Twenty-Five Years," by Lee Mitchell, July, 1939.

"The Town That Is a Theatre," by Anthony F. Merrill, July, 1939.

"Tributary Tours," by Rosamond Gilder. Illustration: Scene from The Carolina Playmakers' Original Production of *Swappin' Fever*, by Lealon N. Jones, July, 1939.

"Fred Howard as Uppowoc, the Indian Medicine Man in *The Lost Colony*" (a photograph), June, 1940.

"Don Rosenberg as Sandy Ochiltree in *The Highland Call*" (a photograph), July, 1940.

Theatre and School (St. Mateo, California).

"Towards an American Folk Drama," by Frederick H. Koch, October, 1933.

Theatre Magazine, The (New York).

"The Carolina Playmakers," by Philip Hettleman. Illustrated. October, 1920.

Illustrations of *Carolina Folk Plays*, May, 1921.

The Forest Theatre and the Bankside Theatre. Illustrations. January, 1922.

"Folk Playmaking," by Frederick H. Koch. Illustrated. October, 1922.

Illustrations of Shakespearean Productions in The Forest Theatre." April, 1924.

Illustrations of *Carolina Folk Plays*, July, 1924.

"The Carolina Playmakers on Tour," by Frederick H. Koch. Illustrated. May, 1925.

The Carolina Playmakers' Production of *Prunella* in The Forest Theatre. Illustrated. July, 1925.

"Dramatic Training in Our Colleges," editorial. Illustrated. January, 1926.

"Harlequinading in North Carolina," by Ethel Theodora Rockwell. January, 1927.

"The Carolina Playmakers Play New York," editorial, February, 1928.

Scenes from The Playmakers' New York Production, March, 1928.

"The Regional Conference on the Drama at Chapel Hill," editorial. Illustrated. July, 1928.

"The Carolina Playmakers Come to Town," by M. E. Kehoe. Illustrated. February, 1929.

Scenes from Forest Theatre Productions: *The Taming of the Shrew* and *Rip Van Winkle*, September, 1929.

Stage Setting of The Playmakers' Forest Theatre Production of *Romeo and Juliet* and Frederick H. Koch as Mercutio, September, 1930.

Theatre Guild Magazine (New York).
"Little Theatre Playwrights: Have Our Amateur Playhouses Created Dramatic Literature?" by Kenneth Macgowan, November, 1929.

Times Herald (Washington, D. C.)
"Chapel Hill Folk Drama in 21st Year," a United Press Release, January 14, 1940.

Times Literary Supplement, The (London, England).
"Plays Racy of the Soil," editorial, September 9, 1939.

Town Hall Crier, The (New York).
"A Christmas Carol," by Frederick H. Koch. Illustrated. December, 1931.

University of Toronto Quarterly (Toronto, Canada).
"Canadian Drama," by Arthur L. Phelps, October, 1939.
"Drama (Gwen Pharis and her plays)," by W. S. Milne, April, 1939.

Vanity Fair (New York).
"The Playboys of the Campus," by Walter Prichard Eaton, May, 1927.

Wesleyan Alumnae, The (Macon, Georgia).
"Something New in Southern Folk Drama." Illustration: Scene from *Washed in de Blood*, May, 1939.

Winston-Salem Journal (Winston-Salem, North Carolina).
"Wolfe's Greatest Ambition Unfulfilled at His Death," by R. W. Madry. Illustration: Thomas Wolfe playing the title rôle in his own play, *The Return of Buck Gavin*, September 25, 1938.
"Scrooge Will Return to Winston-Salem—Professor Koch to Read *Christmas Carol* Next Sunday," by Pete Ivey, December 3, 1939.
"Koch Stirs Capacity Audience With Presentation of

Dickens' Beautiful *A Christmas Carol*," by Harvey
Dinkins, December 11, 1939.

World's Work, The (New York).
"North Carolina Dramatizing Its History," editorial, December, 1922.

Woman's Home Companion (New York).
"Own Your Own Little Theatre," by Constance D'Arcy
MacKay. Illustrated. May, 1928.

IV. BOOK REVIEWS

1. CAROLINA FOLK PLAYS[1]

Asheville Citizen, The (Asheville, North Carolina)
"Carolina Folk Plays Given in New Volume." November
14, 1924.

Billboard, The (Cincinnati, Ohio)
"American Folk Plays–Carolina Folk Plays," by Gordon
Whyte. January 6, 1923.

Book Review Digest, The (New York)
"Carolina Folk Plays," January, 1925.

Charlotte News, The (Charlotte, North Carolina)
"Carolina Playmakers Publish Fourth Book," January 24,
1932.

Chronicle, The (San Francisco, California)
"One Act Plays Offer Varied Appeal to Reader and Actor,"
by George C. Warren, January 28, 1925.

Courier-Journal, The (Louisville, Kentucky)
"The Literary Lantern," a syndicated column, by Elizabeth Lay Green, January 3, 1932.

Daily Tar Heel, The (Chapel Hill, North Carolina)
"'Carolina Folk Comedies' Title of New Series," January
10, 1932.

---

[1] *Carolina Folk Plays, First Series* (1922), *Second Series* (1924), *Third
Series* (1928). New York: Henry Holt and Company. (Illustrated.) *Carolina Folk Comedies.* New York: Samuel French, 1931. (Illustrated.)

Dispatch, The (Richmond, Virginia)
"On the Library Table," by Hunter Staff, January 22, 1925.

Durham Morning Herald, The (Durham, North Carolina)
"New Volume of Five Carolina Folk Plays Has Been Issued," November 16, 1924.

Equity (New York)
"All Kinds of One Act Plays," November, 1923.

Ex Libris (Paris, France)
"Carolina Folk Plays," by Prue Durant Smith, January, 1924.

Freeman, The (New York)
"Carolina Folk Plays," by M. L. M., April 11, 1923.

Greensboro Daily News (Greensboro, North Carolina)
"Drama of the Plain People," by Gerald W. Johnson, December 17, 1922.
"The Literary Lantern," by C. A. Hibbard, November 23, 1924.
"Doing Some Thinking," editorial review, by Lenoir Chamber, November 9, 1924.
"Make Collection of Carolina Folk Plays," by Robert Madry, November 16, 1924.
"The Literary Lantern," a syndicated column, by Elizabeth Lay Green, January 3, 1932.

Hartford Daily Courant, The (Hartford, Connecticut)
"Some Choice Items for Play Readers," February 14, 1932.

Herald, The (Louisville, Kentucky)
"Carolina Folk Plays," February 1, 1925.

Herald and Tribune, The (New York)
"Carolina Folk Plays," by Walter Prichard Eaton, February 8, 1925.
"Drama and Some Plays—Carolina Folk Comedies," by Walter Prichard Eaton, March 6, 1932.

Judge (New York)

"Not Letting George Do It," by Walter Prichard Eaton, February 10, 1923.

Literary Review of The New York Evening Post, The (New York)

"Carolina Folk Plays," December 30, 1922.

Literary Digest, International Book Review, The (New York)

"The Changing Art of the Modern Playwright," by Lloyd Morris, March, 1923.

News and Observer, The (Raleigh, North Carolina)

"Carolina Playmakers Form an Oasis in Our Artistic Desert," by Nell Battle Lewis, February 11, 1923.

"Carolina Players Reveal the True Carolina Flavor," by Nina Holland Covington, January 14, 1923.

New York Evening Post, The (New York)

"Carolina Folk Plays," by Charles Pike Sawyer, January 17, 1923.

New York Tribune, The (New York)

"Carolina Folk Plays," by Roscoe W. Brink, January 21, 1923.

New York Times Book Review, The (New York)

"Carolina Folk Plays," (Illustrated.) February 4, 1923.

New York World, The (New York)

"Carolina Folk Plays," by Maxwell Anderson (Pendragon), January 21, 1923.

San Diego Union (San Diego, California)

"Carolina Folk Comedies," February 21, 1932.

Survey, The (East Stroudsburg, Pennsylvania)

"Tarts and Comfits," by Hunter Stagg, February 15, 1925.

Times, The (Roanoke, Virginia)

"Carolina Folk Plays Published in Volume," November 17, 1924.

Theatre Arts Monthly (New York)

"Carolina Folk Plays," April, 1925.

"Carolina Folk Comedies," by Carl Carmer, February, 1933.

Transcript, The (Boston, Massachusetts)
"More Carolina Folk Plays," March 11, 1925.

Town Hall Crier, The (New York)
"Carolina Folk Comedies," by G. V. D., March, 1932.

Washington Post, The (Washington, D. C.)
"Professor Frederick Koch Comes Forward with a Series of Very Commendable *Carolina Folk Plays*," by Frances L. Baer, December 10, 1922.
"Carolina Folk Plays," by Gordon Whyte, November 29, 1924.

Washington News, The (Washington, D. C.)
"Carolina Folk Plays," by Frank Taylor, January 24, 1923.

Worcester Sunday Telegram (Worcester, Massachusetts)
"Carolina Folk Comedies," by M. G. P., June 19, 1932.

2. AMERICAN FOLK PLAYS[1]

Associated Press: A syndicated review published in many American newspapers. "Calls Plays Edited by Koch Most Significant," by John Selby, Book Editor, the Associated Press, June 25, 1939.

Alumni Review, The (Chapel Hill, North Carolina)
"Folk Play Volume," by Walter Spearman, June, 1939.

Dallas Morning Star, The (Dallas, Texas)
"History in Folk Playlets," by Hilton R. Greer, June 23, 1939.

Dallas Texas Times-Herald (Dallas, Texas)
"Folk Plays by Students Form New Collection," July 9, 1939.

Herald-Tribune—Book Section (New York)
"American Folk Plays," by Walter Prichard Eaton, July 23, 1939.

[1] New York: D. Appleton-Century Company, 1939. (Illustrated.)

Nashville Tennessean, The (Nashville, Tennessee)
"A Flavor of 'Just Folks,'" by O. K. Barnes, June 11, 1939.

National Historical Magazine, published by the Daughters of the American Revolution (Washington, D. C.)
"American Folk Plays," by Dorothy K. Cleavland, August, 1939.

New York Post (New York)
"A Foreword Which Does Not Help A Volume," by John Mason Brown, May 25, 1939.

Newark Evening News (Newark, New Jersey)
"American Folk Plays," June 21, 1939.

News and Courier (Charleston, South Carolina)
"Folk Plays From All America," by R. W. T., June 25, 1939.

North Georgia Review, The
"American Folk Plays," by Sterling A. Brown, Spring, 1940.

One-Act Play Magazine (New York)
"Editorial Review of Professor Koch's Published Volume of One-Act Plays," by William Kozlenko, February, 1940.

Oregonian, The (Portland, Oregon)
"American Folk Plays." (Illustrated.) October 18, 1939.

Pasadena Star-News (Pasadena, California)
"American Folk Plays," June 24, 1939.

Plain Dealer (Cleveland, Ohio)
"American Folk Plays," June 11, 1939.

Players Magazine (Peru, Nebraska)
"American Folk Plays," by A. B. Joder, July–August, 1939.

Quarterly Journal of Speech (Baton Rouge, Louisiana)
"American Folk Plays," by B. H., February, 1940.

Recreation Magazine, The (New York)
"American Folk Plays," December, 1939.

Rural America (New York)
"American Folk Plays," October, 1939.

Salt Lake Tribune (Salt Lake City, Utah)
"Writers of Rocky Mountain West," July 2, 1939.

Saturday Review of Literature, The (New York)
"The Native Theatre," by Stephen Vincent Benét. (Illustrated.) July 1, 1939.

Savannah Morning News (Savannah, Georgia)
"American Folk Plays," June 4, 1939.

Southern Folklore Quarterly (Gainesville, Florida)
"American Folk Plays," by William Peery, December, 1939.

Southern Literary Messenger (Richmond, Virginia)
"American Folk Plays," by Caroline B. Sherman, October, 1939.

Southern Speech Bulletin, The (Tuscaloosa, Alabama)
"American Folk Plays," by Leroy Lewis, November, 1939.

Springfield Republican (Springfield, Massachusetts)
"Two New Books Recommended to Theatre Workers," September 30, 1939.

Sunday Standard Times (New Bedford, Massachusetts)
"Enthusiasm and Sincerity Characterize Folk Plays," June 25, 1939.

Telegram (Worcester, Massachusetts)
"On American Folk Drama," by M. P. (Illustrated.)

Theatre Arts Monthly (New York City)
"American Folk Plays," editorial, September, 1939.

Times, The (Madison, Wisconsin)
"American Folk Plays," by J. S., July 2, 1939.

Times Literary Supplement, The (London, England)
"Plays Racy of the Soil," editorial review, September 9, 1939.

Times-Picayune, The (New Orleans, Louisiana)
"American Folk Plays," by R. M. S., July 9, 1939.

Waco Tribune-Herald (Waco, Texas)
  "American Folk Plays," in Sunday Book Corner, by William Stanley Hoole, July 9, 1939.
Youngstown Vindicator (Youngstown, Ohio)
  "20 One-Act Plays in Book," by John Selby, July 2, 1939.

NORTH CAROLINA NEWSPAPERS

Asheville: *The Asheville Citizen-Times*, "Valuable Contribution to American Drama," by G. de R. Hamilton, Jr., May 28, 1939.

Chapel Hill: *The Daily Tar Heel*, " 'Proff' Koch's Classes Edit New *American Folk Plays*," by Gladys Best Tripp, May 26, 1939.

Winston-Salem: *Journal and Sentinel*, "Koch Gathers *American Folk Plays*," by Eleanor L. Follin, May 28, 1939.

Durham: *Herald-Sun*, "Dr. Koch Edits Play Collection," by Steed Rollins. (Illustrated.) May 28, 1939.

Charlotte: *The Charlotte Observer*, "Dr. Koch Edits New Book of *American Folk Plays*," by Legette Blythe. (Illustrated.) May 28, 1939.

Greensboro: *Daily News*, "Founder of Playmakers Scores with His *American Folk Plays*," by Fritz Raley Simmons. (Illustrated.) June 4, 1939.

"*Literary Lantern, The*" (Syndicated Column) by Caro Green Russell, June 4, 1939.

Raleigh: *News and Observer*, "Transcontinental Journey," by Jonathan Daniels. (Illustrated.) June 4, 1939.

APPENDIX III

I. ORIGINAL PLAYS PRODUCED

1. FULL-LENGTH PLAYS

A Pageant of the North-West, an historic drama, written in collaboration by eighteen under-graduate students, under the direction of Professor Frederick H. Koch of the Department of Dramatic Literature, produced in the Bankside Theatre, May 28–29, 1914.

Shakespeare, the Playmaker, a communal Masque, written by twenty under-graduate students, under the direction of Professor Frederick H. Koch of the Department of Dramatic Literature, produced in the Bankside Theatre, June 12–13, 1916.

2. ONE-ACT PLAYS

FIRST SERIES, DECEMBER 19, 1916.

Turribly Sot, a comedy of New England life, by Clara Struble.

The Long Exile, a tale of Russian prisoners in Siberia, by Arthur Cloetingh.

SECOND SERIES, JANUARY 25, 1917.

Wanted—A Farmer, a comedy of farmers in Chicago, by B. Melvin Johnson.

Becca, an adaptation of Kipling's story, "Lispeth," by Agnes O'Connor.

Turribly Sot, a comedy of New England life, by Clara Struble.

Are You Guilty? a satire on college life, by Arthur Cloetingh.

THIRD SERIES, FEBRUARY 15, 1917.

Butterflies, a romance of a university town, by Clara Struble.

475

Patsy Puts It Over, a comedy of the Turtle Mountains of Dakota, by Agnes O'Connor.

April Showers, a play of the North-West, by Howard Huston.

Beyond the Steppes, a tragedy, suggested by a story by Tolstoy, by Arthur Cloetingh.

FOURTH SERIES, FEBRUARY 22, 1917.

Beyond the Steppes, a tragedy, suggested by a story by Tolstoy, by Arthur Cloetingh.

Turribly Sot, a comedy of New England life, by Clara Struble.

April Showers, a play of the North-West, by Howard Huston.

Patsy Puts It Over, a comedy of the Turtle Mountains of Dakota, by Agnes O'Connor.

FIFTH SERIES, MARCH 15, 1917.

Morgan of Hinchinbrook, a drama of the Alaskan frontier, by Howard Huston.

Back on the Old Farm, the education of a country boy, by Arthur Cloetingh.

Moonlight, a romance, adapted from a story by de Maupassant, by Benjamin F. Sherman.

SIXTH SERIES, DECEMBER 20-21, 1917.

The Spirit of Christmas, a poetic drama, by Franz and Lillian Rickaby.

SEVENTH SERIES, JANUARY 31, FEBRUARY 1, 1918.

Me an' Bill, a tragedy of the Great Plains, by Benjamin F. Sherman.

How Daddy O'Donnell Had His Way, a comedy of an autocrat in a farm home, by Karl Einarson.

Dakota Dick, a comedy of the Dakota Bad Lands, by Harold Wylie.

EIGHTH SERIES, FEBRUARY 21-22, 1918.

A Vacation Tragedy, a satire of college life, by Karl Einarson and Vilhjalmur Steffansson.

Me an' Bill, a tragedy of the Great Plains, by Benjamin F. Sherman.

The Home Fires, a patriotic play of today, by Harold Wylie.

NINTH SERIES, APRIL 12–13, 1918.

Barley Beards, a play of the Dakota harvest fields, by Howard DeLong.

A Sorority Flurry, a comedy of university life, by Agnes O'Connor.

For the Colleen, a romance of a prairie pioneer, by Agnes O'Connor.

II. THE DAKOTA PLAYMAKERS TOURS

1. TOURING WITH PROFESSIONAL PLAYS

FIRST TOUR OF NORTH DAKOTA, JUNE, 1906.
The Rivals, by Richard Brinsley Sheridan.

SECOND TOUR OF NORTH DAKOTA, JUNE, 1907.
Tom Pinch, by Charles Dickens.

THIRD TOUR OF NORTH DAKOTA, JUNE, 1908.
The Love Chase, by James Sheridan Knowles.

2. TOURING WITH ORIGINAL NATIVE PRAIRIE PLAYS

FOURTH TOUR OF NORTH DAKOTA, APRIL, 1917.
Turribly Sot, by Clara Struble.
Wanted—A Farmer, by B. Melvin Johnson.
Morgan of Hinchinbrook, by Howard Huston.
Back on the Old Farm, by Arthur Cloetingh.

III. PROFESSIONAL PLAYS PRODUCED

1. FULL-LENGTH PLAYS

The Rivals, by Richard Brinsley Sheridan, June, 1906.
Tom Pinch, by Charles Dickens, June, 1907.
The Love Chase, by James Sheridan Knowles, June, 1908.
Twelfth Night, by William Shakespeare, June, 1910.
Everyman, April, 1911.
The School For Scandal, by Richard Brinsley Sheridan, June, 1911.

Nathan Hale, by Clyde Fitch, April, 1912.
The Professor's Love Story, by James M. Barrie, June, 1912.
Little Eyolf, by Henrik Ibsen, 1914.
The Devil's Disciple, by George Bernard Shaw, May, 1915.
Much Ado About Nothing, by William Shakespeare, April, 1916.

2. ONE-ACT PLAYS

Spreading the News, by Lady Gregory, March 31, 1913.
Riders to the Sea, by John M. Synge, March 31, 1913.
The Hour Glass, by William Butler Yeats, March 31, 1913.
A Pot of Broth, by William Butler Yeats, November 23, 1916.
Hyacinth Halvey, by Lady Gregory, November 23, 1916.
The Rising of the Moon, by Lady Gregory, November 23, 1916.
How He Lied to Her Husband, by George Bernard Shaw, November 29, 1917.
The Death of Robin Hood, by Alfred Noyes, November 29, 1917.
The Swan Song, by Anton Chekhov, November 29, 1917.

APPENDIX IV

THE DAKOTA PLAYMAKERS: A SELECTED BIBLIOGRAPHY

September 1, 1905 to September 1, 1918

I. PUBLICATIONS OF THE DAKOTA PLAYMAKERS

1. PUBLISHED PAGEANTS AND MASQUES

A Pageant of the North-West, an historic drama, written in collaboration by eighteen under-graduate students under the direction of Professor Frederick H. Koch of the Department of Dramatic Literature. (Grand Forks, N. Dak.; The University of North Dakota, 1914.) Ill.

Shakespeare, the Playmaker, a Tercentenary Masque, written in collaboration by twenty under-graduate students under the direction of Professor Frederick H. Koch of the Department of Dramatic Literature. (Grand Forks, N. Dak., The University of North Dakota, 1916.) Ill. Also in *The Quarterly Journal* (Grand Forks, N. Dak.; The University of North Dakota, July, 1916.)

The Book of the Dickey County Pageant, written by twenty members of the community in collaboration, under the direction of Mattie Crabtree, of The Dakota Playmakers. (Ellendale, N. Dak.; The Dickey County Leader, 1917.)

The New Day, a Masque of the Future, by Margaret Plank Ganssle, of The Dakota Playmakers. (Grand Forks, N. Dak.; The Grand Forks Herald Co., 1918.)

The Book of the Patriotic Pageant of Dickey County, written in collaboration by eleven Dickey County people, under the direction of Mattie Crabtree, of The Dakota Playmakers. (Ellendale, N. Dak.: The Dickey County Leader, 1918.)

The Selish, An Indian Pageant-Masque, written and produced by students of the University of Montana, with the cooperation of the community of Missoula, Montana, under the direction of Margaret Plank Ganssle, of The Dakota Playmakers, July 30, 1919. (Missoula, Montana: The University of Montana, 1919.)

2. Plays Published Separately

The Christmas Spirit, a poetic fantasy in two acts, by Franz and Lillian Rickaby. (Boston: Walter H. Baker and Company, 1922.)

II. PERIODICAL REFERENCES TO THE DAKOTA PLAYMAKERS

American Magazine of Art, The (Washington, D. C.)
"The Dakota Playmakers," by Frederick H. Koch. Illustrated. December, 1918.

American Review of Reviews, The (New York)
"Communal Playmaking," editorial. Illustrated. September, 1916.

Architectural Review, The (Boston)
"Some Garden Theatres," by Frank A. Waugh. Photograph and drawing of the Bankside Theatre. September, 1916.

Bellman, The (Minneapolis)
"The Craze For Little Theatres," by Montrose J. Moses. Illustrated. March 17, 1917.

Boston Evening Transcript, The (Boston)
"Dakotan Discoveries in Dual Dramaturgy," by Hiram Moderwell. Illustrated. September 30, 1916.

Community Center, The (New York)
"Communal Authorship," editorial. March 17, 1917.

Country Life in America (Garden City, New York)
"The Pageant in America," by Frances Gilchrist Wood. Illustrated. November, 1916.

Current Opinion (New York)
"The New Art of Pageantry in the United States," editorial. Illustrated. September, 1914.

Drama League of America, Report of the Second Annual Convention (Chicago)
"The University Theatre," by Frederick H. Koch. April 24, 1912.

Drama League of America Year Book (Chicago)
"Amateur Values in Pageantry," by Frederick H. Koch. 1915–16.

Drama League Monthly (Chicago)
"The University Laboratory and Festival Theatres," by Frederick H. Koch. September, 1916.

Drama Magazine, The (New York)
"The Dakota Playmakers," editorial. October, 1922.

English Journal, The (Chicago)
"Useful Documents," editorial. June, 1919.

Independent, The (New York)

"The Little Theatre Revolt," by Montrose J. Moses. Illustrated. May 12, 1917.

Journal of Education, The (Boston)

"Communal Play Making," by Frederick H. Koch. October 26, 1916.

"Shakespeare, the Playmaker," by President Frank L. McVey of the University of North Dakota. October 26, 1916.

Literary Digest, The (New York)

Illustrations of the Bankside Theatre and scenes from "*A Pageant of the North-West*," July 25, 1914.

Manitoban, The (University of Manitoba, Winnipeg, Canada)

"The Drama and the People, A Challenge to Us," editorial. March, 1918.

Minnesotan, The (Minneapolis)

"Sidetracking the Movies," editorial. Illustrated. November, 1916.

Pittsburgh Sun, The (Pittsburgh)

"Drama Leaders Attending Convention," editorial. Illustrated. April 25, 1917.

Playground, The (Cooperstown, New York)

"Imaginative Rural Recreation," by Constance D'Arcy Mackay. May, 1920.

Quarterly Journal of Public Speaking, The (Chicago)

"Amateur Values in Pageantry," by Frederick H. Koch. October, 1915.

Quarterly Journal of the University of North Dakota, The (Grand Forks)

"The Question of the Theatre," by Frederick H. Koch. July, 1911.

"Literary Value in the Modern Drama," by Frederick H. Koch. April, 1913.

"Dedication of the Bankside Theatre," editorial. Illustrated. July, 1914.

"Making 'A Pageant of the North-West,'" by Frederick H. Koch. July, 1914.

"The Pageant of the North-West," editorial. Illustrated. July, 1914.

"Toward the Municipal Theatre," by Frederick H. Koch. January, 1916.

"The Amateur Theatre in the University," by Frederick H. Koch. July, 1916.

"The Bankside Theatre," by Frederick H. Koch. Illustrated. July, 1916.

"Shakespeare, the Playmaker," text of the play. July, 1916.

"An Historical Sketch," by Frederick H. Koch. Illustrated. October, 1918.

"The Construction of the Play-Stage," by Albert John Becker. Illustrated. October, 1918.

"Towards a New Folk Theatre," by Frederick H. Koch. May, 1930.

School of Education Record of the University of North Dakota, The (Grand Forks)

"Lines and Cues," by Franz Rickaby. December, 1921.

Survey (New York)

"A Pageant of the Prairies," editorial. Illustrated. July 4, 1914.

"Caliban of the Yellow Sands," by John Collier. Illustrated. July 1, 1916.

Theatre Magazine (New York)

Illustration of the Bankside Theatre. September, 1918.

"Amateur Theatricals—The Dakota Playmakers," by H. Foster Jones. August, 1919.

Woman's Home Companion, The (New York)

"From Nothing Up," by Constance D'Arcy Mackay. Illustrated. April, 1921.

Youth (Cambridge)

"The Poetry of a Cultural Frontier," by Franz Rickaby. June, 1919.

APPENDIX V

Observations on the Pronunciation of the Dialects of North Carolina

With a few obvious exceptions, the personages depicted in the dramas here printed speak one or another of the dialects used by the uncultured whites and negroes of North Carolina. In connection with this effort to utilize for dramatic purposes the folk speech of a relatively small district of the South, several facts should be borne in mind. In the first place, it is an error to assume, as appears to be done frequently outside the South, that all Southern whites speak practically alike and that the difference between their speech and that of Southern negroes is insignificant. Although, it is true, certain peculiarities of pronunciation and certain turns of phrase are more or less common to all speakers of English in the South Atlantic States, considerable differences both in vocabulary and in pronunciation are discernible between numerous districts of this section, in some instances even when these districts adjoin each other. The dialect spoken by the native whites of eastern North Carolina, for example, is markedly different from that of the Carolina highlands, and among the Blue Ridge and Alleghany mountains clear variations in language may sometimes be noted as one passes from valley to valley or from "cove" to "cove." Again, although it is true that the English-speaking negroes of the South, having borrowed their language from the whites, have much in common with them and have even exerted an appreciable influence upon the speech of their white neighbors, yet no Southerner would confuse the dialect of a typical uneducated Carolina negro with that of even the most backward Carolina white. Moreover, in North Carolina, as elsewhere, dialect varies from family to family and from individual to individual, and even the same person changes his speech to suit his humor, his company, or other occasional circumstances.

What Horace Kephart says of the Carolina mountaineer is true of the uncultured throughout the State. "The same man," writes the author of *Our Southern Highlanders*, "at different times may say *can't* and *cain't*, *set* and *sot*, *jest* and *jes'* and *jist*, *atter* and *arter*, *seed* and *seen*, *here* and *hyur* and *hyar*, *heerd* and *heern* and *heard*, *took* and *tuk*." These facts, obvious as they are to the Southerner, need to be emphasized if this volume is to be read intelligently outside the South.

It should also be observed that the dialects of North Carolina, like those of other districts, cannot be correctly represented by any conventional system of printed signs. As Professor Sheldon has pointed out, "the written [language] . . . is, speaking generally, only a later and inexact representation for the eye of the language as spoken, that is, of the real language," and, with an alphabet so imperfect as ours, it is clearly impossible to depict accurately even the more obvious peculiarities of Southern pronunciation, to say nothing of the subtler differences between the various speech-islands of the South. Few of the differences between North Carolinese and standard American English are capable of exact representation by ordinary letters; most of them are so elusive as to escape even the most elaborate system of phonetic symbols. In the words of a distinguished authority on the history of English speech, "You could not denote [such variations in language] if you would and if you could, you would be encumbered, rather than aided, by the multiplicity of signs." Or, to adopt the language of a queer old eighteenth century spelling reformer, "delicate ears alone can discern what only delicate organs can convey."

In view of these difficulties, it became necessary to adopt an arbitrary standard of spelling for the dialects represented in this volume. In establishing this norm the editors have been guided by several considerations. To begin with, as may be observed in the work of Synge and other serious writers of dialect literature, successful dialect writing depends rather upon picturesqueness of vocabulary and idiom than upon spelling. In the best dialect literature spelling is of purely incidental value. Again, in the case of many words and phrases the difference between North Carolinese and American English as spoken by all except the most careful speakers outside the South, is too slight to justify any change in the accepted spelling. On the other hand, the combined labors of Southern dialect writers for nearly a century have established for certain words and phrases a conventional standard which has come to be associated in the public mind with any effort to represent on paper the speech of the typical Southerner. In considering the matter of traditional dialect spelling, a distinction should, however, be made between legitimate variations from standard practice and those spellings which are of no assistance in pronunciation and are merely "bad." Josh Billings, it is recorded, began his career as a humorist by changing his famous "Essa on the Muel" from ordinary to "phonetic" spelling, but most of Josh Billings' spellings, however funny they may have been to our fathers, have little justification phonetically. The same is true of much of the spelling used by Artemus Ward, Petroleum V. Nasby, Sut Lovingood, and other humorous writers who have helped to establish the tradition of dialect spelling in America. For many words contained in the dramas here printed, new spellings could be devised which, regarded phonetically, would perhaps represent the actual Carolina pronunciation more accurately than either the standard or the traditional orthography; yet any such gain in accuracy would in most cases be more than offset by a resulting loss in intelligibility. In view of these facts and of the alarm with which spelling reforms are liable to be regarded by the average reader, it has been deemed advisable to depart from standard usage only in those cases where traditional practice in Southern dialect literature clearly points the way or where the use of "phonetic" spelling runs no risk of irritating or distracting the reader.

Although nothing short of an intimate acquaintance with spoken North Carolinese can insure an absolutely correct pronunciation of the written language, the following observations may be of assistance to readers who know the dialects of the South chiefly through the medium of the printed page. Owing to limitations of space, only the more general and characteristic peculiarities of the Carolina dialects can be considered here.

As regards consonantal sounds, the spelling adopted in this volume requires little comment. In general the consonants, except *r*, may be understood to have the same value as in standard American English. For practical purposes it may be assumed that *r* is omitted by native Carolinians whenever it stands before other consonants or is final. The result is usually a slight change in the quality or length of the preceding vowel. Thus *floor* and *tore* are practically indistinguishable in pronunciation from *flow* and *toe*, and the Carolina pronunciation of *corn* rhymes with the standard pronunciation of *dawn*. There is also a strong tendency to omit the *r*-sound between vowels (as in *be'yin'* for *burying* [a funeral] and *ve'y* for *very*), and even in some cases when it stands after a consonant and before a vowel (as in *hund'ed* for *hundred* and *p'oduce* for *produce*). In order to avoid undue distortion in the form of the words, *r* is generally retained in the spelling here used except in forms such as *cuss* for *curse*, *fust* for *first*, and *nuss* for *nurse*, where the meaning is easily identified and the spelling is clearly justified by tradition. The combination *er* is also freely used, especially in final position, to represent the indistinct sound heard in the Carolina pronunciation of such words as *tobacco* but lacking in more exact speech.

As appears from the examination of a large body of dialect literature, the practice of spelling together groups of words pronounced as a unit is frequently open to objection; hence it has been followed here only in a few well established cases such as *gimme* for *give me*, *mebbe* for *maybe*, and *nemmine* for *never mind*. The highly characteristic Southern pronunciation of *you all* (practically *yawl*) is indicated merely by a hyphen (*you-all*).

Of the many phonetic differences between the dialects

of North Carolina and standard American or English usage, several require special attention.

For the short *o* sound heard in the standard English pronunciation of *cob, dog, fog, frog, God, gone, gospel, hog,* and similar words, the typical uncultured North Carolinian generally substitutes a sound closely approximating that of the vowel in *law*. Or, to put it another way, in North Carolina *God* rhymes with *sawed,* and *hog* is pronounced as though it were spelled *hawg*.

The dialects of North Carolina show few traces of the so-called "broad *a*" and none at all of the middle or Continental *a* recommended by the dictionaries for such words as *branch, can't, France,* and *grass*. Except before *r* the sound in such cases is usually that of *a* in *lamb,* sometimes slightly drawled. The same vowel is heard in the Carolina pronunciation of *ant, aunt, bath, calf, dance, gape, half,* and similar words. Thus, in eastern North Carolina, *calm, palm,* and *psalm* rhyme with *dam*. When the *a* sound (written *a* or *ea*) precedes *r,* the *r* practically disappears and the vowel approaches the sound of *aw* in *law* so closely as to be easily distinguishable from the New England pronunciation of *a* in the same position. Thus, in North Carolina *yard,* though not quite a perfect rhyme for *sawed,* is much more nearly so than it is for *hard* as pronounced by the New Englander. (Cf. *Dialect Notes,* I, 34.) As elsewhere in the South Atlantic States, the "broad *a*" is most frequently heard in the eastern Carolina pronunciation of *ask, ma, master, pa!* A characteristic though not exclusively Carolina pronunciation is *cain't* (cf. *ain't*) for *can't*. In *calf, can't, car, carpet, Carter, garden,* (*re*)*guard*(*s*), and other words in which the accented *a* is preceded by a *c* or *g*(*u*), the glide-sound following the consonant and popularly supposed to be an earmark of aristocracy in eastern Virginia and North Carolina, is seldom heard except among negroes and whites of the older generation.

In the North Carolina pronunciation of *apple, ash, bag, candle, cash, have, rabbit, saddle, spasm,* and similar words, the accented vowel is generally somewhat flattened and is occasionally drawled. Important exceptions are *ketch* for *catch*, *chomp* for *champ*, *flop* for *flap*, *stomp* for *stamp*, *strop* for *strap*, *tossel* for *tassel*, and *tromp(le)* for *tramp(le)*. A similar substitution is frequently heard in the pronunciation of *barrel*, *barrow*, *narrow*, *spargus* (asparagus), and *sparrow*.

The short *e* sound heard in the standard pronunciation of *any*, *bed*, *bury*, *dead*, *friend*, *heifer*, *Reynolds*, *said*, *says*, and similar words is not uniformly preserved in the dialects of North Carolina. A frequent and characteristic substitute is short *i*, especially as in Anglo-Irish, before *m* or *n*. Thus *end* becomes *ind*; *Evans*, *Ivans* or *Ivins*; *fence*, *fince*; *Jenny*, *Jinny*; *men*, *min*; *pen*, *pin*; *yesterday*, *yistidy*. Short *i* is also the accepted vowel in the Carolina pronunciation of *again*, *get*, *kettle*, *project*, *ten*, and *yet*. Again, among negroes and uneducated whites the accented vowel of *dead*, *edge*, *leg*, *neck*, and *sedge* is frequently replaced by the sound of *a* in *age*. *Keg*, *wrestle*, *yellow*, *yes*, and a few other words occasionally have the same accented vowel as *rag*, and in the more remote districts *deaf* rhymes with *leaf*.

Among negroes and certain rustics *bear*, *declare*, *fair*, *stair*, *pair*, *swear*, *their*, *there*, and similar words frequently have the same accented vowel as *bar* and *star*, but *care*, *scare*, and *scarce* are pronounced as though spelled *keer*, *skeer*, and *skeerce*. In the pronunciation of negroes *scarce* rhymes with *face*.

The obscure vowel sound heard in the standard pronunciation of the unaccented syllables of such words as *ago*, *children*, *China*, *cupboard*, *famous*, *liquor*, *mother*, and *nation* is not only preserved in the Carolina pronunciation of these and similar words, but is often substituted where in more precise enunciation other vowels are required. Its extensive occurrence is one of the chief indications of the "laziness" frequently charged against Southern speakers generally. Because of the practical impossibility of representing with ordinary letters the more difficult examples of slurring in the dialects of North Carolina without deforming the words beyond recognition, the standard spelling is preserved except in a few cases where tradition justifies the substitution of *o*, *a*, or *er*.

For the short *e* sound heard in the standard pronunciation of *certain*, *learn*, *search*, *serve*, and similar words, mountaineers and negroes are likely to substitute the *a* sound of *Clark*. *Heard* is frequently pronounced *hyeard*. *Girl* may become *gall*; the pronunciation *gyerl* is confined to a few older whites and negroes.

In *been*, *breeches*, *sleek*, *teat*, and a few other words, the accented vowel of standard pronunciation is uniformly replaced by that of *bit*. *Creature* is pronounced *creeter* or *critter*.

For the accented short *i* heard in the standard pronunciation of such words as *bring*, *dinner*, *hinder*, *linen*, *miracle*, *pith*, *pin*, *since*, *spirit*, *thin*, *thing*, *think*, the uneducated Carolinian is likely to substitute a short *e* sound. That is to say, in the mouth of the typical uncultured speaker the accented vowel of *pith* and *hinder* is that heard in the standard pronunciation of *death* and *tender*. Other noteworthy departures from standard pronunciation are *genuaine* for *genuine*, *favoraite* for *favorite*, *highstrikes* for *hysterics*, *reptaile* for *reptile*, *eetch* for *itch*, and *mischeevous* for *mischievous*. In North Carolinese the universal pronunciation of *Mrs.* is merely *Miz*, with the final consonant somewhat prolonged. (Cf. Krapp, *The Pronunciation of Standard English in America*, New York, 1919, p. 122.)

For the accented vowel of *boar*, *bore*, *door*, *floor*, *force*, *gourd*, *porch*, *pork*, and most other words of the same class, the native Carolinian substitutes a long *o*. The *r* is of course lost. Thus, in typical North Carolinese of the remote rural districts *boar*, *door*, *floor*, and *sore* are homonymous respectively with *beau*, *dough*, *flow*, and *sew*. Noteworthy also are the pronunciations *janders* for *jaundice*, *sassy* for *saucy*, and *faward* for *forward*.

The *u* sound heard in the standard English pronunciation of *lose* requires special consideration. As in certain sections of America outside North Carolina, *food, proof, roof, root, soon, spoon,* and certain other words have the sound of *oo* heard in *balloon,* whereas *butcher, broom, coop, Cooper, hoof, hoop, Hooper,* and *room* have a short *u* sound like that heard in the standard pronunciation of *bush.* Again, in the Carolina pronunciation of *cute, dew, due, duty, stew, tune,* and *Tuesday,* the accented vowel is preceded by a glide sound as though the words in question were spelled *cyute,* etc.; in *absolute(ly), blue, deuce, glue, Lucy, Luke, rude, Sue, true,* and most other words of this class the glide is never present. In North Carolina, as elsewhere in the South, the "correct" differentiation in this matter is one of the best criteria of native speech. No North Carolinian of uncontaminated linguistic habits would, for example, pronounce "New tunes are due to Sue," *Noo toons are doo to Syue.*

A noteworthy departure from the accented vowel heard in the standard pronunciation of such words as *pull, woman, wood,* are *put, took,* and *soot,* which among older speakers generally rhyme respectively with *gut, tuck,* and *smut.*

For the so-called "long *i*" of standard usage the Carolina lowlander frequently substitutes a sound composed of the *u* of *but* followed by the vowel of *tea.* In a number of words— notably *advice, (al)might(y), bite, cipher, (de)light, disciple, ice, like, mice, nice, night, right(eous), title, trifle,* and *twice*— the latter is the accepted pronunciation along the coast as in other parts of the South Atlantic seaboard, and its "correct" usage is one of the best linguistic earmarks of the native Southerner. In the matter of "long *i*" the Carolina mountaineer is much closer than the lowlander to the ordinary pronunciation in the North and the Middle West.

Analogous to the treatment of "long *i*" is that of the *ou* sound heard in the standard pronunciation of *couch* and *town.* Most words containing this sound are pronounced much as they are outside the South, but in certain cases— notably *doubt, house, louse, mouse, mouth,* and *south*—the first element of the diphthong is replaced by the vowel of *met.* Less frequently the same combination of short *e* and *u* is heard in *cow, cloud, down, flour, flower, found, foul, fowl, how, howl, now, plough,* and *sow* (a female hog). The ability to use this sound "correctly" is another excellent test of Southern speech. Among the mountains the *au* sound appears to be the rule. Except in the most remote districts the diphthong lacks the flat, nasal drawl adopted by many Northerners who attempt to imitate Southern dialect.

For the *oi* sound heard in the standard pronunciation of such words as *anoint, hoist, join(t), joist, point, poison, spoil,* and *tenderloin,* negroes, mountaineers, and other ultra-conservative speakers substitute "long *i.*"

Tom Peete Cross.

The University of Chicago.

APPENDIX VI

DEDICATION OF

THE PLAYMAKERS THEATRE

November 23, 1925

by
FREDERICK H. KOCH
Founder of The Carolina Playmakers
and
HARRY WOODBURN CHASE
President of the University of North Carolina[1]

Seven years ago The Carolina Playmakers presented their initial group of folk-plays on a makeshift stage which they designed and constructed in the auditorium of the Chapel Hill High School. To-night we have come to dedicate this historic building as The Playmakers Theatre.

They were simple plays,—these first plays—the work of youthful writers. But they interpreted in new dramatic forms the life and ways of their own people.

[1] Now Chancellor, New York University.

Since then The Playmakers have produced forty-two of their Carolina plays, representing thirty different authors. Three volumes of the plays have been published; two, the work of various members of the group; and one, the plays of a single author. These plays are recognized as marking the beginnings of an authentic American folk drama.

To be sure they are plays of a single locality,—but they have a wider significance. For the locality, if it be truly interpreted, is the only universal. It has been so in all lasting art.

In dedicating this building North Carolina takes a unique place in these United States; for our theatre is really a State Theatre—the first in America to be devoted to the making of its own native drama.

We conceive of our state university as the intellectual and cultural center of North Carolina, and it is fitting that North Carolina should establish here at Chapel Hill a building dedicated to the expression of the lives of her people in the dramatic arts.

And so we have a distinct responsibility,—an important work to do in the dramatic renaissance of which we are a part. May our peoples theatre of to-day interpret the struggle and the vision of our common life towards a new republic of enduring literature.—*F. H. K.*

Through the joint action of the Carnegie Corporation and the University, this building has been made available as a permanent home for The Carolina Playmakers. That it will be worthily used the extraordinary achievement of the Playmakers during the years gives every assurance. We therefore dedicate it to-night in the confidence that it may make possible about our common life a little more of the stuff that dreams are made of; that its existence here shall mean a little less monotony, a little more glamor about our days; that the horizons of imagination shall by its presence here be enlarged so that we shall come more steadily and wholly to see the place of beauty and of its handmaiden, art, in a civilization not too much given to its encouragement. To such purposes, Mr. Director, this building, the first permanent provision for any of the fine arts at the University, is from this night set apart.

To you and the group you have built up here, the University wishes godspeed as in these surroundings, themselves beautiful and historic, it follows the gospel of beauty through the years.—*H. W. C.*

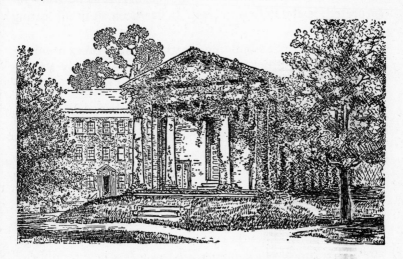

THE PLAYMAKERS THEATRE

CHAPEL HILL, NORTH CAROLINA

This historic building, originally the University Library and Ballroom, and later the School of Law, has been reconstructed and equipped as a permanent home for THE CAROLINA PLAYMAKERS. *It is the first state-owned theatre in America to be devoted to its own native drama.*